Regional
Encyclopedia of Business
and Management

Management in the
Emerging Countries

Titles from the International Encyclopedia of Business and Management series

International Encyclopedia of Business and Management
6 volume set, hardback, 0-415-07399-5

Concise International Encyclopedia of Business and Management
1 volume edition, hardback, 1-86152-114-6

Pocket International Encyclopedia of Business and Management
Paperback, 1-86152-113-8

IEBM Dictionary of Business and Management
Paperback, 1-86152-218-5

The IEBM Encyclopedia of Marketing
Edited by Michael J. Baker
Hardback, 1-86152-304-1

The Regional Encyclopedia of Business and Management
4 volume set, hardback, 1-86152-403-X

IEBM Handbook Series

The IEBM Handbook of Human Resource Management
Edited by Michael Poole and Malcolm Warner
Hardback, 1-86152-166-9

The IEBM Handbook of Information Technology in Business
Edited by Milan Zeleny
Hardback, 1-86152-308-4

The IEBM Handbook of International Business
Edited by Rosalie L. Tung
Hardback, 1-86152-216-9

The IEBM Handbook of Management Thinking
Edited by Malcolm Warner
Hardback, 1-86152-162-6

The IEBM Handbook of Organizational Behaviour
Edited by Arndt Sorge and Malcolm Warner
Hardback, 1-86152-157-X

Regional
Encyclopedia of Business
and Management

Management in the

Emerging Countries

Edited by
Malcolm Warner

Business Press
Thomson Learning™

Australia • Canada • Denmark • Japan • Mexico • New Zealand • Philippines
Puerto Rico • Singapore • South Africa • Spain • United Kingdom • United States

The Regional Encyclopedia of Business and Management: Management in the Emerging Countries

For more information, contact Business Press, Berkshire House, 168–173 High Holborn, London, WC1V 7AA or visit us on the World Wide Web at: http://www.itbp.com

---

British Library Cataloguing-in-Publication Data
A catalogue record for this book is available from the British Library

---

ISBN 1-86152-407-2

Other titles in the Regional Encyclopedia of Management set:

ISBN 1-86152-404-8 (Americas)
ISBN 1-86152-405-6 (Asia Pacific)
ISBN 1-86152-406-4 (Europe)
ISBN 1-86152-403-X (4-volume boxed set)

First edition published 2000 by Thomson Learning

Typeset by HWA Text and Data Management, Tunbridge Wells
Printed in the UK by TJ International, Padstow, Cornwall

Contents

List of contributors. vii
Introduction, *Malcolm Warner* 1

General themes
Management in the emerging countries, *Tomás O. Kohn
and James E. Austin*. 9
Perspectives on globalization, big business and the emerging
countries, *Peter Nolan* 26

Specialized themes
Accounting in the emerging countries, *Peter Walton* 41
Banking and finance in the emerging countries, *Morgen Witzel*. 50
Business cultures, the emerging countries, *Rabindra N. Kanungo* 60
Economies of the emerging countries, *John Cathie*. 68
Human resource management in the emerging countries,
Manuel Mendonça 86
Industrial relations in the emerging countries, *Segun Matanmi*. 95
Management education in the emerging countries, *Peter Blunt* 105
Management of technology in the emerging countries,
Richard A. Ouma Onyango 117
Manufacturing in the emerging countries, *Axèle Giroud*. 129
Marketing in the emerging countries, *John Ford*. 142
Strategy in the emerging countries, *Shekhar Chaudhari*. 154
World Trade Organization (WTO), *Alan M. Rugman* 163

Country profiles
Africa
Management in Africa, *Tayo Fashoyin* 169
Management in Algeria, *Boualem Chenoufi and David Weir* 176
Management in Botswana, *John Cathie*. 182
Management in Ghana, *Yaw Debrah* 189
Management in Kenya, *John Henley*. 198
Management in Nigeria, *Pikay Richardson*. 206
Management in South Africa, *Frank M. Horwitz* 214
Management in Tanzania, *Henry Mapolu* 221
Management in Uganda, *Moses N. Kiggundu* 228
Management in Zambia, *Victor H. Muhandu* 237
Management in Zimbabwe, *Zivanayi Tamangani and Zororo Muranda* 245

Asia
Management in Bangladesh, *Shahid Uddin Ahmed*. 255
Management in India, *Monir Tayeb*. 263
Management in Pakistan, *Shaista E. Khilji* 271

Contents

Management in Sri Lanka, *Austin Fernando* 280

Middle East

Management in the Arab world, *David Weir* 291
Management in Egypt, *Mahmoud Salem* 301
Management in the Gulf States, *David Weir* 308
Management in Iran, *Monir Tayeb* 316
Management in Jordan, *David Weir* 324
Management in Lebanon, *Yusuf M. Sidani* 332
Management in Saudi Arabia, *Mahmoud Salem* 340

Index 359

List of contributors

Professor Shahid Uddin Ahmed
Professor of Management
Department of Management
University of Dhaka
Bangladesh

Dr James E. Austin
Richard P. Chapman Professor of
Business Administration
Graduate School of Business
Administration
Harvard University
Boston
Massachusetts
USA

Professor Peter Blunt
Professor of Management
Graduate School of Business
Northern Territory University
Darwin
Australia

Dr John Cathie
Assistant Director of Research
Department of Land Economy
University of Cambridge
England

Professor Shekhar Chaudhuri
Professor of International Management
and Business Policy
International Management Group
Indian Institute of Management
India

Dr Boualem Chenoufi
University of Eastern Cyprus
Gazimagusa
Cyprus

Dr Yaw A. Debrah
Senior Lecturer
Cardiff Business School
University of Wales, Cardiff
Wales

Professor Tayo Fashoyin
ILO/SAMAT
Harare
Zimbabwe

Austin Fernando
Executive Director
Resources Development Consultants
Limited
Migrant Services Centre
Sri Lanka

Dr John B. Ford
College of Business and Public Admin
Old Dominion University
Norfolk
USA

Axèle Giroud
Lecturer in International Business
Bradford Management Centre
University of Bradford
Bradford
England

Professor John Henley
Business School
University of Edinburgh
Scotland

Professor Frank Martin Horwitz
Graduate School of Business
University of Cape Town
Cape Town
South Africa

Professor Rabindra N. Kanungo
Faculty Chair Professor
Faculty of Management
McGill University
Montreal
Canada

Shaista E. Khilji
PhD Candidate
Judge Institute of Management Studies
University of Cambridge
England

Professor Moses N. Kiggundu
Professor of Management and Strategy
School of Business, Carleton University
Ontario
Canada

Dr Tomás Kohn
Boston University
Massachusetts
USA

Henry Mapolu
Director
Redma, Management Trainers and
Consultants for Eastern and Southern
Africa
Dar Es Salaam
Tanzania

Dr Segun Matanmi
Associate Professor
Faculty of Social Sciences
Lagos State University
Nigeria

Professor Manuel Mendonça
Faculty Lecturer, Organizational Behavior
and Human Resource Management
Faculty of Management
McGill University
Montreal
Canada

Victor Muhandu
Zambia Privatisation Agency
Lusaka
Zambia

Zororo Muranda
Lecturer in Marketing
Department of Business Studies
University of Zimbabwe
Harare
Zimbabwe

Professor Peter Nolan
Jesus College
University of Cambridge
England

Dr Richard Allen Ouma Onyango
Lecturer
Department of Library and Information
Studies
University of Botswana
Gaborone
Botswana

Dr Pikay K. Richardson
Fellow in Economics of Business
and Director, India Research and
Development Unit
Manchester Business School
University of Manchester
England

Dr Alan M. Rugman
Thames Water Fellow in Strategic
Management
Templeton College
University of Oxford
England

Professor Mahmoud Salem
Professor and Head
Department of Management
Sultan Qaboos University
Muscat
Oman

Dr Yusuf Sidani
Graduate School of Business and
Management
American University of Beirut
Beirut
Lebanon

Dr Zivanayi Tamangani
Lecturer in Management
Department of Business Studies
University of Zimbabwe
Harare
Zimbabwe

Dr Monir Tayeb
Senior Lecturer
Department of Business Organization
Heriot-Watt University
Edinburgh
Scotland

Professor Peter Walton
Professor of Accounting
HEC Management Studies
University of Geneva
Switzerland

Professor Malcolm Warner
Fellow, Wolfson College
and Judge Institute of Management
Studies
University of Cambridge
England

Professor David Weir
Newcastle Business School
University of Northumbria
Newcastle-Upon-Tyne
England

Morgen Witzel
London Business School
and Durham University Business School
England

Introduction

'Emerging markets' have dominated the headlines in the business press and even many academic publications for the last decade or more. Investors' confidence in these areas was then buoyant; banks' exposure to them was also considerable, although not as much as in the 1980s. Most recently, the shock-waves of the Asian crisis have helped discourage investment in many such emerging markets. 'Emerging markets' may not however be entirely synonymous or co-terminous with 'emerging countries' but there is a major overlap. Some other parts of the world like Russia are termed as emerging markets but this is because they were not 'market economies' until recently. In this volume, we have for the most part dealt with the poorest countries and those who are, most strictly speaking, spoken of as 'emerging countries' in terms of their level of economic development (see ECONOMIES OF THE EMERGING COUNTRIES).

Confidence has of late flagged in many markets, particularly as financial crises have arisen in countries in Africa, Asia and Latin America and so on. Many large Western banks have faced considerable financial embarrassment and losses as a result of unwise investments in emerging markets. Third World indebtedness has also become a talking-point. The poorest emerging economies have no doubt had the worst problems and probably have the strongest case for debt-cancellation; on the other hand, fearful of 'moral hazard', international bankers do not want to make concessions too easily. The recent Asian economic crisis has heightened their fears in this regard. They believe that rescuing countries from debts arising from the misjudgements of their governments and corporations may encourage others to be cavalier about risk. Others have spoken of making the International Monetary Fund (IMF) an international 'banker of last resort'. Without a doubt, debate will continue on this point for some time to come. But the G7 countries have a responsibility of awesome proportions in the context of possible 'global meltdown'. However, fine words and pious intentions may not be enough. Reflating the world economy may be rather difficult if demand falters from these parts of the global market and their banking systems are in financial difficulties. The vulnerability of both national and international financial systems is now in question (see BANKING AND FINANCE IN THE EMERGING COUNTRIES).

Political and company governance reform is another theme that has surfaced in the context of the recent crises. 'Cronyism' and 'lack of transparency' have been put up as possible causes of unsound lending to emerging markets. How such reforms can come about in any broad-brush manner is moot. Moreover, it is not only emerging countries which have been accused of such practices; the case of Japan comes to mind here. Yet it is in the emerging countries that the worst examples of unsound practices have taken place (see BUSINESS CULTURES, THE EMERGING COUNTRIES). In some parts of Africa, as well as Asia and Latin America for instance, it is likely that Western and Japanese investors will keep their distance for some years to come. The impact of such financial disasters on institutions like the IMF and their willingness to lend may thus have long-term implications for development. On the other hand, some commentators believe that the conditions imposed by lending bodies like the IMF impose overly-strict demands on such economies *vis-à-vis* proposed structural reforms which may lead to a sharp cut in the living standards and jobs of the poor. The policies imposed on many African countries, as well Latin American and South East Asian ones in recent years have been attacked as overly harsh in terms of their impacts on the most economically vulnerable. Even liberal economists, such as Jeffrey Sachs of Harvard University, have attacked the IMF-type policies as inappropriate in the current conditions. Some even propose cancelling their debts.

Political opposition to the acceptance of international rescue packages may lead to economic, political and social instability, with the prospects of riots and disorder fed by the discontent of the urban and rural poor. Opposition may come from a more respectable quarter, with the prospect of capital-controls becoming more attractive to many, as the middle classes in some of these parts of the world see their life-savings wiped out as a result of the most recent economic and financial upheavals. This single factor in itself may put the future of the 'globalization' model at risk and less likely to be uncritically taken up in future. At best, we may see emerging economies becoming pragmatic in their attitude as to how far they are integrated into sources of global finance. Whether you think this is a good idea depends on your view of how the world economy can best develop and the stability of the system. Economic nationalism, as exemplified recently by the reactions of some leaders in southeast Asia, may become increasingly attractive if threats in the economic environment become stronger.

Economic and financial problems are not the only constraint. Management in emerging economies is, it is generally agreed by most experts in the field, relatively less well developed than in mature ones, although there is often a 'dual' structure whereby the advanced sector, dominated by the MNCs, may represent a 'benchmark' for the more traditional or less advanced set of firms (see MANAGEMENT IN THE EMERGING COUNTRIES; MANUFACTURING IN THE EMERGING COUNTRIES). The hope is that more sophisticated management techniques may filter down to the SMEs there. But in many cases, the trickle-down theory has not worked out. Technology-transfer is however problematic as 'intermediate development' techniques may be more appropriate in many cases. However, to be cut off from the 'global digital highway' may not be an option (see MANAGEMENT OF TECHNOLOGY IN THE EMERGING COUNTRIES). Whether the infra-structure of many poor countries can sustain complex computer networks is another matter, as power supplies often fail even *vis-à-vis* conventional manufacturing technology. Power failures in many emerging countries are alas quite 'normal' phenomena. Achieving a robust infra-structure and managing well depends on sound investment strategies by governments in areas like power-generation. Investment in 'hardware' is not only important but also in 'software', such as education and human resources. World Bank loans here are substantial but are not always well spent. Private capital now contributes to many infra-structural projects but is less likely in future as economic conditions deteriorate and risk increases. Managing the infrastructure well is an essential ingredient in growth; public administration training has not always been up to the task in many cases.

Management in emerging economies, whether in the public or private sector, is also of mixed quality (see MANAGEMENT IN THE EMERGING COUNTRIES). It ranges from relatively well-trained, as is the case of countries like the Republic of South

Africa, to relatively undeveloped as in the case of many poorer African nations like Tanzania. Management in the Indian sub-continent may vary in rigour and training from the more advanced sectors, such as airlines (for instance Air India or Pakistan Airlines) or the newly developed 'high-tech' industries in India), to the backward sectors in say, Bangladesh's rural textile industry. Overall, the robustness of much management in emerging countries leaves a great deal to be desired and there is a need for more investment in human resources in these parts of the world but development which is 'appropriate' and tailored to the needs of the economy and sector in question. A 'one size fits all' solution is decidedly not needed.

Whereas in much of the post-independence period, many emerging markets were run as 'planned economies' rather than market-oriented ones, as the 'state socialist model' was held up as one to be copied, international investment has encouraged the more liberalized course and 'privatization', rather than 'parastatal monopolies'. Some economies have gone further down this road than others; for example, in the 1990s, Ghana has emerged as a 'model' *vis-à-vis* its African neighbours (see MANAGEMENT IN GHANA), whereas India has only recently taken this path. The latter had been under the influence of 'socialist' influences since independence and had public ownership and a centralist administrative structure, partly taken over from the Raj and partly because of ideological reasons (see MANAGEMENT IN INDIA). Export-led growth, on the lines of East Asian 'little Dragon' economies was late in coming and only recently *de rigueur*; since the recent Asian crisis, however, confidence in this route has been rather muted. Economies less linked to global markets, like the Indian example, have on the other hand been less adversely affected by the turn-down. However, the worldwide deflation has involved falls in commodity prices that have afflicted many emerging countries' economies, such as Zambia, with its reliance on exports of copper (see MANAGEMENT IN ZAMBIA). Many countries have seen a fall in the price of oil, such as Nigeria, which have cut their GDP as well as governmental revenues. The market for Western goods in these countries has fallen more than proportionately as recession has struck (see MARKETING IN THE EMERGING COUNTRIES). It will no doubt take some years for commodity prices to recover and prosperity to return to these producer-nations. Deflation may now be a long-term and world-wide phenomenon.

We have in this volume, we should note here, mostly restricted our coverage of the problems of development to emerging countries as a special category. In this particular volume, examples are mostly located in Africa, the Indian subcontinent, the Middle East and so on, although examples may also be given in the thematic chapters from other emerging economies we have included in our regional volumes on Asia and the Americas, especially Latin America. For example some contributors have included here the People's Republic of China, featured in the volume evoted to the Asia Pacific region. China is 'emerging' in one sense but is also at a transitional stage *vis-à-vis* 'economic superpower' status. It is clear that there are not always very rigid boundaries between several of the themes and regional areas we have covered (see PERSPECTIVES ON GLOBALIZATION, BIG BUSINESS AND THE EMERGING COUNTRIES).

Management values in emerging countries have had less attention than they deserve in the last few decades. Many writers in this field have copied Western 'sacred cows' uncritically. They may have believed that traditional values were inimical to economic development and that the absence of the so-called 'Protestant work-ethic' made economic growth less likely. Less attention has been paid to the distinct environmental conditions in what was for years called the 'Third World'. Values in management there may often be different from those in the advanced societies; managers may be more authoritarian and paternalistic, with a high power-distance, to use Hofstede's term, more common. Collectivist rather than individualistic scores may be higher; masculine rather than feminine values predominate. Uncertainty avoidance may be greater. Techniques common in the West, such as 'Management by Objectives', may simply not work or function less well where values are different (see BUSINESS CULTURES, THE EMERGING COUNTRIES).

Studies of management in developing or emerging nations may have lagged behind those of its counterpart in more mature economies for understandable reasons. Normally, it requires field work in far-flung places. Many studies may have been the result of local postgraduate students pursuing doctoral studies in Western universities and then writing-up empirical data derived from their local sites. This is not to say that there are no books or articles under this or approximate headings. But such publications are few in number *vis-à-vis* their counterparts on advanced economies. There is however a burgeoning literature in the field of international business and multinational corporations that concerns itself with how such firms operate in those countries, which varies in quality and sophistication. Discussion and analysis of how indigenous business and management models function there has attracted less attention, although the role of national entrepreneurs, firms and state enterprises has been relatively more explicitly noted in the development economics literature (see BUSINESS CULTURES, THE EMERGING COUNTRIES). Many of these texts here cover national experiences, such as those of specific African economies, for instance. The World Bank has many publications in this genre.

Greater attention to emerging markets and their economic development is noteworthy for instance in the African or Indian subcontinent contexts. Western economists or management academics may specialize in one or more area but these are not commonly found in many business schools and rather locate themselves in development studies institutes or departments. Moreover, writers and scholars working in those countries do publish a great deal on those specific instances, although it may not be widely available outside those countries. The World Bank, the International Monetary Fund, the International Labour Organization, amongst others, also publish highly specialized studies both across-the-board as well as on specific countries. Comparative studies of emerging countries in the business and management domains are thin on the ground. The need for thematic and national treatments is therefore imperative for both students, teachers and practitioners of management.

What has been emphasized in this volume both in the general as well as the country-specific chapters is that there is no single model of management which fits all the countries we have covered, no 'one best fit'. It is clear that there is no one 'best practice' model when studying management in advanced economies; even less so in the case of emerging ones. We must look at contingencies like the level of development, local institutional factors, national norms and so on. For example, accounting practices in such countries diverge greatly in their applications. Amongst other factors, they also derive from several external models (see ACCOUNTING IN THE EMERGING COUNTRIES). For years, they followed colonial examples but more recently a growing number of countries in this category are adopting international accounting standards, with varying degrees of success. Similarly, banking and finance practices are also often nation-specific. Frequently, practices follow colonialist models from the pre-independence period, as is the case with industrial relations legal frameworks as well as personnel and HRM practices, for instance (see INDUSTRIAL RELATIONS IN THE EMERGING COUNTRIES). Past influences have often been other than beneficial, as in the case, say, of technology management. It is vital therefore that the local circumstances and contexts in emerging markets be taken into account when analysing specific themes in their development.

Management education and training as a category in emerging markets does, for example vary enormously from one region to another. It is most advanced in southeast and east Asia, moderately developed in the Indian subcontinent and rather backward in much of Africa outside the Republic of South Africa. Whether Western-style business schools are appropriate is also debatable, as is sending young managers abroad to do MBA programmes *vis-à-vis* the needs of local economies. Indeed, setting MBA courses on site, whether national or foreign, may not necessarily be appropriate. However, national governments have aspirations to follow Western models, often at the expense of relevance or cost. Also what is taught is as important as how it is taught. Methods derived from external models may not be the most suitable. Investment in education and training at a lower level in the national infrastructure may yield greater returns. It is often said that greater investment in primary education and vocational training may be more advisable than spending too much on tertiary-level courses. A small percentage of managers may need advanced training, such as at the MBA level. They may however need specialist disciplinary training in subjects such as engineering, computer technology, etc., then hands-on experience both at home and abroad, prior to higher management studies (see MANAGEMENT EDUCATION IN THE EMERGING COUNTRIES).

The *Regional Encyclopedia of Business and Management* was created to remedy the lack of up-to-date description and analysis in these domains and to present a chart to understanding how there are many different routes to economic and management development. The growing importance of globalization of business in the twentieth century has highlighted the need for a comprehensive set of books which looks at management in a specific regional area, covering not only general themes relevant to its functioning but also *vis-à-vis* specific countries. An authoritative and comprehensive reference book, such as the *Regional Encyclopedia of Business and Management*, sets out to dispel the confusion as well as provide much needed guidance on the origins, scope and practice of international management.

The *Regional Encyclopedia of Business and Management* is split into four volumes, covering Management in the Americas, Management in Asia Pacific, Management in the Emerging Countries and Management in Europe. The editorial perspective is both comparative and interdisciplinary. We intend to compare and critically analyse the different management structures and styles across the world in order to establish a more sophisticated understanding of their distinctiveness as well as commonalties. The volumes are interdisciplinary in that the contributions try to relate the approaches of specialists to themes that cut across the national boundaries in the geographical areas covered in the particular volume.

The *Regional Encyclopedia of Business and Management* seeks to recognize both these facets in a comprehensive and rigorous way. Each volume consists of three parts, providing a consistent treatment of themes of general and specialist interest as well as specific country profiles. In doing so, we hope to provide an indispensable work of reference for both academics and students, as well as practitioners of management.

Part One deals with general themes covering the overall state of management in the geographically defined region. Part Two covers specialized themes relevant to the region, such as accounting, banking and finance, human resource management, marketing, strategy and so on. Part Three consists of country profiles, whereby we define and analyse management in the countries in the geographically-defined area. Each chapter includes the management traditions, infrastructure, and managerial styles in each country as well as information on education and training.

Finally, this project has come about through the hard work and dedication of many people. I should here like to thank all the authors for their commitment to the project, the publishing team at ITBP in particular Kay Larkin, So-Shan Au, Fiona Freel and Sophie Durlacher, as well as Morgen Witzel who has been an 'honorary' member of the team.

MALCOLM WARNER
AUGUST 1999

General themes

Management in the emerging countries

1 **Understanding the environment**
2 **Factors**
3 **Levels**
4 **Business–government relations**
5 **Finance**
6 **Production**
7 **Marketing**
8 **Organization**
9 **Conclusion**

Overview

Some may argue that in any business, regardless of location, there is a need for well-developed strategies and proper strategy implementation processes. While this is true, it is necessary to recognize that strategy definition and implementation are inextricably tied to the business environment, and that environment is fundamentally affected by a country's level of development and by the dynamics of the development process.

One reason for focusing on emerging or developing countries is their absolute and growing importance in the global business arena. Almost 80 per cent of the world's consumers are in developing countries and almost all of the population-based market expansion in the twenty-first century will occur there. Although poorer, the developing countries' economies are growing faster than those of developed countries. Developing countries are an increasingly significant part of the global economy, as recipients of growing foreign direct and portfolio investments and as competitors in export markets. The proliferation of business opportunities in developing countries, their growing competitive significance, and the contribution that businesses can make to these nations' development, make them a priority item on the agenda of forward-thinking business executives.

Since the business environments in emerging countries are different along several dimensions from those in developed countries, it is necessary to understand the forces shaping the lesser developed countries' environments and the resulting distinctive issues that must be dealt with when managing there, particularly the challenges of dealing with much greater instability and uncertainty. This entry sets forth a framework to analyse emerging countries' business environments and delineates guidelines for managing in those environments. In this entry we use the terms 'emerging countries' and 'lesser developed countries' (LDCs) interchangeably. Other labels exist, such as 'newly industrialized countries' (NICs), 'Third World nations' and 'developing economies and countries', each carrying different references and connotations. Our terminology is used without any intended value judgement and is used mainly to facilitate reading.

1 Understanding the environment

To function effectively in emerging countries, managers must be able to scan, analyse, understand, and react to the environmental forces that surround the firm. Developing countries' contexts are complicated, continually in flux, and highly diverse (see ECONOMIES OF THE EMERGING COUNTRIES). A standard 'blueprint' of a developing country's business environment is not feasible because countries fall at varying points on the development continuum and have heterogeneous contexts. What is possible is to present a conceptual 'map' that can help identify systematically the critical contextual variables to examine and the analytical pathways to follow in probing the managerial implications of environmental forces.

A tool for such analysis is the environmental analysis framework (EAF) (Austin 1990) represented schematically in Figure 1. It enables managers to examine the business environment systematically, to decipher its managerial implications, and to answer key strategic and managerial questions. In the EAF, external forces are

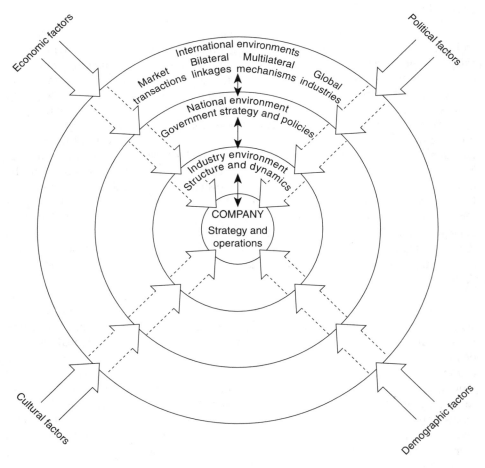

Figure 1 Environmental analysis framework
Source: Austin (1990)

categorized into four factors – economic, political, cultural, and demographic – that effect the business environment at four levels – international, national, industry, and company. While the EAF provides a comprehensive analytical tool, managers may find it convenient to use selective portions of the framework according to their needs. In effect, a manager should be scanning the environment always from the perspective of the fourth level, the company, so as to interpret the implications of a given piece of environmental analysis in terms of the firm's particular circumstances.

2 Factors

It is important to understand how the environmental factors tend to differ among lesser developed countries (LDCs), and between LDCs and developed countries, so as to grasp better the nature of the business environment and to indicate the likely directions of change as countries develop. The manager's task is to identify which variables should be examined and how they should be analysed. Table 1 specifies variables in the four factor categories and the following sections illustrate some of the analyses. Managers should note that the approach presented deals with the environment's complexity by first looking at distinct factors, so data may be systematically collected and examined. The second, and critical, step is the analysis of interdependencies among the factors that results in a clearer perception of the whole, based on a greater understanding of the pieces. It is the manager's role to identify the managerial implications of these environmental characteristics.

Economic factors

The most often quoted economic factor, per capita gross national product (GNP), is used to define a country's level of development. Emerging countries are those classified as low- and middle-income economies by the World Bank (see ECONOMIES OF THE EMERGING COUNTRIES). The resulting wide range of income levels (from per capita GNP under US$100 to over US$8,000) indicates different levels of demand among LDCs and highlights one element of the diversity among these countries. Differences in aggregate gross domestic product (GDP) (ranging from over US$500,000 million to under US$100 million), GDP growth rates (ranging from over 10 per cent to under –5 per cent per annum), and inequality of income distribution (measured by the GINI coefficient) (Kakwani 1980; Lecaillon 1984) create different business opportunities and risks and call forth distinct management practices. (The GINI coefficient measures the extent to which there is inequality in the distribution of income among a group of people. If the distribution is 100 per cent equal, namely every one per cent of the population receives one per cent of the total income, the GINI coefficient is 0. Total inequality, where one person receives 100 per cent of a society's income, would result in a GINI coefficient of 1. In practice, the GINI coefficient ranges between approximately 0.25, for countries with very equal income distribution, to approximately 0.75 for countries with very unequal distribution.)

Table 1 Summary of environmental factors

	Development level (GNP per capita)		
	Low	*Middle*	*High*
Economic factors			
Natural resources			
importance to economy	high	⟶	lower
availability	under-developed	⟶	developed
Labour			
skilled human capital	scarce	⟶	abundant
% workforce in agriculture	>60%	± 40%	<15%
Capital			
GNP per capita (US$)	<$1,000	⟶	>$15,000
savings rates	low	high	somewhat high
income equality	medium	high	low
financial institutions	weak	⟶	strong
inflation	moderate	high	low
capital flight	outflow	⟶	inflow
Foreign exchange			
exchange-rate volatility	low	high	low
trade deficits	medium	high	low
range of exports	narrow	⟶	broad
debt service burden	high	⟶	low
concessional foreign aid	recipient	⟵	donor
Infrastructure			
physical infrastructure	weak	⟶	strong
information availability	low (unreliable)	⟶	high (reliable)
Technology			
technology flows	recipient	⟶	supplier
sophistication	low	⟶	high
industry structure	dualistic	⟶	unitary
Political factors			
instability	high	medium	low
political institutions	weak	⟶	strong
international links	dependent	⟶	more autonomy
Cultural factors			
social structures	more rigid	⟶	less rigid
religious influence	stronger	⟶	weaker
gender roles	very distinct	⟶	less distinct
language	high diversity	⟶	low diversity
Demographic factors			
annual pop. growth rate	approx. 2%	approx. 1.5%	approx. 0.5%
age structure	young	⟶	older
life expectancy	approx. 60 yrs	approx. 68 yrs	approx. 77 yrs
urbanization (% total pop.)	approx. 30%	approx. 60%	approx. 80%
urbanization (growth)	approx. 4.7%	approx. 3.2%	approx. 0.8%
migration	low	high	high

Source: Based on Tables 3.2, 3.8, 3.9 and 3.11 (Austin 1990) and World Bank 1994 *(World Development Report)*
Note: The most often quoted economic factor, per capita GNP, is used to define a country's level of development. Developing countries are those classified as low and middle income

Natural resources

Managers need to monitor closely the natural resources sector when it is central to a country's economy, since any changes are likely to have major spillover effects on the economy and on government policies (see ECONOMIES OF THE EMERGING COUNTRIES).

Labour

The scarcity of skilled human capital makes it difficult to implement complex projects; something that must be considered in their design and implementation phases. Special attention needs to be paid to human resource management practices to train and retain employees. On the other hand, the abundant supply of low-cost labour is a source of significant cost advantages for the manufacture of labour-intensive products and creates the need to adapt production technologies accordingly (see HUMAN RESOURCE MANAGEMENT IN THE EMERGING COUNTRIES).

Capital

Capital scarcity and low-income levels in many LDCs limit the nature of demand and often preclude the existence of mass markets, except in the megapopulation countries where even the smallest per capita demand for a product gives rise to significant market opportunities. Low income and low savings rates combine to create the need for special marketing practices, where consumer credit and specialized product design play a central role for products from food and clothing to consumer durables and housing. Capital scarcity and weak financial institutions constrain financing in most LDCs. That weakness, however, opens up opportunities for providers of financial services and gives rise to alternative mechanisms, such as business groups. The opportunities to finance projects are further complicated by the pernicious effects of high inflation. A high-inflation environment places a special strain on all corporate activities, including planning, controlling, purchasing, and marketing. The capital scarcity in LDCs is often compounded by capital flight. Managers must monitor capital flight since it may signal underlying problems that trigger sudden changes in currency values and in government intervention and controls (see BANKING AND FINANCE IN THE EMERGING COUNTRIES).

Foreign exchange

Capital flight also signals (and may actually cause) currency devaluations that exacerbate the instability in many LDCs' currencies. Such instability requires careful assessment since exchange rate fluctuations can drastically alter a firm's cost structure and competitiveness, both domestically and in the international marketplace. Exchange rate instability is often the result of a narrow export base and persistent trade deficits that also result in foreign exchange shortages. Managers must be aware of foreign exchange scarcity and adopt practices that economize this scarce resource. In a foreign exchange shortage environment, exporters, especially those involved in non-traditional exports, are likely to be in a favourable bargaining position with governments (see ECONOMIES OF THE EMERGING COUNTRIES).

Infrastructure

The lack of infrastructure affects many aspects of a company's operations. When there is the need to include access roads, generators, water treatment facilities, and other items, projects become more costly and less of a competitive threat. Poor energy supply results in production and maintenance problems. Inadequate telecommunications services affect the ability to coordinate with suppliers and to provide adequate sales and service support. Of course, the lack of adequate infrastructure creates major opportunities in the building infrastructure business (see MANUFACTURING IN THE EMERGING COUNTRIES).

Technology

Given the low technological level in most LDCs, managers must seek appropriate technology. Key issues are technology adaptation and transfer and dealing with the tensions that develop between sophisticated installations and the surrounding low technology environment (see MANAGEMENT OF TECHNOLOGY IN THE EMERGING COUNTRIES).

Political factors

In addition to the economic factors discussed so far, managers need to deal with other factors that shape the environment. One characteristic of many LDCs is their political instability that creates uncertainty, increases indirect costs, interferes with planning activities, and often leads to bureaucratic bottlenecks. Drastic political changes can result in economic upheavals that disrupt a firm's ability to operate normally. The polarization of views often brings with it increased security risks for personnel, especially expatriates. The challenge for managers is to understand the sources of instability and assess how the firm may be affected. Political risk is a company-specific, and sometimes even project-specific, phenomenon.

Ideology

A country's political ideology plays an important role in shaping the business environment. While the ideological struggle between socialism and capitalism continues, the effects of nationalism often overshadow the debate. To manage relations with governments properly, managers need to understand the national ideology and how it is shifting.

Institutions

Relations with governments are carried out at the personal level and through institutions. The weakness in these institutions makes the process difficult, unreliable and further complicates the task of managing in LDCs. Because of weak institutions, government services are provided inefficiently and are often costly; there is a tendency for arbitrariness in decision making, and pressures for bribery to secure permits and approvals abound. In such an environment, managers need to identify and understand the key political actors. This task is complicated by the multiplicity of political actors in LDCs, including, in addition to the governmental institutions, the military, university students, labour unions, ethnic groups, and so on. The range of political actors opens up opportunities to form coalitions that may be helpful in bargaining situations.

Most LDCs' economies are closely tied to the international economy. These ties often follow old political or colonial linkages that influence the business environment. Managers, especially of multinational enterprises, must be aware of existing links, since they influence the perceived dependencies between home and host countries and may affect the firm's dealings with government institutions and other political actors.

Cultural factors

While culture is a complex and hard-to-define phenomenon, there are aspects that lend themselves to analysis and understanding (see BUSINESS CULTURES, THE EMERGING COUNTRIES).

Social structure and dynamics
The social structure and dynamics can be examined in terms of attitudes towards others (ranging from individualism to collectivism), the structure of relationships (ranging from hierarchical to egalitarian), and decision-making styles (ranging from autocratic to participatory). Where collectivism is important, kinship and other group ties may determine the environment. Managers need to understand these variables and tailor human resource management policies, managerial practices and interpersonal communications to fit the cultural norms. Since cultural patterns influence industry structure, managers must be aware of the resulting effects. Narrowly defined social structures may limit access to group-controlled activities. However, if properly understood and cultivated, there are opportunities for careful market segmentation and for preferential access to such activities.

Human nature perspective and time and space orientation
Access is likely to be possible if managers understand the society's attitudes towards human nature and towards time and space, and translate that understanding into appropriate actions.

Religion, language and gender
These actions are likely to be most appropriate when they also take into account religious, linguistic and gender characteristics and sensitivities.

Demographic factors

Demographic characteristics of a country define the last set of factors that need to be incorporated into the EAF.

Growth rates
High population growth rates in developing countries create market opportunities, especially for basic consumer goods. However, high population growth rates restrict per capita income and contribute to labour and social unrest that may affect political stability.

Age structure

The age structure in LDCs is dominated by young people. This restricts the savings rate and reduces funds available for investment. Much of the surplus labour in LDCs is made up of inexperienced and unskilled young workers. While this poses short-term staffing problems, it also offers some benefits; a young workforce is highly trainable, enabling managers to develop a motivated and dedicated workforce. Given that 45 per cent of the LDCs' population is under 20 years of age compared to 28 per cent for developed countries, there are very different product needs and market segments between these countries.

Urbanization and migration

In LDCs, agriculture tends to represent a larger share of the national economy, with industry and services playing lesser roles. However, as countries develop, the share of agriculture in the economy tends to decrease, while the share of industry and services increases (see annual *World Development Report* (World Bank)). With further development, telecommunications, financial, professional and other supporting services tend to increase faster than industry. Given these patterns, the opportunities for investment change as a country develops. These changes take place not only between sectors but also within sectors. In services, for example, the growth in demand for telecommunications and transportation usually precedes the growth in financial and professional services.

The high rate of growth in urbanization in emerging countries creates consumer goods markets that can be served relatively easily (see MARKETING IN THE EMERGING COUNTRIES). It also creates demand for housing and infrastructure. Migrants from rural areas or other countries increase the supply of labour available in cities. However, these workers are likely to require special training to help them adapt to an urban setting. Fast urbanization rates result in congested and poorly planned cities, making it difficult for the movement of people and products. Fast growth rates combined with inadequate zoning laws often create problems for factories which get established in industrial settings and suddenly find themselves surrounded by residential units.

Health

The relatively low life expectancy in developing countries is a reflection of these countries' poor sanitation, nutrition and inadequate health facilities and education. Managers need to be aware of these realities and adopt practices such as in-house education and healthcare, supplemental food programmes, and so on. Such programmes increase employees' loyalty, boost worker productivity, and may result in competitive advantages. Inadequate healthcare facilities create opportunities for the supply of medical and pharmaceutical products and services. A measure that captures the effects of several demographic factors is the 'physical quality of life indicator' (PQLI). It is a composite index based on a country's literacy rate, infant mortality rate, and life expectancy (Sewell *et al.* 1985) and, as such, suggests the quality of human resources available in a country. Given that a country's PQLI rank might differ significantly from its rank based on other economic indicators, the added information of this index is useful for business decision makers and further highlights the diversity among developing countries. The factors discussed above influence events in the international arena, shape governments' development strategies and policies, affect the structure and competitive dynamics of the company's industry, and directly impinge on specific activities of the company. An understanding of these different levels of the business environment is the second component of the EAF.

3 Levels

International level

Given that LDCs are an integral part of the international economy, the first level of analysis consists of integrating international aspects into an understanding of national, industry and company dynamics. To do so, one must examine the ways in which a country is linked to others through cross-border flows of resources, bilateral agreements, multilateral agreements, and by the actions of players in global industries. These international linkages are influenced by the economic, political, cultural and demographic factors mentioned earlier and influence the environment in which managers and businesses operate.

National level

In LDCs, more so than in developed countries, governments play a central role in shaping the business environment. Therefore, managers must interpret national development strategies and assess their effects on the industries in which they operate and on their firms. To facilitate such interpretation, managers can use the 'Public-policy impact chain' described schematically in Figure 2.

There are two main approaches Third World countries have taken to foster development: import substitution (IS) and export promotion (EP). These approaches result in widely distinct policies that affect industries and firms differently. Import substitution creates protected markets and success often depends on the ability to establish manufacturing facilities within a country. Export promotion focuses on external markets and success depends on achieving international competitiveness. Given that countries following EP strategies have grown faster than those following

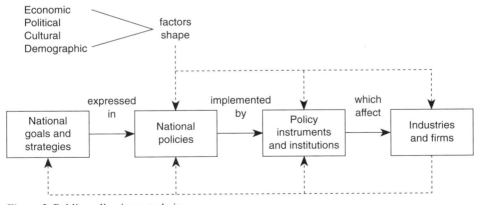

Figure 2 Public-policy impact chain

Table 2 Policy areas and instruments

| Policy instruments | Policy areas | | | | | |
	Monetary	Fiscal	Trade	Foreign investment	Incomes	Sectoral
Legal	Banking reserve levels	Tax rates subsidies	Government import controls	Ownership laws	Labour laws	Land tenure laws
Administrative	Loan guarantees	Public service fees	Import quotas and tariffs	Profit and capita; repatriation	Price controls	Industrial licensing
	Credit regulations	Tax collection	Exchange rates and controls	Investment approvals	Wage controls	Resource concessions
			Export controls			Domestic content
						Technology licensing
Direct market operations	Loans	Government purchases	Government imports	Joint ventures	Government wages	Government research
	Money creation	Government sales	Government exports	Sale of SOEs to foreign investors		Sectoral SOEs

IS, there is a trend away from IS. This trend has been accompanied by market liberalization, including a move away from state-owned enterprises. Such a move has further increased the level of competition in LDCs and requires firms to base their strategies on real competitive advantages.

While economic growth is a widespread national goal, managers must understand that governments have multiple goals, such as consumption, equity, employment, technological progress, national sovereignty and political survival. The policies adopted to achieve them and the implications for business vary substantially.

Governments implement policies through institutions using a variety of policy instruments applied in several policy areas, as summarized in Table 2. The move towards privatization and market liberalization is an ongoing shift in the relative importance and availability of policy instruments.

A policy's impact on a firm depends on the instruments used and the institution that implements it. Managers need to understand institutions' organizational structures, capacities and motivations to assess the best way of interacting with them. Managers also need to be aware of the ways in which policies impact on the firm. To do so, it is useful to identify the points, within the company, where different policies have their greatest effects. By doing so, managers can delegate to the appropriate levels the task of monitoring and reacting to government actions.

Industry level

As illustrated in the public–policy impact chain, government actions affect the competitive dynamics and structure of industries: the third level of analysis required in the EAF. While there are well-known approaches to industry analysis in developed countries, such analyses must be modified in LDCs to consider explicitly the powerful influence of governments and the diverse types of players who participate in LDCs. These players, with different competitive strengths and weaknesses, are local firms and cooperatives, state-owned enterprises, business groups, informal sector producers and multinational corporations. The government, in particular, may alter the bargaining power of suppliers or of buyers, may raise or lower barriers to entry, can create or eliminate substitution pressures, and can affect the intensity of rivalry within an industry. Because of the privatization of state-owned enterprises that is taking place in many LDCs, managers must carefully monitor and react to the resulting sudden changes in industry dynamics.

Company level

The fourth environmental level is the firm itself. The goal of the EAF is to focus on the environment's impact on the firm. Further analyses of the interrelation between the environment and the firm are discussed next.

4 Business–government relations

The environmental analysis framework provides managers with the tools to assess the managerial implications of the business environment. Since that environment is greatly affected by government, we focus first on managing business–government relations.

Dealing with the government is often the key external relationship of a developing country firm. It is essential to manage this relationship effectively, and specific strategies to do so must be developed. In formulating such strategies the manager must answer three questions: (1) What do I need from whom in the government? (2) What does the government entity need that I have and how much does it need it? (3) How should I interact with the government? Once the firm's needs are clearly defined, the task of identifying and understanding the government's needs begins. This is complex, given that the government is not a unitary force. There is a multiplicity of actors with a variety of, often conflicting, goals. It becomes necessary to create a political map of actors – such as national-level officials, bureaucrats, political party officials, labour leaders, state-owned enterprises, and a variety of pressure groups – and identify their interests and power so as to assess how well the company may contribute to the actors' (and government's) needs, thereby understanding its bargaining power.

Such understanding is essential, since the business–government relation is a power relationship. The manager who can achieve company–government congruency is likely to succeed in negotiations with the government (Austin 1990: 156–65). One can construct a 'congruency matrix' that compares company resources to government needs to identify intersecting areas. However, one must understand that a company's bargaining power tends to erode over time and needs to be reassessed periodically by asking the same questions over and over again. By understanding the relative power of the firm and assessing the importance of issues under negotiation, managers can adopt a strategic approach to government relations. Schematically, the strategies of the firm faced with government actions can be represented as in Figure 3. Sometimes the firm needs to alter the government's positions, while at other times it may accede to

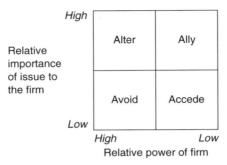

Figure 3 The '4a' approach to strategic government relations

government requests. Alternatively, the firm may seek allies to improve its bargaining position or may avoid the issues altogether by changing its strategies (the '4A' approach).

In their dealings with governments, managers often encounter the problem of corruption. The need, real or perceived, to pay someone in order to receive a service is pervasive and creates practical, legal and ethical dilemmas. On the practical side, refraining from bribery requires patience and perseverance, but can – and often does – produce superior long-term results. On the legal side, bribery is generally not condoned, and in the case of US multinationals is punished under the Foreign Corrupt Practices Act of 1977. On the ethical side, the presence of corrupt practices makes it necessary for managers and companies to state their positions clearly, including establishing corporate codes of conduct.

5 Finance

Special challenges in the financial management of LDC companies are the problems associated with inflation, exchange rate instability and capital scarcity (see BANKING AND FINANCE IN THE EMERGING COUNTRIES). Inflation creates havoc with management control tools by giving rise to illusory profits when companies use 'generally accepted accounting practices'. Illusory profits lead to incorrect decisions and result in excessive tax burdens. Inflation can also lead to liquidity problems and complicates relations with suppliers, customers and employees. To manage in inflationary environments managers need to understand the forces that lead to price increases and forecast such changes. The need to forecast is paramount, since products will cost more and money will be worth less. Therefore pricing must be based on replacement costs rather than accounting historical information. It is feasible to handle the complexities of high inflation and companies that do so effectively will create competitive advantages.

Closely tied to inflation is exchange rate instability. There are two issues managers need to understand: how best to forecast shifts in the value of the local currency and how to deal with them. While purchasing power theory provides much guidance for exchange rate forecasting based on relative inflation rates, it is important for managers to understand that other forces also influence exchange rates (Salvatore 1995). One such force is the country's ability to generate the foreign exchange it needs for its imports. In this regard, managers should monitor countries' balance of payments statistics for the sources and uses of foreign exchange. Important items to monitor include the trade balance, debt-service payments, foreign aid and remittances, inflow of foreign capital, outflow of domestic capital and the level of foreign reserves. When monitoring foreign capital flows it is important to distinguish between direct investments, which tend to be stable and long term, and portfolio investments, which tend to be unstable and may create significant pressures on a country's reserves with slight changes in the international financial market's perception of a country's investment risk.

In LDCs, import and capital controls, combined with direct government intervention, often drive exchange rates. Since devaluations do not affect all groups equally, it is important to understand the power and interest of different groups who may influence government actions. To deal with exchange rate fluctuations managers must manage the three types of risk that exposure to such fluctuations creates.

Transaction exposure arises out of transactions denominated in a currency whose value changes relative to the home currency during the life of the transaction. To deal with such exposure managers may avoid entering into foreign currency transactions or hedge their exposure in the foreign currency futures market.

Translation exposure arises out of multinational companies' need to translate foreign subsidiary's financial statements. While certain measures can be taken to reduce translation exposure, managers must recognize that translation charges are accounting entries and often do not reflect economic realities. Therefore, one must caution against actions that are taken to minimize translation losses at the expense of sound management practices.

Operating exposure arises when changes in the real, not the nominal, exchange rate affect the relationship between revenues and expenses of a company or alter the relationship between the costs of different competitors in an industry. Since operating exposure affects the essence of firms' profitability, managers must be alert to the adjustments needed to prevent a loss of competitive advantage. Such adjustments may include alternative sourcing practices, different marketing strategies, and creative approaches to financial issues.

Because of the scarcity of capital in most LDCs, firms need to economize on capital uses with appropriate choices of technology and of management practices. The interest in emerging economies' equity markets creates the opportunity for firms to raise equity capital, and the growing integration of capital markets enables firms to tap into international financial sources through American Depository Receipts (ADRs) and Global Depository Receipts (GDRs). To do so, firms must adopt management and accounting practices that enable them to be viewed as reputable well-managed operations. Equity financing may also be found in private placements or joint ventures. Debt financing is sometimes available on preferential terms to local firms while multinationals benefit from access to international lending institutions.

6 Production

A critical aspect in a company's operations is its choice of technology (see MANAGEMENT OF TECHNOLOGY IN THE EMERGING COUNTRIES; MANUFACTURING

IN THE EMERGING COUNTRIES). While some technological innovations originate in LDCs, most come from developed countries and need to be transferred, and often adapted, to the host country. The efficiency of the transfer is affected by the mechanisms used. Foreign direct investment creates a long-term link between the technology supplier and user and often results in creative multi-directional technology flows. Licensing can also yield long-term flows and separates technology transfer from ownership issues. Governments often scrutinize technology transfer agreements to prevent the inclusion of unduly restrictive clauses. LDC companies can also acquire technology through equipment purchases, technical services and training programmes, access to public information and the hiring of trained employees. A country's and a company's goal should be to move up the technological capability ladder by creating the human skills needed to deal with the complexity involved in going from adopting to adapting to enhancing and, finally, to creating new technology.

A firm's technology choice needs to take into account the relative factor costs in a country, market requirements (both local and international), technical constraints, availability of inputs (such as skilled labour, raw materials, energy and support services) and competitive dynamics. Because of inadequate availability of inputs in many LDCs, firms often find that they consider two options that they would not necessarily consider in developed countries: backward vertical integration (BVI) and structured subcontractor assistance programmes. While BVI has the advantage of greater control and possibly reduced cost, it has the disadvantage of reduced flexibility, increased capital requirement, and increased managerial complexity. The need for production and technology strategies that are consistent with the local business environment is increasingly important because of the growing emphasis of LDC governments on export promotion, the intensified competition as LDCs liberalize their economies, and the growth of global industries where manufacturing strategies are sources of competitive advantage. Also, given that governments and companies are becoming more concerned with the ecological implications of development, ecologically sensitive production processes will be the rule of thumb in the future.

7 Marketing

Emerging country environments pose several key challenges to marketing managers (see MARKETING IN THE EMERGING COUNTRIES). Product policy must be adapted taking into account demographic, economic, political, and cultural factors. Pricing in the low per capita income and often inflationary LDC environments poses special challenges. Promotional strategies are influenced by media availability, population distribution, literacy rates, mail and telephone service availability and linguistic and cultural diversity. Distribution systems need to take into account infrastructure deficiencies and local customs and practices. Often, aspects of a country's commercial network are controlled by certain ethnic groups, restricting access to outsiders and creating advantages for those who penetrate the system. The ability to develop marketing strategies is hampered by the inability to obtain sufficient and accurate information. It may also be hampered if marketers do not ensure that their products, and the way they market them, are compatible with consumers' circumstances and contribute to enhance their well-being.

Given the emphasis for exports in most LDCs, a critical marketing task is often the ability to succeed in the international marketplace. Managers must be aware that although they may have cost advantages in manufacturing, there are significant barriers to exports that need to be overcome. These include unacceptable product quality, unreliable delivery, insufficient manufacturing capacity, inadequate information of markets and export processes, limited access to distribution channels, logistical difficulties, high costs (sometimes caused by overvalued exchange rates) and trade restrictions. Some of these barriers are reduced when exporting among developing countries, and the growth of regional free-trade areas such as Mercosur and the Andean Pact enable LDC companies to learn how to overcome their exporting handicaps.

8 Organization

We highlight here three organizational issues that companies need to address when entering a developing country market. The first is 'entry form', with different levels of resource commitment and risk, ranging from exporting from the home country to licensing or subcontracting a local firm to foreign direct investment (FDI) in the host country. Using the EAF managers can evaluate systematically the desirability of different options. The chosen alternative should be the result of evaluating the country's economic (market size, labour costs and skills, managerial capacity, infrastructure adequacy), political (stability, governmental receptiveness of FDI, regulatory environment) and cultural (compatibility) characteristics, the industry dynamics, and the company's product, technology, managerial and financial resources and globalization strategy (see PERSPECTIVES ON GLOBALIZATION, BIG BUSINESS AND THE EMERGING COUNTRIES).

The second is 'ownership strategy'. In the case of FDI, the firm must decide between a joint venture and a wholly-owned investment. On the positive side, joint ventures can provide resources (capital, technology, management know-how and so on) needed by the partners, can serve as political insurance, and create competitive advantage. Local partners can be cultural guides and provide political access (know-who). On the negative side, problems can arise from conflicting priorities, loss of control, and excessive costs of interaction and coordination. Managers must assess the pros and cons of alternative ownership strategies and devise optimal solutions taking into account the business environment. Since conditions change over time, ownership strategies may also have to change, and managers should contemplate this in the arrangements they make at the outset.

Finally, 'organizational design and processes' need to be established taking cultural factors into consideration. This can be done by relating cultural values, attitudes, and behaviour to the organizational areas they most affect. For example, social structures will have an impact on organizational structures, societal relationships will influence manager–employee relations, interpersonal orientation will affect group processes, motivation will colour the nature of incentive and evaluation systems, perception of time will influence planning processes, and perception of space will affect office and factory layout. In general, one can ascertain that cultural sensitivity along with economic acumen and political dexterity are necessary to manage successfully in LDCs.

9 Conclusion

Doing business in emerging countries is extremely difficult, yet the importance of doing it well and the opportunities available make confronting these difficulties a growing managerial imperative in conducting international business (see Warner 1997). Developing the capabilities needed to deal effectively with the contextual uncertainties and complexities will be a source of competitive advantage. The environmental analysis framework can be a powerful companion in achieving managerial competency. Also, the journey towards excellence must be accompanied by a leadership perspective that understands business's important contribution to, and responsibility for, improving the economic and social well-being of developing countries. Competency and commitment will foster meaningful progress.

TOMÁS O. KOHN
BOSTON UNIVERSITY
SCHOOL OF MANAGEMENT

JAMES E. AUSTIN
HARVARD UNIVERSITY

Further reading

(References cited in the text marked *)

* Austin, J.E. (1990) *Managing in Developing Countries: Strategic Analysis and Operating Techniques*, New York: The Free Press. (Analysis of the dynamics of the Third World business environment where, unlike the West, government is what the author terms a 'megaforce'.)

Austin, J.E. and Kohn, T.O. (1990) *Strategic Management in Developing Countries: Case Studies*, New York: The Free Press. (Collection of case studies designed to add substance to the points made in *Managing in Developing Countries*.)

Buckley, P. and Mirza, H. (eds) (1996) *International Technology Transfer by Small and Medium-sized Enterprises: Country Studies*, London: Macmillan. (Addresses a number of key issues related to technology transfer by small- and medium-sized enterprises, most especially whether such companies are more effective transferors than larger transnational corporations.)

* Kakwani, N. (1980) *Income Inequality and Poverty*, New York: Oxford University Press, published in association with the World Bank.

Kenwood, G. and Loughheed, A. (1999) *Growth of the International Economy*, London: Routledge. (A useful account of the growth of the world economy 1820–2000.)

* Lecaillon, J. (1984) *Income Distribution and Economic Development: An Analytical Survey*, Geneva: International Labour Office.

Porter, M.E. (1980) *Competitive Strategy*, New York: The Free Press. (Addresses major questions of concern to managers, and presents a comprehensive set of analytical techniques for understanding a business and the behaviour of its competitors.)

Porter, M.E. (1985) *Competitive Advantage*, New York: The Free Press. (Introduces a tool that may be used to diagnose and enhance competitive advantage: the value chain.)

* Salvatore, D. (1995) *International Economics*, Englewood Cliffs, NJ: Prentice Hall. (Presents international economics, emphasizing the relevance of concepts and theories through numerous real-world examples.)

* Sewell, J., Feinberg, R.E. and Kallab, V. (eds) (1985) *US Foreign Policy and the Third World: Agenda 1985–1986*, New Brunswick, NJ: Transaction Publishers.

Stobaugh, R. and Wells, L.T. (eds) (1980) *Technology Crossing Borders: The Choice Transfer, and Management of International Technology Flows*, Boston, MA: Harvard Business School Press.

* Warner, M. (ed.) (1997) *Comparative Management,* London: Routledge. (A 4-volume set of readings on comparative management. The fourth volume deals with the emerging countries.)

Wells, L.T. (1983) *Third World Multinationals: The Rise of Foreign Investment from Developing Countries*, Cambridge, MA: MIT Press.

World Bank (1993) *The East Asian Miracle*, New York: Oxford University Press. (Study examines the public policies of eight high-performing Asian economies from 1965–90.)

* World Bank *World Development Report*, New York: Oxford University Press, published annually. (Annual report on the world economy and the state of social and economic development.)

See also: BUSINESS CULTURES, THE EMERGING COUNTRIES; ECONOMIES OF THE EMERGING COUNTRIES; HUMAN RESOURCE MANAGEMENT IN THE EMERGING COUNTRIES; INDUSTRIAL RELATIONS IN THE EMERGING COUNTRIES; MANAGEMENT EDUCATION IN THE EMERGING COUNTRIES; MANAGEMENT OF TECHNOLOGY IN THE EMERGING COUNTRIES; MANUFACTURING IN THE EMERGING COUNTRIES; MARKETING IN THE EMERGING COUNTRIES

Related topics in the IEBM regional set: MANAGEMENT EDUCATION IN ASIA PACIFIC; MANAGEMENT EDUCATION IN LATIN AMERICA; MANAGEMENT IN ASIA PACIFIC; MANAGEMENT IN LATIN AMERICA

Perspectives on globalization, big business and the emerging countries

1 Introduction
2 Big business and catch-up in the past
3 The big business revolution in the West since the 1980s
4 Conclusion

Overview

This contribution examines the changing nature and extent of the gap between big businesses in advanced capitalist countries and businesses in the emerging countries. First, it looks at the way in which big businesses have grown in capitalist latecomer countries; these have almost entirely been with extensive state support. There is hardly a single example of a successful big business emerging without state support in latecomer countries. Next, the entry examines the dramatic transformation in the nature of capitalist big business since the 1980s, in the epoch of explosive liberalization and globalization, a process that is still in its infancy. It argues that the gap between the dominant big businesses of advanced capitalism today and those of the emerging countries is becoming rapidly wider. The height of the barriers to entry is growing at high speed in the new epoch. Central goals of capitalist big businesses are to capture market share and, from this position, create barriers to entry. As the successful globalizing large businesses establish themselves, so they establish global 'first mover advantage', and it will become more and more difficult to dislodge them from their position of market dominance. In the new environment of liberalized international trade and capital flows, and with ever more stringently enforced intellectual property rights, it becomes ever more difficult for emerging countries to imagine that they can successfully develop their 'own' big businesses to challenge those of the advanced economies.

1 Introduction

The great challenge for policy makers in emerging countries is to determine the degree to which it is desirable and feasible to attempt to construct indigenously owned businesses, which can challenge the global giants (see STRATEGY IN THE EMERGING COUNTRIES). Given that capital has no nationality, is there any point in attempting to construct one's own 'national big business'? If a given country, even a huge one such as China, attempts to do so, what are the costs that might be involved in the attempt, in terms of sheltering inefficient industries? In the long run, will globalizing big business possess any 'nationality'? Will the ownership and the core of operations naturally gravitate in the long term towards the main locations of the market and global income?

2 Big business and catch-up in the past

Centrality of big business in the West

The earliest forms of the modern industrial enterprise were found in the railways of the United States and Europe in the mid-nineteenth century. These quickly developed into the world's largest business institutions, often with tens of thousands of employees. Such vast organizations quickly developed hierarchical professional bureaucracies, and associated impersonal procedures for coordinating and monitoring the large numbers of employees. The railways mobilized vast sums of investment funds from an increasingly widespread body of shareholders (Schmitz 1993: 19–21). These characteristic features of the modern industrial enterprise quickly spread to other parts of the economy in which large business emerged. These were industries characterized by greater economies of scale, greater potential gains from vertical integration, greater speed and coordination of production flows, as well as greater gains from high-volume marketing. These were notably the food, chemicals, primary metals and transportation equipment sectors. By the 1930s, the one hundred largest firms accounted for around one-quarter of total manufacturing output in Britain and the United States. By the 1960s the share had risen to one-third or more (Schmitz 1993: 35).

The most usual path for pre-war giant firms to grow was through vertical integration. Purchase of a large array of inputs through the market was judged to involve relatively high transaction costs in relation to such issues as ensuring timeliness of supply and product quality, and it was thought to be cheaper to produce the inputs within the firm. The large multi-plant firm was a central force in cost reduction and technical progress. It often benefited from economies of scale at the plant level, associated with reduction in unit costs. In many sectors plants of less than a certain scale faced substantial unit cost disadvantages. Large firms often benefited also from economies of 'scope' arising from product diversification associated with reduced transaction costs involved in multi-plant operation. Large, multi-plant firms may benefit from lower unit costs in purchasing inputs, reduced transport costs, superior research and development, reduced risk from operating in several markets or across several products, lower capital costs, the capacity to create a brand name, credit provision to customers and after-sales service (Chandler 1990: 200). In many sectors firms that do not operate several plants are at a competitive disadvantage (Scherer and Ross 1990: 115 and 140). The modern industrial enterprise 'played a central role in creating the most technologically advanced, fastest growing industries of their day'; these industries, in turn, were 'the pace-setters of the industrial sector of their economies' (Chandler 1990: 593).

Mergers and acquisitions played an important role in the emergence of the giant corporations of the advanced capitalist economies. Merger activity has typically intensified in the final phase of a bull market on the stock exchange, as firms use their increased stock market 'wealth' to finance take-overs. Sixty-three of the 100 largest US firms in 1955 experienced their main spurt of growth as a result of merger activity, including 20 in the 1895–1904 merger wave; in Britain, more than 75 per cent of the increase in market share of 600 leading firms between 1919 and 1930 is accounted for by mergers (Schmitz 1993: 47–8).

The state and the rise of big business in the West

Far from arising completely spontaneously through the free play of market forces, even the rise of big business in the West was strongly influenced by the state: 'Virtually all of the world's largest core firms have experienced a decisive influence from government policies and/or trade barriers on their strategy and competitive position. History matters! There has never been a "level playing field" in international competition, and it is doubtful whether there ever will be one' (Ruigrok and Van Tulder 1995: 221).

Britain's Industrial Revolution was enormously shaped by state intervention. By the 1840s Britain had become the home of free trade, imposing the doctrine of *laissez-faire* upon its vast colonial territories. However, Britain's own business revolution took place under an explicitly Mercantilist philosophy of high protection and export promotion, not to speak of massive territorial conquest largely in pursuit of economic benefit. Its infant industries were heavily protected, denying the massive textile industries of China and India access to the British market (Smith 1776: vol. 1, book iv, chapter 2), and gave Britain's infant textile industries the chance to mature. Moreover, while Britain's authoritarian state had no laws to prohibit capitalists from combining to lower the price of labour, it had 'many [laws] against [workmen] combining to raise it' (Smith 1776: vol. 1, chapter viii, 74–5). By the mid-nineteenth century Britain's 'big business' (compared to the rest of the world) was able to prosper with free trade. It is highly questionable whether Britain would indeed have been the 'First Industrial Nation' without extensive state intervention.

The USA in the nineteenth century unashamedly industrialized behind high protectionist barriers, 'free riding on free trade' (Lake 1988: chapter 3). For almost two centuries, US tariffs rarely were below 30 per cent, and often much higher (Ruigrok and Van Tulder 1995: 211–12). By the inter-war period, US firms dominated big business globally, with around two-thirds of the world's top fifty companies. Despite extensive public discussion and academic analysis of big business, there is little evidence that antitrust law in the USA did much to hinder the rise of large US firms. Indeed, it has even been argued that the key piece of American antitrust legislation, the Sherman Act of 1890, actually promoted the growth of big business. It is argued that it encouraged the abandonment of cartels in favour of large, integrated firms. During the First World War and much of the Depression of the 1930s, federal government effectively ignored antitrust law, in order 'to stimulate the economy' (Schmitz, 1993: 55).

East Asian latecomer countries

The large firm has been central also in the late industrializing economies of East Asia; this phenomenon points to important lessons for emerging countries elsewhere. The extent of state support required to develop powerful indigenous large firms was even greater than that required in Britain in the Industrial Revolution, or in the UA in the late nineteenth century. As the technical and institutional gap between latecomers and the advanced economies rose, so the extent of necessary state intervention increased.

Japan: the entrepreneurial state

In Japan the catch-up process after the Second World War was facilitated by the Japanese government, the Ministry of International Trade and Industry (MITI) in particular, through a wide array of trade and industrial policies that went counter to mainstream economic theory (Johnson 1982). As one of the key bureaucrats in MITI said: '[w]e did the opposite of what the American economist told us to do. We violated all the normal concepts' (quoted in Ruigrok and Van Tulder 1995: 214). In 1962, Japan had 31 of the world's 500 largest enterprises: by 1992 the number had risen to 128 (Amsden and Singh 1994: 115). By 1997, Japan had 26 of the world's 100 largest corporations (by value of sales) (*Fortune* 3 August 1998).

In the early post-war period, the US occupying forces imposed American anti-trust laws upon Japan. Initially these were strictly applied. They led to the dismantling of the leading pre-war *zaibatsu*, the large industrial groups which had dominated the inter-war Japanese economy. However, under pressure of the Cold War, there occurred 'a rapid erosion of the competition laws, both *de facto* and *de jure*' (Amsden and Singh 1994). The government encouraged the reconstruction of the *zaibatsu*, albeit in a somewhat looser form, known as *keiretsu*. The goal of the Japanese government was explicitly to create oligopolistic competition (Okimoto 1989: 12–13, quoted in Amsden and Singh 1994: 943–4).

MITI, the government's planning body, actively encouraged mergers between leading firms in key industries. It was only able to allow competitive large firms to develop through 'draconian import controls' (Amsden and Singh 1994: 946). However, the government was acutely aware of the need to avoid monopoly and encourage oligopolistic rivalry. It closely monitored market shares and prevented any single investment from being big enough to destabilize the market. International competitiveness was powerfully encouraged through the use of exports and international market share as the performance goals with which to evaluate the extent of government support for big businesses through different policies: 'Protection, together with restrictions on domestic competition, provided the Japanese companies with a captive home market leading to high profits which enabled them to undertake high rates of investment, to improve the quality their products, and also to capture market abroad' (Amsden and Singh 1994: 945–6).

Most large Japanese companies are members of a small number of industrial groups, the *keiretsu*; it usually owns less than 2 per cent of any other member firm, but it typically has a stake of that size in every firm in the group, so that between 30 and 90 per cent of a firm is owned by other group members. Japanese corporations have about 70 per cent of their shares held by other corporations (Aoki 1994: 21). The system is a kind of 'collective defence to maintain the control by management over ownership' (Suzuki 1991: 78–9). Under this system, there was only a low level of merger and acquisition. The removal of ownership control means that the unconstrained Japanese managers can afford to ill-treat owners with impunity. In 1990, the total dividend payout of all public corporations in Japan was 30 per cent of profits compared with 50 per cent in Germany, 54 per cent in the US, and 66 per cent in the UK. Japanese managers were able to ignore short-term profitability as a measure of their performance and concentrate instead on 'Schumpeterian' competition, such as foreign market penetration, quality control, and long-term product development. 'Share price increase' is their least important target, and 'market domination' their most important one (Best 1990: 10).

Taiwan and South Korea: the developmental state

In Taiwan and South Korea the state went far beyond influencing the environment within which big business operated. In both cases, the state played an important role in the construction of large-scale business through the direct operation of upstream, heavy industry, which the private sector was unable or unwilling to undertake.

Taiwan

The state concentrated its influence upon the relatively large-scale firms (over 300 employees), which accounted for around 60 per cent of the total value of industrial output in the 1980s, 'leaving the downstream smaller-scale firms much freer' (Wade 1990: 73 and 110). Through its extensive ownership and operation of vital upstream industries, as well as numerous other measures, such as import controls, tariffs, entry requirements, domestic content requirements, and concessional credit, the Taiwanese state has strongly influenced the operation of the private sector. Taiwan has thirteen of the top 100 Asian business (by market capitalization; *Financial Times* 24 January 1997), and six of the world's top fifty multinationals (ranked by foreign assets) based in emerging countries (UNCTAD 1996: 34–5).

South Korea

The South Korean government actively encouraged the growth of powerful, large-scale private businesses, the *chaebols*, by providing them with a protected domestic market, and supplying them with tightly controlled, but low-interest credit from the state-owned banking system (Chang 1994). Like the Japanese state, South Korea was acutely aware of the importance of maintaining competition among its large oligopolistic firms. It went out of its way to ensure that big business did not collude, by allocating subsidies only in exchange for strict performance standards (Amsden and Singh 1994: 948). Moreover, like Japan also, its exports were a major criterion on which the state provided policy and financial support to developing big business. It was prepared to provide long-term support until the businesses became internationally competitive, enabling firms to have long time horizons for their investment plans (Amsden and Singh 1994: 949). Like Japan, the economy was massively protected from import competition for a long period while its big businesses were nurtured.

By 1985, South Korea had 35 of the top 200 largest industrial enterprises in emerging countries, including 11 of the 29 'high-tech' companies and 13 of the 'mid-tech' companies within this group (Amsden 1994: 302). Uniquely among emerging countries, by 1993, South Korea had no fewer than four companies in the Fortune 100 list of the world's largest companies, namely Samsung, Daewoo, Ssangyong and Sankyong (Ruigrok and Van Tulder 1995: Table 9A).

3 The big business revolution in the West since the 1980s

Direct importance of big business in advanced capitalism

In recent years, there has been a sharp increase in the role of small and medium-sized firms, leading many commentators to believe that the age of the large firm is over. Using computer numerically controlled machine tools, firms frequently replace conventional automated production with flexible manufacturing systems. A large increase has occurred in outsourcing of components and service activities by large firms. The early 1990s saw a considerable 'downsizing' in employment in large firms associated with the cyclical downturn in demand in the OECD (Organization for Economic Cooperation and Development) countries: total employment in the firms included in the Fortune 500 list fell from over sixteen million in 1990 to under twelve million in 1994. Despite the belief in the growing importance of small and medium-sized businesses, big businesses still occupy centre stage in the advanced capitalist economies. Huge corporations with tens or even hundreds of thousands of employees stand at the centre of the capitalist system. In 1990, the share of the largest 100 manufacturing firms stood at 20 per cent of GNP in Europe, 24 per cent in the USA and 30 per cent in Japan (Ruigrok and Van Tulder 1995: 155).

The share of the largest firms within any given economy or region fails to capture the real nature of the global business revolution in the 1990s. The dramatic shift towards focus on core business and the explosion of multinational investment has produced a extraordinarily rapid process of concentration of economic influence in sector after sector. In the 'first round' of concentration, the main impact was felt upon globally powerful brand names, those with special R&D capabilities and the ability to achieve systems integration. Ten or twenty years ago, a 'powerful' company might achieve a national market share of, say, 25 per cent. Today, 'powerful', 'competitive edge' companies achieve global market shares of 20–25 per cent. Facilitated by the stock market, mergers and acquisitions have led at high speed to the dominance of just three or four companies in sector after sector, not just in national or even regional markets, but across the world.

'Global Toyotism' in advanced and emerging countries

The relative cost of purchasing inputs through the market, as opposed to production within the firm, has fallen radically in recent years. This reduction has been partly due to explosive changes in communications technology and partly due to increased access by large firms to cheap, non-unionized labour forces both within advanced economies and in emerging countries (see INDUSTRIAL RELATIONS IN THE EMERGING COUNTRIES). Changes in labour law in many advanced economies have made it much less difficult to shift vast ranges of functions out of the firm into the hands of specialist suppliers. As specialist suppliers of goods and services themselves consolidate, so they also can become better able to invest in R&D and information systems, enabling them to supply improved products at falling real prices. It has become less necessary to organize a wide range of activities within the firms, and the costs of attempting to do so, compared to purchasing such products from specialist suppliers, has risen steadily.

Through the *'external' firm*, or myriad of related businesses across the globe, the modern capitalist big business stands at the centre of a vast network of other businesses, all dependent upon the core business for their success. Networks of 'aligned' suppliers and purchasers of the core companies' products are fast developing. The growth and prosperity of the small and medium-sized enterprises (SMEs) is closely dependent on the global success of the large firms to which they are suppliers (see MANUFACTURING IN THE EMERGING COUNTRIES). Moreover, an important process of consolidation is now taking place among first-tier suppliers in industry after industry.

In industries as diverse as soft drinks, aerospace and automobiles, manufacturers are selecting a greatly reduced number of 'aligned' suppliers to establish global supply systems. The companies that are successful in this 'industrial policy', organized by big business, are able to use their success to acquire other suppliers and establish leading positions in their respective sectors. Each of them is able to benefit from high levels of R&D, global procurement systems and enhanced resources to spend on information technology, mimicking the development of globalizing core businesses. In time, the concentration process is likely to cascade downwards to include second-tier suppliers. In pursuit of competitive edge as world-class suppliers of goods and services, a small number of globally dominant businesses has emerged in almost every sector that is a 'first tier' supplier to globally powerful companies.

Around 37,000 transnational corporations (TNCs) worldwide directly employ around 73 million people, or around 20 per cent of the employment of the advanced capitalist countries, and account for one-fourth of all global technological innovations. However, such firms increasingly stand at the centre of an industrial 'web' of suppliers who depend on them for their existence and prosperity, in a new global form of the late medieval 'putting out system'. These account for at least as many 'indirect employees' as are directly employed by the giant firms. The TNCs' total share of employment in the advanced economies may be around 40 per cent: 'There is dire need for new statistical techniques to assess the influence of "transnationals" on indirect employment and to cope with the paradox that core firms with a Toyotist concept of control have increased their structural influence over the economy, because they have lowered their number of directly employed workers' (Ruigrok and Van Tulder 1995: 155).

Merger frenzy of the 1990s

The 'core' of the world's most powerful firms is growing fast, despite outsourcing and disposal of 'non-core business. In the 1990s the rapid liberalization of world trade and investment flows (see ECONOMIES OF THE EMERGING COUNTRIES) has allowed a rapid growth in both developed and developing economies, and in particular a powerful tendency towards concentration of ownership. In industry after industry there has occurred a rise in the global market share accounted for by a small number of firms expanding to some degree through organic growth, but above all, by merger and acquisition within their core competence as the size of competitive global markets has massively increased (see MARKETING IN THE EMERGING COUNTRIES). The full flowering of the innate oligopolistic tendencies of capitalism are finally being realized, at high speed.

The pace of transnational merger and acquisition in the 1990s has gathered pace at extraordinary speed. From $156 billion in transactions in 1992, the global total nearly doubled to $290 billion in 1994, and then soared to $1,100 billion in 1997 (Morgan Stanley Dean Witter 1998: 4). Eight of the world's ten largest mergers took place in 1998, with a total value of $563 billion. The total value of mergers and acquisitions in 1998 was over $2,000 billion (*Fortune* 11 January 1999). The Morgan Stanley survey of 'competitive edge' companies noted the following in relation to the new pattern of mergers: 'First, mergers have become favoured over take-overs. In particular, mergers of companies of equal size and position in the same industry have become a key method of improving sales per employee and market position. Second, the strategic rationale for many transactions has changed in the last decade. In surveys of European companies, diversification was cited as one of the top reasons for M and A activity ten years ago. More recently, focus and consolidation – along with cost reduction – have been given as the top reasons' (Morgan Stanley Dean Witter 1998: 5).

Hardly a sector has not seen this process. The 1990s have witnessed a unique epoch of concentration of economic power. There has been a powerful trend towards concentration in almost every sector. Some of the more prominent examples include aerospace, defence equipment, power equipment, farm machinery, automobiles, automobile components, pharmaceuticals, soft drinks, alcoholic drinks, snack foods, household goods (from detergents to shampoo and toothpaste), telecommunications, chemical fertilizers, pulp and paper, power generation, hotels, travel agents, advertising, retailing, financial services, accountancy, and legal practices.

It will be seen below that the 1990s are witnessing a massive process of asset reorganization within giant capitalist firms. Following the extensive diversification of the 1980s, the 1990s have seen a dramatic change in big business philosophy and practice. Firm after firm has shed non-core business in order to focus on the areas in which the firm can compete globally. This sharp focus has enabled businesses to develop vast global businesses within a much narrower range of competence than previously. Moreover, the sharpening of focus has meant that large businesses can now devote much greater resources to their chosen activities. They can do so in order to develop distinctive, proprietary technologies, in order to develop the company's brand name through diverse, aggressive marketing across the globe, and in order to develop competitive advantage through the skills and technology, especially information systems, needed to knit together the value-chain upstream and downstream. Under the new paradigm of globalizing business systems, the barriers to entry for businesses in emerging markets have thus dramatically increased. Indeed, a major goal of mergers and acquisitions has been precisely the creation of barriers to entry (an issue of great relevance to poorer economies, for example in South Asia and Africa).

Globalization and the Anglo-Saxon business model

Furthermore, the global business revolution of the 1990s saw a sharp change in the relative economic fortunes of different parts of the advanced capitalist system. In the 1980s a large part of business economics was concerned with explaining the relative success of East Asian latecomers, such as Japan and South Korea. There was a large literature on the apparent disadvantages of the Anglo-Saxon business structure. The capitalist stock market-based system was argued to be disadvantageous for long-term growth and competitiveness. The 1990s have seen a dramatic turnaround in relative economic performance, with a sharp improvement in the relative performance of US firms: 'The US has the lion's share of those corporations equipped to exploit global markets. It also supplies the bulk of the technology that knits those markets together' (*Financial Times* 14 June 1997). The Anglo-Saxon big businesses have absorbed many of the lessons of the East Asian model, especially those of Toyotist downsizing and outsourcing. The 1990s 'business revolution' has shown that the stock market can be seen as perfectly compatible with long-term perspectives. Indeed, it may even be argued that the extraordinary surge in stock market valuations for globalizing, downsizing, big businesses has demonstrated an irrational excess of optimism about the long-term growth prospects for big businesses in the epoch of globalization.

This view is reinforced strongly by the *Competitive Edge* studies published by Morgan Stanley Dean Witter (Morgan Stanley 1997, 1998 and 1999). These studies ranked companies by their capacity to have a sustainable 'competitive edge' in the global economy. Morgan Stanley's objective was to 'identify companies with a meaningful advantage in their global sectors'. Their objective was to assemble 'a comprehensive view of the competitive landscape, country by country, and industry by industry' (Morgan Stanley 1998: Introduction). They ranked large quoted companies in terms of their competitive advantage in their respective sector. A key issue was global market share, which strongly influences the capability of new entrants to catch up: the higher the share, the more sustainable was the firm's leadership judged to be. In 1998, they identified a total of 250 companies that were 'world leaders'. Of these, no fewer than 133 were North American. Japan had just 21 companies that were identified as 'world leaders'.

Leading US companies have taken on the 'just-in-time' management practices of their Japanese competitors, but have gone much further in downsizing employment and investing in new technology: 'Throughout the 1990s corporate America, which grew lazy in the 1970s and early 1980s, has been in the throes of a far-reaching restructuring – much of it learned from Japan. Displaying remarkable flexibility, many US industries have regained their competitive edge … and this has helped power an extraordinary bull market in equities' (*Financial Times* 24 January 1997). In the top 100 companies ranked by value of overseas assets, the USA has no less than 32 entries (UNCTAD 1996: 33).

A 'business revolution' is being forced upon formerly distinctive business structures. To be successful on the 'global level field' requires focus on core business and a global capability. The frame of reference for competitive success has become the world's leading-edge firms, instead of national or regional leading firms. What we may call a 'global business revolution', in tandem with the Asian crisis of 1997/98, has forced drastic restructuring of East Asian businesses along Anglo-Saxon lines.

In 1998, South Korea's top five *chaebols*, Hyundai, Samsung, LG, Daewoo and Sk, agreed to a government-orchestrated restructuring. Having renationalized the big banks, the government is able to use credit control as an instrument to impose restructuring upon the *chaebols*. They agreed to halve their total number of subsidiaries and participate in a comprehensive asset-swapping exercise that would enable much firmer focus on core business, to enable benefits from economies of scale. The goal was to reduce the number of Korean competitors to just two in critical export industries. After the asset swaps, Hyundai and Daewoo will be the only car manufacturers, Samsung and LG/Hyundai will be the only semiconductor manufacturers, and Samsung and LG will be the only consumer electronics groups (*Financial Times* 8 December 1998). Samsung is merging its petrochemicals and aerospace divisions with another *chaebol*. Hyundai is merging its petrochemicals, power generation and railway rolling stock operations with a rival *chaebol*.

Most large Japanese companies are in a desperate state, with deep structural problems exacerbated by the Asian crisis. The 'global business revolution' has seen a dramatic turn-around in the fortunes of Japan's leading companies. In 1990, six of the world's top ten companies by market capitalization were Japanese. By 1998, there were none. In 1998, Japan had just 46 companies in the FT's Global 500 list, and only two in the Global 100 (*Financial Times* 28 January 1999). In 1990, Japan's share of the world's stock market value was 41.5 per cent. By 1998 this had fallen to a mere 10.5 per cent (*Financial Times* 8 December 1998). In 1998, Japan still had eighteen of the world's top fifty corporations by value of sales, but had only one company in the top fifty by total profits (*Fortune* 3 August 1998).

The *keiretsu* system allowed allocation of capital within the group with little regard to returns achieved. An analysis by investment bankers Goldman Sachs shows that Japanese non-financial groups in the Nikkei 300 collectively failed to achieve a return above their cost of capital after 1990; 'Since that date they have destroyed value of Y3,000 billion a year, a cumulative Y21,000 billion, by investing in project and plants that generated negative returns' (quoted in the *Financial Times* 8 December 1998). The degree of internal restructuring has so far been quite limited. In part, this is due to the limitations imposed by the cross-holding system, which makes it difficult to achieve domestic mergers unless the numerous participating parties are agreed. Instead, a revolutionary process of international acquisition of Japanese companies has begun. Merrill Lynch has bought the branch network of Yamaichi Securities. GE Capital has acquired the leasing operations of Japan Leasing, Japan's second-biggest company in this sector. Travellers is buying Nikko Securities. Goodyear (US) has, effectively, taken over Sumitomo Rubber, Japan's third-biggest tyre company. Finally, Renault has taken a controlling stake in Nissan Motors. Some Japanese industry officials see the 'surrender into the arms of Renault' as symbolic of 'a fall from grace for Nissan and the entire automotive industry'; one former official from the Ministry of International Trade and Industry called the Renault–Nissan alliance a 'national disgrace' (quoted in the *Financial Times* 23 March 1999).

The impact of the rise to dominance of the Anglo-Saxon business system is thus not confined to Asia. The 'global business revolution, as we have dubbed it, has forced dramatic changes also on the business system of continental Europe, from the Nordic countries through to France and Germany. By the late 1990s, most large European industrial corporations had in turn wholeheartedly embraced the philosophy of globalization, shareholder value, cost cutting and focus on core business.

4 Conclusion

Latecomer countries thus face severe difficulties in competing with large firms from the advanced economies across a wide range of industries, not just in the 'high-tech' sectors. The barriers are much higher than even in the recent past. Emerging big businesses in emerging countries encounter high barriers to entry in the shape of continuous development of new products, new processes for old products, brand-name power in the consumer goods industries, high expenditures on information systems and the ability of globally powerful core firms to integrate globally across the value chain within the relevant sector. Such barriers clearly put new entrants, in poorer economies, at a distinct disadvantage.

This process is being accelerated by the current merger frenzy in the advanced capitalist countries. Hardly a single globally powerful firm in the early- or the late-industrializing countries grew to power without some form of state assistance. The recent rapid rise in barriers to entry across a wide range of industries means that the extent of state intervention required to help the poorer, emerging countries build at least some globally powerful firms has increased. However, the need for greater state intervention has occurred at a time when the political feasibility of such intervention has drastically declined. Moreover, the greater the degree of state intervention, the greater the chance that intervention generates long-term processes detrimental to efficient growth. This presents policy makers today with a new and difficult situation to deal with if they attempt to replicate the oligopolistic structure of advanced capitalism. It has become ever more difficult for emerging countries to imagine that they can successfully develop their own 'big businesses' to challenge some of the advanced economies. The example of successful late-industrializing countries such as Japan, South Korea and Taiwan cannot be easily replicated in today's political and economic environment either within Asia itself or in poorer parts of the world like Africa. The 'global business revolution' thus forces a radical rethink of industrial policy in emerging countries.

PETER NOLAN
JUDGE INSTITUTE OF MANAGEMENT STUDIES
UNIVERSITY OF CAMBRIDGE

Notes

The research for this paper was funded by the ESRC (grant number R00055235) for the project 'The emergence of the modern industrial corporation in China since 1970s', administered by the Department of Applied Economics, University of Cambridge, and by the China Big Business Programme, at the Judge Institute of Management Studies, University of Cambridge.

Further reading

(References cited in the text marked *)

* Amsden, A.A. (1989) *Asia's next giant: South Korea and late industrialization*, New York and Oxford: Oxford University Press. (An early classic study of South Korea's emergence as an international power.)

* Amsden, A. and Singh, A. (1994) 'The optimal degree of competition and dynamic efficiency in Japan and Korea', *European Economic Review* 38: 941–51. (Incisive article on efficiency levels in Japan and Korea.)
* Aoki, M. (1994) 'The Japanese firm as a system of attributes: A survey and research agenda', in Aoki, M. and Dore, R. (eds), *The Japanese Firm: The sources of Competitive Advantage,* London: Oxford University Press. (A good analytical chapter on the characteristics of the Japanese firm.)
* Best, M. (1990) *The New Competition*, Cambridge: Polity Press. (A critical study of industrial policy and its implications for governments.)
* Chandler, A.D. (1990) *Scale and Scope: The Dynamics of Industrial Capitalism*, Cambridge, MA: Harvard University Press. (Chandler's seminal work follows up the logic of his earlier work.)
* Chang, H. (1994) *The political economy of industrial policy*, New York: St Martin's Press. (An interesting authoritative study of the Korean chaebols.)
* Johnson, C.A. (1982) *MITI and the Japanese miracle*, Stanford: Stanford University Press. (An excellent analysis of Japan's state intervention in its economic development.)
* Lake, D.A. (1988) *Power, Protection and Free Trade*, Ithaca: Cornell University Press. (Useful account of protectionism, with examples from US experience.)
* Morgan Stanley Dean Witter (1997, 1998, 1999) *The Competitive Edge*, New York and London: Stanley Dean Witter. (An up-to-date analysis of large companies' ability to compete in international markets.)
* Okimoto, D.I. (1989) *Between the MITI and the market*, Stanford: Stanford University Press. (A scholarly account of Japanese industrial policy.)
* Ruigrok, W. and van Tulder, R. (1995) *The logic of international restructuring*, London and New York: Routledge. (An interesting account of the role of large firms in the world economy.)
* Scherer, F.M. and Ross, D. (1990) *Industrial Market Structure and Economic Performance*, 3rd edn, Boston: Houghton Miflin Company. (A standard work on industrial and economic policy.)
* Schmitz, C.J. (1993) *The Growth of Big Business in the United States and Western Europe, 1850–1939*, Basingstoke: Macmillan. (Seminal historical work on the growth of large firms, up to 1939.)
* Smith, A. (1976, first published 1776) *The Wealth of Nations*, Chicago: University of Chicago Press. (Classic exposition of laissez-faire but with important qualifications.)
* Suzuki, Y. (1991) *Japanese Management Structures, 1920–80*, Basingstoke: Macmillan. (A systematic analysis of the growth of large Japanese firms and their management.)
* UNCTAD (United Nations Conference on Trade and Development) (1996) *World investment report 1996. Investment, Trade and International Policy Arrangements*. Geneva: UN Publications. (Authoritative international assessment of world development in the mid-1990s.)
* Wade, R. (1990) *Governing the market: Economic theory and the role of government in East Asian Industrialization*, Princeton: Princeton University Press. (Scholarly account of the role of the state in Asian economic development.)

See also: ECONOMIES OF THE EMERGING COUNTRIES; INDUSTRIAL RELATIONS IN THE EMERGING COUNTRIES; MANUFACTURING IN THE EMERGING COUNTRIES; MARKETING IN THE EMERGING COUNTRIES; STRATEGY IN THE EMERGING COUNTRIES; WORLD TRADE ORGANIZATION

Related topics in the IEBM regional set: ASIA-PACIFIC ECONOMIC COOPERATION; ASSOCIATION OF SOUTH-EAST ASIAN NATIONS; ECONOMIES OF ASIA PACIFIC; ECONOMIES OF LATIN AMERICA; MANAGEMENT IN ASIA PACIFIC; MANAGEMENT IN CHINA; MANAGEMENT IN JAPAN; MANAGEMENT IN LATIN AMERICA; MANAGEMENT IN NORTH AMERICA; MANAGEMENT IN SOUTH KOREA; MANAGEMENT IN TAIWAN; NORTH AMERICAN FREE-TRADE AGREEMENT

Specialized themes

Accounting in the emerging countries

1 Introduction
2 Accounting heritage
3 British heritage
4 Countries with no dominant accounting tradition
5 Communist countries
6 Conclusion

Overview

An accounting infrastructure is increasingly being considered as an essential prerequisite for economic development. Such an infrastructure consists not only of accounting regulations but of an indigenous supply of suitably qualified professionals and the educational and ethical structures to support them. The existence of such elements is generally an accident of colonial history, with former British and French colonies having reasonably well evolved, although different, accounting systems, but with Communist countries and others having to create a Western structure without any roots.

Many emerging economies are installing accounting rules based on the rules of the International Accounting Standards Committee, the international regulator. These are not, however, applied strictly and the lack of an appropriate auditing and surveillance system is noticeable. In addition, while these rules may be appropriate for companies active in capital markets, they are not designed for small business, nor has any specially adapted system yet been evolved, although there is a new initiative in franco-phone West Africa which goes in this direction. The problem is particularly difficult in the People's Republic of China where not only has an accounting culture to be created but an enterprise culture has to precede it.

The nature of indigenous professional structures is highly variable and while some countries have professional organizations which operate high-level examinations as the barrier to entry, others have associations which do not impose conditions of competence. It is therefore difficult for outsiders to know what is the level of assurance provided by local professionals. The World Bank and the United Nations (UN) are both active in trying to build quality professional bodies and help establish high standards of competence.

1 Introduction

Until relatively recently, accounting has not been seen as a major issue in relation to emerging countries. If considered at all, it has been perceived as merely part of the normal baggage of an economy which arrives with economic development (see ECONOMIES OF THE EMERGING COUNTRIES). However, views have changed and accounting is increasingly seen as a necessary pre-condition for an economy to develop, and also high-quality accounting is seen as being essential to the maintenance of an efficient advanced economy.

In economies that are at a relatively early stage of development, such as Cameroon or Kenya, it is now accepted that without some kind of workable accounting infrastructure, the economy cannot develop (see ECONOMIES OF THE EMERGING COUNTRIES). Aid donors are reluctant to give aid and sponsor development programmes if there is no guarantee that there are properly trained staff available to control the funds and report on their use. Commercial investment needs the same assurances. Indigenous small businesses are held back from growth because they do not have reliable figures with which to manage their business and to support loan applications, nor access to reliable financial management advice if debt finance is provided.

The World Bank has been a leader in recognizing this problem and sponsoring training programmes to encourage the development of local accounting skills and auditing. The United Nations' intergovernmental working group of experts on International Standards of Accounting and Reporting (ISAR) has also been active in drawing attention to this problem and trying to find solutions, not least by obtaining financial aid and supervising local training programmes in countries such as Azerbaijan and Uzbekistan, and developing a model professional qualification. International professional organizations such as the Association of Chartered Certified Accountants (ACCA) also offer technical assistance both in training and in creating the necessary professional support structures.

At the more advanced end of the spectrum of emerging economies, countries such as Indonesia, Thailand, Taiwan, etc. have developed major indigenous companies, but lack both the detailed accounting rules and the auditing capability and culture which lead to the provision of the transparent financial statements necessary for the smooth running of financial markets. A report commissioned by ISAR in 1998 laid a major portion of the blame for the Asian crisis on poor accounting and disclosure (Rahman 1999). The ISAR report noted that indigenous rules were frequently lacking requirements to report on issues such as the level of foreign exchange risk and related party transactions, as well as any requirements to report economic substance rather than legal form.

Investors were misled as to the real level of borrowing of many companies, because this was often hidden through off-balance-sheet arrangements, and the foreign currency make-up and term structure of debt were not disclosed. Once exchange rates moved dramatically, these problems became evident and investors reacted, perhaps too sharply, by withdrawing from the market. With better financial disclosure, it is argued, investors would have had a better appreciation of the risk; expansion might have been slower but investors would not have fled in panic when the market turned. The report also criticizes the role of the international accounting firms (the 'Big Five') in allowing local members of the international firm to sign clean reports on accounts where there was less than transparent disclosure, even if this was in line with local requirements.

The Asian crisis illustrates well the problem that it is not sufficient to develop economic activity in isolation: for this to be sustainable there needs to be both an institutional and a cultural framework which provides for the efficient operating of the market. As far as accounting is concerned, this means that the capital markets only work efficiently if investors are sure that the information they are given is viable. This is arrived at through demanding accounting rules and an audit profession which can police their application effectively, as well as investors who understand the financial information and can react appropriately to it. Accounting rules are easily available from the International Accounting Standards Committee (IASC), the recognized standard setter for international business, and auditing rules from the International Auditing Practices Committee (IAPC), but the development of a sophisticated structure of financial statement preparers, users and auditors is more complex and requires education programmes and the creation of appropriate professional organizations with real sanctions for unprofessional behaviour.

2 Accounting heritage

The label 'emerging countries' takes in a very wide range of countries running from poor African states with a low level of literacy through to the 'Tiger' economies of South East Asia and to China (see MANAGEMENT IN THE EMERGING COUNTRIES; PERSPEC-TIVES ON MANAGEMENT IN THE EMERGING COUNTRIES)). The range of problems encountered is very wide and the environments within which accounting has to operate are very diverse. The cultural heritage varies from one country to another, involving differing problems of reorientation as far as accounting and financial information is concerned. For accounting purposes it is useful to identify four types of economy:

1 Former French colonies
2 Former British colonies
3 Countries with no dominant accounting tradition
4 Communist countries

Both French and British colonial administrators left their former colonies with relatively well-developed accounting infrastructures (Ollier 1998), but countries such as Korea, Indonesia and Thailand have no long tradition of financial reporting, while China and Vietnam have to build entirely new systems, involving a radical shift in attitude.

The colonial heritage has proved to be more useful in some countries than in others. Under both French and British rule, accounting regulations created in developed Western economies were transplanted, generally without modification, into colonies at different stages of development, and local professional organizations were started, generally with the help of their European counterparts (e.g. Parker 1989). Such cultural exports have had the effect that countries such as Burkino Faso have an accounting infrastructure which is in no way organized to meet their real needs, while countries such as Malaysia and Singapore have been able to sustain their financial markets better as a result of having a long period to adapt to accounting rules and professional structures appropriate to a more developed economy.

Former French colonies such as Tunisia, Morocco, Mauritania, Mali, Ivory Coast, Guinea, Cameroon and Benin all have accounting rules based on the French *Plan Comptable Général* (PCG – General Accounting Plan) and have audit professions modelled, at least, on the French institutions. The PCG, in its modern elaborated form, includes rules of accounting and a compulsory chart of accounts which determines how the accounting database is structured, as well as some advice on management accounting.

The particular advantage of a chart of accounts is that it simplifies teaching basic accounting, ensures that all accounting records are the same, and therefore makes for easier auditing and transfer of staff between businesses and lower training costs. In addition, the French approach includes a view that all businesses should prepare some form of accounts and that these should correspond closely with tax rules. On the positive side, this has the result that some form of accounting is taught automatically in business courses. On the negative side, there is a strong identification between accounting and tax, which may mean that small traders prefer not to keep any accounts, seeing these as a tool of government control rather than having any connection with business management. The PCG has its origins in reporting the results of individual companies, and is not particularly oriented around the needs of capital markets. Consequently it is a better tool for small and medium-sized companies than for stock exchange reporting.

Countries such as Tunisia have pursued their own evolution of the French model to take account of the advances in their own development and to align themselves with International Accounting Standards (Colasse 1997). In West Africa, several states cooperated in the 1990s to produce a common updated accounting plan. These states had previously used either the 1957 version of the French PCG, or an African adaptation of it, the Plan OCAM. However, from 1998 they have agreed to use the *Système Comptable Ouest-Africain* (SYSCOA), which is part of a plan to create a common economic area with shared financial institutions and comparable company law and accounting rules.

SYSCOA is in line with the modern French PCG in that it includes accounting rules as well as a chart of accounts, and proposes different versions of the same basic system which are adapted to companies of different sizes (Trotman 1999). At its most sophisticated level it provides rules for the consolidated accounts of groups of companies, while the basic version is intended for the individual accounts of small companies. A major innovation, though, is that in addition to these related versions, which are all based on using standard accruals accounting (transactions recognized when an economic event takes place, irrespective of when cash changes hands), SYSCOA also has a cash accounting variant intended for the micro-business for which more developed accounts are too much of a luxury (cash accounting involves simply recording cash inputs and outputs, without regard to the timing of the economic transaction to which they relate). This is intended to address the needs of the numerous small traders who form a large slice of the economic activity of the least developed countries. While most tax authorities accept such accounts as better than nothing, this is the first time that they have been explicitly recognized within a formal government-controlled system.

3 British heritage

Former British colonies typically have local legislation based on the British 1948 Companies Act (this was even the model for Australian legislation in the 1960s). This is a relatively sophisticated piece of legislation which includes a requirement for the preparation of consolidated accounts for groups of companies. The 1948 Act reflected a major reform of British company law in 1947 following on from the recommendations of the Cohen Committee (1945). It is still the basis of company reporting in the UK even though it has been modified (1982) in respect of the detail of disclosures in the profit and loss account and (1989) the criteria for including related companies in the group accounts, both changes as a result of European company law directives.

The export of the 1948 Act to the British Commonwealth is an example of what is seen as wholly inappropriate transfers of technology by colonial powers. Developed in the context of an advanced economy which is home to the most important European stock exchange, and in a tradition of regulating only the accounts of larger businesses, this legislation did not correspond to the accounting needs of emerging countries. It was, however, used in countries such as Cyprus, Nigeria, Ghana, Malaysia and Singapore as well as Australia (Walton 1986). However, as these countries have developed, some of their economies have in a sense caught up with the accounting infrastructure.

One feature of the 1948 Act is that it requires an independent audit of the annual accounts, and in the British version requires that this is done by members of professional bodies recognized by the Secretary of State. The requirement for an independent, professional audit was therefore transmitted to the countries that adopted the 1948 Act. This was in part made possible because most British colonies had developed professional associations in line with the Anglo-Saxon model, often helped by the British professional bodies.

Many of the indigenous bodies offer professional examinations to a high standard and ensure an appropriate level of competence (e.g. India, Hong Kong, etc.). However, this is not always the case, particularly in smaller countries. For example, for many years admission to the Cypriot body was conditional on obtaining an appropriate UK qualification, but there was no Cypriot examination as such. In other countries, such as Kenya, membership of the local body was conditional upon having some activity as an accountant, without necessarily having completed a specific professional examination requirement. The evolution of local professional bodies has been helped by inputs both from multilateral donors such as the World Bank and the European Union (EU) and from technical assistance from bodies such as the ACCA. The UN's ISAR has developed a global professional qualification benchmark with the objective of providing a uniform standard against which emerging countries may compare their local requirements. Aside from the waste of resources inherent in each country going through its own qualification development programme, the global benchmark is intended to provide, through an assessment and endorsement agency, assurance of standards and wider acceptability and recognition of new qualifications.

In addition to the question of a viable local professional organization to maintain standards of audit and ethics, there is a need for education to prepare indigenous students for accounting examinations. In Botswana this has been addressed by the provision of a government-backed accounting training institute, but the provision of professional education remains a problem in many countries where government resources are stretched and accounting education is seen as not the highest priority. In

Kenya, for example, state schools are frequently closed, and there is a private sector accounting college, but few individuals have the personal resources to follow this route, or are obliged to take major breaks during the course of the programme. External donors have funded colleges in Malawi and Zambia, but without donor support their continued existence is threatened.

While the French approach to accounting and the British one are not the same, they are both the product of developed economies, and their export to French and British colonies over a long period, while arguably inappropriate at the time, has had the benefit of creating some kind of tradition of accounting, and some respect for its role in the economy. While it would be quite wrong to suggest that attitudes to accounting in these countries correspond to Western European attitudes, there is generally an infrastructure and approach which make evolution to a local developed economy less problematical as concerns accounting.

4 Countries with no dominant accounting tradition

It may well be this lack of a long accounting tradition that has created difficulties in the 'Tiger' economies such as Indonesia and Thailand which have no strong accounting tradition. Here it is more obvious that the link between good financial disclosure and efficient financial markets does not form part of the cultural tradition, and the idea of independent audit has yet some way to evolve in this context. Aside from the British heritage in Malaysia, Singapore and Hong Kong, and leaving aside Japan as an economy which has emerged rather than being emerging, the influences on the other economies have been the USA and lately some initiatives through the Association of South-East Asian Nations (ASEAN) to harmonize along the lines of International Accounting Standards. Older colonial influences such as France and the Netherlands have left little surviving trace.

The USA has been influential in Korea, Taiwan and the Philippines in the period after the Second World War, but this has stopped some way short of adoption of US accounting in these countries. Professional bodies have been established, but these are not up to the standard of the American Institute of Certified Public Accountants, and in particular it seems that client relationships are different in nature.

The professional bodies in ASEAN countries have formed the ASEAN Federation of Accountants and are also generally members of the International Federation of Accountants (IFAC), the global representative of the profession, and the issuer of audit standards through the IAPC. The ASEAN bodies have declared their intention to harmonize their accounting on International Accounting Standards, and their membership of IFAC presupposes auditing standards of a similar quality. In a number of ASEAN countries the professional body is also the accounting standard setter, so that the means of harmonization are within their hands. However, obstacles to this process are, first, local reluctance to accept aspects of standards which are seen as being in conflict with the emerging country environment, and second, the fact that the International Standards themselves are still in a state of evolution, so that a country may have adopted International Standards and then become de-harmonized by a change at the IASC (Carlson 1998). Equally, having the 'right' rules in place is a different thing from having an institutional and cultural framework that supports these and users, preparers and auditors necessarily being in tune with this (see BUSINESS CULTURES, THE EMERGING COUNTRIES).

Worldwide, there are very few countries that have any kind of surveillance mechanism for financial reporting, or any specialist court to which accounts may be referred in the case of doubt. Legal sanctions for failure to respect the rules usually exist, but bringing them to bear upon a particular case is usually a very difficult process and so prosecutions are extremely rare. In these circumstances, the whole burden of policing companies' application of accounting and disclosure rules falls on the auditors. The auditors are, however, usually paid by the companies whose actions they may be called upon to query, and this situation places a severe burden on the auditors' ethical standards and sense of independence. The situation is difficult enough in developed economies where the role of the profession is well established and the number of clients available is large. It is much more problematical where there is little or no tradition of audit and disclosure, and clients are few.

5 Communist countries

In some senses, the greatest challenge is to be found in China and Vietnam where the government remains Communist but has decided to move towards a market economy. This creates the major problem of having to introduce an enterprise culture and train executives in all kinds of skills, including accounting, which were either not necessary before, or done in a quite different fashion. Communist accounting is more to do with recording use of assets than profit and performance measurement (Richard 1998). Introducing enterprise accounting means creating an entirely new set of rules, and also educating accountants and business managers to use them.

In Vietnam, much effort has been spent in introducing new rules, but it remains unclear as to what extent they are actually applied by anyone. In China, however, a more systematic approach to the change has been taken, with an acknowledgement that a phased programme of development is necessary, including the establishment of training schools in accounting, intended for practitioners but also for government officials and business managers.

The first public accounting firm opened in China in Shanghai in 1981 and practices, mostly funded by different government agencies, and therefore under their influence, have grown since then. In 1989 the Ministry of Finance formed the Chinese Institute of Certified Public Accountants (CICPA) and in the early 1990s issued a regulation providing basic Accounting Standards which came into force in 1993. This was intended to apply first to joint ventures with foreign companies and then to be extended progressively to listed companies and then to all enterprises. China became an observer at the IASC in 1998. The CICPA started to issue auditing standards from 1994 and became a member of IFAC in 1997.

While a major effort has been made to introduce international accounting standards and a viable auditing profession, there has been opposition and difficulties in implementation which have slowed the process. In particular, appointment as an auditor was in the past often seen as a retirement job for government officials, with no particular relevant training or knowledge. Since 1991 the CICPA has run professional examinations, leaving a profession with a major age gap. In addition, there are many cases of audit failure, and the Ministry of Finance has started a campaign to punish these, with jurisprudence establishing both criminal and civil liabilities for fraudulent auditing and accounting. In 1999 the Chinese government has decided to set up three accounting training schools, the first of which will be in Beijing. These are aimed at reinforcing understanding of the new accounting.

China has made considerable progress in introducing enterprise accounting, and has demonstrated an understanding that the problems are not just technical but also cultural. However, its accounting infrastructure remains dominated by the state, so that the CICPA is really a government agency, not a free-standing members' association, and audit firms have strong links to government banks and other government agencies. While all the paraphernalia of a Western accounting system appears to be in place – it is all controlled by the government.

6 Conclusion

Accounting in emerging economies is in a state of rapid evolution. In the less developed states there are a number of initiatives in hand, including the UN and the IASC, which may well produce some useful inputs to the development of accounting structures which are better adapted to local circumstances and may make it easier for businesses to evolve successfully. In the more developed countries, the Asian crisis has put accounting under the spotlight and it is clear that while the drive towards expanding these economies has followed a track of mimicking the accounting of Western developed countries, this has not been very successful. It seems likely that it will take time either for these structures to function as they do in the West, or for alternative structures (for example, alternative means of checking compliance with accounting rules such as state auditors) to be developed which fit more comfortably into the local environment.

PETER WALTON
UNIVERSITY OF GENEVA

Further reading

(References cited in text marked *)

* Carlson, P. (1998) 'IASC financial reporting standards in ASEAN', *Accounting & Business*, April. (An analysis of the extent to which countries in South East Asia have adopted International Accounting Standards into domestic regulation.)
* Colasse, B. (1997) 'Du nouveau système comptable des entreprises en Tunisie: alignement ou adaptation aux normes comptables internationales ?', *Revue Française de Comptabilité*, April. (This explains the main aspects of the reform of accounting in Tunisia, and is written by one of the main advisers to the project.)
  Nobes, C. (1998) *Accounting in developing countries: questions about users, uses and appropriate reporting practices*, London: ACCA. (A useful survey of the literature on accounting in emerging countries and of the gaps in knowledge.)
* Ollier, C. (1998) 'Accounting standards in Africa', *Accounting & Business*, March. (A current review of the main trends in accounting in sub-Saharan Africa.)
* Parker, R.H. (1989) 'Importing and exporting accounting: the British experience' in Hopwood, A.G. (ed.), *International Pressures for Accounting Change*, Hemel Hempstead: Prentice Hall

International. (A discussion of the extent to which British colonial administrators encouraged British professional bodies to develop similar bodies in the colonies.)

* Rahman, Z. (1999) *The Role of Accounting Disclosure in the East Asian Financial Crisis*, Geneva: UNCTAD. (A research report which analyses the accounts of Asian banks and their audit reports and concludes that they are not sufficiently transparent.)

* Richard, J. (1998) 'Accounting in Eastern Europe: from Communism to capitalism' in Walton, P. Haller, A. and Raffournier, B. (eds), *International Accounting*, London: International Thomson Business Press. (A quality analysis of the evolution and objectives of Communist accounting.)

Sian, S. (1998) 'Opening the door for microbusinesses', *Accounting & Business*, October: 30–31. (An article which looks at the interaction between accounting and the provision of finance for small enterprise in Kenya.)

* Trotman, M. (1999) 'A new accounting plan for French-speaking West Africa', *Accounting & Business*, February. (Details of the main aspects of the latest evolution of the French accounting plan in Africa.)

United Nations (1991) 'Accountancy development in Africa, challenge of the 1990s', New York: United Nations. (A paper prepared by UNCTAD which highlights the lack of development of an indigenous accounting profession in Africa.)

Wallace, R.S.O. (1993) 'Development of accounting standards for developing and newly-industrialised countries', *Research in Third World Accounting* Vol. 2, JAI Press, pp. 121–65. (An academic analysis of the evolution of accounting rules in emerging countries and the influence of the International Accounting Standards Committee.)

* Walton, P. (1986) 'The export of British accounting legislation to Commonwealth countries', *Accounting & Business Research*, Autumn. (A survey of the transmission of UK companies statutes to British colonies and former colonies.)

Walton, P. (1997) 'Special rules for a special case', *Financial Times*, 18 September: 11. (Newspaper article which outlines the nature of the accounting needs of African countries.)

See also: BUSINESS CULTURES, THE EMERGING COUNTRIES; ECONOMIES OF THE EMERGING COUNTRIES; MANAGEMENT IN BOTSWANA; MANAGEMENT IN THE EMERGING COUNTRIES; MANAGEMENT IN GHANA; MANAGEMENT IN KENYA; MANAGEMENT IN NIGERIA; MANAGEMENT IN ZAMBIA

Related topics in the IEBM regional set: ACCOUNTING IN ASIA PACIFIC; ACCOUNTING IN EUROPE; ACCOUNTING IN LATIN AMERICA; ACCOUNTING IN NORTH AMERICA; ASSOCIATION OF SOUTH-EAST ASIAN NATIONS; MANAGEMENT IN CHINA; MANAGEMENT IN INDONESIA; MANAGEMENT IN JAPAN; MANAGEMENT IN TAIWAN; MANAGEMENT IN THAILAND; MANAGEMENT IN VIETNAM

Banking and finance in the emerging countries

1 Introduction
2 Key characteristics of emerging countries
3 Transnational institutions
4 National institutions
5 Problems and outlook

Overview

Many emerging countries have experienced considerable growth and expansion in their financial sectors over the past decade. Economic liberalization has meant that banks have been able to compete more effectively and also invest in new banking technologies. Many countries have seen considerable growth in the numbers of banks and bank branches. In countries such as Brazil and, especially, India the growth of the financial sector has played a key role in economic and social development. However, the most important institutions in terms of banking and finance in emerging countries remain the transnational institutions such as the World Bank, the African Development Bank, the Asian Development Bank and so on. These are able not only to provide finance on a considerable scale, but also to impose their own development agendas in exchange for capital.

1 Introduction

Banking and finance in emerging countries can take many different forms, depending on the stage of economic development reached by the particular country. In general, however, emerging countries can in this respect be said to exhibit two key characteristics: the state plays a very important role in terms of national institutions, and transnational or international institutions play a large, sometimes dominant role. As the economies of these countries are often very fragile: the banking systems are also usually highly fragile; both businesses and the population at large may be unwilling to place much faith in local banks, preferring to deal with branches of major international banks from the industrialized nations; alternatively, there is a reliance by some sectors of the population on 'unofficial banks', or moneylenders. In addition, banking supervision and control are often still in their infancy, meaning that corruption is a problem in some countries.

The key financial needs of emerging countries are in most cases for capital to finance development projects, whether these are undertaken by the state or by the private sector (this again will vary from country to country depending on the prevailing ideology, although the private sector is much more prominent now than it was two decades ago). However, the political and economic uncertainties that plague many emerging countries mean that finance is often interrupted or made highly conditional by the finance provider.

The present situation is usually seen as unsatisfactory by all parties. Emerging countries are often urged to reform their economies and lift restrictions on currency and capital flows, but it is not altogether certain that this would result in the provision of the capital required for development.

2 Key characteristics of emerging countries

The term 'emerging countries' can have a number of different meanings. Here, it is taken to refer to countries which are still in the process of industrializing, which still have immature economies, which still rely heavily on agriculture or resource extraction, and which have high levels of poverty (see ECONOMIES OF THE EMERGING COUNTRIES). Within this group, there is considerable variation in terms of wealth, income, culture and political structure. Some countries in this group (Brazil, India, the Philippines) actually have strong industrial sectors in some areas, while other areas remain underdeveloped.

Given these variations, in terms of banking and finance, emerging countries can be said to have the following characteristics.

- Controlled or unstable exchange rates. Nembhard (1996) points out that most countries in the world – and this includes most emerging countries – maintain some form of exchange rate controls, either fixed pegs or floating within narrow bands. Those emerging countries that have not fixed exchanged rates tend to find that the value of their currency fluctuates, sometimes uncontrollably.

- Fluctuations in monetary systems. Emerging countries, through either a lack of economic sophistication, pressure from international institutions, or both, frequently tinker with their financial systems in hope of achieving greater stability. The result is frequently the opposite, as each change introduces fresh uncertainty. Argentina, for example, had three currencies in the space of a decade.

- Capital scarcity. Nearly all emerging countries suffer from this problem. Most have by definition low income levels; many have high inflation, and both these factors lead to low savings and investment rates. Inevitably they are forced to rely on foreign capital, but this tends to take flight whenever levels of risk and uncertainty begin to rise; this in turn forces devaluation.

- Weak institutions. Domestic banking institutions, both private and state sector, tend to be fragile, undercapitalized and overexposed. Banking failures are common in times of economic shock.

- A strong informal banking sector. With weak banks and a shortage of capital, the population at large (especially the working classes) often resorts to the informal sector, turning to moneylenders to meet their daily financing needs. In Bangladesh, a system of community banks has been established with villagers pooling their savings and lending out of a common fund, thus keeping control of both lending and borrowing within the community; this is proving to be an effective and viable alternative to the moneylenders.

- Inefficient or weak government. Emerging country governments are not always inefficient, but they are nearly always in a position of weakness when it comes to bargaining with foreign powers, especially the major international lenders. The latter are usually able to force their own economic agenda on the borrowing countries, sometimes to the detriment of the latter.
- Unfavourable balance of payments. Most emerging countries rely on commodity exports to pay for imports, and worldwide declines in commodity prices over the past two decades have left many with unfavourable balances of payments. Those countries that have been able to diversify and build 'parallel' industrial sectors, such as Brazil and India, are less exposed in this fashion, but there is still much pressure to import, and only rarely do these nations have positive balances.
- Vulnerability to shocks. A combination of weak institutions, reliance on commodity exports and reliance on imports for energy and capital goods means that these countries are particularly vulnerable to economic shocks. The first oil price shock, for example, affected the African economies long after the West had ridden out the effects. The case of Brazil, which has been forced into devaluation in January 1999 as a result of the East Asia crisis, is another example.
- High levels of risk. All of the above factors mean that operations in these economies are fundamentally risky, for domestic and foreign firms alike. Financial institutions can be reluctant to lend. Alternatively, as happened in the 1980s, they can overlend on risky ventures, and then call in loans in times of crisis (Curran 1979), with negative consequences for lenders and borrowers alike.

3 Transnational institutions

Transnational institutions play a very important, if not dominant role in banking and finance in emerging countries. There are a wide variety of these, some operating under the aegis of the United Nations and some functioning independently. Some are worldwide in focus, others have a particular regional focus. Apart from the International Monetary Fund and the World Bank, the most common form of transnational institution is the development bank, a banking institution usually owned by a group of member countries which exists to channel finance into development projects. There follows a brief summary of some of the more important institutions.

International Monetary Fund

The International Monetary Fund (IMF) was established in 1945, with the aim of facilitating international monetary cooperation, encouraging international trade and promoting exchange rate stability. Part of its remit was also to make loans to member nations in time of need. The current membership is 182 countries, the majority of which fall into the classification of emerging countries. It is the IMF's lending policies that have caused most controversy. Particularly during the 1970s and 1980s, the IMF set harsh conditions for the granting of loans to emerging countries, and its policies of 'structural adjustment' (requiring borrowers to undertake economic reform as a condition of the loan being granted) have been harshly criticized (Hellheiner *et al.*

1997). The IMF lends directly to member states, and does not undertake specific project financing.

World Bank

The World Bank (officially known as the International Bank for Reconstruction and Development) was also established in 1945 under the terms of the Bretton Woods Agreement. Its role is to provide finance specifically for development projects in a variety of guises. In 1999 the Bank listed six key development goals:

- reducing by half the proportion of people in extreme poverty by 2015;
- achieving universal primary education in all countries by 2015;
- demonstrating progress towards gender equality and the empowerment of women by eliminating disparities in primary and secondary education by 2005;
- reducing by two-thirds the mortality rates for infants and children under five by 2015;
- providing access to reproductive health services for all individuals by 2015;
- implementing national strategies for sustainable development by 2005.

As these goals indicate, the World Bank's primary focus has been on social change and the elimination of poverty rather than on economic development (although some finance initiatives for small businesses have been established under World Bank auspices). The World Bank too has been harshly criticized for inappropriate policies (see, for example, Brown 1997). The gap between the World Bank and the IMF – the provision of finance for economic development – has been largely left to the regional development banks.

African Development Bank

Founded in 1963, the African Development Bank is the most important development finance institution in Africa. It is owned by its 77 member states, with the 53 African members owning two-thirds and the 24 European, Asian and American members owning one-third. The bank's headquarters is in Abidjan in the Ivory Coast. It is governed by a board of directors, one from each member state; the board elects a president, who is always from Africa. The Bank's aims are the provision of development finance and capital for business ventures in member states, and also to encourage and attract investment to the region more generally (Rocco 1986; African Development Bank 1999). A particular aim is to help member countries diversify their economies and increase export earnings, so improving economic stability. By 1999 it was the world's second largest development funder, after the World Bank; at the end of 1997 the Bank's authorized capital was $23.3 billion.

The Bank provides project finance and funding in a variety of industrial sectors, although emphasis is laid on agriculture, public utilities, transport and communication, and social services. The typical loan has a maturity period of 12–20 years; grace periods of up to five years are common. The Bank also funds studies in the above field, and also provides consultancy and assistance in areas such as structural adjustment and technical support. The Bank also administers the African Development Fund, which exists specifically to provide development finance for projects in the very poorest African countries, at extremely low rates of interest. Finally the Bank administers the Nigeria Trust Fund, established in 1976 by the government of Nigeria to aid its poorer neighbours.

Asian Development Bank

Founded in 1966, the Asian Development Bank, like the African Development Bank above, is loosely patterned on the World Bank but also has a greater interest in financing economic development projects. The Bank has 57 members, 41 from the Asia-Pacific Region and 16 from Europe and the Americas. The USA and Japan are the largest shareholders, having between them subscribed 16 per cent of the Bank's capital. Overall 63 per cent comes from the regional members, while 37 per cent comes from the non-regional members. The Bank states its purposes as extending loans for equity investments, providing technical assistance, promoting and facilitating other public and private capital investment in development projects, and coordinating development plans and policies within the region. The Bank's headquarters is in Manila; its current president is Mitsuo Sato (many of the Bank's presidents since foundation have been from Japan). There are resident missions in countries where the Bank is particularly active in terms of financing projects; regional offices have recently been opened in Vanuatu, Kazakstan and Uzbekistan (Asian Development Bank 1999). Outstanding loans at the end of 1998 totalled $3.3 billion, over half of which had gone to Indonesia.

Inter-American Development Bank

The oldest of the multilateral development banks, the Inter-American Development Bank (IADB) was founded in 1959, with the mission of accelerating economic and social development in Latin America and the Caribbean. The impetus for the foundation came from Brazil, which had called for a cooperative effort to be made to further development in the region; the Organization of American States provided the framework for the Bank's establishment. Current membership of the Bank is 46 nations, with 28 from the Western hemisphere and the remainder from Europe and Asia (Inter-American Development Bank 1999). Headquarters is in Washington, DC.

As in the two cases above, the IADB both provides direct project financing and technical support and helps to coordinate investment from other sources. Social projects such as health and education development had an early priority, but more recently the IADB has been devoting more effort to assistance for business ventures, particularly in the agricultural sectors. The IADB also administers the Inter-American Investment Corporation, which provides direct loans, lines of credit and equity investments to businesses, as well as fee-based consultancy services. The main focus here is on business start-ups and on businesses seeking to modernize or upgrade their skills and technology.

As well as the above, there are a variety of other institutions working to provide finance and investment in emerging countries. Mention should be made in this context of the North American Development Bank, the Caribbean Development Bank, the East African Development Bank, the Border Environment Cooperation Commission, the Development Assistance Committee of the OECD (Organization for Economic

Cooperation and Development), the International Fund for Agricultural Development, the OPEC (Organization of Petroleum Exporting Countries) Fund for International Development, the European Investment Bank, and the United Nations Development Programme, the latter of which provides mainly support services for development initiatives.

4 National institutions

Most emerging countries have a banking sector, though in some cases this will be quite small. Emerging countries' banking and financial institutions usually parallel those of the developed nations in terms of structure, with a central bank (itself usually controlled directly by the government) governing a network of state financial institutions and commercial banks. Of the latter, three main types exist: domestic private sector banks, domestic state-owned banks, and branches or subsidiaries of foreign banks. The presence of each type depends to a large extent on the prevailing ideology of each country's government, but in most emerging countries at the present time, examples of all three types will be found.

Two national examples give some idea of the nature and diversity of banking systems in emerging countries, and also of the problems these countries face.

Brazil

Brazil offers a good example of the kind of banking diversity that can be found in many emerging nations. Brazil is still technically an emerging nation; it has a strong industrial base and is the world's eighth largest economy, but many of its 145 million people still live in what might be termed emerging country conditions. The central bank, the Banco Central do Brasil, was established in 1964, and is directly controlled by the National Monetary Council. The central bank and the state-owned Banco do Brasil are the main instruments for the implementation of fiscal and monetary policy; the central bank is also responsible for bank supervision and the management of financial reserves and foreign debt.

The Brazilian economy has been subject to extreme shocks in the last several decades, with hyperinflation in the early 1990s and more recently the devaluation of the real. Lack of investment in the 1980s nearly crippled its emerging industrial base. Despite these problems, Brazil has in the 1990s been able to develop an extensive and modern banking system. There are around 300 banks in Brazil, in both the state and private sectors, and by 1990 banking accounted for 13 per cent of Brazilian gross domestic product (GDP) (Vorst 1995: 127).

Although there are large numbers of Brazilian private banks, they are of relatively small size; until very recently, government policy restricted private banks to regional operations. For example, regional banks had to have 80 per cent of their branches within three or fewer states. As a result, Brazilian banks are not large by international standards, and overseas expansion has been limited. During the 1980s Brazilian banks suffered heavy losses during the country's economic crises, and there were a number of failures. More recently, Brazilian private banks have been exploiting Internet technology to expand their operations. Bradesco and Banco Real, for example, now offers 24-hour banking and bank machine services throughout Brazil. Brazil 1 is

Brazil's first 'virtual' bank. There is also a merchant banking sector, as exemplified by institutions such as the Banco Mercantil de São Paulo Finasa, which has survived since 1938.

State-owned banks suffered fewer restrictions, and the Banco do Brasil, the main state-owned commercial bank, is one of the world's 50 largest banks. Other important state-owned banks include the Banco Nacional de Desenuolvimento Economico, which provides finance for industrial ventures; the National Housing Bank, which finances social and housing projects; and the Banco de Estado do Ceará.

Foreign banks are beginning to be represented. Banco de Boston, for example, is a subsidiary of the US-based Boston Bank, and offers links with its parent corporation as well as a full range of banking services.

Thus Brazil has a diverse and well-developed banking sector, encouraged by economic and political liberalization over the past decade. Nonetheless, its banking system remains highly frangible and subject to problems arising from the extreme conditions in which the Brazilian economy so frequently finds itself.

India

Like Brazil, India has many of the characteristics of both an emerging and a developed economy (see MANAGEMENT IN INDIA). This has led to what are in effect two banking systems, what Yousefi (1995) calls the 'organized' and the 'traditional' sectors. The organized sector includes the Reserve Bank of India (the central bank), the State Bank of India, commercial banks, development banks, cooperative banks and a variety of non-banking institutions (insurance companies, investment funds and so on). The traditional banking institution is defined by Yousefi as including 'indigenous bankers' and village moneylenders who provide financial support for small enterprises, farms and consumers.

The organized sector, as above, is divided into state-owned and privately owned institutions. At the centre of the banking system is the Reserve Bank of India, the Central Bank, which is responsible for all bank regulation and supervision. As well as the usual central bank functions of credit and exchange control, monetary and fiscal policy implementation and so on, the Reserve Bank has also taken the lead in planning the expansion of the banking sector in India.

During the 1950s and 1960s many banks in India were nationalized, along with other financial institutions such as life insurance companies. At the same time there was a rapid increase in numbers of banks, and even more so in numbers of branches. This expansion was particularly intense among the regional rural banks, where the government's aim was to displace the 'traditional' sector, encourage saving by the population, and provide investment for rural enterprises. The domestic banking sector was thus used as a direct agent to stimulate social change.

In 1992, the Gandhi government's economic liberalization plan included opening up the banking sector to greater competition, but the state still controls many of the major banks, including the State Bank of India, the Indian Bank, the Syndicate Bank and the Bank of India. The Industrial Development Bank of India is another state-owned institution, which exists to provide finance for business and economic development.

Older private sector banks continued during the period of nationalization, but the period since liberalization has seen many new banks spring up. There are well over 300 banks in India, many fairly small. Most are regional based; the Bank of Punjab, founded in 1994, appeals mainly to the Sikh population of the Punjab, and the Federal Bank had its origins in Kerala. The Bank of Baroda and the Bank of Madura are other examples of regional-based banks. Some of these banks have since expanded across India; the Bank of Baroda, for example, has 2500 branches and claims 20 million customers. Many of the commercial banks have now moved into 24-hour and Internet banking services. Foreign banks are well represented, for example Citibank and the Abu Dhabi Commercial Bank.

Along with commercial banks, there are a number of other financial institutions worth noting. The post office maintains a savings bank system similar to that of the UK, on which the former is patterned. State Financial Corporations have been established in each of India's 18 states to provide financing for businesses; these are part-private, part-public owned. The aforementioned Industrial Development Bank of India, along with the Industrial Credit and Investment Corporation and the Industrial Finance Corporation, are national institutions likewise dedicated to the provision of business finance. The Industrial Development Bank, along with the National Bank for Agriculture and Rural Development, also provides finance specifically for agricultural institutions. Investment companies and other non-bank institutions are also important sources of finance.

The formal banking and finance sector is growing rapidly, and is considered among the strongest in Asia. At the same time, the 'traditional' sector has begun to decline in importance. Village and community banks and moneylenders still play an important role, especially in the agricultural communities of central and southern India, but their importance in terms of overall finance provision is declining.

4 Problems and outlook

The examples given in the previous section offer an optimistic picture of banking and finance in emerging countries. In both cases, particularly since economic reforms began, the banking sectors have made significant strides in closing the gap with emerging countries. New banking techniques and technologies have been adopted and new markets opened up. Further, especially in India, banks have played a significant role in encouraging economic and social development.

There are, regrettably, examples to the contrary. In Nigeria, for example, the banking sector remains crippled by lack of reform, state interference and economic uncertainty (see MANAGEMENT IN NIGERIA). Nigeria has several parallel economies in this respect; one is devoted solely to hard currency and uses foreign banks, while another is wholly unofficial and relies on networks of moneylenders; both have strong connections with the black market. The official banking sector remains weak. There is little trust in the banking system, and at times too, it seems, little comprehension of the principles of banking and finance. In 1986, when the government of the day devalued the naira, a former head of state denounced the central bank for 'lack of patriotism'. Any crisis seems enough to spark off a capital flight, with domestic as well as foreign capital seeking havens abroad.

Opinions differ as to how instability of this nature is best tackled. Previous orthodoxy was that liberalization offered the best chance of stability, and the example of India seems to support this. However, it is worth noting that in India the state continues to play a major role in the provision of finance. States also continue to rely on capital and currency controls to protect their domestic economies, and here again there is an increasing view that such controls may be a short-term necessity (Nembhard 1996).

Another of the problems plaguing the financial sector in emerging countries is lack of adequate supervision. Foreign bank branches are often preferred over domestic banks because the latter are usually supervised by their parent institutions according to home-country rules; ANZ Grindlays, for example, which has a large network of banks in emerging countries, audits its branches in these countries by the same rules as would apply in Australia or the UK. One of the reasons for the India success story would appear to be the strength of the regulatory and inspection powers of the Reserve Bank of India, which controls bank licensing, branch expansion and liquidity, and administers the Deposit Insurance Corporation which pays out should savers lose their deposits.

How things can go wrong can be illustrated by the collapse of the Bank of Credit and Commerce International (BCCI), which conducted much of its business in emerging countries and was brought down in the early 1990s by a combination of fraud and mismanagement. Such examples are relatively rare; much more common is the problem encountered by the African Development Bank (Rocco 1986: 70) when attempting to fund a joint venture in Liberia. After long negotiations, the project broke down; the foreign partner insisted on using a New York bank, while the Liberian partner, under pressure from the Liberian government, insisted on using a Monrovian bank (which was subject to less scrutiny and control).

Economic stability and improved regulation and accountability are the chief barriers to growth in banking in emerging countries, as the recent Asian economic crisis has revealed. Nevertheless, great advances have been made over the past decade. As the case of India shows, a healthy domestic banking sector is critical to internal development, and the development of domestic banks in partnership with transnational institutions must be a key goal for the opening decades of the twenty-first century.

MORGEN WITZEL
LONDON BUSINESS SCHOOL

Further reading

(References cited in the text marked *)

Africa and the African Development Bank (1989) London: Euromoney Publications. (Now dated but detailed and still useful study which includes a description of the African Development Bank and its role as a finance provider.)

* African Development Bank (1999) main home page at http://afdb.org. (Links to a number of well-designed and informative information pages.)

* Asian Development Bank (1999) main home page at http://www.adb.org/mainpage. (Links to a series of pages on the ADB; links not always reliable.)

Brahm, L.J. (1992) *Banking and Finance in Indo-China*, Hemel-Hempstead: Woodhead-Faulkner. (Detailed though now dated study of the banking systems of Vietnam, Laos and Cambodia.)

British Library for Development Studies (1999) 'Eldis', at http://www.ids.ac.uk/eldis. (Very useful source page for information on development banks and international financial institutions.)

* Brown, M.B. (1997) *Africa's Choices after Thirty Years of the World Bank*, Boulder, CO: Westview Press. (Argues strongly that the World Bank has failed in its mission in Africa, and calls on the African countries to produce their own development solutions.)

* Curran, W. (1979) *Banking and the Global System*, Cambridge: Woodhead-Faulkner. (Thoughtful discussion of the globalization of banking by a US investment banker.)

Economist Intelligence Unit (1998) *EIU Country Report: Brazil*, London: Economist Intelligence Unit. (Up-to-date summary of the Brazilian economy and financial system.)

Economist Intelligence Unit (1998) *EIU Country Report: Nigeria*, London: Economist Intelligence Unit. (Up-to-date summary of the Nigerian economy and financial system.)

* Hellheiner, G., Berry, A., Stewart, F. and Culpeper, R. (eds) (1997) *Global Development Fifty Years After Bretton Woods: Essays in Honour of Gerald Hellheiner*, New York: St Martin's Press. (Includes essays reviewing the impact of the IMF and its policies on emerging countries.)

IfBG Göttingen (1999) 'World Banks (Brazil)', at http://www.gwdg.de/~ifbg/both_bra.htm. (Links to web pages of Brazilian banks.)

Inter-American Development Bank (1994) *Economic and Social Progress in Latin America*, New York: Inter-American Development Bank. (General description of the economic state of Latin America in 1993, when the crisis of the early 1990s was having a serious impact.)

* Inter-American Development Bank (1999) home page, at http://www.iadb.org.exr. (Introduction to the work of the Inter-American Development Bank.)

* Nembhard, J.G. (1996) *Capital Control, Financial Regulation and Industrial Policy in South Korea and Brazil*, Westport CT: Praeger. (Compares and contrasts the effectiveness of fiscal controls in a newly-industrialized country and a less developed one.)

* Rocco, F. (1986) *The African Development Bank*, London: Middle East Economic Digest. (Useful, but again dated, information largely superseded by the Bank's own web site.)

* Vorst, K.S. (1995) 'The Brazilian financial system', in Gale, J.R. (ed.), *Banking and Financial Systems in Selected Countries,* Lampeter: Edwin Mellen. (Good summary of the Brazilian system, though statistics require updating.)

World Bank (1999) home page, at http://www.worldbank.org/html. (The primary web site of the World Bank, with menus leading to a variety of information and reports.)

* Yousefi, M. (1995) 'The banking and financial system in India', in Gale, J.R. (ed.), *Banking and Financial Systems in Selected Countries*, Lampeter: Edwin Mellen. (Good summary of the Indian system.)

See also: ACCOUNTING IN THE EMERGING COUNTRIES; ECONOMIES OF THE EMERGING COUNTRIES; MANAGEMENT IN AFRICA; MANAGEMENT IN THE ARAB WORLD; MANAGEMENT IN THE EMERGING COUNTRIES; MANAGEMENT IN INDIA; MANAGEMENT IN NIGERIA

Related topics in the IEBM regional set: BANKING AND FINANCE IN ASIA PACIFIC; BANKING AND FINANCE IN EUROPE; BANKING AND FINANCE IN LATIN AMERICA; BANKING AND FINANCE IN NORTH AMERICA; MANAGEMENT IN ARGENTINA; MANAGEMENT IN BRAZIL; MANAGEMENT IN THE PHILIPPINES

Business cultures, the emerging countries

1 Introduction
2 Institutional level culture
3 Societal level culture
4 Internal work culture
5 Conclusion

Overview

Effective operation of business in the international arena requires an understanding of business cultures of different countries. The increasing globalization of business and the liberalization of economies in all parts of the world has made this requirement imperative. This is particularly true for the economically developing or emerging countries of Asia and Africa. There are three reasons why it is so important to study business cultures of these countries. First, with globalization of business there is an increase in interdependence among the newly emerging and the more industrialized countries in the world economy. Such interdependence is reflected in the fact that these emerging countries act as significant buyers, suppliers, competitors and capital users (Austin 1990). Second, in an interdependent global economy, the responsibility for the development of the emerging countries is no more limited to these countries alone, but as Kiggundu (1989) pointed out, it is the responsibility of other industrialized countries as well. Finally, the creation of various economic trading blocks such as NAFTA (North American Free Trade Agreement), suggests that both developed and emerging countries are realizing the benefits of expansion of their business operations worldwide in a free-market liberalized world economy. Expansion of business is perceived to be the best way to realize the full potential of a country, and in this regard, the world's major economic trading blocks have come to appreciate the importance of the business culture in the emerging countries.

1 Introduction

Business and government organizations are complex systems operating within dynamically interacting environmental forces (see MANAGEMENT IN THE EMERGING COUNTRIES). Effective management of such complex systems requires an understanding of both internal and external environments of these organizations. The internal environment refers to the socio-technical systems within the organization, and the external environment is represented by the economic, political, legal and socio-cultural characteristics of the country in which the organization operates. How business is conducted in these organizations depends on their adaptive and coping responses to both the internal and external environmental demands. These adaptation modes in the form of norms, values, beliefs, assumptions and practices are embodied in what is referred to as the 'business culture'. Integration of business on a global scale requires an analysis of business cultures of different countries, particularly those of the developing countries that are emerging in the economic arena. Before analysing the business cultures of emerging countries, the meanings of the two concepts, 'emerging countries' and 'business culture' need to be clarified.

The emerging countries represent most of the developing nations located in Asia (e.g. India, Pakistan) and Africa (e.g. Kenya, Uganda). Although there are significant differences among these countries, as a group, they exhibit a common pattern distinct from Western industrialized nations (see MANAGEMENT IN INDIA; MANAGEMENT IN KENYA; MANAGEMENT IN PAKISTAN; MANAGEMENT IN UGANDA).

The emerging countries can be characterized in three different ways. First, these countries have a similar historical experience. They came under the influence of foreign invasions and alien rules and gained their independence in the later part of the nineteenth century. It is during the post-independence era that they have begun to industrialize by borrowing Western capital and technology.

Secondly, in terms of economic, political and demographic contexts, these countries, as a group, provide a distinct pattern. As Adler and Boyacigiller (1995) point out using data from Austin (1990), these countries 'tend to be characterized by weak infrastructures, the lack of a skilled labor force, and low technological levels. They tend to be politically unstable. Culturally, developing countries tend to be characterized by rigid social structures, distinct gender roles, strong religious influences, and high levels of cultural diversity. Demographically, they usually experience high birth rates and thus have relatively young population' (Adler and Boyacigiller 1995: 5).

The third distinguishing characteristic can be observed in the socio-cultural environment. The emerging countries have been found to exhibit certain socio-cultural values that are, on the average, different from those of the developed countries. For instance, Jorgensen (1995) assessed the cultural closeness of East Africa relative to other countries on five socio-cultural dimensions (individualism, power distance, uncertainty avoidance, masculinity and dynamic Confucianism). He clearly found two clusters: one representing the industrially developed countries (e.g. Japan, the UK, Germany, the USA and Canada) and the other representing mostly the emerging countries (e.g. East and West Africa, and India).

The meaning of 'business culture' depends on how one defines the term 'culture'. Although there are many definitions of culture, the most comprehensive one has been offered by Kroeber and Kluckhohn (1952). According to these authors, 'Culture consists of patterns, explicit and implicit, of and for behaviour acquired and transmitted by symbols, constituting the distinctive achievements of human groups, including their embodiments in artifacts; the essential core of culture consists of traditional (i.e. historically derived and selected) ideas and especially their attached values' (Kroeber and Kluckhohn 1952: 181). Business culture therefore refers to a set of beliefs, assumptions, values and habitual behaviour patterns related to how things are done in a business or in organizational contexts.

The business culture in a given country manifests at three different levels. At the most basic individual level, it manifests as the internal work culture operating within an organization. It is a pattern of shared managerial beliefs and assumptions about workers and work behaviours that determines managerial practices within the organization (Schein 1992). This internal work culture however is influenced by two other levels of culture manifestations: the institutional/corporate level culture and the societal level culture (Kanungo and Jaeger 1990; Kanungo *et al.* 1998). The institutional level business culture is determined by the demands of the external economic, political and legal environment. The societal level business culture is influenced by the demands of the socio-cultural environment in which the business separates. The three levels of business cultures in emerging countries are described below.

2 Institutional level culture

Soon after their independence from colonial rule the emerging countries assigned centrally controlled state and public sector enterprises to play a dominant role in the economy. These enterprises are either commercially oriented or oriented toward meeting national developmental strategies for socio-economic growth. They manage not only manufacturing, marketing and finance, but also transportation, communication, energy and agriculture. But during the 1970s and 1980s, many of these state-owned enterprises experienced low capacity utilization, over-manning, low productivity and high unit cost leading to huge accumulated losses. State control also resulted in the perpetuation of the political patronage system that created inefficiency and mismanagement. As a result many of these countries faced severe balance of payment crises, budgetary deficits and inflation. In order to stabilize their economy, they resorted to loans and assistance from the International Monetary Fund (IMF), the World Bank and other donor agencies such as the United States International Development Agency (USAID). The assistance from these agencies was received with conditions attached requiring macroeconomic stabilization measures and decontrol or liberalization of the economy allowing foreign private investments and making it possible for private enterprises to compete in a free market (Faini *et al.* 1991). Such demands from the loan granting agencies have led to the restructuring of public enterprises and increasing privatization in the emerging countries. The pace of such liberalization of the economy however varies from country to country. Counties in south Asia, plus Bangladesh and Pakistan chose rapid privatization, while India and SriLanka have opted for a longer liberalization completed in phases.

In India, there has been a shift from the position in 1956 of a government regulated economy along socialist lines to the situation in 1991 after implementing a liberalization policy following the structural adjustment guidelines of the IMF and the World Bank. This has resulted in a gradual lowering of tariff protection, a reduction of price and output controls, a greater reliance on market forces, easier entry into industries, reductions of restrictions on foreign private investment and foreign exchange transactions, and some deregulation of investment decisions (Khandwalla 1996). By and large, the structural adjustment reforms of 1991 have led to increased private domestic and foreign sector participation in the energy, communication, transport and finance sectors.

In the East Africa, the impetus for structural adjustment reforms came from the financial crisis caused by oil price stocks in the 1970s and low export earnings in the 1980s. This led to negotiations with the World Bank for structural adjustment loans. As a result, the governments of Kenya, Tanzania and Uganda have pursued a course of restructuring to reduce government bureaucracy in resource allocation and to increase managerial autonomy of public enterprises. The various forms of structural adjustment include currency liberalization, increased prices paid to agricultural producers, a rationalization of state industry, controls on the size of the public service, a reduction in state intervention in the economy, a reshaping of the competitive framework by removing entry barriers, the development of a client–service orientation, and improving credit facilities, industry infrastructures and standards (Jorgensen 1995).

In addition to reshaping their economic environment, organizations within the emerging countries are beginning to put greater emphasis on managing their human resource more effectively. More and more attention is being paid to improving employee motivation, and in planning for performance improvement, organizational learning and manpower development (Jorgensen 1995; Venkata Ratnam 1995).

A notable feature of the institutional level culture in the emerging countries is that the primary responsibility for socioeconomic development rests with the state governments. For this reason, one finds a number of strategic developmental organizations (as opposed to commercially oriented profit making organizations) in these countries. These are macro-level organizations responsible for the development of other organizations in various sectors of the economy. Their performance is directed at sustaining structural adjustment reforms and outcomes.

There are three types of strategic developmental organizations (Khandwalla 1990). One type are the sectorially apex organizations like the Reserve Bank of India, responsible for the coordination and regulation of the banking sector. Other apex organizations are ministries of finance, agriculture, industry, etc. which initiate development programmes, disburse funds to public and private agencies, monitor performance and regulate growth of their respective sectors.

The second type are the spearhead organizations such as public enterprises in a particular industry sector. These organizations (e.g. Uganda Railways, Steel Authority of India) are a vital part of the development strategies related to industries such as heavy machinery, metal, oil, fertilizers, heavy chemicals, etc.

Finally, the third category of developmental organizations includes private organizations, foreign owned enterprises, small producer cooperatives, voluntary organizations and small scale industries in the rural sector. They act as catalysts for economic and social development and depend heavily on government support. Because of their resource dependence on government, they tend to chose bureaucratic conformity as their operating style.

3 Societal level culture

The above mentioned structural adjustment reforms at the institutional level are intended to effectively manage business in various economic sectors. However, managing business requires more than just following the structural adjustment guidelines. In order to run a business one has to adapt to the demands of the socio-cultural environment or the societal level culture from which the business draws the human resources for its operation, the customers for its products and services and other stockholders with whom it transacts for its success.

The societal level culture is represented by a set of common beliefs, values and norms, theories of behaviour or mental programmes that are shared by people living in a society. There are seven major dimensions on which the societal level culture of emerging countries has been characterized (Hickson and Pugh 1995; Hofstede 1991; Triandis 1994; Trompenaars 1993). Compared to Western industrialized nations, the emerging countries exhibit higher levels of loyalty toward community (or collectivistic orientation), power distance, paternalism, femininity, uncertainty avoidance, fatalism and context dependence. These cultural characteristics manifest themselves in business in a number of ways. Because individuals in these countries maintain the tradition of extended and joint family systems, they feel a strong sense of loyalty to their families and communities. As a result business is often run by fulfilling personal obligations toward in-group members rather than by meeting contractual organizational and task demands. In-group membership is often based on ethnicity, caste, tribe, family, language and religion. Work goals are accomplished by individuals and work teams primarily because of personalized relationships with supervisors, subordinates and co-workers and not because of the individual employee's work contract with the organization. The characteristic of high power distance stems from the rigid and hierarchical structure of social institutions in these countries. People accept the unequal distribution of power in organizations as a part of the human condition and value the role of formal authority and status in inducing compliance among subordinates.

The combined effect of high community loyalty and high power distance manifests itself in paternalism in business. Paternalism characterizes the supervisor–subordinate relationship within the organization. Supervisors in positions of authority assume the role of a parent and consider it an obligation to provide support and protection to subordinates under their care. Subordinates, in turn, reciprocate such care, support and protection of the parental authority by showing loyalty, deference and compliance to the supervisor. A whole range of managerial practices in these countries result directly from the beliefs in group embeddedness and hierarchy. The power of decision making is largely concentrated in the higher rungs of the organization. Subordinates seek guidance, direction, affection and patronage from their superiors, not only in job related matters, but also in career and family matters.

High femininity as a cultural characteristic of emerging countries implies that in business, interpersonal harmony, the quality of personal relationships and a caring attitude towards others are valued more than task performance. The existence of high uncertainty avoidance implies that people are more reluctant to take risks. They look for clear direction in the form of rules and regulations to guide their behaviour. Finally, the cultural characteristic of fatalism implies that people do not believe that they have the power to control their own destiny. As a result, very often, planning for the future is considered a futile exercise. Thus, business tasks are handled as they come up, and problems are seldom anticipated in sufficient time to make adequate preparations for solving them.

The high context-dependent characteristic of emerging countries implies that people in these countries have a tendency to utilize salient contextual experiences to justify their behaviour instead of using logical principle-based norms. People belonging to Western industrialized societies apply logical principles and generalized norms to justify their behaviour because they presume that their social and physical environment is stable and governed by universal laws and principles. But people belonging to the emerging countries find their environment unstable and unpredictable, and consequently look for a contextual justification for their behaviour. This is reflected in their approach to business. Behaviour on the job is guided more by the demands of the immediate context (e.g. meeting unanticipated demands from family, boss, community, etc.) than by a work ethic or principles governing the work place. Since context plays an important role in determining an individual's perceptions, attributions and behaviours, face-to-face interaction in business communications is valued more in these countries than in Western industrialized countries, where communication through electronic media tends to be preferred.

4 Internal work culture

The internal work culture of a business organization is largely a reflection of the shared managerial values, beliefs, norms and behaviour patterns in the organization. The internal work culture is affected by both institutional and societal level cultures, and has a more direct impact on organizational policies and practices (see HUMAN RESOURCE MANAGEMENT IN THE EMERGING COUNTRIES).

The management values, and the climate of beliefs and assumptions in business that characterize the internal work culture have been grouped under two broad categories (i) descriptive assumptions about human nature, and (ii) prescriptive assumptions about the guiding principles of human conduct (Kanungo and Jaeger 1990). The first category describes assumptions about human nature along the following dimensions: causality and control of outcomes, creative potential, malleability, time perspective and time units for action. The emerging countries differ significantly from Western industrialized countries on each of these dimensions. In emerging countries, because of the belief in fatalism at the societal level culture, workers (including managers) exhibit a high dependence on outside forces for their outcomes (external locus of control). Human resources are viewed as less malleable and with limited creative potential. The time perspective tends to be less future-oriented and more past and present oriented. The preferred time unit for action is short-term because long-term planning is considered futile in the context of environmental volatility and unpredictability.

The second category spells out the normative assumptions about whether to adopt a proactive or reactive stance to task performance; whether to judge success on a moral or a pragmatic basis; whether to promote a collegial/participative or an authoritarian/paternalistic orientation; whether to base one's behaviour on predetermined principles or on the exigencies of the situation. In this category too, there are substantial differences between the emerging countries and the Western industrialized countries. In the emerging countries, workers take a more passive or reactive stance to task performance. They shy away from taking initiatives because, for them, personal initiative heightens the uncertainty of making mistakes and incurring the displeasure of superiors. They therefore prefer to follow the rules and direction of their superiors. Very often, success or failure of performance in business is judged on moral grounds, derived from past traditions and religious practices, rather than on pragmatic grounds.

Interpersonal relationships in organizations tend to be paternalistic rather than collegial/participative. The demands of the immediate context override work principles when judging one's performance in business.

5 Conclusion

The business cultures of the emerging countries are the byproduct of two major sources of influence. One source is from the Western donor communities and agencies such as the IMF and the World Bank. This source of influence has led to various forms of structural adjustment reforms. The other source of influence is from the socio-cultural traditions within the emerging countries themselves. The interaction of these two sources of influence has created business cultures in these countries that often signify conflicting modes of business practices. For instance, the influence of indigenous societal level culture manifests itself through in-group embeddedness (familism and community loyalty), power hierarchy, paternalism and patronage. On the other hand the Western influence leading to structural adjustment reforms calls for modernization trends that promote individualistic achievement, performance focus and egalitarian values.

Indigenous experience with the uncertain and unpredictable environment often results in a compulsion to avoid future planning and taking on risky ventures. The Western influence on the other hand is forcing business to opt for long-term planning and moderate risk taking behaviour. Finally, religious traditionalism and prevailing rural and agricultural values have led to moralism and an excessive concern for economic security in business. This situation is gradually being replaced by pragmatism and economic growth orientation in business because of the Western influence. The increasing presence of multinationals in the emerging countries has made it necessary to pay more attention to the issue of integrating Western and indigenous influences on business cultures and practices.

RABINDRA N. KANUNGO
FACULTY OF MANAGEMENT
MCGILL UNIVERSITY, MONTREAL, QUEBEC

Further reading

(References cited in the text marked *)

* Adler, N.J. and Boyacigiller, N. (1995) 'Going beyond traditional HRM scholarship' in Kanungo, R.N. (ed.), *New Approaches to Employer Management Volume 3: Employee Management in Developing Countries*, Greenwich, Connecticut: JAI Press, pp. 1–13. (Advocates internationalization of the traditional field of HRM.)

Atiyyah, H.S. (1992) 'Research in Arab countries, published in Arabic', *Organization Studies* 13: 105–10. (Summarizes the features of Arab management culture.)

* Austin, J.E. (1990) *Managing in Developing Countries: Strategic Analysis and Operating Techniques*, New York: The Free Press. (An analysis of problems and techniques of management in developing countries.)

Blunt, P. and Merrick, L.J. (1992) *Managing Organizations in Africa*, New York: De Gruyter. (Focuses on management issues in organizations in Africa.)

* Faini, R., de Melo, J., Senhadji, A. and Stanton, J. (1991). 'Growth-oriented adjustment programs: A statistical analysis', *World Development* 19: 957–67 (An analysis of structural adjustment programmes.)

* Hickson, D.J. and Pugh, D.S. (1995) *Management Worldwide*, London: Penguin Books. (An analysis of the impact of social culture on organizations around the globe.)

* Hofstede, G. (1991) *Cultures and Organizations: Software of the Mind*, London: McGraw-Hill. (An analysis of the impact of societal culture on organizations.)

* Jorgensen, J. (1995) 'Restructuring public enterprise in East Africa: The human resource management dimension', in Kanungo, R. N. (ed.), *New Approaches to Employer Management Volume 3: Employee Management in Developing Countries*, Greenwich, Connecticut: JAI Press, pp. 35–66. (Deals with the methods to improve public enterprises in East Africa.)

* Kanungo, R.N. and Jeager, A.M. (1990) 'Introduction: The need for indigenous management in developing countries', in Jeager, A.M. and Kanungo, R.N. (eds), *Management in Developing Countries*, London: Routledge, pp. 1–19.

* Kanungo, R.N., Aycan, Z. and Sinha, J.B.P. (1998) 'Socio-culutral environment, work culture, and managerial practices: The model of culture fit' in Larsy, J.C., Adair, J.G. and Dion, K.L. (eds), *Latest Contributions to Cross-Cultural Psychology*, Amsterdam: Swets and Zeitlinger. (A comparison of work cultures in India, USA and Canada.)

* Khandwalla, P.N. (1990) 'Strategic developmental organizations: Some behavioural properties', in Jeager, A.M. and Kanungo, R.N. (eds), *Management in Developing Countries*, London: Routledge, pp. 23–42.

* Kiggundu, M.N. (1989) *Managing Organizations in Developing Countries: An Operational and Strategic Approach*, West Hartford, CT: Kumarian Press. (An analysis of strategic and operational issues in management in developing countries.)

* Krober, A.L. and Kluckhohn, C. (1952) *Culture: A Critical Review of Concepts and Definitions*, Cambridge, MA: Peabody Museum. (A critical analysis of the concept of culture.)

Parker, B. (1999) *Globalization and Business Practice*, London and Thousand Oaks, CA: Sage. (Up-to-date text; chapter 4 deals with global business culture in detail.)

* Schein, E.H. (1992) *Organizational Culture and Leadership* (2nd edn), San Francisco, CA: Jossey-Bass.

* Triandis, H.C. (1982) 'Review of culutres' consequences: International differences in work-related values', *Human Organization* 41, 86–90. (A review of Hofstede's empirical work on work values.)

* Trompenaars, F. (1993) *Riding the Waves of Culture*, London: Brealey. (An empirical analysis of the impact of social culture on organizations.)

* Venkata Ratnam, C.S. (1995) 'Social and labor issues of privatization in South Asia: A comparative study', in Kanungo, R.N. (ed.), *New Approaches to Employer Management Volume 3: Employee Management in Developing Countries*, Greenwich, Connecticut: JAI Press, pp. 67–91. (Analysis of issues related to employment under privatization programmes in South Asia.)

See also: ECONOMIES OF THE EMERGING COUNTRIES; HUMAN RESOURCE MANAGEMENT IN THE EMERGING COUNTRIES; MANAGEMENT IN THE EMERGING COUNTRIES; MANAGEMENT IN INDIA; MANAGEMENT IN KENYA; MANAGEMENT IN PAKISTAN; MANAGEMENT IN SRI LANKA; MANAGEMENT IN TANZANIA; MANAGEMENT IN UGANDA

Related topics in the IEBM regional set: BUSINESS CULTURES, ASIAN PACIFIC; BUSINESS CULTURES, EUROPEAN; BUSINESS CULTURES, LATIN AMERICAN; BUSINESS CULTURES, NORTH AMERICAN

Economies of the emerging countries

1 **Introduction**
2 **International economic institutions and the economics of emerging countries**
3 **Trade and aid policy issues**

Overview

The economics of emerging countries are concerned with those major theories and policies that may bring economic growth and prosperity to poor countries in the world economy. Since the emergence of the idea of emerging countries, in the period since 1945, the means to achieve economic growth has been subject to changing fashions in economic theory and policy practice. The experience of economic development in the world economy has been mixed, with sub-Saharan Africa having had a poor economic growth performance since the 1960s, while southeast Asia has recorded high and sustained rates of economic growth. The multilateral economic institutions, namely the International Monetary Fund, the World Bank and the General Agreement on Tariffs and Trade (GATT), now the World Trade Organization (WTO), have promoted policies to encourage free trade in the world economy, while the Food and Agricultural Organization, the United Nations Conference on Trade and Development and the European Union have promoted policies to intervene in markets, either by the nation state or by agreements among nation states, to achieve particular economic and social objectives in addition to economic growth. The economics of emerging countries is concerned with the selection of appropriate trade policy or policies to promote growth and development.

Free trade has not been universally considered as the best policy for primary commodity producing countries, largely because of the decline in the terms of trade and the perceived bias of the trading system in favour of the rich and industrialized countries. Policies to promote industrialization through import substitution and state intervention through economic planning, in most emerging economies resulted in inward-looking strategies which did not provide the basis for lasting and sustained economic growth. The combination of import protection of industry and state intervention in the economy often resulted in unsustainable inflation and the collapse of economic growth. The combination of the protection of industry through import substitution policies and direct state intervention in the economy either resulted in economic stagnation, as in sub-Saharan Africa, or unsustained inflation and economic collapse, as in South America. In southeast Asia, however, state intervention in the economy to promote industrialization and economic growth through the outward-looking strategies of selling manufactures on world markets, provided the basis for the sustained and lasting growth of the economies known as the Asian Tigers.

Economic aid, or the transfer of resources from rich to poor countries, while contributing to the social and economic welfare of some emerging countries, has not universally proved to be as effective a means of promoting growth and development when compared with trade. Agricultural growth, while having increased in both the developed and the emerging countries, has not meant that hunger and malnutrition has been eradicated in the world. The growth of the world population, particularly among poor countries, taken together with increasing environmental degradation, poverty and food insecurity, suggest that the economics of emerging countries will continue to cause concern that economic growth, stability and prosperity eludes so many of the poor countries in the world.

1 Introduction

In the world economy, countries are grouped into different categories according to their relative prosperity or poverty (see WORLD TRADE ORGANIZATION). This economic condition is measured by the proxy of per capita income, which is the gross national product (GNP) divided by the population of the nation-state concerned. Per capita income, expressed in dollar terms, provides a very approximate measure of relative prosperity or poverty. In 1989 Mozambique had a per capita income of 80 dollars, whereas Switzerland had some 29,880 dollars per capita. The average annual growth rate between 1965 and 1990 of countries ranged between Botswana growing by some 8.5 per cent and Kuwait by some –4.0 per cent.

The categorization of countries as being either rich or poor, is too general a classification and does not sufficiently allow for the explanation of the factors that have contributed to their relative prosperity or relative poverty. The economics of emerging countries is concerned with explaining the underlying factors, both the economic theory and policy, that have contributed, or not, to the economic progress of nation-states.

The causes of economic growth are as central a concern in the 1990s as they were in 1776 when the economist Adam Smith first published his famous *Wealth of Nations*, where he explored and explained the process of growth and the distribution of wealth among nation states. Explaining the processes of economic growth and the distribution of income is still today the essential purpose of the economics of emerging countries.

The economics of emerging countries have provided a forum for alternative views as to what is the most appropriate means to achieve the eradication of poverty and provide the basis for sustained economic growth and prosperity. Emerging countries as a category, came into being during the period of decolonialization and the cold war struggle of economic ideas (and political frameworks) was very much a part of economic policy debates. These policy debates have preoccupied development specialists over the last 50 years (Bauer 1991; Lal 1983).

Poor countries have been variously described in the last 50 years as backward, low income, underdeveloped, Third World, peripheral (as in metropolitan, peripheral areas), South (as in North/South) or as low- and middle-income emerging countries, and fashions with regard to economic theory and policy that may alleviate conditions of poverty and provide the basis for sustained economic growth have been the central concern of development economics, or the economics of emerging countries, since the period of the 1940s (Brandt 1980). During the 1980s countries in the world economy were categorized into low-income, medium- and high-income countries, and in the

1990s former medium-income emerging countries were considered as emergent market economies with prospects for foreign private capital investment obtaining a higher rate of return than in the rich countries. Former Soviet bloc eastern European economies are referred to as transitional economies. International multilateral economic institutions have played a central part in the ideas and thinking on the economic development of poor countries.

The economics of emerging countries have been concerned with recurrent themes, *inter alia*:

1   the measurement of poverty and the meaning of development, including the importance of population growth;
2   what are the appropriate macroeconomic, microeconomic, international trade and payments policies to achieve economic growth on a regular and continuing basis;
3   the provision of economic aid from rich countries to contribute to the well-being and growth of poor countries and policies to promote the redistribution of wealth on a global scale.

The economics of emerging countries have been concerned with identifying the appropriate policies for sustained economic growth and the alleviation of poverty. Since the idea of emerging countries emerged in the immediate post-war period, there has not been a consensus among development economists as to what are the appropriate economic policies for the transformation of poor countries into prosperous ones. The idea that the economic policies pursued by emerging countries, as opposed to developed countries, has a separate body of theory and practice, has been a recurrent theme and concern for most of the last 50 years. Economic policy recommendations towards poor countries, were inextricably interwoven with the politics of the cold war period, where the role of the State as the agent for progress and prosperity contrasted sharply with the alternative view that unrestrained free trade and free markets would provide the basis for lasting growth and economic development (see PERSPECTIVES ON GLOBALIZATION, BIG BUSINESS AND THE EMERGING COUNTRIES).

At the heart of all major policy debates on the process of economic development lies a sharp contrast between arguments that propose the State as the agent of economic change and those that propose free markets and free enterprise as a superior agent for change. The issues are often contrasted by policies which emphasize redistribution of resources for purposes of social planning and political objectives such as equity. Improving the distribution of income and direct poverty alleviation is considered to have a direct trade-off with allocative efficiency and economic growth. Free market economics has an implicit theory of distribution (known as 'trickle-down') that emphasizes the primacy of economic efficiency and growth over redistribution of wealth as the means of providing economic development. The free market theory of distribution argues for economic growth as the means to improving the distribution of income in an economy and, for that matter, for the distribution of income in the world economy taken as a whole. As an economy grows, so more people will be drawn into the growth process and prosperity will spread. Interventionist theories (or structuralist theories as they are sometimes known) consider direct intervention by the State into the economy for the purposes of improving the distribution of income in favour of the poor as a more appropriate means to overcome poverty and economic backwardness.

Interventionist policies are justified on the grounds of the failure of markets due to the existence of monopoly, externalities such as pollution or instabilities (adverse prices or terms of trade) inherent in the market system, taken together with bottlenecks (such as a shortage of capital) that prevent sustained growth and therefore an improving distribution of income in favour of the poor. The State is considered as the agent of economic change for overcoming the failures or excesses of the free market system, and it is believed that state planning can provide a framework for allocative and distributive justice that will simultaneously achieve both equity and growth.

There is, of course, a middle ground between the market and the State, where in the economics of emerging countries pro-market theorists concede that on issues of poverty alleviation the poor can be targeted directly, provided that the cost of government programmes does not undermine economic efficiency and economic growth. The State has played a direct role in formulating investment and economic growth policies in the Asian Tigers or Dragon economies (South Korea, Taiwan, Hong Kong, Singapore) but within the context of promoting trade (see PERSPECTIVES ON GLOBALIZATION, BIG BUSINESS AND THE EMERGING COUNTRIES). These economies have had exceptionally high rates of sustained economic growth since the 1960s until the present time. Over the last five decades free market economics have gradually come to dominate the economic policy framework for the emerging countries and particularly since 1989 with the emergence of the eastern European countries (transitional economies) in the post-cold war capitalist world economy. The promotion of free market economic ideas and policy frameworks has largely been the concern of three multilateral economic institutions which were established in the 1940s (see Mehmet 1999).

2 International economic institutions and the economics of emerging countries

The ending of the Second World War saw a rethinking of the framework for international economic policy which would provide a guide for the capitalist economies and their conduct of international economic relations during the cold war period (1950–89). The conduct of economic policy between the First and Second World Wars had resulted in worldwide protectionism, depression and the collapse of world trade and economic growth, policies which in turn had contributed to the war itself. The economic order which emerged during the immediate post-war period was designed to provide the basis for world economic growth and prosperity. To this end the principles on which it rested were those of the nineteenth-century liberal economic tradition which had emphasized the centrality of the doctrine of free trade and the importance of the adherence to comparative advantage in the conduct of economic policy on the world economy. Nations should compete with each other on the basis of their costs of production and their economic efficiency and the State should provide a minimalist role in terms of its intervention in economic affairs. The role of the State should be to uphold law and order, national security and not to engage in direct economic activity, although this minimalist view was somewhat moderated by Keynesian ideas on macroeconomic management during the 1950s and 1960s. The shortage of capital and the non-convertibility of the currency of many nation states provided a rationale for the giving of economic support by way of economic aid from rich to poor countries (Lewis 1978).

Multilateral institutions were established to oversee the conduct of economic policy in four key areas: international finance and payments; investment and development; international trade policy; and international agricultural and food policy.

The International Monetary Fund

The International Monetary Fund (IMF) was established together with the International Bank for Reconstruction and Development (IBRD), or the World Bank as it has come to be known, at Bretton Woods in New Hampshire, USA, in 1944. Both these international agencies are based in Washington, DC. The IMF had originally been conceived as a world monetary authority and was to operate in the world economy as a world central bank with powers analogous to a central bank in a nation state. The IMF does not, in fact, act as a world central bank, but more as a coordinator of exchange rate, monetary and related policy issues among its members. The IMF has been concerned to promote international monetary cooperation, to aid the expansion and balanced growth of trade, to promote exchange rate stability, to assist in the establishment of a multilateral system of payments, and to give confidence to members by making its resources temporarily available to decrease the intensity and duration of balance of payments disequilibria. There are currently 179 member countries of the IMF. The role of the IMF has evolved over the last half century with a particular emphasis upon providing policy advice and short-term financial support to emerging countries. The general policy framework in which the IMF support is given is known as conditionality, whereby countries are entitled to financial support conditional on liberalizing their economy and adopting economic policy measures that will address their underlying economic problems. These problems are invariably related to the rate of inflation, overvalued exchange rates, budgetary deficits and balance of payments deficits. Members of the IMF can draw upon their subscription to membership of the fund and in addition there are financial facilities of varying degrees of 'conditionality' in terms of repayment. Drawing from the IMF beyond the quota system entitlement involves financial penalties that approximate free market rates of interest and stricter terms of repayment. The IMF economic policy framework nearly always emphasizes monetary contraction; devaluation, either implicit or explicit; the redirection of government intervention in the price system or the promotion of privatization; internal financial reform and the raising of interest rates; external liberalization, through the reduction of barriers to trade and the freezing of wage demands with a view to cut inflationary pressure. IMF policy draws heavily upon orthodox neo-classical economic theory and policy (see BANKING AND FINANCE IN THE EMERGING COUNTRIES).

The World Bank

The World Bank as a sister institution to the IMF was concerned with providing loans on both a grant and concessional basis for the reconstruction of war-torn Europe and as such operated as a development fund rather than as a bank. While the IMF has been largely concerned with short-run to medium-term monetary, financial and balance of payments problems in emerging countries, the World Bank has focused its policy on the medium- to long-run issues concerning project investment and appraisal and sectoral development. The World Bank specialized in project development, infrastructure and the identification of both projects and programmes to promote economic growth and development in recipient emerging countries. Cost-benefit analysis became a major tool for the identification of appropriate projects during the period from the late 1960s until the 1980s. While cost-benefit analysis still provides a major means to identifying and evaluating appropriate projects, the Bank has gradually shifted its policy from an almost exclusive microeconomic emphasis to that of a both a micro- and macroeconomic framework (known at first as programme lending). The Bank's approach to lending is known as structural adjustment policy.

Structural adjustment lending is concerned with identifying investment in projects, programmes and general budgetary support for the promotion of sustainable economic growth in emerging countries in receipt of World Bank funds. The World Bank group includes the original organization (the IBRD) and three other specialist lending agencies. World Bank funds are given on a concessional basis to emerging countries which, in due course, repay these monies to the Bank. World Bank lending is undertaken by the group of four institutions: the IBRD which makes market-rate loans and offers training and technical advice; the IDA (International Development Association), established 1960, which provides interest-free loans, training and technical advice; the IFC (International Finance Corporation), established 1956, mobilizes capital for private ventures; and the MIGA (Multilateral Investment Guarantee Agency), established 1986, insures foreign direct investment against political risk and provides advisory services to help countries attract private foreign investment.

It was increasingly recognized that the policy framework of both the IMF and the World Bank overlapped and a emerging country that failed to meet IMF conditionality would not receive IBRD structural adjustment funding. The policy overlap of the sister institutions required a greater coordination, if contradictory policy advice and support was to be avoided. To this end, IMF and World Bank policies are complementary and not separate from their common purpose of promoting sustained economic growth through liberalized trade in the world economy. Periodically calls are made for the unification of both organizations. This has hitherto been rejected, although both organizations are increasing their levels of joint work and cooperation on the framing of development policies. The lines between their respective areas of policy advice and development funding are becoming blurred.

The General Agreement on Tariffs and Trade/World Trade Organization

The General Agreement on Tariffs and Trade (GATT) was established in Geneva to supervise the development of a world system of free trade (see WORLD TRADE ORGANIZATION). Since 1947 signatories to the GATT have increased to include all countries in the world economy, with the exception of China which now seeks to become a member. Unlike the IMF and the World Bank, the GATT has a legal framework for its trade policy which is binding on its membership. Free trade is promoted by the GATT through its legal framework and by periodic trade negotiations among its members, known as 'trade rounds'. Each trade round has considered both the rules on trade as well as specific types and categories of trade. Free trade has been gradually extended and deepened over the last half century, from the deepening of trade in industrial products to the extending of new areas such as the inclusion of agricultural trade policy in the Uruguay round. The GATT trade negotiations of the Kennedy round of 1967, the Tokyo round of 1979 and the recently completed Uruguay round 1994, have reduced the level of protection in the world economy and thus have contributed to world economic growth. The GATT has been superseded by a new World Trade Organization (WTO) in 1995 (see WORLD TRADE ORGANIZATION). Over the last half century, the GATT has successively widened its scope and the principles of free trade have extended over a wider range of products and services and world trade as a whole is freer today than it was in the immediate post-war period (Meerhaeghe 1974).

Food and Agricultural Organization

The Food and Agricultural Organization of the United Nations became operational in Rome in 1945 and was to be concerned with policies to alleviate world hunger and poverty. Its advocacy of policies to intervene in world agricultural trade and promote agricultural commodity stabilization schemes was considered to be incompatible with the principles of free trade and consequently its role was limited and has largely been confined to that of gathering data and technical information on aspects of world agriculture. Issues of world hunger and poverty have seen the proliferation of world food agencies (all Rome based). In addition to the FAO (proposed in 1943 at Hot Springs), the World Food Programme (WFP) was established in 1961 to use food aid to promote economic and social development in the Third World; the world food crisis of 1972–4 saw the establishment of the World Food Council (WFC) and the International Fund for Agricultural Development was established in 1977 to improve the lives of the rural poor, the thirteenth UN Agency (Talbot 1990).

The economics of emerging countries have been influenced by the ideas and thinking of the free trade multilateral institutions of the IMF, GATT and the World Bank, as well as by the more interventionist thinking of the FAO and the three other Rome food and agricultural agencies. The earlier focus of the GATT in the 1950s and 1960s saw many agriculturally and primary commodity based emerging countries excluded from the benefits of trade negotiations that were concerned with industrial products. Partly as a result of this exclusion, the United Nations Conference on Trade and Development (UNCTAD) (1964) urged policies for intervention in commodities to offset the adverse effect of a decline in their terms of trade. Prices of commodities (other than energy products) are near their lowest levels in real terms this century (see Figure 1). The trend in these commodity prices has been downward over most of the past 95 years. The UNCTAD proposals argued for an extension of commodity agreements and arrangements on the lines of the Wheat Trade Convention of 1933, the International Sugar Agreement of 1937, the International Coffee Agreement of 1957 and the International Tin Agreement of 1934. The agreements had sought to stabilize production and output by various means, such as buffer stocks, production quotas and

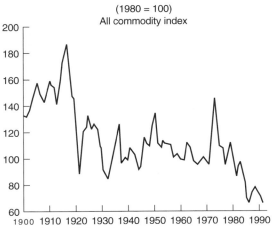

(1980 = 100)
All commodity index

Figure 1 Commodity prices in the 20th century

price agreements in order to regulate trade and offset any deterioration in the terms of trade of producer countries and to smooth the variability of prices that many commodities were liable to experience. The UNCTAD proposal culminated in a scheme for a multi-commodity fund to intervene in international commodity trade in the late 1970s. The period of the 1970s saw considerable instability in world commodity markets with the world food crisis and the formation of the Organization of Petroleum Exporting Countries (OPEC) and its successful but temporary quadrupling of the price of oil. The policy options of emerging countries in response to the secular deterioration of their terms of trade is either to adopt measures in a vain attempt to offset this decline or to diversify their economies.

In addition to multilateral institutions, the economic policy prescriptions, concessions and finance of the bilateral aid agencies have played a major part in the formulation of the policy and the economics of many emerging countries. The USA particularly, through its influence upon the Bretton Woods Agencies, the GATT and the Organization for Economic Cooperation and Development (OECD), was the dominant bilateral country in the formulation of economic policy towards emerging countries and in the provision of economic assistance towards their economic development. The communist bloc influenced the formulation of economic policies in many emerging countries through its advocacy of 'economic planning' in the form of state ownership and control of industry and agriculture. Heavy industrialization was a favoured but unsuccessful policy prescription. The collectivization of agriculture in the Soviet bloc and in the People's Republic of China, as well as attempts made in emerging countries, proved, with experience, to be unsuccessful, and agricultural output invariably fell as a consequence of these policies. The failures of Stalinist agricultural policies in the 1930s undermined agricultural output and the policies of the 1950s were on similar lines until the collapse of the Berlin Wall. Maoist agricultural policies resulted in a major famine in China in the 1960s as the policies of Stalin had done in the Soviet Union in the 1930s. In Africa a collectivist agricultural and rural social policy in Tanzania, known as Ujamaa, failed to sustain agricultural output and was subsequently abandoned. The communist bloc did not provide economic aid to emerging countries on anything near the scale of the capitalist West. Indeed, communist aid tended to favour high-profile projects such as the Aswan Dam in Egypt or the provision of military aid to its client states. Military aid was also provided by the West to bolster regimes in the emerging world, particularly those countries that were on cold war frontiers such as South Korea.

The United States Agency for International Development (USAID) and its allied agencies provided aid to emerging countries. Economic aid was considered an essential transfer to poor countries to underpin the process of economic growth and development. The USA was the major aid donor during the 1950s and 1960s although other rich countries had their own bilateral aid programmes. In the 1960s the Pearson Commission (established by the IBRD) reported recommendations to the United Nations that rich countries should endeavour to allocate one per cent of their GNP per annum to poor countries in the form of economic aid. Apart from the Scandinavian countries and the Netherlands, who have accepted this aid target, other rich countries have not reached as much as one per cent of their GNP in their aid contributions (Brandt 1980).

European Union

During the 1960s the European Community (now the European Union (EU)), developed its own distinctive aid and trade policies towards the emerging world. The European Union trade policies towards emerging countries are under the Lome Conventions, of which there have been four. Each Lome agreement runs for a five-year period and each new agreement is renegotiated with the ACP (Africa, Caribbean and Pacific) countries. Members of Lome were essentially former colonies of the European Union countries. The EU has established preferential trade access to ACP countries through the Generalized System of Preferences (GSP). The USA has also introduced a generalized system of preferences in its sphere of influence (in response to the EU initiative), an agreement with South American countries known as the Punta del Este agreement.

European Aid Policies are operated through the European Development Bank (EDB) and the European Bank for Reconstruction and Development (EBRD), the latter having been established to assist the new transition economies of Eastern Europe. The EBRD also has funding from the USA and other non-EU rich countries. Its development lending is limited to help the former Soviet bloc economies to transform their institutions and economy to free market policies. EBRD lending policy is constrained, in so far as almost half of its funds must be directed to the private sector. EU trade policies towards emerging countries are unified into a single policy but European aid policies co-exist with the bilateral aid policies of member states.

These various international institutions, by a combination of resources and policy prescriptions, have had a major influence on the economics of emerging countries during the cold war era and are likely to continue to do so. The emphasis now is on channelling multilateral funding to private sector development as witnessed by the changes in policy of the IBRD and the introduction of the EBRD policy emphasis upon encouraging the private sector. Since 1989 the economics of emerging countries have highlighted the role of the private sector in policy changes, particularly within the multilateral institutions. Policy is being increasingly formulated to facilitate private sector development, the government sector is receiving policy advice to liberalize, and development funds are being directed to promote these objectives. In theory, as markets fill the role as providers of capital for development, then the need for multilateral development agencies will lessen, if not entirely disappear.

Over the last 50 years and particularly since 1989, free-trade and free-market policies are in the ascendant, and these policy prescriptions are likely to be reinforced by increased economic growth in the world economy. They are also likely to be moderated if global economic prospects go awry. The global depression of the 1930s set the economic agenda for most of the twentieth century in so far as post-Second World War economic policy has sought to undo the policies of the inter-war period.

3   Trade and aid policy issues

In the period when the classical doctrine of free trade was being enshrined at Bretton Woods as a fundamental doctrine for the post-war economic order and as an operating principle for the new international institutions, doubts were being expressed as to whether free trade would be beneficial to poor countries taken as a whole. Those countries emerging from colonialism had an economic structure that had been established to provide raw materials for their colonial masters. Their economies were highly specialized in the production of primary commodities, which were subject to wide fluctuations in price on world markets. This specialization provided commodity price instability to emergent emerging countries and undermined their prospects for economic growth and development. The collapse of commodity markets in the 1930s had seen the introduction of marketing boards with monopoly powers to purchase commodities and to try to stabilize commodity prices. The marketing boards also used buffer stock as part of their stabilization policy. In West Africa the newly independent countries, for example, inherited these boards which had accumulated considerable funds which in turn were to be applied for the general development of the new states. The colonial legacy had left behind economic institutions that did not operate on the basis of free trade, and indeed these marketing boards taxed producers to raise general revenues. The result of these revenue raising policies had a profound effect on the pattern of production of primary commodities. In West Africa the monopoly commodity boards' taxation policy resulted in a supply response from producers that either caused the output of commodities to decrease, or led producers to find, through smuggling, alternative markets, usually in neighbouring countries. The marketing boards, in their internal price policies and taxation policy, eventually undermined their own production base which in turn resulted in a revenue crisis for the state concerned (see MARKETING IN THE EMERGING COUNTRIES).

The dependence of emerging countries upon primary commodities, in addition to providing a rationale for monopoly policies within countries, resulted in attempts by the emerging countries themselves to cartelize commodity trade through producer agreements and the regulation of trade. Free-trade policy was being challenged as the first best policy for emerging countries through the terms-of-trade hypothesis.

The terms of trade

Studies by Hans Singer and Raul Prebisch in the late 1940s suggest that the trading system was not neutral towards the prospects for primary producing countries. These studies indicated that the terms of trade worked against the interests of poor countries and in favour of rich countries. The Singer–Prebisch hypothesis (or the terms-of-trade hypothesis) provided a powerful argument for interventionist policies in international trade through direct intervention in trade policy itself to correct the bias towards rich countries in favour of poor countries (Meier and Seers 1984). The fall in commodity prices meant that commodity-dependent countries found that increases in their productivity resulted in lower prices and lower government revenues. These lower revenues in turn made development financing more difficult, and in times of commodity-price instability revenues were unpredictable. The benefits of primary commodity productivity were being passed on to rich countries in lower prices and not being retained by the poor countries. The terms-of-trade hypothesis and the non-neutrality of the international trading system provided the basis, in the 1960s and 1970s, for the development of dependency theories which argued that the economic order of the post-war world was a continuation of the exploitative nature of international trade that had been central to the colonial system of economics which had shaped the nineteenth and early twentieth centuries. Trade according to this school had become a mechanism for the extraction of profit from the poor countries to the rich.

Allied to this view of the exploitative nature of the trade system itself, was a further view that multinational corporations (MNCs) were the institutional mechanism for the expropriation of profits from emerging countries. MNCs were said to practise 'transfer pricing', which was the charging of prices not according to costs and profits but for the purpose of concealing their profitability and overcoming emerging country government policy to retain profits in the country of origin.

The Singer–Prebisch hypothesis also provided an additional argument for economic aid from rich countries to poor countries. The terms-of-trade hypothesis proves to be a resilient idea and provides an alternative theoretical focus, or an exception for many, to the doctrine of free trade. The bias of the trading system is not considered by all economists (or multilateral institutions) as having been proven and over the last 50 years numerous studies have tried to refine the hypothesis or refute it. The decline in the terms of trade suggests for IMF analysts that the economy concerned should diversify to other economic activities and not to put in place policies to resist the decline. In addition to the terms-of-trade hypothesis, trade pessimism also saw the re-emergence of the Infant Industry or Infant Economy argument for protectionism. Classic free-trade theory and its modern refinements such as the Heckscher–Ohlin theory, saw trade as the engine of economic growth, and free trade as the means to establish the fastest rate of growth for the world economy as a whole since free trade provided both static and dynamic gains to a country engaged in it. Since the nineteenth century, when John Stuart Mill argued that countries which did not have industries but wished to establish them, it had been considered reasonable to protect the fledgling industry as a parent would an infant, until such time as the child could take care of itself. Mill had provided an argument for a limited period of protection of new industries or new economics. The infant industry argument lent itself to justify tariff barriers (or quotas) or producer subsidies in emerging countries where import substitution policies were being established as some poor countries sought to industrialize. Producer subsidies were considered as less pernicious than tariffs and less damaging to trade. The weakness of the infant industry or economy argument is that once protectionism has been established it becomes difficult to know when it will give way to free trade – indeed it may become endemic to an economy. Rich countries protect their older industries (senile industries) on the basis of a similar argument to that of the infant industry argument – once protectionism is established it can be difficult removing it.

Import substitution and industrialization policies

Import substitution policies stressed industrialization as a means to rapid economic growth and development, since the rate of productivity increase in industry was higher than that possible in agriculture. Economic development that embraced industry would produce higher and faster growth than agriculture alone. Policies to promote industrialization as a means of faster economic development were also influenced by the cold war. The Soviet Union had followed a policy of promoting heavy industry in the form of capital goods. The planning system was considered, at that time, as being superior for the purpose of creating heavy industry. The idea of state planning or the command economy gained considerable support during the first three decades of the cold war, with the Soviet model being considered in countries such as India. The Chinese model, emanating from the cultural revolution, of small-scale production as in the case of iron, proved to be a fiasco. In India the Mahalanobis plan for industrialization, in which heavy industry was to be promoted by the State through state investment and forced savings, was adopted. This policy was not successful.

Economic planning

Economic planning was considered as the essential framework, with the State guiding the economy to economic growth and prosperity. National plans were produced and planning periods became the norm for many emerging countries. Five-year development plans were produced in the hope that economic aid would be forthcoming from rich donors, but these plans more often than not were wish-lists and could not and did not achieve their targets. State planning did not provide a panacea for underdevelopment, but provided a justification for the direct intervention of government into economic activity which, in most emerging countries, government was singularly ill equipped to carry out successfully. Where government operated industry directly the results were not usually efficient, although countries such as South Korea did successfully operate import substitution policies under the guidance of the State (see Rowley and Bae 1998). In this case the State set industrialization priorities for the private sector and backed them with state resources.

Throughout the 1970s and 1980s, the failures of economic policy in many emerging countries were becoming apparent with low growth, high unemployment and increasing poverty. State intervention into economic policy was coming to be seen not only as an inappropriate means to promote economic growth but also as positively harmful to growth. The policy failures of economic planning were being characterized as government failure rather than market failure. Government intervention had produced rent-seeking behaviour on the part of entrepreneurs and businessmen. State intervention in the economy through excessive regulation (such as import and export licences) had caused business to spend increasing time, effort and money on overcoming these impediments to growth. Rent-seeking activity was therefore positively unproductive and contributed to low economic growth. The role of the State in the direct conduct of economic planning, including direct ownership and control of business, was not a success.

Economic aid

Economic aid from rich countries to poor countries had emerged at the end of the Second World War when the USA had provided economic assistance for the restructuring of the economies of Europe under the Marshall Plan. This aid was short term but substantial and allowed Europe to overcome shortages and bottlenecks which had resulted from the devastation of war, and put these countries on the path to reconstruction and economic recovery. The success of the Marshall Plan indicated that transfers from government to government in the form of grants and concessional loans could enable economic recovery and economic growth. While under the Bretton Wood system economic growth was to be achieved by the promotion of free markets, private foreign investment and the expansion of world trade, it was also recognized that this was unlikely to happen spontaneously in the dollar shortages of the 1950s, and therefore transfers of resources would be beneficial to both donors and recipients of those transfers. Economic aid would help to pump prime the economies of the newly emerging emerging countries.

The cold war had a particular influence upon policies of the aid donor countries. Development countries receiving economic aid, more often than not received it on the basis of the foreign policy concerns of the donor rather than on the intrinsic needs of the recipient economy. Economic aid was not given on the basis of need or of strictly economic criteria, but often for purposes of global foreign policy which were determined by the cold war.

Economic aid from rich countries to poor countries became a prominent feature of the economics of emerging countries during the cold war period. The lack of convertibility of the currency of most emerging countries and their balance of payments difficulties provided an impediment to the growth of international trade. To some degree, the transfers from donors alleviated these currency and convertibility bottlenecks.

Transfers of economic aid from rich to poor countries took a number of forms. Tied aid was transfers given to specific projects and programmes in emerging countries, the donor specifying the aid either in kind or in terms of the donor currency. Military aid, technical aid and commodity aid (food aid) are highly tied and the sourcing for tied aid was invariably the donor country. While tied aid may provide benefits to the recipient, it also provided benefits to the donor. The industries in donor countries producing military equipment, or the farmers producing food surplus to effective demand, or the construction companies building a dam, all benefited from aid programmes. The aid programmes of most donor countries were strongly supported by vested interests within the donor country.

Transfers of freely convertible untied aid were less frequently given than tied aid. It has been suggested that tied aid would allow the donors to account for the way that the aid is used in the recipient country, as often it is more difficult to account for untied financial aid. However, aid switching or fungibility would be possible. If the recipient country had already allocated resources in its development budget for a project or programme that the aid could meet, the resources could be used for alternative purposes. Since the giving of economic aid was predominantly a government-to-government activity, this encouraged the public sector rather than the private sector. Multilateral economic aid also consisted of transfers and support for the government sector.

Tied aid did not allow emerging countries to look for the lowest cost available on world markets for their economic projects and was therefore potentially less efficient than financial transfers. Aid in general also encouraged government economic activity over that of private enterprise. The effects of economic aid on the development of poor countries was a mixed picture; in the cases of some countries aid had provided benefits to both donor and recipient, and in others it had not. By the late 1970s, the effectiveness of aid was being called into question.

The 1970s were a watershed in terms of policy prescriptions from the rich countries to the poor. The efficacy of economic aid was being called into question by both donors and recipients alike. Third World countries through UNCTAD and the example of OPEC were advocating policies for direct intervention in the world trading system to transfer greater resources for their economic and social development. Calls were made for a new international economic order (NIEO) to benefit poorer countries, and the rich countries (the North) and the poor countries (the South) sought different remedies for economic development. The Brandt Commission published a report that emphasized the need for greater transfers of economic aid and greater intervention in the world economy to assist the South. The recommendations of the Brandt Commission Report (1980) and those of the UNCTAD integrated commodity proposals were not acceptable to the rich countries who did not support these.

The economics of emerging countries during the 1980s through the Bretton Woods institutions re-emphasized the primacy of free markets, private foreign investment and the growth of international trade. Both the IMF and the World Bank promoted and funded policies that provide a framework for macroeconomic stabilization that is dependent upon conditionality and structural adjustment within emerging countries. These policies stress the importance of privatization, 'getting the prices right', financial reform, particularly with regard to exchange rate policy, and monetary and interest rate policy as the basis of sound and stable growth. The distribution of income was to be left almost entirely to market forces, through the process of trickle-down. However, dire poverty could be exceptionally considered by government, provided market forces were not thwarted and the programmes and policies adopted were targeted to the specific needs of those poor who would be unable to benefit from growth. Welfare programmes should focus upon those poor who would be excluded from economic prosperity and expenditure would be specific to their needs but not general budget welfare expenditure. The emergence of the eastern

European economies has reinforced their view that economic development is dependent on free markets and free trade. The macroeconomic stabilization policies of the Bretton Woods institutions are designed to enhance economic growth and stability within a free-market, free-trade world economy.

Asian Tigers

The experience of the Asian Tigers or Dragons (South Korea, Taiwan, Hong Kong and Singapore) during the 1970s, 1980s and even into the 1990s, was considered to be a model for economic growth and prosperity. These economies had consistently grown at an annual rate well in excess of eight per cent per annum and continue to grow at amongst the highest rates of economic growth in the world economy. These Tiger economies prospered by emerging their manufacturing industries exporting for world markets. Although the experience of each of these economies is unique, they did have a number of factors in common. The economies were relatively open economies dependent upon world markets for their growth. They all have high rates of savings and investment and government has encouraged industry by cooperation with private investment. The State in these countries has facilitated investment and growth and these economies have adjusted to export objectives as primary objectives of economic policy. While these economies have depended on world markets for their growth, both Taiwan and South Korea have developed an industrial organization on conglomerates. These organizations (*chaebols*) are similar to Japanese industrial organizations although not the same. The South Korean *chaebols* are active participants in the formulation of government economic policy on a regular basis. While South Korean economic policy is market orientated, it is not free from government supervision and indeed support. South Korea is often cited as a model of *laissez-faire* economics and the benefits of such a framework for policy are held up as an example. However, the role of the State as a promoter of South Korean policy was interventionist in so far as industrial and trade policy was state determined. These hyper-growth Asian economies or NICs (newly industrialized countries) have evolved an economic policy formula that may not be easily replicated in other parts of the world. Their largely Confucian cultural heritage (and the homogeneous nature of their society) may account for a large part of their success, rather than the application of market principles on their own.

Food and agriculture

The economics of emerging countries have been influenced by changing fashions in economic policy as well as by poverty, hunger and malnutrition (Foster 1992). In spite of the growth of the world economy and the emergence of many emerging countries on to a path of sustained economic growth, the persistence of poverty in many low-income countries has prompted policies from rich countries to alleviate these problems. Food aid has been given from the rich countries, most notably the USA, Canada, Japan and the European Union, as well as from the World Food Programme of the United Nations, to over 100 emerging countries. This form of development assistance has proved to be controversial, since it is a form of aid that has the capacity to displace agricultural markets, both those of the recipient of the aid and of third-party agricultural producers. Food aid as emergency aid to meet famine, drought and dislocation of economies from civil war forms a small part of the total food commodity aid that is given. Its contribution to recipient economies takes the form of general economic aid since many food aid programmes allow the sale of the aid on their internal market, thus providing government revenues and foreign exchange savings. The sale of food aid may displace local producers of similar foodstuffs if the pricing policy in the country concerned is set below the cost of production.

The FAO and the EU advocate policies for the instigation of national food plans in emerging countries with reserves of food stocks to offset any shortfall in supply that might result from higher world food prices or drought. The holding of food stocks is very costly and it also requires the intervention of a government agency to manage these stocks. The Bretton Woods institutions do not favour this approach to the food problem in emerging countries, since it involves state intervention in markets. Their preferred options for a food security policy is one based on government holding financial reserves for the import of food, should that be necessary.

The problem of food shortages and food insecurity in many emerging countries is regarded by many development economists as being unlikely to be solved by market mechanisms alone. The Theory of Entitlements provides a framework for the understanding of hunger and famine within a social and institutional setting that suggests public or state action to deal with food shortages (Dreze and Sen 1989).

Agricultural productivity has increased remarkably in the world economy since the Second World War. Agricultural production in the developed world underwent a massive increase in output and with it the growth of agricultural trade. This fact explains why world population growth has increased, outwitting the Malthusian spectre. The productivity increase in the developed world was due to government intervention to support agriculture, particularly prices and trade, as well as the introduction of new technology in the form of fertilizers, hybrid seeds and mechanization. In the emerging world the introduction of improved seed varieties and fertilizers has contributed to a remarkable increase in output which has come to be known as the Green Revolution. The Green Revolution was a major initiative of the Ford and Rockefeller research institutes over many years and has undoubtedly contributed to an increase in the world food supply. These productivity increases are, however, unlikely to balance against the absolute increase in world population.

The emergence of the environment as an issue in the economics of emerging countries has focused on urbanization, poverty, food insecurity and population policies. The Brundtland Report (1987) highlighted these issues and suggested policy prescriptions which involved the direct involvement of the State and international actions to alleviate these problems.

The UN population conference in 1994 recommended an explicit population policy to limit the growth of world population through contraception and family planning. Religious groups have reluctantly accepted these proposals but their response is unlikely to promote such policies. The UN population conference in 1967 had advocated economic development as the best population policy since economic growth is usually accompanied by smaller family sizes.

The economics of emerging countries have been influenced by many factors, including the cold war and this has taken the general form of policy recommendations that have advocated free markets or state planning and intervention to achieve economic growth and welfare. Emerging economies, particularly the NICs, have shown that high rates of economic growth and industrialization can provide the basis for economic prosperity and welfare. The State has provided the framework for economic activity in many emerging countries, including some of the NICs. The replication of a country's economic performance by another country may not always be successful since there are unique factors in the situation of each country. It is not possible for all the countries of the world economy to industrialize and therefore different policy prescriptions will apply to different country circumstances (North 1990; Mehmet 1999). The emergence of the transitional economies of eastern Europe and the emergent markets in the world economy – together with growing environmental concerns, not least the rapid growth of world population – suggest that the economics of emerging countries are likely to be a continuing focus for policy prescriptions that oscillate between free-market and state solutions. Trade, technology, institutions and the environment, as well as continuing poverty and hunger, are likely to determine the economics of emerging countries.

JOHN CATHIE
UNIVERSITY OF CAMBRIDGE

Further reading

(References cited in the text marked *)

* Bauer, P.T. (1991) *The Development Frontier*, Hemel Hempstead: Harvester Wheatsheaf. (Collection of essays on development economic issues with a pro-free-market emphasis.)
* Brandt, W. (1980) *North–South: A Programme for Survival. Report of the Independent Commission on International Development Issues*, London: Pan. (Covers a wide range of development issues which in the event were not acted upon in terms of recommendations to the rich countries.)
* Brundtland Report (1987) *Our Common Future, World Commission on Environment and Development*, Oxford: Oxford University Press. (An excellent report which looks at the range of environmental problems in the Third World and offers proposals for tackling them.)
* Dreze, J. and Sen, A.K. (1989) *Hunger and Public Action*, Oxford: Clarendon Press. (Comprehensive analysis of hunger and famine in emerging countries; gives an indication of policy options.)
* Foster, P. (1992) *The World Food Problem: Tackling the Causes of Undernutrition in the Third World*, London: Adamantine Press. (Comprehensive textbook analysis of the problems of world hunger.)
  Godement, F. (1997) *The New Asian Renaissance*, London: Routledge. (A good account of development from colonialism to post-Cold War.)
* *IMF Survey* (1994) 'Adjustment, not resistance, the key to dealing with low commodity prices', October, occasional paper no. 112, Washington, DC: IMF. (Regular publication of IMF)
* Lal, D. (1983) *The Poverty of 'Development Economics'*, Hobart paperback 16, London: Institute of Economic Affairs. (A very readable polemic against 'unorthodox theories' of development.)
* Lewis, W.A. (1978) *The Evolution of the International Economic Order*, Princeton, NJ: Princeton University Press. (Classic short essays on trade and aid policy in the Third World.)
* Meerhaeghe, M.A.G., van (1974) *International Economic Institutions*, 2nd edn, London: Longman. (Good account of the origins of the IMF, World Bank, GATT and commodity agreements, the EU and OECD.)
* Mehmet, O. (1999) *Westernizing the Third World*, London: Routledge. (An attack on the Eurocentricity of economic development theories.)

* Meier, G.M. and Seers, D. (eds) (1984) *Pioneers in Development*, New York: Oxford University Press. (Excellent collection of essays by major contributors to development economics. Very readable and comprehensive.)
* North, D. (1990) *Institutions, Institutional Change and Economic Performance*, Cambridge: Cambridge University Press. (Classic work on economic growth and institutions.)
* Rowley, C. and Bae, J. (eds) (1998) *Korean Business*, London: Frank Cass. (Useful collection on the South Korean model of industrialization.)
  Shin, Y.-S. (1996) *The Economics of Latecomers*, London: Routledge. (A scholarly account of technology transfer and catching up by emerging countries.)
* Smith, A. (1776) *Wealth of Nations*, Harmondsworth: Penguin, 1976. (Systematic analysis of the causes of economic growth and prosperity that remains influential today.)
* Talbot, R.B. (1990) *The Four World Food Agencies in Rome*, Ames, IA: Iowa State University Press (Good factual account of Rome food and agricultural agencies.)

See also: BANKING AND FINANCE IN THE EMERGING COUNTRIES; HUMAN RESOURCE MANAGEMENT IN THE EMERGING COUNTRIES; MANAGEMENT IN THE EMERGING COUNTRIES; PERSPECTIVES ON GLOBALIZATION, BIG BUSINESS AND THE EMERGING COUNTRIES; WORLD TRADE ORGANIZATION

Related topics in the IEBM regional set: ECONOMIES OF ASIA PACIFIC; ECONOMIES OF EUROPE; ECONOMIES OF LATIN AMERICA; ECONOMIES OF NORTH AMERICA; EUROPEAN UNION; MANAGEMENT IN CHINA; MANAGEMENT IN HONG KONG; MANAGEMENT IN JAPAN; MANAGEMENT IN SINGAPORE; MANAGEMENT IN SOUTH KOREA; MANAGEMENT IN TAIWAN

Human resource management in the emerging countries

1 Introduction
2 Human resource management
3 Impact of societal and work cultures on design of HRM practices
4 Strategies to ensure the culture fit of HRM practices
5 Conclusion

Overview

The desire in the emerging or economically developing countries to share in the benefits of modern science and technology has provided a strong impetus for business and governments to adopt the successful management practices of the developed countries of Europe and North America. The increased interaction between the emerging and developed countries that has resulted from the current trend towards a free-market, liberalized world economy provides more opportunities for the adoption of these practices. However, it is important to recognize that the 'state-of-the-art' management practices and techniques, evolved in the context of Western cultural values, cannot be uncritically adopted in emerging country organizations that operate in a fundamentally different sociocultural environment. This issue of cultural fit is particularly vital for human resource management practices. Therefore, a two-step approach is required to ensure the cultural fit of these practices in emerging country organizations. The first step is to identify the cultural characteristics that facilitate or hinder the effectiveness of these practices and, secondly, to initiate strategies that build on the cultural facilitators and overcome the cultural constraints.

1 Introduction

The primary objective of human resource management (HRM) is to acquire and develop human capital through which organizations achieve their objectives. 'Expertise in the human resource area' has been ranked as second in importance after 'expertise in strategy formulation', for achieving objectives, and as the most important means of improving quality (Miner and Crane 1995). The recognition of the strategic and operational importance of HRM by management practitioners and scholars in the West has led to continuing developments in processes and techniques that foster, promote, support and reinforce employee effectiveness.

These processes and techniques can be equally effective in emerging county organizations provided that the implementation mode is adapted to fit the organizations' societal and internal work cultures. The 'emerging countries' represent most of the developing nations located in Asia (e.g. India, Pakistan, Indonesia) and Africa (e.g. Kenya, Uganda) (see MANAGEMENT IN KENYA; MANAGEMENT IN

UGANDA). They tend to be similar in terms of historical experience, economic, political and demographic features, and societal and internal work cultures (Kanungo 1998).

The sections that follow discuss the human resource management practices critical to emerging countries, the impact of societal and work cultures on the design of human resource management practices, and specific strategies to ensure the culture fit of these practices (see BUSINESS CULTURES, THE EMERGING COUNTRIES).

2 Human resource management

There are two views of HRM. One view sees it as the function of the human resource professionals, usually in the human resource department, who develop human resource management processes and tools for recruitment and selection, training and development, compensation, employee and labour relations. The other view sees HRM as the managing of human resources by line managers who manage the 'people' resource in their work units or departments using the expertise provided by the human resource professionals. The two views, thus, complement each other. However, since managing people is the core work of management, we focus on human resource management practices that are critical to the line managers in emerging country organizations. The critical practices are *performance management* and *reward systems*. These practices are designed to improve the employee motivation that is crucial to addressing the issue of low productivity, and increasing the effectiveness of organizations in emerging countries. What is also pertinent is that these practices are directly within the control of line managers, unlike decisions on recruitment and selection, and labour relations that are generally centralized at the corporate level in the private sector, or in a specialized agency in the public sector. Each practice and the conditions conducive to its effectiveness are described below.

Performance management

Managing employee performance is an ongoing cyclical process involving four basic steps. In the first step, the manager defines the subordinate's job – that is, identifies all the important aspects of the job, and clarifies how it is related to the objectives of the work unit and of the organization. Involving the subordinates in the job definition process leads to an agreed understanding of, and commitment to, the appropriate job behaviours. The second step is the setting of expectations or the standards by which the job performance will be appraised. Employee performance is greatly enhanced when the job standards constitute goals that are difficult but attainable, and are specific but appropriate to organizational objectives. The participation of the employee in this step is crucial because it contributes to the setting of performance standards and measures that are reasonable, realistic and appropriate (Locke and Latham 1984).

In the third step, the manager monitors the performance and provides ongoing feedback. The manager functions as a coach, praising good performance, and picking up on specific behaviours with detailed suggestions on how to correct performance deficiencies. In their coaching stance, managers are careful to create an open, relaxed atmosphere that encourages employees to seek guidance in sorting out priorities or in resolving problems. The fourth step is the formal appraisal review, at the end of a pre-determined performance period, during which managers function as judge and coach. As judge, the managers record their assessment of the subordinate's performance. As coach, they adopt the problem-solving mode to identify obstacles to required performance levels and formulate developmental plans that will enable the subordinate to do better in the next performance period.

Reward system

There are two approaches to reward system design and management. One, a reward system based on the intrinsic–extrinsic rewards dichotomy; the other, is a system based on the reward characteristics of saliency, valence and contingency.

According to the intrinsic–extrinsic rewards classification, intrinsic rewards alone motivate employees to high work performance; extrinsic rewards only serve to reduce employee dissatisfaction (Herzberg 1966). Examples of intrinsic rewards are autonomy, recognition, challenging assignments; examples of extrinsic rewards are pay, benefits, vacations. There are serious problems with the intrinsic–extrinsic dichotomy approach. It assumes that all workers seek to satisfy their growth needs at work; therefore, only rewards that satisfy their growth needs – such as challenging assignments, will motivate them. The relevant research contradicts this motivational assumption and shows that the intrinsic–extrinsic rewards dichotomy is conceptually flawed (Kanungo and Hartwick 1987). Furthermore, the intrinsic–extrinsic dichotomy is completely at variance with the fact that, in emerging countries, as will be seen later, economic and social security is considered more important to life than are freedom and control at the workplace (Kanungo 1979). Consequently, extrinsic rewards can and do serve as motivators to workers in these countries.

The alternative approach to reward systems is founded on the constructs of the expectancy theory of work motivation. It recognizes that rewards, be they intrinsic or extrinsic, will motivate the desired employee behaviour only when these are perceived to be salient, valued and contingent on that behaviour (Kanungo and Hartwick 1987; Kanungo and Mendonca 1988). The characteristic of reward contingency needs to be especially emphasized. Any contingent reward, whether one chooses to term it intrinsic or extrinsic, is directly linked to, and is derived from, job performance. For example, the dollars involved in the salesperson's commission (an extrinsic reward) are as directly linked to and derived from the sale that is made as the formidable challenge (an intrinsic reward) experienced by the salesperson in making that sale. The approach, just discussed, permits the design of a reward system that takes into account and provides for culture-based value and need differences. It is, therefore, ideally suited, with appropriate modifications to be discussed later, for emerging country organizations.

3 Impact of societal and work cultures of emerging countries on HRM practices

We first consider the impact of the societal culture, and then that of the internal work culture on HRM practices in emerging country organizations.

Societal culture of emerging countries

Societal culture constitutes a particular pattern of ideas, values and norms of behaviour that are shared by members of a society. Kanungo (1998) characterized the societal culture of emerging countries, compared to the Western industrialized nations, as relatively high on: collectivistic orientation, power distance, femininity, uncertainty avoidance and context dependence; he has also described the way in which these cultural characteristics manifest themselves. We draw on this description to discuss how the characteristics of the societal culture of emerging countries impact on the HRM practices of: (i) performance management; and (ii) the reward system.

Impact of societal culture on performance management
In a collectivistic orientation, work is not an act of self-fulfilment or self-expression, but is primarily a means to fulfil one's obligation to the family. It shifts the focus away from job objectives and objective performance standards. Hence, it acts as a cultural constraint to effective performance management. All the critical activities in goal setting, job performance and appraisal require the manager to function as a coach and mentor to his or her subordinates; it presupposes a relationship of openness and free exchange of views and ideas. High power distance is not compatible with this nature of a manager–subordinate relationship; nor is it compatible with the joint problem solving so essential to successful performance management. Considerable inter-personal relations, with a focus on job objectives and performance, are involved in the performance management process. High femininity implies that employee orientation is toward people or a focus on 'personalized relationships' rather than on performance. Consequently, high femininity can contaminate or adversely affect the interpersonal relations. For example, feedback by the supervisor might be misconstrued as attacks on the person rather than on the observed behaviours. Furthermore, performance appraisal will always be problematic because employees believe that loyalty to the superior, just like loyalty to the head of the family, is more important and expected, rather than meeting the contractual obligations of the job.

Performance management requires employees to be involved in the goal setting process – that is, setting difficult but attainable goals. Because high uncertainty avoidance discourages risk taking, it becomes a severe constraint on effective performance management. Effective performance management also requires that employees abide by a specific set of agreed goals to be attained by specific time targets according to a specific action plan. Context-dependent thinking emphasizes context-determined rather than principle-dominant behaviour. Such an emphasis is not conducive to job behaviours which managers and subordinates have jointly agreed to be the required standards of performance. The context dependent thinking will cause employees to be highly unpredictable with regard to performing the required job behaviours.

Impact of societal culture on reward system
The collectivistic orientation does not favour contingent rewards based on the individual's performance; group performance would be a preferred basis. It would, however, favour non-economic rewards that recognize the individual's contribution to

significant others in the job context. Employee participation is crucial in the design and implementation of reward techniques – in particular, those techniques that can affect the fairness or equity of the system (see INDUSTRIAL RELATIONS IN THE EMERGING COUNTRIES). High power distance discourages such participation. Also, the unquestioning acceptance of the superior's decisions on rewards, inherent in high power distance, often conflicts with the employee's belief of equity that, although never vocalized, in reality adversely affects the individual's performance motivation. High femininity does not encourage performance-based rewards; instead, it facilitates non-economic rewards that satisfy affiliation needs.

The unwillingness to take risks, inherent in uncertainty avoidance, is not conducive to performance-based pay that, in essence, is at-risk pay. It also inhibits the use of non-economic rewards that satisfy growth needs, such as challenging assignments because of the risks involved in such assignments. In situations of context-dependent thinking, the employees' approach to the job is not guided by principle-dominant behaviour. Consequently, it will hinder the use of performance-based pay.

Internal work culture

The internal work culture of an organization can be understood in terms of the basic managerial assumptions which explain the organization's beliefs, values and practices (Schein 1985), that are also influenced by the prevailing societal culture. Kanungo and Jaeger (1990) have grouped the management assumptions that characterize the internal work culture, into two categories: (i) the descriptive assumptions about human nature, and (ii) the prescriptive assumptions about the guiding principles of human conduct. Thus, in emerging country organizations, management views their employees: as having an external locus of control; as less malleable with limited development potential; with a time perspective that is past and present oriented; and preferring short-term rather than long-term planning (see MANAGEMENT EDUCATION IN THE EMERGING COUNTRIES). In terms of the prescriptive assumptions, employees in the emerging countries are encouraged to be passive and reactive, rather than proactive, in task performance; judge success on a moral basis; adopt a paternalistic orientation; and let the demands of the immediate context override principles and rules. We now discuss how these characteristics of the internal work culture of emerging countries affect the HRM practices relating to: (i) performance management; and (ii) the reward system.

Impact of internal work culture on performance management
The workers' belief in the external locus of control will cause managers to be apprehensive that the subordinates, being risk averse, will not work toward goals involving the risks of failure; therefore, managers will hesitate in setting difficult goals. When managers view their subordinates as having limited potential for development, they will consider it futile to invest time and effort in their development. Inherent in the performance management process, is the need for managers to adopt a future orientation – be it in goal setting, removal of organizational obstacles to effective performance, or employee training and development. The managers'

assumptions about the employees' past and present orientation and their short-term perspective will prevent them from engaging in long-term planning.

The successful approach to managing subordinates' performance requires that managers anticipate what needs to be done and initiate appropriate actions and procedures to meet the established job objectives; neither, the passive nor reactive stance to task performance is conducive to such an approach. To effectively manage the subordinates' performance, the manager should objectively assess the degree of success in attaining job objectives. The norm of moralism does not permit an objective and rational assessment. The paternalistic orientation, inherent in the internal work culture, operates against the joint problem-solving approach that is necessary to effectively manage performance. The internal work culture's norm that behaviour be context dependent will likely prompt managers to be more tolerant of and accept the fact that the subordinates' social obligations which are totally unrelated to the job can take precedence over performance of job tasks and duties.

Impact of internal work culture on reward system
The managerial assumptions of employees' external locus of control and their limited and fixed potential inhibit the use of non-economic rewards such as challenging assignments and participation in decision making; instead, the reward system will be characterized by the carrot-and-stick approach. Because of the past and present orientation and the short-term perspective assumptions, the reward system, even if it is performance-based, will reinforce short-term objectives and, as a consequence, further perpetuate the dysfunctional effects of such a time perspective. Implicit in the passive/reactive stance, is the notion that individuals are not encouraged to change themselves to meet the task demands or cope with environmental pressures. Therefore, the reactive and passive stance is not conducive to performance-based rewards. Employee involvement in reward system design enhances their perceptions of reward saliency, valence and contingency and, as a result, the effectiveness of the reward system (Kanungo and Mendonca 1997). The paternalistic norm is incompatible with employee participation in reward design and implementation; it will, therefore, be an impediment to designing effective reward systems. The norm that behaviour should be context dependent is not conducive to effective reward system design because it is incompatible with performance-based rewards.

4 Strategies to ensure the culture-fit of HRM practices in emerging country organizations

In order to ensure the culture-fit of the human resource practices, emerging country organizations do not need to resort to policies and practices that would coerce employees into giving up their deeply held cultural values and beliefs. Instead a systematic approach is discussed that enables emerging country organizations to remove the cultural constraints, and build on the cultural facilitators to ensure the effectiveness of HRM practices relating to: (i) performance management; and (ii) the reward system.

Strategies to ensure culture-fit of performance management

First, set goals that are within the employee's competency level, and gradually increase the complexity and responsibility level as the employee feels more capable. At the same time, enhance the employee's self-efficacy belief through empowerment strategies. These interventions will address the constraining effects of high uncertainty avoidance. When managers function as coach and mentor, subordinates find in their interaction a personalized and supportive relationship that addresses the adverse effects of high power distance. To overcome the constraining effects of femininity, make subordinates aware of the job's potential contribution to departmental and organizational goals that ultimately serve some community or national good. Also, use performance feedback opportunities to underscore the positive or negative impact of the performance on others. In this way, the job also becomes a means to satisfy the relationship orientation.

To overcome the inhibiting effects of context dependent thinking, set goals in terms of observable behaviours with specific time frames. During feedback, focus on actual behaviours and the time taken in relation to the agreed time targets. Also, every feedback session should lead to action plans with specific performance targets and completion schedules. In order to build on the cultural facilitator of collective orientation, set group goals, if feasible. To orient subordinates toward personal task accomplishment, assure them that the needed support systems will be available, and use feedback sessions to identify training and development needs, and to point out the positive effect of goal attainment on significant others. The ongoing dialogue with constructive, positive and encouraging discussion will reinforce and enhance the employees' self-efficacy belief, and contribute eventually to the development of an internal locus of control and a proactive approach to job performance.

Strategies to ensure culture-fit of reward system

The principal objective of the interventions is to make rewards contingent on performance. An effective first step would be to forge a close link between rewards and the performance management process. When performance expectations are set, the rewards that will follow should also be clearly stated and emphasized. Initially, the at-risk pay should be a minimal component of the total compensation; as the subordinates feel more able to cope with more difficult goals, the at-risk pay component of total compensation should be gradually increased. The rewards linked to performance expectations should also be emphasized during feedback sessions, together with assurances of support and guidance to help subordinates meet and even exceed the performance standards. The open climate created by the manager's role of coach and mentor can facilitate discussions of whether the rewards are perceived to be salient and valued, whether the rewards satisfy their salient needs and, more importantly, whether these are perceived to be fair and equitable. Approached in this way, the reward system also serves to reinforce the employees' self-efficacy beliefs and, thereby, becomes a potent vehicle to shift their locus of control beliefs from the external to the internal.

To ensure congruence with the collectivistic orientation, design group-based contingent rewards if the work technology or structure permits it. Nevertheless, the reward package should include the non-economic rewards that satisfy the needs for recognition. In a collectivistic orientation, even when employees perform well they do not get satisfaction from 'work well done', but from 'work well recognized'. The modalities for public recognition could include mention in bulletin boards, in-house publications, work-unit or department meetings, award ceremonies that piggy-back on significant festivals or social events.

The nurturant-task leadership style

Fundamental to the success of the modalities of implementing a performance management and rewards system as described above, is the adoption and implementation of the nurturant-task leadership style (Sinha 1980), and its empowering strategies. The *task* component of this style essentially serves to remedy the dysfunctional effects of uncertainty avoidance, high power distance, and context dependent thinking. It does this by reorienting the subordinate's focus on job content through specific job performance action plans, time targets, assistance in problem solving and valued rewards. The *nurturant* component relies on empowerment strategies that enhance the subordinates' self-efficacy beliefs. In addition to reducing the dysfunctional effects of high power distance and uncertainty avoidance, nurturant leadership also builds on the facilitating features of the collectivistic orientation and femininity.

5 Conclusion

The human resource is a particularly critical resource for emerging country organizations as they strive to seize the opportunities and cope with the challenges of technological developments, business alliances, trading blocks, and increasing globalization. New processes, techniques and tools for the effective management of human resources in these changing times will undoubtedly emerge in both the emerging and industrialized countries. However, changes in the organization's current human resource management practices or the adoption of new processes and techniques will be fruitful only to the extent that such changes are congruent with the organization's societal and internal work cultures.

MANUEL MENDONÇA
FACULTY OF MANAGEMENT
MCGILL UNIVERSITY, MONTREAL, CANADA

Further reading

(References cited in the text marked *)

Aycan, Zeynep, Kanungo, R.N. and Sinha, J.P. (1999) 'Organizational culture and human resource management practices: the model of culture fit', *Journal of Cross-Cultural Psychology* (Discusses the empirical data on managerial perceptions of human resource management in several developing countries.)
* Herzberg, F. (1966) *Work and the Nature of Man*, Cleveland, OH: World. (Presents the two-factor theory which became one approach to designing work rewards.)
* Kanungo, R.N. (1979) 'The concepts of alienation and involvement revisited', *Psychological Bulletin* 86: 119–38. (Examines under what conditions need satisfaction leads to employee involvement.)

* Kanungo, R.N. (1998) 'Business cultures, the emerging countries', *The IEBM Regional Set*. (Explores business cultures in emerging countries.)
* Kanungo, R.N. and Hartwick, J. (1987) 'An alternative to the intrinsic–extrinsic dichotomy of work rewards', *Journal of Management* 13: 751–6. (Discusses the empirical support for the characteristics of effective rewards.)
* Kanungo, R.N. and Jaeger, A.J. (1990) 'Introduction: The need for indigenous management in developing countries', in Jaeger, A.M. and Kanungo, R.N. (eds), *Management in Developing Countries*, London: Routledge. (Presents a model of the culture fit of management practices.)
* Kanungo, R.N. and Mendonça, M. (1988) 'Evaluating employee compensation', *California Management Review* 31: 23–39. (Explores the empirical evidence for the critical steps in reward system design and management.)
  Kanungo, R.N. and Mendonça, M. (eds) (1994) *Work Motivation: Models for Developing Countries*, New Delhi, India: Sage Publications. (Explores the issues of work motivation in developing countries, and discusses related practical strategies.)
* Kanungo, R.N. and Mendonça, M. (1997) *Compensation: Effective Reward Management* 2nd edn, Toronto, Ont: John Wiley & Sons. (Covers compensation system design and management, including performance management.)
* Locke, E.A. and Latham, G.P. (1984) *Goal setting – a motivational technique that works*, Englewood Cliffs, NJ: Prentice-Hall. (Identifies the characteristics of the goal setting process that is crucial to the performance management process.)
* Miner, J.B. and Crane, D.P. (1995) *Human Resource Management: The Strategic Perspective*, New York, NY: Harper Collins. (Covers human resource management policies and techniques.)
* Schein, E.H. (1985) *Organizational Culture and Leadership*, San Francisco, CA: Jossey Bass. (An analysis of organizational culture – what it is, and how it develops and changes.)
* Sinha, J.B.P. (1980) *The Nurturant-Task Leader*, New Delhi, India: Concept. (Presents case studies to support the use of the nurturant-task leadership style in developing countries.)

See also: BUSINESS CULTURES, THE EMERGING COUNTRIES; ECONOMIES OF THE EMERGING COUNTRIES; HUMAN RESOURCE MANAGEMENT IN THE EMERGING COUNTRIES; INDUSTRIAL RELATIONS IN THE EMERGING COUNTRIES; MANAGEMENT EDUCATION IN THE EMERGING COUNTRIES; MANAGEMENT IN THE EMERGING COUNTRIES; MANAGEMENT IN INDIA; MANAGEMENT IN KENYA; MANAGEMENT IN PAKISTAN; MANAGEMENT IN UGANDA

Related topics in the IEBM regional set: HUMAN RESOURCE MANAGEMENT IN ASIA PACIFIC; HUMAN RESOURCE MANAGEMENT IN EUROPE; HUMAN RESOURCE MANAGEMENT IN LATIN AMERICA; HUMAN RESOURCE MANAGEMENT IN NORTH AMERICA

Industrial relations in the emerging countries

1 Introduction
2 Colonial impact
3 Nationalism, post-colonial states and crises of development
4 Role of government, political problems and instability
5 Collective relations
6 Structural adjustment programmes
7 The democratic challenge
8 Demands of social partnership
9 Conclusion

Overview

Industrial relations in emerging countries have been products of both endogenous and exogenous factors. In several countries, predominantly former colonial dependencies, the sudden creation of the original and formal cradle of industrial relations – wage-employment – had been externally induced. Subsequently, these initial structures gradually grew in the designated countries and remained intact for varying periods beyond political independence and through the 1970s. But, for reasons also internally and externally accounted, the industrial relations institutions in these countries have undergone further regimes of transformation and regeneration – sometimes chaotic and disruptive of macrolevel development – through the 1980s and 1990s.

The major elements of industrial relations in emerging countries have been: the colonial impact; nationalism, post-colonial states and crises of development; an overbearing role of government, coupled with political problems and instability; the impact of structural adjustment programmes; the democratic challenge; and the emergent demands of social partnership.

The patterns of industrial relations in emerging countries are still largely disparate, but with a few coherent features gradually emerging. The continuity of these in the very long term, and the probable additional benefits of social well-being and political peace in these nations, should strengthen the overall framework of relationships.

1 Introduction

The emerging countries are comparatively new nations in the geopolitical sense of nationhood. Therefore, industrial relations or patterns of the employment relationship that are associated with them are also relatively new and still evolving. It should be borne in mind that much larger proportions of the total and economically active population in virtually all of these countries still lie outside the formal wage-employment sector – where, technically, industrial relations exist (see ILO 1990a, 1990b).

The term 'emerging countries' is a generic conceptual label for that large and diverse group of nations, mostly located in Africa, Asia, Latin America (central and south America), and the Caribbean. Perhaps the amorphous composition of this group is best depicted by its varying characterization in the subject matter literature (see MANAGEMENT IN THE EMERGING COUNTRIES; PERSPECTIVES ON GLOBALIZATION, BIG BUSINESS AND THE EMERGING COUNTRIES). For example, Yesufu (1966: 90–1) included the following in his index of 'under-development': low average per capita national income, low standard of living and social welfare, an unbalanced – often monocultural – economic structure, and general poverty of the population. Similarly, Bean (1994: 208) has defined 'developing or third world societies' broadly in terms of per capita gross domestic product (GDP) levels, increasing social and political modernization, and predominant spatial or geographical location. Thus, the generality of emerging countries exhibits various development needs and gaps in all ramifications of socio-economic life, particularly when standard international parameters are applied.

However, when viewed either in terms of their present levels of development or on account of their industrial relations, these countries are far from monolithic. The contiguous sub-Saharan African countries, as a case, even with their identical configuration, are still very different in levels of infrastructural acquisition for expanding the wage-employment and industrial sectors. The overall scale of comparison further widens when these countries are compared with regionally faster-growing and relatively more rapidly industrializing South Africa, or with the industrial 'models' of Latin America such as Mexico, Venezuela and Brazil. The same is true of the north African and the Asian countries, with differential social background, population density and natural endowment, and therefore different economic structures and orientations (Yesufu 1966: 91; Bean 1994: 208–9; ILO 1994a: 11–26; World Bank 1995: 249; see also Poole 1986: 11–37).

2 Colonial impact

The origin of industrial relations in emerging countries is generally traceable to the creation and popularization of wage work during the period of colonial rule. Given the backdrop of the mainly agrarian and rural economies that sustained the traditional societies in Africa, Asia, Latin America and the Caribbean, the introduction of wage labour and gradually, later, the modern work method, by the colonial powers – for example, in sub-Saharan Africa from about the late nineteenth century onwards – was new and different from the indigenous values and traditional non-pecuniary mechanisms of compensation for individual or communal labour. One immediate salutary effect was the sudden activation of individual-level motivation to work for monetary or material utility.

Thereafter, and through several decades of elaboration before eventual political independence from British, French, German, Spanish or Portuguese hegemonies, the colonial powers had gradually expanded the wage-employment sectors (largely public but also private or business) in these countries and, through these initial basic structures, also created the early necessary legislative framework that legitimized trade unionism as well as provided the instrumentality for the concession of a semblance of labour rights that lasted until national independence at different periods by the countries.

However, the scope of the wage-employment sector in these countries (which is still largely urban-skewed) and the associated labour force relative to the total population (that is, the economically active proportion) has remained small (ILO 1990a, 1990b). This reflects the status and structure of the countries' economies, and the fact that even when they are rapidly pursuing industrialization, they are mostly (with the exception of pockets, particularly in east and southeast Asia, as well as in Latin America) at considerably low levels of economic growth and subject to serious crises (ILO 1994: 25–6). In another sense, that situation also portrays the overall scope of industrial relations (see HUMAN RESOURCE MANAGEMENT IN THE EMERGING COUNTRIES).

3 Nationalism, post-colonial states and crises of development

In emerging countries, there was affinity between the early labour movement and nationalistic opposition to colonial hegemonies. Yesufu has noted of these countries that:

> The most significant trade union development started after the Second World War, and thus coincided with the period of intense nationalist agitation. Although the size of the labour force organised in trade unions was (often) small ... their value to the nationalist movement and the struggle for political advance and independence was immense ... . Accordingly, the recruitment of the trade unions into the nationalist movement was vital to its success.
>
> (Yesufu 1966: 104–5)

The colonial administrators did not initially tolerate this, as it was reflected in series of anti-labour and anti-political legislation in the strongholds of colonial power before the dawn of independence. However, the benefits to nationalists and trade unions were mutual in the short term, as the pro-independence struggles also promoted labour unionism. But the post-colonial experience of trade unions in emerging countries did not necessarily reflect the rapport of the previous nationalism era. The hitherto robust relations with the new indigenous governments were soon deflated, especially when the astute unions became critical of their blunders. The impatient post-colonial governments often became fascist and repressive (Kraus 1994). Against all odds, the labour movement in many of these countries – through the benefit of labour education over the years and the larger assistance of international organizations such as the ILO (International Labour Office) – has produced formidable leaderships with cross-national recognition. These leaders have been able to influence policy and participate in the tortuous development process – even under hostile regimes in some of these countries – apart from the pursuit of business unionism.

4 Role of government, political problems and instability

A recurring theme in industrial relations in emerging countries has been the conspicuous presence of government (see ECONOMIES OF THE EMERGING COUNTRIES). The logic of state intervention, particularly in an emerging country, has often been defended. The major thrust of the apologists is that government can probably best protect public good (for example, quality of life, greater employment generation, human resource development, and accountability for development finance) (Yesufu 1966: 90–2). More specifically, the provision of an enabling framework for positive industrial relations, in the form of legislation to moderate the employment relationship and protect vulnerable workers, is also an appealing rationale.

However, when the government role in industrial relations becomes all-pervading and overbearing, as in the emerging countries – where for reasons of malfeasance or outright ineptitude labour policies are sometimes inconsistent or not enforced at all (see Fashoyin, 1992) – such a government presence is futile. Bronstein (1995: 163–4) has found that ' ... two most distinctive characteristics of Latin American industrial relations systems are the legal (heteronomous) regulation of employment and working conditions and the very high degree of state intervention in collective labour relations'. The implication is that free collective bargaining, in particular, is often stifled. Although some social gains in these countries have been reported on the front of 'human rights – freedom of association and autonomous collective bargaining' (Bronstein 1995: 185), he cautions that only future trends will confirm the stability of these changes.

The situation in Africa also conforms to the foregoing profile of government (see MANAGEMENT IN AFRICA). For example, in Nigeria, the degree of robustness of labour rights has been very much a function of the relative dispositions of successive national governments from colonialism to the present era of protracted military dictatorship. The general pattern has been government's penchant for taking complex industrial and labour relations actions by fiat (for example, wage determination in the public sector, with often serious inflationary consequences). This has accounted for the poor record of collective bargaining in the public sector, which commands the largest proportion of wage-earning population, and from where the first three trade unions – of civil servants, railway workers and teachers, respectively – had emerged in the country during the colonial period. On the contrary, the culture of collective relations has endured in the private sector.

In general, the larger environment of industrial relations in emerging countries has been a burden. In almost all cases, the new sovereign states were highly pluralistic right from their creation or independence and, in addition, lacked democratic culture as well as the maturity and tolerance of political leadership to carry along the wider populace. Hence the pursuit of often parochial interests in the face of widespread poverty and scarcity soon fanned the embers of inter-ethnic confrontation. The human vices of official corruption, greed and conspicuous consumption have not aided the conservation of pockets of affluence and natural endowment, such as the crude oil, gold and diamonds in the African and Latin American continents, which could prudently have been harnessed for the public good (see Gabre-Michael 1994: 211). So the characteristics of structural instability that persisted in the new nations also tended to boomerang into serious political and economic development problems that have remained. This, too, has been an issue of grave concern, both to the international community because of the potential conflagration effect, and also to the creditor nations. Nevertheless, there are real pressures for comprehensive change through democratization and good government in these societies.

5 Collective relations

The practice and benefits of collective bargaining – an ideal democratic and self-regulating system for governing employer–employee relations, and therefore the heart of industrial relations (see Kochan and Katz 1988: 1) – gradually accompanied the evolution and development of trade unionism and employers' associations in emerging countries. However, from the beginning, the entire course and pattern of collective relations in these nations have always been determined by the demands of their individual systems, and particularly by the framework of labour laws.

Mostly within the first four decades of the twentieth century, the early trade union movement – initially generally organized along house or craft/enterprise unionism – emerged in the regions. With the additional aid of the early scanty legislative provisions that were made by the colonial governments, these developments immediately facilitated collective relations, although on a lesser scale. The legal frameworks had conceded critical labour (or collective) rights and these were embodied in labour codes or Acts, particularly the right to organize and to bargain collectively, including the stipulation of grievance procedures for trade dispute processing.

Countries like Egypt and Somalia have, for example, fully-fledged labour codes containing various provisions. Ghana, Nigeria, Kenya, Zambia and Mauritius – to mention just a few – have adopted specific industrial relations Acts that also recognize various rights (ILO 1983: 28–9). In Latin America, Chile in 1924, Guatemala in 1926 and Ecuador in 1928 adopted acts on labour contracts, followed by Mexico in 1931, Brazil in 1934 and Venezuela in 1936 (Bronstein 1995: 164).

As indicated earlier, the scope of both labour policy or legislation and collective relations was rather limited until the 1970s or 1980s, depending on the individual country. For example, in Africa, even now, with the exception of Egypt, Ethiopia, Libya and Tanzania, existing legislation has yet to include the rural (traditional) and the urban informal sectors (ILO 1983: 31; The World Bank 1995: 5) – partly a fall-out of the highly urban-skewed wage-employment sector mentioned in the discussion of colonial impact.

In other emerging areas of Africa, Asia and Latin America, the main reasons for the restriction of collective relations have included: the unequal bargaining power relations between workers and the capitalist owners, especially in the context of development and largely unfavourable economic trends in the 1980s and 1990s (Fashoyin 1992); governments' predilection to 'keep unions in check' and therefore create practical obstacles in the way of development of collective bargaining (Bronstein 1995); and the relatively new experience of workers with the tool skills and strategy of collective bargaining. In the long term, sustained stewardship training and general labour education will serve the workers and their unions well on tool orientation.

Another common and comparatively new pattern in emerging countries is industrial unionism, whereby workers in the same industry, irrespective of occupational or skill differentiation, belong to the same union. The earlier existing unions were often, through state policy, reorganized along predominantly industrial lines. The various national unions normally operate from designated labour centres (central labour organizations).

It cannot be overemphasized that the primary function of a trade union as an organization is the continuous representation and protection of workers' interests. A complementary perspective is that trade unions also have social responsibility in contributing to the development of society (Kochan and Katz 1988). This overlapping continuum and periodic sliding between 'bread and butter' and the wider social unionism have been reflected in the pursuits of labour movements in emerging countries from colonialism to the present.

The emergence of seemingly powerful industrial unions in the critical sectors of many of these countries – for example, in Ghana, Nigeria, Zimbabwe, India, Argentina and Brazil (because of the implication of centralized and multi-employer bargaining) – has also influenced the proliferation of employers' associations and federations. It is significant that tripartite organizations have increasingly included members of unions, employers' associations, and government. A further development has been the deregulation or decentralization of machineries of collective bargaining, mainly as a result of the recession and continuing predicament of these emerging countries.

The original centralized structures of bargaining have been strained and rendered unviable, with the implication that aspects of national labour contracts, even under multi-employer bargaining, are increasingly being subjected to individual employer conditions. Although this is one dimension of the new flexibility in the labour markets, it is an important instrument of the ascendancy of concession bargaining, and the new economy-imposed challenge of employer–employee cooperation, in these countries.

6 Structural adjustment programmes

Most of the emerging countries, whether in Africa, Latin America or Asia, had been under one form of structural adjustment programme (SAP) or another by the mid-1980s. These are economic recovery strategies comprising a battery of policy measures aimed at finding effective solutions to macroeconomic problems. The problems generally include monoculture, lack of self-reliant growth and development, low productivity and stagflation, serious imbalance of payments, huge external debts, and government budget deficit. Moreover, the SAPs have often been prescribed by the Bretton Woods institutions (the International Monetary Fund and the World Bank), on whom the crisis-laden economies of these nations are dependent for development credit and finance (Simpson 1994: 191–200).

Unfortunately for these countries, a lot appears to be wrong with the instrumentation of the SAPs. Policy demands are overwhelming. The prescriptions are usually comprised of the following: devaluation, removal of subsidies on basic commodities, reduction of government expenditure, labour market reforms, reduction of trade protection, and increased incentives for the traditional sector (agriculture and mining) (Simpson 1994: 193). As the doses have so far not jolted the countries into early signs of possible recovery, the industrial relations actors – in many societies, as a result of the human toll, the larger populace – have been unanimous in protesting against the pangs of structural adjustment.

In the main, the effects of SAPs on industrial relations have been unfavourable to the emerging countries. These are: gross union membership decline with the contraction of the formal employment sectors; growing informalization of the economy; the toughening of collective bargaining as a result of unfavourable pressures on job security and employee welfare, for example, through deregulation and other institutional realignments; the ascendancy of concession bargaining; and the continuing precarious predicament of the national labour forces (Fashoyin, *et al.* 1994: 1–38; Bronstein 1995: 167–9).

SAPs have generally adversely impacted labour-market policies and approaches as well as industrial relations in these countries (Simpson 1994: 191–200), and it is probably a vicious circle. But since most of the adjustment programmes began around the mid-1980s, the long-term effects should crystallize by the year 2000.

7 The democratic challenge

One of the structural elements differentiating modern industrial relations in the West from practices in the emerging countries has been the political framework of relations. Although it took the advanced countries of the West several generations of experimentation with the tenets of liberal democracy to attain their present status, democratic values and institutions in particular have survived. In essence, the principles of democratic society (see Adams 1995) have also influenced the tradition of industrial relations in western countries; one of these is the mechanism of collective bargaining in the wider context of industrial democracy.

In the emerging countries, the principles of democratic society are hardly embraced, to the effect that government is omnipresent even in the sphere of industrial relations, and autocratic labour policies have been the norm. One illustration of the spill-over effect is the fact that not only the unions and employers but the entire citizenry are expected by government to subordinate individual and collective trade interests to that of the nation (ILO 1995: 70). Such a development burden could be a positive impetus to widespread nationalistic consciousness and patriotic feeling, but the exigencies of the times have been causing gradual social and political transformation in these countries, especially in the 1990s. In Africa, for instance, industrial relations have had to subsist under changing political institutions. Just as most African economies are being rapidly deregulated and governments are suddenly opening up channels of participation with other actors (employers and unions), the larger political context is also increasingly being pressured for democratic changes (Gabre-Michael 1994). The same processes are occurring in Latin America, for example, Argentina, Chile, Uruguay, Brazil and El Salvador (see Bronstein 1995), as well as in Asia, for example, India, where major institutional changes have taken place, or where new developments are rapidly unfolding, in favour of ultimate democratization of workplace management and the necessary synergy between the major actors, such as through increasing social unionism and concertation (a consonance between labour, management and the State in favour of positive employment relationships) (Mankidy 1995: 41; see also Verma *et al.* 1995).

By and large, it is noted that there is uneasy political calm, especially in Africa and Latin America – mostly enforced with military hardware – and a protracted political transition. But events of the future years will reveal the extent of democratization of the political machinery of governance in these countries, and the degree of flexibility of industrial relations.

8 Demands of social partnership

The logical conclusion from the account so far is that industrial relations in emerging countries will particularly benefit from new alliances, positive orientations and approaches. The other side to the challenge of ongoing changes is that these have opened new possibilities for concertation and accommodation by the partners in industry, that is employers, labour and government. All of the latter – being the principal stakeholders – should embrace the culture of tolerance, consultation, compromise and cooperation. The horrendous problems of these nations demand collective effort, trust and goodwill to be tractable, perhaps in the very long term.

9 Conclusion

Empirical evidence obviates further explanation of the perceived direct relationship between good industrial relations policies and practices, and the probable achievement of social and economic development. Human resources and solid employment relationships in collective output are critical for this development. The objective records of the Western (developed) nations and the track record of industrial democracy have clearly shown a positive correlation with the attainment of appreciable levels of social and economic development. The various cross-national accounts have shown how employment policies and general industrial relations practices, such as wage determination, trade union status and collective relations, are products of specific systems and contexts of industrial relations. Thus, the comparatively poor record of labour policies and practices, and the continuing labour market rigidities in the emerging countries, are further impediments to their overall social and economic development.

As a concrete example, this is the major thrust of the work by Roy Adams (1995). Further, both the ILO (1995) and the World Bank (1995) have drawn attention to these various shortcomings on the part of the emerging countries, and as contributory to the existing development gaps.

The trends in industrial relations in the emerging countries are major elements in the calculus of functions that block the necessary development process. In mathematical language, an 'equation' or algorithm is made up of given functions or individual elements that serve to explain a given problem or situation. When such elements or functions are summed up, this is calculus. Hence, the prevalence of less than positive industrial relations policies and practices (in the emerging countries) has tended to compound the development process in the sense of conspicuous State presence and authoritarian tendencies, high frequencies of industrial conflict and consequent productivity losses having negative ramifications for development. National planners and change agents in these countries cannot downplay the role of the industrial relations climate, particularly as a barometer of the degree of labour market well-being and as a guarantee of human resources rights – the benchmarks of quality of the contemporary world of work.

In the years ahead, industrial relations in emerging countries will continue to attract international attention and interest because the environment of work and contextual factors in these countries, which often contrast with those in the advanced countries of the world, have been changing rapidly. The direction of this change and a proper comprehension of the various internal and external agencies will further determine the trajectory of future relations and the extent to which enduring models of the employment relationship will emerge.

It is important to point out that, beyond industrial relations, the general economic and political problems of the emerging countries have global overtones and indirect ramifications for the developed nations, because of the potential threats of social poverty and instability to international order (see Parker 1999).

There is a continuing need for general institution building in these countries to strengthen the existing machineries for collective labour relations. In particular, strategic human resource management, including training and other development processes, will improve these countries' capacity for promoting favourable overall climates of stable employment relationships, and social development itself.

SEGUN MATANMI
LAGOS STATE UNIVERSITY

Further reading

(References cited in the text marked *)

* Adams, R.J. (1995) *Industrial Relations Under Liberal Democracy: North America in Comparative Perspective*, Columbia, SC: University of South Carolina Press. (A treatise on North American industrial relations and the structure and processes of differences as compared with the European and Asiatic models.)
* Bean, R. (1994) *Comparative Industrial Relations: An Introduction to Cross-National Perspectives*, London: Routledge. (A synthesis of comparative evidence on cross-national practices of industrial relations.)
* Bronstein, A.S. (1995) 'Societal change and industrial relations in Latin America: trends and prospects', *International Labour Review*, 134(2): 163–86. (This journal contribution portrays the complexity, change and diversity that characterize Latin American industrial relations.)
* Fashoyin, T. (1992) *Industrial Relations in Nigeria*, Lagos: Longman Nigeria. (This is an appraisal of past and present policies and practices in industrial relations, and views collective bargaining as realistic for determining wages and other conditions of employment.)
* Fashoyin, T., Matanmi, S. and Tawose, A. (1994) 'Reform measures, employment and labour market processes in the Nigerian economy: empirical findings', in T. Fashoyin (ed.), *Economic Reform Policies and the Labour Market in Nigeria*, Lagos: Friedrich Ebert Foundation/Nigerian Industrial Relations Association. (The product of a formative research on the impact of structural adjustment programmes on the Nigerian labour market.)
* Gabre-Michael, M. (1994) 'Second sub theme: changes in the roles of public authorities, employers' organizations and trade unions: an overview', in International Labour Office, *Political Transformation, Structural Adjustment and Industrial Relations in Africa: English-speaking Countries*, Geneva: ILO. (A comprehensive review of tripartite roles in African industrial relations.)
* ILO (International Labour Office) (1983) *Labour Relations in Africa: English-speaking Countries*, Geneva: ILO. (One of the critical and usually comprehensive ILO accounts of labour–management relations in Africa.)

* ILO (International Labour Office) (1990a) *Yearbook of Labour Statistics*, retrospective edition on population censuses, 1945–89, Geneva: ILO. (A rare data bank, particularly on the emerging countries – where empirical data are a problem – but also on the developed ones.)
* ILO (International Labour Office) (1990b) *Yearbook of Labour Statistics, 1989–90*, Geneva: ILO. (An update on previous longitudinal data.)
* ILO (International Labour Office) (1994) *World Labour Report*, Geneva: ILO. (A yearly overview of the employment situation and regional patterns throughout the world.)
* ILO (International Labour Office) (1995) *World Labour Report*, vol. 8. Geneva: ILO. (An account of significant events, trends and indicators in connection with international and comparative industrial relations.)
  Kiely, R. and Marfleet, P. (1998) *Globalization and the Third World*, London: Routledge. (A useful collection of case studies, with relevance to industrial relations.)
* Kochan, T.A. and Katz, H.C. (1988) *Collective Bargaining and Industrial Relations*, 2nd edn, Homewood, IL: Irwin. (A foundation text on the role of collective bargaining in the employment relationship.)
* Kraus, J. (1994) 'Trade Unions and Democratization in Africa', in M. Doro (ed.), *Africa Contemporary Record 1989–90*, New York: Africana Publishing. (This chapter discusses the predicament of African unions within the overall political framework.)
* Mankidy, J. (1995) 'Changing perspectives of worker participation in India with particular reference to the banking industry', *British Journal of Industrial Relations*, 33(3): 443–58. (A situation account of industrial democracy in a critical south Asian industry.)
  Parker, B. (1999) *Globalization and Business Practice*, London and Thousand Oaks, CA: Sage. (Chapter 6 on global labour problems is especially relevant.)
* Poole, M. (1986) *Industrial Relations: Origins and Patterns of National Diversity*, London: Routledge & Kegan Paul. (The book employs comparative analysis to explain the phenomenon of national diversity in industrial relations.)
* Simpson, W.R. (1994) 'First sub theme: structural adjustment and its impact on labour relations', in International Labour Office, *Political Transformation, Structural Adjustment and Industrial Relations in Africa: English-speaking Countries*, Geneva: ILO. (A position paper on ILO views on structural adjustment programmes and their effects on African industrial relations.)
* Verma, A., Kochan, T.A. and Lansbury, R.D. (1995) *Employment Relations in the Growing Asian Economies*, London: Routledge. (A most recent reader on industrial relations and human resource management in the relatively faster-growing and more rapidly industrializing emerging countries of the Asia region.)
* World Bank (1995) *World Development Report*, New York: Oxford University Press. (An updated multilateral account of development trends around the world with copious use of international and comparative social statistics.)
* Yesufu, T.M. (1966) 'The state and industrial relations in emerging countries', in A.M. Ross (ed.), *Industrial Relations and Economic Development*, London: Macmillan. (A formative work on the state's role in industrial relations in emerging countries.)

See also: ECONOMIES OF THE EMERGING COUNTRIES; HUMAN RESOURCE MANAGEMENT IN THE EMERGING COUNTRIES; MANAGEMENT IN AFRICA; MANAGEMENT IN EGYPT; MANAGEMENT IN THE EMERGING COUNTRIES; MANAGEMENT IN GHANA; MANAGEMENT IN INDIA; MANAGEMENT IN NIGERIA

Related topics in the IEBM regional set: HUMAN RESOURCE MANAGEMENT IN ASIA PACIFIC; HUMAN RESOURCE MANAGEMENT IN EUROPE; HUMAN RESOURCE MANAGEMENT IN LATIN AMERICA; HUMAN RESOURCE MANAGEMENT IN NORTH AMERICA; INDUSTRIAL RELATIONS IN ASIA PACIFIC; INDUSTRIAL RELATIONS IN EUROPE; INDUSTRIAL RELATIONS IN LATIN AMERICA; INDUSTRIAL RELATIONS IN NORTH AMERICA; MANAGEMENT IN ARGENTINA; MANAGEMENT IN BRAZIL

Management education in the emerging countries

1 **Regional perspectives**
2 **Means for improvement**
3 **Conclusion**

Overview

Management education in emerging countries in Africa, Asia and Latin America is influenced by a number of factors which both determine the form such education takes and strongly influence its chances of success. One major influence is the environment within which management education is delivered, which is itself a function of variables such as governance, culture and resource availability. Other factors include the models and methods of management education employed, teacher qualifications and experience and the nature of institutional structures for the delivery of management education. Taking these factors into account, there are a number of ways in which management education in emerging countries could be improved.

Management education is defined here as including all learning activities concerned with the acquisition by managers of skills, knowledge, attitudes and values which are deemed relevant to improving their managerial performance. Under this definition, management education also includes fields such as management training and development.

Much has been said and written about the poor management of organizations in emerging countries. Public organizations in particular have been and continue to be criticized for inefficiency, waste, overstaffing and ineffectiveness. These claims have considerable validity (although poor performance is by no means uniform) and organizational dysfunction in emerging countries is a serious impediment to development. Lack of management capability is one of many factors contributing to this condition.

In industrialized nations such as the USA and the UK it is widely assumed that management education is good for managers, organizations and economies, and as a result large, sophisticated management education industries have developed in these countries. But while the same assumption is made in many emerging countries, facilities for management education are comparatively few in number, small in scale and of more variable quality.

In contrast with the industrialized nations, most management education in emerging countries is directed at public sector rather than private sector managers. The private sectors of many emerging countries are of small size and simply do not employ as many managers as do the frequently overstaffed public sectors. While this balance is likely to change as more and more emerging countries are persuaded to reduce the size of their governments and encourage private sector growth, the speed of this change will vary considerably from one country to another. A further reason for the prominence of public sector management education in emerging countries is that, even under conditions of smaller government, the public sector will clearly continue to be crucial to effective national governance through its responsibilities for policy implementation in areas such as education and health, regulation and protection of the environment, and the creation of environments which are conducive to entrepreneurial activity. Effective public sector management is indispensable to sustainable economic and human development, and its needs take priority over those of private sector management in emerging countries.

However, the need to make a distinction between management education for the public and private sectors is diminishing as worldwide trends towards economic and political liberalization continue to blur the distinctions between the management of public and private organizations. The dominance of the free-market economic paradigm has put pressure on governments everywhere to become smaller and to operate their institutions in a manner more similar to organizations in the private sector (World Bank 1994).

1 Regional perspectives

Africa, Asia and Latin America offer contrasting pictures of economic and human development. In Asia, the latter part of the twentieth century marks the beginning of a remarkable era of economic and political revolution. Despite the recent downturn in the region, the economic success of Japan and the 'tiger' economies of South Korea, Taiwan, Singapore and Hong Kong has been the catalyst for a major shift in the global balance of economic and strategic power. Once recovery is underway in these economies along with those of middle-income countries such as Malaysia and Thailand and the economic emergence of poorer countries such as China, India and Vietnam is confirmed, this will establish east and southeast Asia as a major world economic centre well into the next century (see PERSPECTIVES ON GLOBALIZATION, BIG BUSINESS AND THE EMERGING COUNTRIES). What are now two of the most populous countries on earth, China and India, may become economic superpowers in the twenty-first century. China is still relatively poor in terms of per capita GDP (gross domestic product), but in the fifteen years between 1980 and 1995 China's overall GDP grew to become the third largest in the world, exceeded only by that of the USA and Japan. It is widely predicted that China's economy will continue to grow rapidly for many years.

In contrast to Asia, most of the economies of sub-Saharan Africa are distinguished by varying levels of poverty and degrees of economic stagnation, although there are some notable exceptions such as Botswana and South Africa. The African continent contains some of the slowest-growing economies and poorest countries on earth. In 1997, nine of the world's ten poorest countries were in Africa (World Bank 1994).

Latin American countries fit in between Africa and Asia, with most economies in the region situated in what the World Bank refers to as the lower middle-income belt. Nicaragua and Honduras are the only Latin American countries ranked by the World Bank among the 40 low-income countries, with a per capita GNP (gross national product) of less than US$675 in 1992 (World Bank 1994). Similar pictures emerge when human development criteria such as longevity, education and income are applied to these three regions (UNDP 1994b); again Asia emerges as the best-developed region and Africa appears the least-developed.

As well as these considerable regional differences, there are also immense cultural variations within the regions themselves, and within countries in each region. All of these variables influence the nature and provision of management education and impact on its potential for success.

Africa

Most management education in Africa has been provided either by universities or by national institutes, such as the Zimbabwe Institute of Public Administration and Management in Harare, or the Eastern and Southern African Management Institute in Arusha, Tanzania. These two are among the few such institutes that are regarded highly or taken seriously by policy makers. Most similar institutions are not well-regarded and are seen as having little ability to make an impact or create improvements in the public sector (Roberts 1990).

In many national institutes, education and training activities consist mainly of standard programmes aimed at middle- and lower-level officials in government organizations and state-run enterprises. Educational material is usually of Western origin and has not been adapted sufficiently to local circumstances. This is partly a result of management educators simply repeating to others what they have learned themselves (mostly in Western universities), despite the limited relevance of this learning to local needs. This problem is exacerbated by the inexperience of educators in teaching, research and consultancy, and by their consequent lack of credibility. Staff quality is not as high as it could be because institute salaries are not competitive, and because institutes do not have sufficient autonomy or influence within government. In addition, relatively little research or consultancy is undertaken and the strategic management of institutes is often deficient.

A jointly-funded programme of technical assistance to strengthen African institutes of management and administration was launched in November 1987 under the auspices of the United Nations Development Programme (UNDP), the Economic Development Institute (EDI) of the World Bank and the International Labour Organization. This programme and other similar programmes such as the African Capacity Building Foundation (which is supported by the African Development Bank, the UNDP and the World Bank) are working to improve the situation. Regional self-help associations with similar objectives have also been established, such as the Association of Management Training Institutes of Eastern and Southern Africa and the Pan-African Institute of Administration. However, progress is slow and there is still some way to go before management education at these institutes reaches an acceptable standard.

Management education programmes in African universities suffer from many of the problems outlined above (Safavi 1981). The situation in South Africa is substantially better than in the rest of Africa, particularly in the former 'white' universities where there are a number of schools of business and public administration of international standard. However, it is the former 'black' universities in South Africa which have been most successful in taking management education to the mass of the people, in some cases by using innovative programmes of applied learning which involve students in business and management practice (Safavi and Tweddell 1990).

Asia

The character of public sector management education in the emerging countries of Asia in the twentieth century has been shaped by two powerful historical forces: first, the rise and fall of the European colonial empires, and second, the growth and decline of the communist regimes in the region. Both these factors have an impact on the nature and quality of management education.

In many former British colonies such as India, Sri Lanka and Pakistan there is a relatively long history of public sector management education which, as in Africa, is usually provided by national institutes of public administration and by the major universities (see MANAGEMENT IN INDIA; MANAGEMENT IN PAKISTAN; MANAGEMENT IN SRI LANKA). In general, national institutes of public administration such as the Sri Lanka Institute of Public Administration (SLIDA) have good reputations and are regarded as being particularly effective in educating middle and junior managers. Institutes such as SLIDA offer relatively competitive salaries and opportunities for salary supplementation through consultancy, with the result that they attract staff of reasonable quality. Innovation in teaching does occur (Jones 1990) but, as in Africa, educational techniques are mostly classroom-based and materials are primarily of Western origin. This is true also of the many MBA programmes offered by universities in this part of Asia.

The relationship between national economic progress and the quality and availability of management education is particularly noticeable in the newly-industrializing countries of Asia. In countries such as Hong Kong, Malaysia and Singapore, which experienced rapid economic growth in the 1980s and 1990s and are no longer regarded as emerging countries, the quality of management education in both national institutes and universities is relatively high. Most management education in these countries is aimed at managers in the private sectors which, in contrast to those of many emerging countries, are very large and dynamic.

This relationship is evident also in countries which are at different stages in the transition from a centrally-planned to a market-orientated economy. In countries which are still at an early transitional stage, such as Cambodia and Burma, institutions capable of providing modern management education are few in number and of relatively poor quality. There is a great need for the establishment of new training institutes and the strengthening of existing ones (Collins 1993).

In China on the other hand, the rate of expansion of modern management education in universities and institutes of finance and economics since 1979 has to some degree kept pace with the rapid growth of the Chinese economy. As in other transitional economies such as Vietnam (Blunt 1992), this expansion was partly a response to the urgent need to transform the thinking of Chinese managers and partly an attempt at import substitution designed to provide a cheaper and safer alternative to sending managers abroad (managers trained at home would be sure to stay in China while those trained abroad might not return). China has progressed further and faster than the other transitional economies mentioned and now has a number of high-quality modern management education institutes, many of which are associated with elite universities such as Beijing University and Qinghua University in Beijing and Fudan University in Shanghai (Warner 1990). One of the best and most prestigious management institutes is the China-Europe International Business School (CEIBS) located in Shanghai, which is a product of international cooperation between the European Union and the Chinese government. CEIBS, which offers an MBA programme and a range of executive short courses, exemplifies the considerable influence of Western models of management education in China.

Developments similar to those which have occurred in China have featured in other transitional economies such as Vietnam and the Commonwealth of Independent States (CIS). Multilateral and bilateral donor agencies are expected to play a major part in these developments. The UNDP is already supporting technical cooperation programmes in management education and institution-building (Blunt and Collins 1994) in Cambodia, China, the CIS, Laos, Mongolia and Vietnam (Collins 1993; UNDP 1994b). Bilateral donor agencies are also active in this field; an example of bilateral technical cooperation in management education and institution-building has been the establishment of a centre for modern management education at the National Economic University of Hanoi, supported by the Swedish International Development Authority.

Despite recognition among indigenous senior managers and outside observers that one of the greatest impediments to management improvement in transitional economies is the need to change the ways in which managers think and behave, an emerging problem in China (Tung 1993) and in other transitional economies is the preference for 'hard' rather than 'soft' management education. Subjects such as finance, statistics, operations research and management of information systems are favoured over those which deal with people, such as human resource management and comparative management. In general, however, Eastern cultures place a high value on education. When this is combined with respect for authority, thrift, productivity and the priority of group over individual interests, as is the case in cultures influenced by Confucian philosophy (Hofstede and Bond 1988), a fertile ground is created in which management education can take hold and flourish. The prospects for management education in Asia seem better than in any other emerging region.

Latin America

Until the 1960s, the development of management education in Latin America was hampered by the traditional reliance on other more prestigious professions, such as law, medicine and engineering, as a source of managers. Law in particular, which has been taught in Latin American universities since the seventeenth century, was seen as an ideal education for the managerial elites of both the private and public sectors (Davila 1991).

It was only in the 1960s that formal management education *per se* began to be established in a number of Latin American countries, mainly as a consequence of support provided by foreign foundations, the US government and a number of international donor agencies. One of the first of such initiatives was the establishment of the Getulio Vargas Foundation in Brazil in the late 1950s; this institution in turn sponsored the establishment of a pioneering and prestigious school of public administration in Rio de Janeiro and a business school in Sâo Paulo. Schools of management and business were established in most countries in the region during the 1960s; most of the new business schools offered US-designed MBA programmes, which were taught by Americans or by indigenous staff educated in the USA. Collaborative efforts by prestigious US universities in various countries, such as Harvard in Nicaragua, Stanford in Peru and Syracuse in Colombia, were in many cases supported by the United States Agency for International Development (USAID).

The Latin American Council of Postgraduate Business Schools was founded in 1967, and most of the top management schools in the region are members. The majority of these management schools are linked to universities, but there are about ten independent institutions.

The foundations laid in the 1960s were built upon in the 1970s and 1980s, to the point where by the mid-1980s about 10 per cent of all students in higher education throughout the region were studying business or management. However, the rapid growth of management education in the 1970s and 1980s resulted in considerable variations in quality between programmes, and in underemployment and unemployment among graduates.

The formal qualifications and research and publication output of faculty, even in the top institutions, continues to fall some way short of standards in developed countries. For example, while 75 per cent of staff in most management schools in the USA hold PhD degrees, the comparable figure for the elite Latin American schools in 1984 was only about 25 per cent. A more recent study conducted in Colombia in 1989 found that in that country's top schools of management only 8 per cent of staff held a PhD. Outside the top schools the picture is even worse: research and publication are rare, teaching skills and resources are frequently less than satisfactory, curriculum design is poor and many staff hold other full-time jobs in order to supplement their incomes. Moreover, the quality gap between the elite management schools and the rest is growing (Davila 1991).

Latin American schools of business and management have also been criticized for their unquestioning acceptance of the North American business school model. Little or no attempt has been made to develop indigenous philosophies, methods, curricula or materials. This in turn has meant that managers have not been sufficiently exposed to such crucial local issues as government–business relationships, privatization, public management in circumstances involving extreme disparities between rich and poor, major regional inequalities within countries, problems of social integration involving ethnic minorities, environmental degradation and rapid population growth. Managers, particularly in public organizations, are therefore often ill-equipped to deal with the complex issues of development that confront them in their work (Davila 1991).

2 Means for improvement

There are at least two broad variables that exert a significant influence on the nature and success of management education. The first variable stems from the extent to which cultures and the institutional environments created by governments attach value to education in general and the outcomes that education is designed to produce. The second variable consists of what is taught, and by whom.

The cultural and institutional environments of management education

The cultural value of education can be gauged partly by the degree to which it is perceived to impart social standing or status within a community. Economic and institutional environments, which are created largely by governments and organizations in civil society (such as professional associations, voluntary organizations and trade unions), attach a value to education to the extent that they reward – even-handedly – educational attainment, and to the extent that they are seen to take seriously the development and maintenance of high-quality educational facilities. Indicators of this value are usually highly visible. If schools of management and administration pay low salaries, are housed in shabby buildings in out-of-the-way locations and are unable to win contracts to undertake government research and consultancy, then the message is clear: government does not attach a high value to management education. In societies where visible symbols of standing are important, as they are in many emerging countries, it is impossible for schools of management to do well in their absence. In countries such as Singapore, however, where the culture and the institutional environment created by government do place a high value on education and openly advocate a meritocratic system which is administered fairly, management and other forms of education are of high quality.

The effects of culture on management education, and possibly on economic success, are particularly noticeable in Asian countries which are influenced by Confucian philosophy. Asian economies such as Japan, South Korea, Singapore, Taiwan and Hong Kong have in common a Confucian cultural heritage which values among other things thrift, discipline, harmony, respect for authority and a high regard for education and the acquisition of knowledge and skill. Emerging countries in Asia which have similar cultures, such as China and Vietnam, are in the process of creating institutional environments which are supportive of the development of high-quality management education.

In many parts of Africa, on the other hand, resources are scarce and the quality of governance and the commitment by government to management education and public management improvement are much more variable. In addition, many African countries lack a relatively homogeneous, unifying cultural heritage. In these countries management education tends often to be of poor quality, and there is no prospect of substantial improvement in the near future (see BUSINESS CULTURES, THE EMERGING COUNTRIES).

Teachers of management and curriculum design

Educational content and teaching methods clearly depend heavily on who does the teaching and on where the teachers themselves were educated. Teachers tend to use the same methods as those by which they themselves were taught. Breaking this pattern is difficult, particularly when there are no alternative curricula to replace those which have been learned and when there is a shortage of role models who have successfully adopted different methods (Blunt and Jones 1997). The situation is complicated by the fact that research in management has yet to determine which aspects of management are culture or situation-free and which are not (Blunt 1990). Accordingly, calls for emerging countries to produce indigenous approaches to management and management education are much more difficult to implement than to pronounce.

None the less, there is a persistent desire in many emerging countries, particularly in the ex-colonies, to do more than simply copy what is done in the West. The motives behind this desire probably have as much to do with discomfort over intellectual dependency as with conviction about the merits of indigenous approaches to management, which themselves are far from being clearly defined or understood. While more texts are being produced which examine the links between Western theory and research and the organizational circumstances of emerging countries (for example, Austin 1990; Austin and Kohn 1990; Blunt and Jones 1992; Blunt *et al.* 1993; Esman 1991; Kiggundu 1989), much work remains to be done on theory development. There is a need to develop case studies which demonstrate how indigenous forms of organization and management can be employed in the interests of development in different national and cultural circumstances (Blunt and Warren 1996).

There is also a need to improve the conventional design features of curricula by making them more relevant to the problems of management – whether public sector or private sector – in emerging countries. In public sector management, for example, managers need to be educated in three broad fields relating to the strategic management of the development process and the organizations responsible for that process.

First, the nature and purposes of sound governance and public sector management under liberalized economic and political regimes should be examined, as should the roles of organizations in civil society such as professional associations, trade unions and non-governmental organizations, whose roles can be complementary to those of government. It is clearly important that public sector managers have a thorough understanding of what governments and other institutional stakeholders are, or should be, trying to achieve in terms of sustainable human development, and how the obstacles to its attainment are manifested in their own national circumstances. Challenges such as reforming economic systems, alleviating poverty, encouraging social integration, improving agricultural performance, providing employment and protecting the environment are common to all emerging countries; but their manifestations and causes will differ, and so too will their priority in national development agendas. Strategies and means for addressing these problems should be adapted accordingly (UNDP 1997).

Public sector managers must also be sufficiently educated in comparative economic and public policy so as to be able to hold balanced discourses with powerful international agencies, whose structural adjustment policies and associated organizational reforms too often appear to be ideologically rather than pragmatically driven. This sometimes results in the underestimation or neglect of the risks of rapid systemic change, the so-called 'big bang' initiatives, which can impose enormous short-term economic and social costs. Management education in the transitional economies in particular should therefore engender informed debate on these issues among public sector managers, rather than simply offering a new dogma to replace an outmoded one.

The second field of management education for public sector managers is the strategic management of public organizations and enterprises in the pursuit of development objectives within the national and institutional framework set by sound governance. Study of this area should encompass such questions as the size of government, the policies, programmes and projects that governments design and implement, their orientations and attitudes to customer service, organizational design and institution-building, employee selection, remuneration and strategic human resource management in general (Collins 1993).

The third field should address the interpersonal and international dimensions of public management. Senior public sector managers in emerging countries must be able to interact effectively and harmoniously with colleagues, experts, donors, entrepreneurs and other representatives from a wide variety of different cultures. Knowledge and skills in such areas as comparative public management, international human resource management, cross-cultural management skills and team building are therefore necessary.

Many emerging countries depend heavily on technical cooperation and finance provided by international agencies. Accordingly, the critical role of international donor agencies and financial institutions such as the World Bank and the International Monetary Fund, as well as their structures, function and internal politics, should also be studied and understood (Graham 1993).

3 Conclusion

Western assumptions about who should teach management should be questioned. It is by no means clear, even in the West, that the academic model which values formal qualifications and research publications over management experience and teaching capability is well suited to educating managers, or whether it simply perpetuates a tradition involving the transmission of management theory and research findings from one generation of business school graduates to the next. This situation reflects an unresolved dilemma in the West as to whether the primary aim of management education should be to provide intellectual training or to provide knowledge and skills which are immediately applicable to the world of work. The immediacy and magnitude of the problems of public sector management in emerging and transitional economies suggest there is a need to concentrate on the latter, at least in the short term.

This concentration in turn calls for a re-evaluation of who should teach management in emerging countries. The scarcity of highly-qualified management academics in many emerging countries should perhaps be seen as an opportunity to employ management educators who possess a better blend of formal qualifications with intellectual and teaching abilities and accomplishment in management practice. Certainly, the cycle of unquestioning dependence on, and transmission of, Western theory, methods and institutional practices by themselves needs to be broken.

PETER BLUNT
GRADUATE SCHOOL OF BUSINESS
NORTHERN TERRITORY UNIVERSITY

Further reading

(References cited in the text marked *)

Adamolekun, L. (1989) *Issues in Development Management in Sub-Saharan Africa*, Economic Development Institute Policy Seminar Report No. 19, Washington, DC: The World Bank. (Analyses institution-building in Africa, including the roles of management training programmes and institutes.)

Ashton, D., Green, F., James, D. and Sung, J. (1999) *Education and Training for Development in East Asia*, London Routledge. (A guide to education and training systems in Asia.)

* Austin, J.E. (1990) *Managing in Emerging Countries: Strategic Analysis and Operating Techniques*, New York: The Free Press. (Examines critical issues of doing business, including government regulations, infrastructure, finance and markets.)

* Austin, J.E. and Kohn, T.O. (1990) *Strategic Management in Emerging Countries*, New York: The Free Press. (Contains detailed case studies of issues surrounding the establishment of foreign companies.)

* Blunt, P. (1990) 'Strategies for enhancing organizational effectiveness in the third world', *Public Administration and Development* 10: 299–313. (Argues the case for a number of culture-free prerequisites for effective organization.)

* Blunt, P. (1992) '*Doi Moi*: Renovating enterprise management in Vietnam', *Journal of Asian Business* 8(2): 5–14. (Outlines case histories of public and private enterprises, and discusses their implications for management education.)

Blunt, P. (1995) 'Cultural relativism, good governance and sustainable human development', *Public Administration and Development* 15: 1–9. (Questions the universal applicability of Western approaches to governance and human development.)

* Blunt, P. (1997) 'Prisoners of the paradigm: Process consultants and "clinical" development practitioners', *Public Administration and Development* 17: 341–9. (Argues that the dominant methods of consulting practice in emerging countries are often adopted for ideological rather than pragmatic reasons.)

* Blunt, P. and Collins, P. (1994) 'Introduction', *Institution Building in Emerging Countries*, special issue of *Public Administration and Development* 14(2): 111–20. (Defines the notion of institution building and analyses its intellectual origins.)

Blunt, P. and Jones, M. (eds) (1991) *Management Development in the Third World*, special issue of *Journal of Management Development* 10(6): 1–83. (Discusses management education in Africa, Latin America and southeast Asia, as well as donor agency perspectives.)

* Blunt, P. and Jones, M. (1992) *Managing Organizations in Africa*, Berlin and New York: Walter de Gruyter. (Synthesizes theoretical propositions, research results, practical experiences and case studies relevant to management in Africa.)

* Blunt, P. and Jones, M. (1997) 'Exploring the limits of Western leadership theory in east Asia and Africa', *Personnel Review* 26(1/2): 6–23. (Examines Western leadership theory in the light of arguments about Western ideological imperialism.)

* Blunt, P., Jones, M. and Richards, D. (1993) *Managing Organizations in Africa: Readings, Cases, and Exercises*, Berlin and New York: Walter de Gruyter. (Companion volume to Blunt and Jones (1992); ideal for management educational and training purposes.)

* Blunt, P. and Warren, D.M. (eds) (1996) *Indigenous Organizations and Development*, London: Intermediate Technology Publications. (Presents numerous case studies from Asia, Africa and Latin America.)

* Collins, P. (1993) 'Civil service reform and retraining in transitional economies: strategic issues and options', *Public Administration and Development* 13: 323–44. (Describes lessons to be drawn from international donor cooperation in policy making, legislative reform and management education.)

* Davila, C. (1991) 'The evolution of management education and development in Latin America', *Journal of Management Development* 10(6): 22–31. (Considers the historical and intellectual origins and the diffusion of management education, and its present state.)

* Esman, M.J. (1991) *Management Dimensions of Development: Perspectives and Strategies*, West Hartford, CT: Kumarian Press. (Argues an approach to development which involves governments, private enterprise and voluntary organizations.)
* Graham, L.S. (1993) 'Revitalising public management training in the Americas', *Public Administration and Development* 13: 95–111. (Analyses curriculum development in the USA for public sector management in emerging countries.)
  Hofstede, G. (1993) 'Cultural constraints in management theories', *Academy of Management Executive* 7(1): 81–94. (Examines the applicability to other cultures of economic and management theory developed in the USA.)
* Hofstede, G. and Bond, M. (1988) 'The Confucius connection: from cultural roots to economic growth', *Organizational Dynamics* 16(4): 5–21. (Gives empirical support to the idea that Confucian cultures are conducive to economic success.)
* Jones, M. (1990) 'Action learning as a new idea', *Journal of Management Development* 9(5): 29–34. (Discusses barriers to action learning in Sri Lanka and ways of overcoming them.)
* Kiggundu, M.N. (1989) *Managing Organizations in Emerging Countries*, West Hartford, CT: Kumarian Press. (Reviews theory and research, and develops a model for managing organizations in emerging countries.)
  Kiggundu, M.N. (1991) 'The challenge of management development in Sub-Saharan Africa', *Journal of Management Development* 10(6): 32–47. (Outlines African experience of management education and infers from this guidelines for improvement.)
* Roberts, L. (1990) *The Policy Environment of Management Development Institutions (MDIs) in Anglophone Africa*, EDI Policy Seminar Report No. 26, Washington, DC: The World Bank. (Analyses the roles, performance and strategies of MDIs in Africa, including a case study of Ghana.)
* Safavi, F. (1981) 'A model of management education in Africa', *Academy of Management Review* 6(2): 319–31. (Surveys fifty-seven African countries and territories, and develops a model of management education.)
* Safavi, F. and Tweddell, C.E. (1990) 'Attributes of success in African management development programmes: concepts and applications', *Journal of Management Development* 9(6): 50–63. (Infers attributes of success from examples of management education in Ethiopia, Kenya and South Africa.)
  Temporal, P. (ed.) (1990) *Management Development in Asia*, special issue of *Journal of Management Development* 9(5): 1–72. (Gives national, cultural and organizational perspectives on management education in Asia.)
* Tung, R.L. (1993) 'Extended review: a comparative perspective on management and industrial training in China', *International Journal of Human Resource Management* 4(1): 241–5. (A review of Warner (1992).)
* UNDP (1994a) *Human Development Report 1994*, New York: Oxford University Press. (Proposes a notion of sustainable human development, a measurement index, and a ranking of countries.)
* UNDP (1994b) *Governance, Public Sector Management and Sustainable Human Development*, New York: UNDP. (Clarifies the concepts, gives examples and considers the role of the UNDP.)
* UNDP (1996) *Human Development Report*, New York: Oxford University Press.
* UNDP (1997) *Reconceptualizing Governance*, New York: Division of Public Afairs. (Outlines a broad concept of the nature of governance, encompassing the state, the private sector, and civil society.)
* Warner, M. (1990) 'Emerging key human resources in China: an assessment of university management schools in Beijing, Shanghai and Tianjin in the decade 1979–88', *International Journal of Human Resource Management* 1(1): 87–106. (Provides data on numbers of graduates, quality of staff, nature of institutions and foreign links.)
  Warner, M. (1992) *How Chinese Managers Learn*, London: Macmillan. (Compares management education programmes in China with those in industrialized and transitionary economies.)
* World Bank (1994) *World Development Report 1994*, New York: Oxford University Press. (Discusses development issues – particularly infrastructure – and provides country rankings on a number of economic indicators.)
* World Bank (1997) *World Development Report*, New York: Oxford University Press.

See also: BUSINESS CULTURES, THE EMERGING COUNTRIES; MANAGEMENT IN THE EMERG-
ING COUNTRIES; MANAGEMENT IN INDIA; MANAGEMENT IN NIGERIA; MANAGEMENT IN
PAKISTAN; MANAGEMENT IN SRI LANKA

Related topics in the IEBM regional set: MANAGEMENT EDUCATION IN ASIA PACIFIC;
MANAGEMENT EDUCATION IN EUROPE; MANAGEMENT EDUCATION IN LATIN AMERICA;
MANAGEMENT EDUCATION IN NORTH AMERICA; MANAGEMENT IN ASIA PACIFIC; MAN-
AGEMENT IN BRAZIL, MANAGEMENT IN CHINA; MANAGEMENT IN HONG KONG; MANAGE-
MENT IN INDIA; MANAGEMENT IN JAPAN; MANAGEMENT IN MALAYSIA; MANAGEMENT IN
MONGOLIA; MANAGEMENT IN SINGAPORE; MANAGEMENT IN TAIWAN; MANAGEMENT IN
VIETNAM

Management of technology in the emerging countries

1 Introduction
2 Context of technology management issues
3 Analysis of management practices
4 Evaluation of prevailing realities
5 Conclusion

Overview

The management of technology in the emerging countries has met with mixed results. There are few phenomenally successful stories among the emerging countries of the Pacific Rim. There are also particularly poor results from Africa. Latin America presents a mixed picture. The failures have been because of widespread misconceptions about technology in general, and the nature of technology sourced from the West in particular. This has misinformed the management processes applied in managing technology. This error has been particularly acute among the emerging countries of Africa. A new approach is required that calls for an explicit and comprehensive understanding of an organization's or country's existing technological strengths and experiences, technology options possible and open to it, and the spectrum of vendors in the market. This is what can be learned from the success stories of the Far East and Latin America. In this pursuit of alternative avenues to effective technology management, the onset of new information and communications technologies (ICTs) presents challenges and opportunities.

1 Introduction

Technology represents the information and knowledge of a society that is used to accomplish tasks, render services or manufacture products. It is all the elements of productive knowledge needed for transformation of inputs into products, in the use of these in the development and rendering of services and also in the generation of further productive knowledge. These elements of productive knowledge and information become condensed into artefact, process or service in order to satisfy a need or want.

This knowledge in society is, however, the culmination of negotiations and compromises on what should constitute the best technical and socially acceptable solutions and positions to be pursued. It means that technology is a product of compromises among the competing interests in a given society. As a result, technological artefacts, such as tools and machines, represent a particular society's packaged compromises aimed at the attainment of a particular goal. This goal could be a solution, a product or delivery of a state of being, such as full employment. What is important to recognize is that technology cannot be universal because it is a package of compromises from the society of its origin and collective decisions on the prevailing priorities it faces. Therefore, all societies generate knowledge and technology which are relevant to their specific environment and which address needs, ongoing changes and such critical issues as sustainability. These, inevitably, vary between societies and the various prevailing environments. Social, economic and political considerations and objectives lead to the development, adoption and deployment of technology for a particular industry, sector or purpose. Technological factors are thus important only so far as they fit into the framework designed by social, economic and political factors. This social specificity of technology by its origins has the effect of limiting the scope of variations and recasting possible at a given time. Management of technology is, therefore, about enabling, at corporate or national level, the mastering of the core of a technology, adapting and diversifying into smaller or related endeavours, and eventually moving towards independent product, service or systems development.

Developments over the past couple of centuries have brought about interactions between different communities and countries of the world. This has led to exchanges in information, knowledge, culture, artefacts and the technologies they encapsulate. The historical consequence of this drift towards global interactions and exchanges has been a dominance, at the international levels of exchange, of those technologies originating in Western Europe and North America (or the West). Historical events have given this region, and the technologies it spawned, particular advantages. This has led to much of the rest of the world setting, and pursuing, the goal of acquiring Western technology and adapting it to local needs. The problem has been that these societies are outsiders with regard to this cultural orbit. The result of their efforts has thus met with mixed results. But these efforts still persist, even among dismal performers.

The reason for this persistence is the demonstrated capacity of Western technology to improve productivity, quality and value and, as a result, the standards of living of those able to exploit it effectively. The phenomenal success of such countries as South Korea in adopting, assimilating and exploiting this technology fans the dream. The effective management of this technology has, therefore, become the urgent goal of many societies and states. It has consumed vast energies and resources at governmental, private, non-governmental and community levels. It has been assumed that the technologies, which have advanced Western countries to such heights of material wealth, should accomplish the same results elsewhere.

2 Context of technology management issues

Among the many emerging countries where technology management met with little success, the diagnosis is their failure to address the culturally specific issues inherent in all technologies (see BUSINESS CULTURES, THE EMERGING COUNTRIES; MANAGEMENT IN THE EMERGING COUNTRIES). They fail to take stock of the technologies already existing in the country, or to evaluate how these relate to or graft onto the new, whether it is going to be possible to develop the newly acquired technology, whether there exists a national capability to adapt imported technology, how long this would take, the resources needed, possible tradeoffs between importing technology now and waiting to develop it at home, or importing now but with the intention of there being no repetitive imports in future, etc. These are critical questions in technology management. This failure has been particularly acute in the emerging countries of Africa where past interactions with the West had been forced, exploitative, traumatic and least beneficial.

The 'miracle economies' of South Korea, Singapore, Taiwan and Hong Kong (and those neighbours striving to emulate them) illustrate that it is possible to manage this technology creatively and productively without research leadership or total mastery of new knowledge generation. Here success appears to have been founded on excellent physical and financial infrastructure, adequate supply of skilled labour, and a pool of technical and scientific information and knowledge nurtured and directed at managing technology. Thus, for instance, South Korea's technology transfer management approach emphasized exhaustive surveys of alternative techniques, technologies, suppliers and markets, as well as the possible combinations of these. It focused on unpackaging technologies as much as possible, avoidance of supplier financing, engaging and negotiating with as many potential suppliers as possible, emphasizing implementation time schedules and capacity utilization, technology diffusion via conferences and trade exhibitions, holding suppliers accountable for undertakings during negotiations, and transparent evaluation of performance. This was measured between related projects, over time, in terms of improved time schedules, higher utility of installed capacity and lower implementation costs.

However, many emerging countries have been concerned more with the availability of technological products, rather than with the complex issues associated with the political, economic and cultural integration of technology (see MANUFACTURING IN THE EMERGING COUNTRIES). They have opted to import 'black-box' and 'turnkey' solutions. They have paid little or no attention to the infrastructures required to support a productive and organic assimilation of an imported technology. The process of choosing technology has tended to be undemocratic in that no comprehensive analysis of national needs and alternative technologies and choices to meet those needs has been undertaken. Nor has regular public consultation on alternatives taken place. Technology policy making, at corporate and national levels, has emphasized operational choices such as procurement and deployment rather than strategic issues like the direction of technological developments and their possible consequences for the acquirer (see STRATEGY IN THE EMERGING COUNTRIES). This has resulted in acquisitions of obsolete and inappropriate technologies. Many industrial landscapes in emerging countries are thus littered with this wreckage.

The technology transfer management has faced the following problems:

- Much of it has consisted of end-products rather than of technology *per se*.
- Much of the technology transfer takes place as intra-firm movements (or internally within a firm and its subsidiaries).
- Many technology contracts result in supplier control and contravene free-market rules.
- The conditions under which transfers take place have been disadvantageous, with technologies sold as complete turnkey packages rather than as component blueprints, and much of it inappropriate, obsolete and over-priced.

In addition, many of these emerging countries and their organizations are afflicted by:

- lack of information and commercial know-how required to assess the merits of what they need;
- limited aptitude for technology unpackaging or unbundling, selection and preparatory work;
- limited information on possible alternative sources, suppliers and markets of, and for, the technologies;
- a preference for finance–technology packages which transfer much decision-making power to suppliers of technology.

Technology management is being further complicated by the onset of information and communications technologies (ICTs). ICTs encompass technologies that enable the handling of information and facilitate communication between people, between people and electronic systems, and between electronic systems. They can be grouped into:

- capturing technologies, which include devices that collect and convert information, such as keyboards, mice, touch screens, barcode readers, image scanners, cam recorders;
- storage technologies, including retrieval, such as magnetic tapes, floppy disks, hard disks, random access memory (RAM) disks, optical disks (like CD-ROMs), smart cards, erasable disks;
- processing technologies covering systems and applications software;
- communications technologies enabling transmission of information such as broadcasting, integrated systems digital networks (ISDN), digital and cellular networks, local and wide area networks (including the Internet), electronic bulletin boards, modems, fibre-optics, cellular phones, fax machines, satellites;
- display technologies that include output devices such as computer screens, printers, video discs, voice synthesizers, virtual reality helmets, etc.

Recent studies, however, suggest that among the low-performing countries, major beneficiaries of this development have been the companies providing the equipment, the banking consortia providing the funding, and local administrative élites using the new technology. Unforeseen negative secondary effects have included balance of payments problems associated with the capital intensity of the new technologies. The possibility of the failure of ICTs to transfer to these countries raises fears of their being cut off from the emerging global digital highway. Without adequate access to this system, these emerging countries will not be able to compete economically. The ongoing 'digital rush' to create and broaden links with electronic networks is thus driven by the recognition of the potential benefits that digital information and communication technologies can bestow.

An example of this is improvements in educational facilities through distance learning and online library access. Electronic networking can improve and cheapen access to quality health services via remote access to diagnostic and healing practices. Remote resource sensing can provide disaster early warning capacity or identify suitable land for crop cultivation, mining explorations, etc. ICTs can assist in technology transfer diffusion management through the option of flexible, decentralized, small-scale industrial production. In the 'miracle' Far East, the introduction of computer-aided manufacturing (CAM) technologies in small-scale industries has been credited with advancing their technological performance. The decentralization of industry, made possible by ICTs, reduces levels of pollution and other negative impacts on the local environment. Another possible benefit is the facility to create a public sphere in 'cyberspace' allowing small remote organizations take advantage of the 24-hour marketing facilities opened up by the World Wide Web (WWW) on the Internet.

Because of the global nature of ICTs, there has been a lot of initiatives at organizational, national, regional and international levels to address the issues. An increasing number of emerging countries have scheduled privatization of their telephone companies in an attempt to attract new and additional capital and technologies. The objective has been to improve and enhance quality of access. India, for example, inaugurated its first digital information network in 1994 and intends to superimpose on this net an ambitious information highway – a network that brings together optical and coaxial cables, microwave links and satellite connections. Between 1994 and 1995, the network grew by almost 23 per cent. India plans to expand its telephone service from its current level of 0.77 per 100 inhabitants to 1.52 by the year 2000. By the turn of the century, China intends to install 100 million digital lines at a cost of US$40 billion. This represents an expansion of telephone service from 0.98 per 100 inhabitants to 3.50. Indonesia opened its telecommunications market to foreign competition in 1995 and expects the installation of 5 million lines by end of 1999. Here ICTs are seen as enabling technologies able to bring information from the grassroots level to the capital, help manage the transport of goods across unforgiving terrain, disseminate life-saving medical know-how to under-skilled practitioners, and process commercial transactions and capital flows in accordance with world best practices.

Korea's Ministry of Information and Communication wants to establish a full-scale information highway by extending the National Information Superhighway into 80 cities across the country. The government aims to provide US$80million for the development of software technology, set up industrial complexes for multimedia industries, and increase investment in research and development. In Latin America the move is towards developing national and regional information infrastructures. The countries are privatizing and developing sophisticated networks. The Plan of Action approved at the summit of the Organization of American States in December 1994 shows a strong commitment to the development of ICT infrastructures. The International Telecommunication Union's (ITU) 1996 report on the region highlights emphasis on joint development of telecommunications policy and the expansion of telecommunications services.

The African initiatives include the 1995 First African Regional Symposium on Telematics for Development and the 21st Session of the Conference of African Ministers responsible for Economic, Social and Development Planning which focused on this sector. These initiatives concluded that without proper national information and communications policies, strategies and implementation plans, African countries would not be able to partake fully in the global information society. Also notable is resolution 795 on 'Building Africa's Information Highway', adopted by the

Conference of Ministers of the United Nations Economic Commission for Africa (UNECA) on 2 May 1995. Another is the deliberations of African ministers for economic and social development which culminated in the report on 'Africa's Information Society Initiative: An Action Framework to Build Africa's Information and Communications Infrastructure' in May 1996. This initiative envisions, by 2010, an information society in Africa in which every man, woman, schoolchild, village, government office and business can access information through computers and telecommunications. It aims for information systems to be in place to support decision making in all major sectors of each country's economy. Access is to be ensured to international, regional and national 'information highways' to support a private sector able to lead Africa's growing information-based economies. African information resources are to be made accessible globally, reflecting content on its tourism, trade, education, culture, energy, health, transport and natural resources management.

On a world level, there are expectations that the new ICTs will improve development and make a contribution to efforts at technology transfer management in the emerging countries. Strong support for the construction of a Global Information Infrastructure (GII) has been expressed by leaders of the G7 countries as well as top management from major private sector players and corporate leaders. But the success of these will depend on *in situ* management practices. This is what determines the approach to such sectoral issues as technology management. In this, Africa particularly faces a precarious position while, again in contrast, the Pacific Rim illustrates an organic integration of Western technology, production methods and organization with oriental cultural nuances of cooperation, patience and endurance. These represent the extreme ends of the technology management practices in emerging countries.

3 Analysis of management practices

Africa has 13 per cent of the world's population, but produces only 1.7 per cent of the world's wealth. The continent's per capita gross domestic product (GDP) was US$620 in 1995 compared to the world average of US$4,880. Between 1985 and 1995 the per capita GDP was declining at the rate of 1.1 per cent per annum. This region faces a productivity crisis that could be exacerbated by the globalization trends founded on ICTs.

Existing training and management practice in Africa is based on an uncritical emulation and extrapolation of Western experiences and economic growth models. This disregards fundamental differences in socioeconomic, political and cultural constraints, conditions and circumstances that face an African manager. This uncritical transfer of management theories and techniques has contributed to organizational inefficiencies and ineffectiveness (see MANAGEMENT IN AFRICA).

By contrast, the Pacific Rim's success formula appears to have been first forged in Japan. This made it possible for other countries to transfer from Japan a tested consensus steeped in their shared traditions based on Confucian values that predominate in the region. South Korea, for example, chose the Japanese development path because it recognized that the Japanese had already adapted Western technology to Eastern social and political mores. In Africa, however, this need to identify, smooth over and compromise local and imported mores is barely recognized. The result has been wasteful irreconcilable conflicts and duplications. Investment in physical and hardware infrastructures, without due regard to procedural, regulatory, institutional and cultural infrastructures, gives sub-optimal returns.

Managing organizations requires a thorough understanding of the dynamic relationships between the internal socio-technical systems and the relationship of this to the external environment with which the system is in constant interaction. Since this external environment is different from that of Western industrialized countries, management theories and practices developed in that context have limited applicability. There is therefore a need to develop indigenous management theories and practices suitable to the emerging countries of Africa, as has happened in the East. This will be critical as this region seeks alternative approaches to the management of technology generally and that of the information and communications technologies in particular.

Dealing with the management of internal and external environments presupposes the existence of a system of management practice and employee behaviour conducive to acceptable levels of work motivation and performance. This comes from managerial and employee acceptance of values, attitudes and beliefs regarding work and organizations – or the corporate culture. Corporate culture influences the behaviour or practices of both management and workers. It represents an organizational reality that shapes both day-to-day practices and behaviours of members and macro-level organizational processes like designing management structures, choice and deployment of technology, and other strategic activities.

The environment in which the organization operates constantly influences this work culture. Organizational survival depends on its ability to respond adequately to external environmental forces by developing appropriate coping strategies that constitute the corporate culture. But this demands sensitivity to environmental constraints and opportunities.

The socio-cultural environment provides challenges for dealing with human resources within the organization and for dealing with the clients (customers or community served) outside of the organization. The socio-cultural environment of any given society determines collective norms and values, plus individual beliefs, attitudes and action preferences. Since an organization is an 'open system', cultural values from the environment are brought into the workplace and have a strong impact on the organization's work culture. Thus, organizational functioning depends on the behaviour and attitudes of people within a given society and their socio-cultural environment.

Studies and experiences confirm that knowledge and technology in one socio-cultural context does not necessarily work effectively in another location because of contextual variables determining organizational functioning and effectiveness. This is why organizational and developmental strategies that utilize the socio-cultural features of the given society are more desirable for overall organizational effectiveness. This is the lesson from the economic 'miracles' of the Far East and Japan. Success of organizations there is attributed to management styles, work attitudes and institutional structures immersed in local traditions. There is, therefore, a need to explore, search for and develop relevant management theories and practices based on local conditions and circumstances. This should begin with an explicit recognition of the different contexts of economic, political and culture faced by, for instance, managers in the emerging countries of Africa.

As an example, the degree of predictability of an environment should determine the ingredients of a corporate culture. Predictable environments make management responsibilities easier to execute and delegate than unpredictable ones. Despite the apparent complexity of developed countries, there is a high degree of predictability at critical points of management. This is because of the developed supporting structures and systems, including reliable supply of trained labour, developed capital markets, stable business–government relations and established legal and arbitration systems.

Management in emerging economies of Africa, on the other hand, faces resources non-availability. The result is incongruence between organizational means and goals. The political and legal climates are unstable and corporate norms underdeveloped. This results in lawless corrupt practices, negligence and dereliction of duty. This creates problems in obtaining required economic, technological and skilled human resources. The challenges faced by such a manager are qualitatively very different. The result is a management style characterized by lack of time management, entrepreneurship and risk taking and behaviour reflecting a lack of trust in 'the system'. The unpredictable and difficult environment has led to a management time perspective that excludes future-orientation and long-term planning. A predictable environment encourages future-orientation and long-term perspective approaches. This, in turn, favours planning. However, in an unpredictable environment, short-termism and present-orientation seem logical. But they do not favour planning. These dysfunctional coping strategies undermine organizational effectiveness. New management theories need to address this. This, however, calls for a clear and explicit definition of the prevailing socio-cultural environment. Japan, for example, acknowledged the disadvantage of lacking natural resources and therefore placed a critical emphasis on high-calibre human resources and information. South Korea also acknowledged its inadequacies and deliberately invested in skills and information pools crafted on its traditional mass education. The new theories must be founded on prevailing realities. The advent of ICTs and the new skills of information management can make a contribution in this effort.

4 Evaluation of prevailing realities

The 1990s witnessed the 'third wave of democratization' and changes in the way many emerging countries are governed. In this wave a large number of military and one-party dictatorships collapsed. The new wave brought with it increasing recognition of political equity as an important aspect of institution building. The steps being taken to craft political systems that reflect the new plural character of societies are also changing the management landscape. Thus hedging in politics is becoming less of an option for many managers. This is because changes are rolling back monolithic politics from the centre stage of national corporate life via privatization and productivity drives. These changes have been felt by most of the emerging countries.

These changes are particularly important for management practices in Africa. Since independence in the 1960s, African business and top management classes have extended their grip on national economies through lobbying for government contracts, import licences, subsidies, loans and preferential treatment. This alliance encouraged and nurtured complacency, corruption and inefficiency. The overwhelming dependence of the business and top management classes on the government and patronage of politicians led to fierce competition for control of the state. This in turn stifled alternative thinking, creativity and enterprise. It fostered the culture of patronage, authoritarianism and the 'total sum game' attitude of winner takes all. At corporate levels this was mirrored in accumulation of capital and static routine and maintenance skills rather than creativity and entrepreneurship. Thus national authoritarianism of governments was replicated in corporate management. Even in Gambia, Senegal and Botswana, where multi-party democracy was retained, the same picture prevailed. This has been attributed to the absence of 'alternation of power' between contending political parties. Power transfer could have supported moderation, compromise and even consensus, and a commitment to live with, and support, plurality, alternative thoughts and solutions. This nurtures a willingness to explore new avenues and practices. In the East, despite a similar lack of political democracy, negotiated consensus and compromises were pursued as a cultural norm where governments invested in infrastructures and business built national wealth.

In Africa, the dominance of politically driven 'total sum' attitudes makes routine management activities such as performance appraisal or personnel selection complex. This uncertainty arises from a wish and need to apply standard techniques for reasons other than performance. This reality is borne out by studies of private and public sector management practices in East and West Africa and in the Southern African Development Community (SADC). It has been confirmed by country-specific studies in Ghana, Kenya and Liberia. The picture reflects few differences in management styles and skills between the public and private sectors. It highlights an array of social, cultural and other obstacles to good management, including inappropriate skills, lack of appropriate resources and funding, shortage of the right staff and lack of motivation. A general lack of participatory decision making is observed. This weakens team spirit and leads to the missing of targets. Many African managers, for instance, admit that essential to managerial success is the building and maintenance of political connections. This is intended to influence policy decisions, the supply of resources and protection against inappropriate policies. This political support is earned through loyalty, not performance and productivity.

It is therefore obvious that Western social science assumptions of purposive and economic rationality in formal organizations have no universal application. Since organizations operate within specific environments, managers need to develop an understanding of these environments if their organizations are to survive and function effectively. Yet many managers in emerging countries, particularly in Africa, have no formal training on how to deal with their environments and have to depend on instincts, trial and error. This results in inefficiency, losses, budgetary burdens, poor products and services and minimal accomplishments. Information about organizational performance is, in such instances, not seriously collected and is sparse. Internal information systems often do not produce data concerning job performance. This results in a shortage of effectively managed organizations with the capacity to deliver development either as public sector environment enablers or as private sector competitive producers of value. This reality inevitably overflows into the management of technology. Managers need to be alerted to the implications of changes in the environment and the importance of the skills of collecting, recording, analysing and synthesizing information. The drive for relevance will require a revisit of indigenous traditions and culture in an effort to determine and define the socio-cultural priorities that drive the societies. The lessons can then be infused into formal organizational management practice. This approach has been a major contributor to the technology management success of the Far Eastern emerging countries.

5 Conclusion

Among the majority of the emerging countries with a poor track record in technology management, the problem is traceable to misconceptions of what constitutes technology as well as a mistaken assumption that Western technology is universal and free of cultural restrictions that can inhibit its transfer. There are several theoretical perceptions influencing strategies for managing the transfer and exploitation of technologies. However, it is critical to acknowledge differences in the various environments and to recognize the need to define the technological location to which the transfer is to be made. This involves an inventory of indigenous technologies and knowledge systems, other technologies already in place, and the levels of skills and history in dealing with these, as well as a comprehensive identification of options available globally. This should strengthen a nation's (or organization's) ability to negotiate for the best terms possible as well as identifying what best suits its needs.

The technology management philosophy underpinning this approach may be described as 'social shaping of technology'. This approach stresses the dynamic interaction between social forces that shape technological development and the technological innovations that affect social relations. It emphasizes the need to understand social forces that give rise to particular technologies, including the socio-economic, political, cultural, gender, geography and market forces. It is imperative for the technology manager to endeavour to understand what forces shape their evolution, and how these forces interact.

Proactive management rests upon the design of visions for a preferred future. It is the basis of sound strategic management. Technology managers should design alternative future courses and then decide on their desirability. Technological solutions can then be sourced and shaped to match these future visions. This is because the course of technological development is always shaped by human beings with particular interests and goals, and a certain (sometimes implicit) view of the future. This future needs to be examined openly and explicitly and not assumed. Management can then seek to influence the selection, design and deployment of new technologies in the ways that are most likely to further the vision and the goals. This approach has the potential to open up, squeeze out and recast abstract technical options and possibilities hidden in new technologies and submerged by the social specificity of the origins of the technologies. It circumvents the confines defined by a manufacturer's manuals which are set out in accordance with the compromises of the society of origin and which are, inevitably, always restrictive.

It is difficult to foresee the implications of the proliferation of ICTs on technology management in emerging countries. It is, however, important to give concerted attention to specifying the social and institutional changes needed to strengthen organizational and national potential for maximizing the possible benefits of this onset. The starting point must, nonetheless, remain an explicit statement of corporate or national goals, followed by an inventory of relevant internal capacities, before a search for and negotiation with better-inclined vendors can be undertaken.

RICHARD A. OUMA ONYANGO
UNIVERSITY OF BOTSWANA

Further reading

Bangwa, Y. (1998) 'Democratization, equity and stability: African politics and societies in the 1990s', *Discussion Paper DP 93*, UNRISD, Geneva. (A good discussion of the social, economic and political changes that have taken place in Africa in the 1990s.)

Blunt, P. and Jones, M.L. (1992) *Managing Organizations in Africa*, Berlin: Walter de Gruyter. (An insightful look at the peculiar features that face a manager in Africa specifically, but in an emerging country, generally.)

Enos, J.L. and Park, W.-H. (1988) *The Adoption and Diffusion of Imported Technology – The Case of Korea*, London: Croom Helm. (Discusses how South Korea successfully managed its technology transfer process. This is based on a sectoral study of four major industries focusing on very sophisticated latest techniques rather than intermediate technology pursued by many emerging countries at the time.)

Goonatilake, S. (1984) *Aborted Discovery – Science and Creativity in the Third World*, London: Zed Books. (Insightfully discusses pitfalls encountered by countries making efforts to attain the scientific capacity to support the management of technology, especially those countries outside the Western cultural orbit generally and the Eastern-oriental states in particular.)

Jaeger, A.M. and Kanungo, R.N. (eds) (1990) *Management in Developing Countries*, London: Routledge. (A good collection of various country and regional studies on management cultures in emerging countries. Constitutes important background reading in the field.)

Montgomery, J.D. (1987) 'Probing Managerial Behaviour – Image and Reality in Southern Africa', *World Development* 15(7): 911–29. (Explains some of the African peculiarities in management practice.)

Ouma-Onyango, R.A.O. (1997) *Information Resources and Technology Transfer Management in Developing Countries*, London: Routledge. (Consists of case studies that bring out technology management cultures in various emerging countries, comparing and contrasting African and oriental approaches.)

Onyango, R. (1990) 'Knowledge industries: aids to technological and industrial development in Africa' in B. Cronin and N. Tudor-Silovic (eds), *The Knowledge Industries – Levers to Economic and Social Development in the 1990s*, London: Aslib, pp. 5–29. (Discusses concepts that can define new approaches to technology management with the onset of the new information and communications technologies.)

Onyango, R.A.O. (1996) 'Indigenous technological capacity: can social intelligence help? A Kenyan case study' in B. Cronin (ed.), *Information, Development and Social Intelligence*, London: Taylor Graham, p.164–81. (Discusses the need for taking stock of indigenous knowledge systems and technologies while exploring technology choices in emerging countries. The focus is specifically on Kenya but global examples are referred to.)

Rahman, A. (1988) 'Science, technology and modernization' in J. Annerstedt and A. Jamison (eds), *From Research Policy to Social Intelligence – Essays for Stefan Dedijer*, London: Macmillan Press, pp. 7–22. (Discusses technology management approach in India based on national skills and natural resources strengths and questions the assumed 'universalities' of advanced technologies.)

Ventura, A.K. (1987) 'Jamaica's bauxite battle' in S. Dedijer and N. Jequier (eds), *Intelligence for Economic Development: An Inquiry into the Role of the Knowledge Industry*, Oxford: Berg Publishers, pp.111–27. (Analyses the management of technology negotiation process whose success was based on an objective inventory of national skills and knowledge as well as comprehensive knowledge of the technology at stake and the capacity of the multinational negotiating partners.)

See also: BUSINESS CULTURES, THE EMERGING COUNTRIES; MANAGEMENT IN AFRICA; MANAGEMENT IN THE EMERGING COUNTRIES; MANAGEMENT IN KENYA; MANAGEMENT IN NIGERIA; MANAGEMENT IN SOUTH AFRICA; MANUFACTURING IN THE EMERGING COUNTRIES

Related topics in the IEBM regional set: MANAGEMENT IN HONG KONG; MANAGEMENT IN JAPAN; MANAGEMENT IN SINGAPORE; MANAGEMENT IN SOUTH KOREA; MANAGEMENT IN TAIWAN; MANAGEMENT OF TECHNOLOGY IN ASIA PACIFIC; MANAGEMENT OF TECHNOLOGY IN EUROPE; MANAGEMENT OF TECHNOLOGY IN LATIN AMERICA; MANAGEMENT OF TECHNOLOGY IN NORTH AMERICA

Manufacturing in the emerging countries

1 Manufacturing capabilities in emerging countries
2 Economic environment and the manufacturing sector in emerging countries
3 Management and the manufacturing sector in emerging countries
4 Factors against the development of firms

Overview

An important trend in the global allocation of manufacturing activities in the 1990s is the shift of location from developed countries such as the USA, Europe and Japan to developing areas in Latin America, east and southeast Asia and Eastern Europe. Thus, some developing countries are able to attract economic activities within their national boundaries and benefit from the increasingly foot-loose location of world production by attracting multinational firms, thanks to the globalization of the world economy. This pattern occurs as developing countries are looking for the most effective means of economic development. The recent attention brought to the beneficial impact of the manufacturing sector on the overall economic results of the country has pushed host governments to adopt active industrial policies. Indeed, one of the main challenges for emerging countries is that of sustainable development, that is a development that provides economic, social and environmental benefits in the long term, having regard to the needs of living and future generations.

The global shift in manufacturing production is however leaving many developing countries behind. One must underline the poor performance of emerging countries in Africa and the Middle East and to a lesser extent in south Asia. After reviewing the overall manufacturing performance of selected emerging countries in Africa, south Asia and the Middle East, the environment within which the breakdown of national economic activity is designed will be emphasized before giving a description of the current managerial situation in these countries.

1 Manufacturing capabilities in emerging countries

During the last two or three decades, considerable efforts have been taken by most developing countries to promote manufacturing industries within their economies (see ECONOMIES OF THE EMERGING COUNTRIES). Industrialization was seen as an engine of growth, because of its linkages to other activities and its potential to offer relief from unemployment, low wages levels and balance of payments difficulties. Whereas in the 1950s, most emerging countries adopted inward-looking, growth strategy based on import substitution industrialization with high levels of protection, since the mid-1970s or earlier for some countries, outward-looking strategies of export-led growth have been adopted. Although such policies have not led to the expected

Table 1 Structure of output

	Gross domestic product US$ million		Agriculture value added % of GDP		Industry value added % of GDP		Manufacturing value added % of GDP		Services value added % of GDP	
	1980	1996	1980	1996	1980	1996	1980	1996	1980	1996
Africa										
Algeria	42345	45699	10	13	54	48	9	8	36	38
Cameroon	6741	9252	29	40	23	22	9	10	48	39
Kenya	7265	9222	33	29	21	16	13	10	47	55
Nigeria	64202	31995	21	43	41	25	8	8	39	31
Tanzania	...	5838	...	48	...	21	...	7	...	31
Uganda	1245	6115	72	46	4	16	4	8	23	39
Zimbabwe	5355	7550	14	14	36	28	25	19	50	59
Asia										
Bangladesh	12950	31824	50	30	16	18	11	10	34	52
India	172321	356027	38	28	26	29	18	20	36	43
Nepal	1946	4456	62	42	12	23	4	10	26	35
Pakistan	23690	64846	30	26	25	25	16	17	46	50
Sri Lanka	4024	13912	28	22	30	25	18	16	43	52
Middle East										
Egypt	22913	67691	18	17	37	32	12	24	45	51
Ethiopia	5179	5993	56	55	12	10	8	..	32	36
Iran	92664	...	18	25	32	34	9	14	50	40
Jordan	3962	7343	8	5	28	30	13	16	64	64
Saudi Arabia	156487	126266	1	...	81	...	5	...	18	...
Sudan	6760	...	34	...	14	...	7	...	52	...
Syrian A. Rep.	13062	17587	20	...	23	...	...	...	56	...
Yemen	...	6016	...	18	...	49	...	11	...	34
Zambia	3884	3388	14	18	41	41	18	29	44	42
World										
World	10704631	28583721	—	—	—	—	—	—	—	—
Low & middle income	3061860	5924712	18	15	42	34	22	22	40	51
East Asia & Pacific	465223	1553518	28	20	44	44	32	33	28	36
Europe & central Asia	—	1118817	—	11	—	36	—	—	—	53
Latin America & Caribbeans	758650	1875727	10	10	40	33	27	21	50	57
Middle East & north Africa	459114	—	12	—	48	—	9	—	40	—
south Asia	219283	480044	38	28	25	28	17	19	37	44
Sub-Saharan Africa	264750	305131	22	24	35	30	14	15	43	46
High income	7810607	22756455	3	—	36	—	24	—	61	—

Source: Data compiled from The World Bank, World Development Indicators 1998

development of the manufacturing sector in all cases, they seem to have recently produced the desired effect on some countries' growth rates.

Most emerging countries in South Asia and the Middle East have achieved high growth rates over the past two decades. Table 2 shows Asian emerging countries' growth rates were above the world average (2.2 per cent) in the 1980s and 1990s, with average annual rates between 4.3 per cent for Bangladesh and 5.8 per cent for India between 1990 and 1996. In the Middle East growth has been substantial in the 1990s, but was less than the world average in the 1980s. Jordan, Sudan and the Syrian Arab Republic have experienced outstanding growth rates of respectively 7.6 per cent, 6.8 per cent and 7.4 per cent over 1990–96. Such high growth levels have not been noticeable in African emerging countries, where recent growth was negative for

Table 2 Growth of output, 1980–90 and 1990–96 (Percentage)

	Gross domestic product		Agriculture		Industry		Manufacturing		Services	
	average annual percentage growth		average annual percentage growth		average annual percentage growth		average annual percentage growth		average annual percentage growth	
	1980–90	1990–96	1980–90	1990–96	1980–90	1990–96	1980–90	1990–96	1980–90	1990–96
Africa										
Algeria	2.8	0.6	4.6	3	2.3	–0.4	3.3	–8.9	2.9	0.8
Cameroon	3.3	–1.0	2.1	2.6	5.9	–5.2	11.8	–2.1	2.6	–0.9
Kenya	4.2	1.9	3.3	0.6	3.9	1.8	4.9	2.5	4.9	3.5
Nigeria	1.8	2.6	3.3	2.4	–1.1	0.5	0.7	–1.5	4.4	4.8
Tanzania	...	...	...	...	...	...	...	...	...	...
Uganda	3.1	7.2	2.3	4	6	12.2	4	13.4	3	8.6
Zimbabwe	3	1.3	2.4	4.5	3	–2.1	2.9	–3.7	2.5	2.5
Asia										
Bangladesh	4.3	4.3	2.7	1.2	4.9	7.2	2.8	7.3	5.7	5.7
India	5.8	5.8	3.1	3.1	7.1	6.8	7.4	7.5	6.7	7
Nepal	4.6	5.1	4	1.9	6	8.5	3.7	12	4.8	6.9
Pakistan	6.3	4.6	4.3	3.8	7.3	5.5	7.7	5.5	6.8	5
Sri Lanka	4.2	4.8	2.2	1.7	4.6	6.6	6.3	8.8	4.7	6.1
Middle East										
Egypt	5.3	3.7	2.7	2.8	5.2	3.9	...	4.3	6.6	3.4
Ethiopia	2.3	3.9	1.4	2.3	1.8	3	2	3.3	3.1	6.7
Iran	1.5	4.2	4.5	4.8	3.3	3.8	4.5	4.6	–0.3	4.2
Jordan	2.6	7.6	6.8	–3.7	1.7	10.9	0.5	10.8	2.1	6.3
Saudi Arabia	–1.2	1.7	13.4	...	–2.3	...	7.5	...	–1.2	—
Sudan	0.6	6.8	0	...	2.8	...	3.7	...	0.4	...
Syrian A. Rep.	1.5	7.4	–0.6	...	6.6	...	...	...	0.4	...
Yemen	...	2.8	...	2.9	...	2.9	...	...	...	2.7
Zambia	0.8	–1.1	3.6	0.5	1	–3.2	4	–1.9	0.1	0.5
World										
World	3.1	2.2	2.8	1.7	3.3	1.6	3.6	1.4	3.3	2.3
Low & middle income	3.1	2.9	3.2	2.8	4.3	...	4.5	...	3.5	4.6
East Asia & Pacific	7.7	10.2	4.8	4	8.9	14.5	9.7	15	8.9	8.3
Europe & central Asia	2.9	–5.4	...	...	...	...	...	...	...	...
Latin America & Caribbeans	1.8	3.2	2	2.5	1.4	2.8	1.2	2.6	1.9	3.8
Middle East & north Africa	0.4	2.6	4.6	3.2	1.3	...	...	2.7	1.2	...
South Asia	5.7	5.6	3.2	3	6.9	6.7	7.2	7.4	6.6	6.7
Sub–Saharan Africa	1.7	2	1.8	2.1	1.1	0.9	1.3	0.8	2.2	2
High income	3.2	2	2.2	0.8	3.2	0.7	3.5	0.4	3.3	1.9

Source: Data compiled from The World Bank, World Development Indicators 1998

Cameroon and very low for Algeria, Kenya and Zimbabwe. Uganda is an exception and has achieved one of the highest growth rates in all three emerging areas with 7.2 per cent over 1990–96.

The structure of output of the emerging countries under study appears in Table 1 for 1980 and for 1996. Manufacturing represents 33 per cent of the Gross Domestic Product (GDP) in east Asia and Pacific countries, 21 per cent in the Latin America and Caribbean, but only 19 per cent in south Asia and 15 per cent in sub-Saharan Africa in 1996. In emerging African countries, manufacturing represents 10 per cent or less of the GDP, which is the lowest level compared to other emerging countries in Asia and in the Middle East. India, Pakistan and Sri Lanka have respective shares of 20 per cent, 17 per cent and 16 per cent in 1996. Such shares have not increased substantially since 1980. In the Middle East, data are often unavailable, however, we can see that in both Egypt and Zambia, manufacturing represents a quarter or more of the GDP. Whereas there is no substantial increase in the share of manufacturing in the GDP of emerging countries between 1980 and 1996, the services sector has increased in many of these countries. Agriculture represents a substantial share in GDP with more than 40 per cent in Cameroon, Nigeria, Tanzania, Uganda, Nepal and Ethiopia. Agriculture is most important in African emerging countries, least in the Middle East.

Looking at growth rates by sector, similar patterns are noticeable. Worldwide, the whole of the Asia Pacific region has achieved the highest growth rates in manufacturing, with 15 per cent annual growth over 1990–96 in East Asia and the Pacific and 7.4 per cent in South Asia, against only 1.3 per cent for sub-Saharan Africa. Growth has been slow in most sectors in African emerging countries, except in Uganda, which has witnessed a 13.4 per cent average annual growth over 1990–96 in the manufacturing sector, against 4 per cent over 1980–90. Developing Asia has achieved impressive growth rates in both manufacturing and the services sector in the past two decades. However, the base level is low in most cases and the manufacturing sector is not diversified. Growth rates in the manufacturing sector were much higher in the 1990s, above 7 per cent for Bangladesh, India and Sri Lanka and a spectacular 12 per cent for Nepal. The highest growth rates in the Middle East took place in the services sector. Jordan however, saw its manufacturing sector increasing by an annual rate of 10.8 per cent between 1990 and 1996.

In terms of employment, the industry represents a very small proportion of the total workforce in African emerging countries with less than 10 per cent of the total, except for Algeria, where industry accounts for 33 per cent of the workforce. The agricultural sector remains the first employer in emerging countries, occupying 93 per cent of total employment in Nepal, 88 per cent in Ethiopia or 86 per cent in Uganda (see Table 3).

Apart from African countries, where they account for one third of the workers, women still represent a minority share in the workforce, especially in the Middle East countries. Illiteracy rates are still high in emerging countries. In Nepal, where 93 per cent of the employment is in agriculture, 73 per cent of the population is illiterate. In most other countries the illiteracy rate is higher than 30 per cent of the population.

Data on the structure of manufacturing are particularly difficult to gather in emerging countries, especially for the period of the 1990s. As appears in Table 4, the most important manufacturing sub-sectors are 'food, beverages and tobacco' and 'textiles and clothing'. 'Food, beverages and tobacco' accounted for at least one-fifth of the manufacturing activity in all emerging economies, reaching 56 per cent in Cameroon, 44 per cent in Zambia, 34 per cent in Kenya and 32 per cent in Pakistan in the 1980s. Where data are available, a similar pattern occurs in the 1990s. The food sub-sector is the major manufacturing activity in Kenya, Cameroon, Zimbabwe, Nepal and Zambia. In Nepal, the textiles and clothing sector represents a third of the manufacturing activity of the country.

Merchandise exchanges in the developing countries do not necessarily follow the world trend. The World Bank Indicators show that the value of merchandise exports has more than doubled since 1980, while manufactured exports have more than tripled. Traditional exports of primary commodities remain important for many developing countries, while manufactured goods increasingly dominate world trade. On the other hand, the majority of imports in developing countries are imports of manufactured

Table 3 Employment profile in African, Asian emerging countries and countries from the Middle East, 1994 (percentage)

	Urban Pop. (1995)	Workers	Employment				Illiteracy (1995)
		Men	Women	Agriculture	Industry	Services	
Africa							
Algeria	54	90	10	18	33	49	38
Cameroon	43	68	32	79	7	14	37
Kenya	26	61	37	81	7	12	22
Nigeria	38	65	35	48	7	45	43
Tanzania	23	53	47	85	5	10	32
Uganda	12	60	40	86	4	10	38
Zimbabwe	31	67	33	71	8	21	15
Asia							
Bangladesh	17	59	41	59	13	28	62
India	26	76	24	62	11	27	48
Nepal	13	68	32	93	0	6	73
Pakistan	34	87	13	47	20	33	62
Sri Lanka	22	73	27	49	21	30	10
Middle East							
Egypt	44	90	10	26	21	37	49
Iran	58	81	19	31	26	44	28
Saudi Arabia	79	93	7	48	14	37	37
Sudan	–	77	23	72	5	23	54
Yemen	32	88	12	63	11	26	–
Jordan	70	89	11	10	26	64	13
Ethiopia	–	64	34	88	2	40	65
Zambia	42	70	30	38	8	54	22

Note: Data on the Gulf States and on Syria were not provided

goods. The impact will vary according to the type of goods, which can be imported capital or consumption goods.

A clear distinction arises when comparing emerging countries in various regions. While the share of manufactures in merchandise exports of emerging countries in Africa and the Middle East is minimal, except for a few countries, that of emerging countries in Asia is very high. 99 per cent of total exports from Nepal is constituted of manufactures, followed by 84 per cent for Pakistan and just above 70 per cent for India and Sri Lanka in 1996.

Import figures prove the high dependence of emerging countries from Africa and the Middle East on external sources for manufactured goods. 79 per cent of Saudi Arabian imports are imports of manufactures and 73 per cent for Zimbabwe. Asian countries distinguish themselves with a smaller dependence on manufactured products and a greater variety in the type of goods imported.

Table 4 Structure of manufacturing, 1980–90 and 1990–96 (percentage)

	Food, beverages and tobacco		Textiles and clothing		Machinery and transport equipment		Chemicals		Other manufacturing	
	% of total value added		% of total value added		% of total value added		% of total value added		% of total value added	
	1980–90	1990–96	1980–90	1990–96	1980–90	1990–96	1980–90	1990–96	1980–90	1990–96
Africa										
Algeria	27	13	18	14	10	15	3	5	43	54
Cameroon	56	31	9	8	4	1	3	3	29	56
Kenya	34	44	12	9	15	10	9	9	30	29
Nigeria	21	...	13	...	13	...	13	...	39	...
Tanzania	23	...	33	...	8	...	6	...	30	...
Uganda	...	...	...	...	...	...	...	...	...	...
Zimbabwe	23	38	17	13	8	11	9	3	42	36
Asia										
Bangladesh	24	...	43	...	4	...	16	...	14	...
India	9	11	21	13	25	25	14	19	30	32
Nepal	...	35	...	34	...	3	...	4	...	23
Pakistan	32	...	22	...	9	...	12	...	25	...
Sri Lanka	...	...	...	...	...	...	...	...	...	...
Middle East										
Egypt	19	...	30	...	11	...	9	...	31	...
Ethiopia	...	...	...	...	...	...	...	...	...	...
Iran	...	...	...	...	...	...	...	...	...	...
Jordan	23	29	7	6	1	6	7	14	62	44
Saudi Arabia	...	...	...	...	...	...	...	...	...	...
Sudan	...	...	...	...	...	...	...	...	...	...
Syrian A. Rep.	...	...	...	...	...	...	...	...	...	...
Yemen	...	...	...	...	...	...	...	...	...	...
Zambia	44	44	13	10	9	5	9	16	25	25

Source: Data compiled from The World Bank, World Development Indicators 1998

2 Economic environment and the manufacturing sector in emerging countries

Substantial lack of data

A major hindrance in the description of the manufacturing sectors in emerging economies is the substantial lack of data. In most of the countries under study, the existing statistical base pertaining to the manufacturing sector does not permit one to readily assess the dynamics of the sector in terms of its size. According to the World Bank, its own figures have to be taken with caution. National accounts in developing countries often include unreported economic activity in the informal or secondary economy (see ECONOMIES OF THE EMERGING COUNTRIES). Such data constraints concern the agricultural production as well as services and the industry. The industry should be regularly measured through censuses and surveys of firms. However, such methods are not always reliable in developing countries, and many results are extrapolated in the World Bank data. Other potential problems in data collection may

Table 5 Structure of merchandise exports and imports, 1980 and 1996 (percentage, US$ millions)

	Merchandise exports US$ millions		Manufactures % of total		Merchandise Imports US$ millions		Manufactures % of total	
	1980	1996	1980	1996	1980	1996	1980	1996
Africa								
Algeria	15634	12609	0	4	10524	8372	72	65
Cameroon	1321	1758	4	8	1538	1204	78	67
Kenya	1313	2203	12	...	2590	3480	56	...
Nigeria	25057	15610	0	...	13408	6433	76	...
Tanzania	528	828	14	...	1211	1642	63	...
Uganda	465	568	1	...	417	725	65	...
Zimbabwe	433	2094	36	30	193	2808	73	73
Asia								
Bangladesh	740	3297	68	...	1980	6898	58	...
India	7511	32325	59	74	13819	36055	39	54
Nepal	94	358	30	99	226	664	73	47
Pakistan	2588	9266	48	84	5350	11812	54	57
Sri Lanka	1043	4097	19	73	2035	5028	52	75
Middle East								
Egypt	3046	3534	11	32	4860	13020	59	60
Ethiopia	424	494	0	...	721	1492	64	...
Iran	13804	22102	5	...	9330	13926	72	...
Jordan	402	1466	34	49	2394	4293	61	61
Saudi Arabia	109113	58177	1	...	29957	27764	82	79
Sudan	584	468	1	...	1499	1439	60	...
Syrian Rep.	2108	3980	7	...	4124	6399	55	...
Yemen	23	4538	47	1	1853	3443	63	59
Zambia	1330	1020	16	...	1100	1106	71	...

Source: Data compiled from The World Bank, World Development Indicators 1998

include the difference in records, the fact that the industrial production may be organized not in firms, but in unincorporated or owner-operated ventures that are not captured by surveys aimed at the formal sector.

Government policies and the manufacturing sector

The world economy is undergoing changes in technological and market conditions which could influence the position of emerging counties and the role they play in the world market (see PERSPECTIVES ON GLOBALIZATION, BIG BUSINESS AND THE EMERGING COUNTRIES). The ability of emerging countries to succeed in this changing world economy will depend on a number of factors.

Macroeconomic policies and especially policies related to the exchange rate seem to have played a substantial role in the emerging economies' industrialization and development experiences in the 1970s and 1980s, mostly because the macroeconomic environment in the developing countries was highly unstable. In Africa, two major oil price shocks, major global recessions, large international interest rate variations and the debt crisis all created severe external pressures. Generally, domestic savings available for productive investment were reduced. Endogenous pressures comprised inappropriate domestic policies, including incentive structures, and mismanagement of public resources. For this reason, industry has been identified as having been responsible for much of the waste of resources and a cure has been sought in diverting resources from industry to other sectors such as agriculture. This, in part, explains why the manufacturing sector is less developed in this region than in others, although governments' attitude has recently changed putting more emphasis on the development of a local industry.

On top of affecting the macroeconomic environment of their country, governments play an important role in the long-run build-up of capacity to undertake efficient industrial production, not only through infrastructural and educational investment, but also through support for R&D, encouragement of technological innovation, provision of finance, and a variety of other 'industrial policies'.

Industrial growth in the 1970s and 1980s was driven, above all, by expanding domestic demand, and increasingly in the 1980s by exports. Therefore, trade policy is commonly seen as a fundamental determinant of economic performance. Liberal policies regarding the inflow of services, technology and capital are also recommended appropriate policies. Analyses of the East Asian successes have called attention to the benefits of selective governmental actions in trade and other areas. As mentioned earlier, many developing countries applied inward-orientated policies in the 1950s and 1960s, which led in the 1970s and 1980s to very small shares of the overall expansion of manufacturing output. Industrial growth associated with overall domestic demand expansion took place in industries that were developed in an earlier import-substituting period. Some of these industries were internationally competitive. Others, however, had originally been established with the help of protection against imports.

In emerging countries, the lack of stability in macroeconomic, industrial and trade policies has therefore been a hindrance to the creation of a local manufacturing base. Only recently have governments in south Asia and Africa adopted more long-term objectives.

Colonial heritage

Countries in the African region inherited a weak industrial base at independence, geared in a typical 'colonial' pattern towards agro-processing activities for export and simple consumer items for the home market.

Public manufacturing enterprises

In many developing countries, public manufacturing enterprises contribute a large proportion of industrial output and are the backbone of the industrialization process (see MANAGEMENT IN THE EMERGING COUNTRIES). Public manufacturing enterprises also contribute substantially to investment, and often state-owned enterprises account for at least a quarter of capital formation. It is not so everywhere. In Sri Lanka, the role of the private sector in industrial production, employment, and the number of establishments far outweighs the public sector. In terms of number of units, value added and employment, private industry clearly dominates the industrial sector.

Ideology, lack of a sufficiently strong private sector, and non-commercial objectives are common reasons for the existence of state enterprises (see BUSINESS CULTURES, THE EMERGING COUNTRIES). For instance, the manufacturing sector has experienced a decline in productivity since the revolution in Ethiopia. The causes are related to the economic dislocation caused by the revolution and the government's dirigiste policies introduced following the 1974 revolution. In 1975, the ruling military government, also known as the Deng Committee nationalized most of the major industries and financial institutions. Most manufacturing activities were exclusively reserved for the state with activities such as entertainment and small-scale food processing and marketing left to the private sector. Private investment could only occur in areas reserved to the private sector.

The performance of public enterprises has often been disappointing, and public firms are generally judged to be less efficient than their counterparts in the private sector. Managers of public firms often lack adequate experience in the management of commercially viable units, and appointments are frequently based on political considerations. Public managers also frequently lack clear objectives, they are seldom evaluated and do not receive incentives to improve their performance. Some exceptions can be found like the 'signalling system', which was installed in Pakistan to monitor performance and provide incentives for improved management of public manufacturing firms.

Role of foreign direct investment

Despite the lack of foreign investment in many emerging countries, they are likely to assume greater importance in the developing countries' industrialization processes as the emphasis in policy discussions shifts to productivity improvement and 'keeping up' with an increasingly integrated world (see ECONOMIES IN THE EMERGING MARKETS). The need for foreign private investment to supplement local capital resources, technology, access to export markets and management know-how has long been recognized in many emerging countries. During the last decades especially, steps have been taken to encourage foreign investment in African and Asian countries, with notably the creation of industrial processing zones. Foreign investors often take a big share in the manufacturing activities of host countries, in terms of both the number of firms and aggregate equity investment. Among the investors in Asian emerging economies, Hong Kong, Singapore and other newly industrialized or industrializing countries occupy predominant positions. Foreign participation in total export is often high. The share of local firms has decreased due to the tendency of the domestic market orientation of these firms. Foreign firms can generally be found in labour-intensive low-technology products such as non-metallic mineral products, rubber goods, footwear and toys. It is unlikely in the short term that the emerging economies under study in this chapter can attract foreign investment in higher-technology areas.

3 Management and the manufacturing sector in emerging countries

In most emerging economies, the majority of manufacturing companies are small and medium-sized firms. In Sri Lanka, the highest proportion of industrial units (86 per cent) have less then 5 employees, and overall, 99 per cent of industrial units fall into the 'less than 50 persons' category. Small industries are generally labour-intensive, and very often their capital to labour ratio is a far inferior to that of manufacturing as a whole.

Typically, the two types of industries include a modern and a cottage industry. The cottage industries sector manufactures, jewellery, handicrafts and the like, while the modern industries are dominated by primary-processing industries, textiles and chemicals. Consumption goods' manufacturing has increased substantially over the past two decades.

Most products are imitations of foreign products, usually products, which were being imported and are now manufactured domestically. Competition in the product market is largely based on price and quality. Although emerging countries produce a wide range of products, they are generally of a considerably lower quality, and often of considerably higher price to that of foreign alternatives. Production has often survived through either market protection, or by serving a separate segment of the market of that met by imports.

There is a substantial lack of local investment, regardless of the sectors. Local firms rarely invest in new plants and equipment or in upgrading their technology. Therefore, older and simpler technology is found in emerging economies. They have an advantage, in that local skills can operate and maintain such equipment more efficiently.

The production structure is such in most emerging countries, that many of the industrial goods currently produced there are clearly not competitive in international terms. Manufacturing firms primarily produce for their domestic market. When they do export, it is usually to nearby countries, and sometimes, smaller volumes to international markets. Exported products generally derive their comparative advantages from access to natural resources. In Asia, the influence of foreign subsidiaries is greater, and export of a variety of labour-intensive products originates mostly from locally based foreign firms.

The strategy of exporting arises for some firms in response to developments in their domestic markets. Most enterprises start by exporting to regional markets, mainly in countries which did not have similar industries.

The presence of MNEs is beneficial for the development of quality managerial and entrepreneurial personnel. In other cases, employees of firms with international links learn management skills through their contact with foreign suppliers and customers. In most emerging countries, the local educational system remains inadequate and insufficiently developed.

The typical local private exporting firms started as family trading enterprises and later moved into the manufacture of products, which were related to their earlier trade activities. Contacts and connections are therefore very useful.

The organization of production is usually very simple, because the majority of local manufacturing firms are small in size. Some firms that engage in exports undertake continuous investments in technology, training and marketing and therefore will also change the way they organize production.

The continued reliance on imported raw materials makes it difficult to sustain the pace of development in the context of foreign exchange shortages in emerging countries. The registered manufacturing sector is largely geared to the use of imported inputs and the pace of industrial development is heavily determined by the availability of these supplies. The lack of alternative good suppliers in the home market is the primary reason for this high dependence.

The regional distribution pattern of private sector industries often shows an overwhelming concentration mainly around major urban areas, such as the Colombo Metropolitan Area in Sri Lanka, which hosts more than 40 per cent of all industrial units.

4 Factors against the development of firms

Firms in the emerging countries have difficulties with changing technology. Also they experience problems in terms of reliability of their supply and the quality of the local inputs. A substitution of local inputs for imported inputs has been one innovative step taken to upgrade their production. The low quality of inputs and the unreliability of supply are, therefore, incentives to use imported inputs. Moreover, firms show a lack of specialization. While supplying the domestic markets, firms adopt the diversification strategy as a growth path where domestic markets for particular products are very small. They therefore lack competitive advantage in particular products. Inter-firm linkages are still very limited, there is little subcontracting of local procurement of manufactured inputs. Unfortunately, foreign firms still generate little positive spill over. In comparison with higher income developing countries, there has been relatively little development of inter-industry linkages through the production of basic industrial intermediates, with a low share of heavy industry intermediates and capital goods in the industrial structure. Finally, problems in infrastructure are an obstacle to attaining and maintaining competitiveness. Expensive, sporadic and unreliable transport and communication and water systems are a serious impediment to the development of competitive local firms. Poor telecommunications and constant power and water interruption cause major disruption in the manufacturing process, and the poor transportation support is an additional cause for unreliable deliveries.

To sum up, recent growth figures show the high potential for emerging economies to develop and take advantage of the globalization of the world economy. However, many difficulties and bottle-necks remain in the expansion of the manufacturing sector.

AXÈLE GIROUD
UNIVERSITY OF BRADFORD

Further reading

(References cited in the text marked *)

Asian Development Bank (1996) *Asian Development Bank Annual Report 1996*, Manila. (Annual report on the multilateral development finance institution engaged in promoting the economic and social progress of its members, published with special themes.)

Bakht, Z. and Batthacharya, D. (1991) 'Investment, employment and value added in Bangladesh manufacturing sector in 1980s: evidence and estimate', *Bangladesh Development Studies* 19(1/2): 1–50. (Reviews the evidence on investment and value added manufacturing sector in Bangladesh in the 1980s, with an analysis of both public and private sectors.)

Bigsten, A. (1997) *Investment in Africa's Manufacturing Sector: A Four Country Panel Data Analysis*, University of Oxford, Centre for the Study of African Economies working paper series, WPS/97-11. (Comments on African manufacturing facilities and firms' investment with case studies on Kenya, Cameroon, Zimbabwe, Ghana.)

Chowdhury, R. and Kirkpatrick, C. (1994) *Project Assistance for Export Marketing in Developing Countries: An Impact Evaluation Study for the Indian Manufacturing Sector*, University of Bradford. Development and Project Planning Centre new series discussion paper, No. 50. (Provides a detailed assessment of an aid-funded project which was intended to promote the export growth of manufactures in India, through the provision of technical and marketing assistance to selected firms in a number of different manufacturing activities.)

Dias, S. (1989) 'Study of the structure and the locational pattern manufacturing industries in Sri Lanka', *Singaporean Journal of Tropical Geography* 10: 119–21. (Describes the role of private and public sectors in the development of manufacturing industries in Sri Lanka.)

The Economist Survey (1998) 'A survey of manufacturing', *The Economist* 20 June. (Reviews recent changes in the world manufacturing outlook and the role of new manufacturing countries.)

Helleiner, G.K. (1994) *Trade Policy and Industrialization in Turbulent Times*, London and New York: Routledge. (On industrial promotion in developing countries, notably through commerce, and commercial and economic policies.)

Helleiner, G.K. (1995) *Manufacturing for Export in the Developing World*, London and New York: Routledge. (On the role of export in the developing world and commercial policies with case studies on Chile, Colombia, Mexico, Turkey and Tanzania.)

Instituto del Tercer Mundo (1997) *The World Guide: a View of the South 1997/98*, Oxford: New Internationalist Publications Ltd. (Information on 217 countries, maps, graphs and statistics and in-depth description of key global issues.)

Krishna, K.L. (1991) 'Technical efficiency in Bangladesh manufacturing industries', *Bangladesh Development Studies*. 19(1/2): 89–106.

South Centre (1997) *Foreign Direct Investment, Development and the New Global Economic Order: a Policy Brief for the South*, Geneva. (Defines policy issues related to inward foreign investment to show how countries can benefit from such investment while remaining attractive locations.)

UNCTAD (1997) *World Investment Report 1997: Transnational Corporations, Market Structure and Competition Policy*, Geneva: United Nations. (Annual report on world investment trends with an emphasis on transnational corporations, market structure and competition policy.)

UNCTC (1990) *New Approaches to Best-Practice Manufacturing: the Role of Transnational Corporations and Implications for Developing Countries*, New York: United Nations. (Report on the role of transnational corporations in enhancing manufacturing capabilities in developing countries.)

Wangwe, S.M (1995) *Exporting Africa: Technology, Trade, and Industrialization in Sub-Saharan Africa*, London; New York: Routledge. (On export performance, business enterprises and international competition in sub-Saharan African countries with case studies on Zimbabwe, Nigeria, Tanzania, Kenya, Ivory Coast and Mauritius.)

Weiss, J. (1991) 'Rehabilitation of manufacturing in sub-Saharan Africa: some macroeconomic issues', in Kirkpatrick, C. (ed.), *Project Rehabilitation in Developing Countries*, London: Routledge, pp. 175–96. (Focuses on the need for market rehabilitation through macroeconomic reforms and domestic market expansion in sub-Saharan Africa.)

World Bank (1998) *World Development Indicators 1998*, The World Bank Publications. (Key world indicators, which include a world view, statistics on people, the environment, the economy, the states and markets, and on global links.)

World Market Research Centre (1997) *World Markets in 1998: Infrastructure Development – Asia*, 6th Annual World Economic Development Congress, The McGraw-Hill Companies, Inc. (Reviews various projects of infrastructure development in Asian countries.)

Wubneh, M. (1990) 'State control and manufacturing labour productivity in Ethiopia', *Journal of Developing Areas* 24: 311–95. (Draws on the need to evaluate long-term development strategies to establish a viable economic system in Ethiopia. It analyses the productivity of the manufacturing sector by testing the structural change in the manufacturing production function between 1960–74 and 1975–84.)

See also: BUSINESS CULTURES, THE EMERGING COUNTRIES; ECONOMIES OF THE EMERGING COUNTRIES; HUMAN RESOURCE MANAGEMENT IN THE EMERGING COUNTRIES; MANAGEMENT OF TECHNOLOGY IN THE EMERGING COUNTRIES; PERSPECTIVES ON GLOBALIZATION, BIG BUSINESS AND THE EMERGING COUNTRIES

Related topics in the IEBM regional set: MANAGEMENT OF TECHNOLOGY IN ASIA PACIFIC; MANAGEMENT OF TECHNOLOGY IN EUROPE; MANAGEMENT OF TECHNOLOGY IN LATIN AMERICA; MANAGEMENT OF TECHNOLOGY IN NORTH AMERICA; MANUFACTURING IN ASIA PACIFIC; MANUFACTURING IN EUROPE; MANUFACTURING IN LATIN AMERICA; MANUFACTURING IN NORTH AMERICA

Marketing in the emerging countries

1 **Introduction**
2 **Context**
3 **Analysis**
4 **Conclusion**

Overview

This entry looks at the challenges and opportunities for marketers when examining emerging nations of the world. Emerging nations are those developing countries with the potential to be major world markets for products and services but which have not yet reached their full potential or economic development. After a general discussion of the marketing opportunities/challenges in emerging countries, three specific country examples are presented (Singapore, China and Nigeria) to illustrate the wide diversity in marketing, consumer income levels and issues facing marketers in emerging nations. The nature of marketing practices is discussed for each of these diverse illustrative countries, and a series of practical suggestions are provided for foreign marketers building upon commonalities that are seen across emerging nations. Finally, a series a suggestions are provided for the reader interested in knowing more about marketing in emerging markets in general or in the illustrative country examples provided.

1 Introduction

There is a great attraction for marketers to establish positions in the emerging countries of the world (see PERSPECTIVES ON GLOBALIZATION, BIG BUSINESS AND THE EMERGING COUNTRIES). It is easy to understand the lure in Asia of 1.2 billion potential customers in China and over 900 million in India, or the sophistication and high discretionary income of the Singaporean and South Korean markets. The continent of Africa presents enormous potential for global marketers with the emerging economic purchasing power of South Africa or the growing interest in imported brands in the highly-populated nation of Nigeria. The recent global competitive successes for the agricultural products of Chile make it an attractive player in South America with a swiftly increasing purchasing power along with the enormous growth in consumer sophistication represented by Brazil. Even the Eastern European nations of Hungary, Poland and the Czech Republic have the potential to be significant players in the world marketplace. The desire for such high-tech products as cellular telephones, VCRs, colour televisions and laptop computers can readily be seen from Beijing and Capetown to Rio and Budapest. Worldwide brands are regularly seen in promotions in these rapidly-developing markets. McDonald's Golden Arches and the image of Colonel Sanders on Kentucky Fried Chicken advertisements are easily visible and recognizable in many emerging markets. Almost any type of marketing tool or approach is available in these markets from outdoor billboards to telemarketing. Even direct marketing has established a toehold in emerging nations as evidenced by the success of Mary Kay Cosmetics and Avon. All ranges of sales promotion tools can also be seen from premiums to free samples, contests/sweepstakes, coupons and trading stamps. Emerging markets are indeed attractive, and the key for marketers is to gain footholds in these markets before they become the intensely-competitive markets that they will inevitably become as their economic development plateaus are reached and their markets become saturated.

2 Context

Nature of emerging markets

Emerging nations, by nature, are countries that have not yet fully reached their economic potential (see ECONOMIES OF THE EMERGING COUNTRIES). They are countries which stand out from the rest of the developing nations of the world due to their enormous growth potential. Developed nations (e.g. the USA, Japan and Germany) look to far slower economic growth rates during the next several decades, and their intensely competitive and saturated markets make them poor prospects for international marketers. As a result, savvy internationally-focused marketers will turn to the emerging markets of the world with their promising growth opportunities and burgeoning consumer product/service markets to gain competitive positions and enhance their chances of long-term success and profitability.

While many developing countries are advancing economically, the emerging nations are those developing countries which have particularly bright futures due to the size and potential purchasing power of their populations, governmental policies which have supported and nourished healthy economic growth rates, and increasingly affluent consumers with tastes for imported products. These countries are characterized by large-scale infrastructural development projects and a clear commitment to economic advancement, and there are often accompanying attractive wage rates for offshore production capabilities and ready supplies of natural resources. These are the prime targets for international marketers to build consumer awareness, understanding, acceptance and ultimately product/brand loyalty. These are such countries as China, India, Taiwan, Indonesia, Singapore and Malaysia in Asia, Hungary, Poland and the Czech Republic in Eastern Europe, Argentina, Chile and Brazil in South America, Mexico in North America, and South Africa and Nigeria in Africa.

Marketing importance of emerging markets

Why are these markets so important? They are important for the profit potential that they provide, the opportunity for more cost-effective geographic expansion rather than new product development, the possibility of entering a new market in an earlier stage of the industry life-cycle, and the obvious potential for gaining access to cheaper labour sources and readily-available raw materials. These are all valid reasons for entering new markets; however, the real advantage lies in the possibility of entering a growing market with a product or service which is new rather than a copy of what is already available. They offer international marketers the chance to build positions while still innovative, rather than merely as imitators. Imitators have a tough time competing in markets against innovators unless they have some easily recognizable competitive advantage. The real battleground for marketers is within the minds of the consumers in their markets before they ever really make the actual product or service purchase, and it is far easier to build a position of strength as an innovator than it is as a follower. The successes of Coke in China demonstrate how important this foothold can be. Coke built its image early, and its presence in and support of the economic development of China put it on the top rung of the soft drink class ladder in the minds of Chinese consumers. As the Chinese economy developed and the discretionary income of Chinese consumers increased, Coke was there for them to purchase and, building up a strong brand image, this position has been an ever-improving one from a financial perspective. The point is that if the brand image is built, the product becomes the obvious choice when a need arises within that product or service category. Emerging markets are prime opportunities for international marketers to establish brand positions in the minds of rapidly-developing middle-class consumers with ever-increasing amounts of readily-available discretionary income, and are an opportunity ultimately to create sustainable competitive advantages.

Marketing challenges of emerging markets

Marketers must also realize that while these emerging markets present tremendous potential, they are also fraught with challenges due to the nature of the developmental process. Since these nations are, by nature, not yet developed, they are subject to a certain amount of volatility, which forces the marketer to be sensitive and observant. The developmental processes are often in flux in these countries with great advances being made but quickly followed by political or economic setbacks. The currencies of these countries may be somewhat unstable. It may be necessary to consider the use of barter and countertrade during particularly unstable periods. It may, in some instances, be necessary for global marketers to make payments to officials to facilitate business dealings which are culturally rationalized as normal ways of doing business rather than as bribery payments. The cultures involved may not in any way see these as inappropriate, and the payments are expected and made with the best and most honourable of intentions (see BUSINESS CULTURES, THE EMERGING COUNTRIES; MANAGEMENT IN THE EMERGING COUNTRIES). Telecommunications may not be readily available, affecting the possible use of telephones for direct marketing purposes or even televisions as a mass marketing advertising vehicle. It may be necessary for the marketer to use print media or even personal salespeople to call on potential customers or groups of customers. There may also be educational limitations, poor to mediocre literacy levels, and limited technological knowledge and experience within the country which may affect not only what you say and how you say it in advertisements, but also, and even more importantly, whether the product or service that is being sold will be able to be adopted by various target markets. Many global marketers have found that their definition of their target markets may need to be modified when dealing with emerging countries. Other infrastructural limitations which may be encountered might involve the lack of financial lending capabilities or the lack of credit to help customers with more expensive purchases or the lack of commercial marketing research firms or advertising agencies to aid foreign marketers in understanding their target audiences and in reaching them in a cost-effective way.

Having presented a number of challenges which marketers must be aware of when dealing with emerging nations, the enormous attractiveness of these rapidly-developing markets often make the impediments pale in comparison to the prospect of longer-term profitability. The next step is to look at the specific marketing practices and strategic marketing issues inherent in these emerging nations.

3 Analysis

Emerging nations represent a wide variety of different societies with varying levels of consumer sophistication and purchasing power as well as marketing infrastructures. There is a vast difference between the low incomes and undeveloped infrastructure of Nigeria (see MANAGEMENT IN NIGERIA) when compared to the high discretionary income as well as sophistication of Singapore. The point is that marketers will experience varying degrees of necessary adaptation in these markets when compared to their own home market experiences, particularly if their home markets are representative of developed nations. The range of marketing tools may be severely reduced given the limitations of the emerging country in question. This does not, by any means, signify that the country does not have the potential for success, it simply suggests that the approach be adapted to coincide with the sophistication of the marketing infrastructure that exists within that country.

Important marketing strategy questions which must be answered when examining different emerging nations for market entry involve:

1   *target market* – is there a viable base of customers with a desire for our products and the incomes to afford repeat purchases?;
2   *entry mode* – can we export to the country and still remain price competitive or do we need to look for a local partner?;
3   *currency issues* – is there a hard currency or would barter/countertrade be preferable?
4   *competition* – who are our competitors and is there room for us?
5   *product configuration* – what product form will best meet the market's needs and is it available already from competitors?
6   *distribution issues* – is there a distribution infrastructure readily available?
7   *promotional issues* – what mix of promotional tools and media are available and appear to be effective?
8   *pricing issues* – can we price our products competitively and maintain profitability while supporting our desired image?

Another major question which the firm must ask itself involves the issue of long-term commitment. Are we willing to make a commitment to this emerging market which will pay back in the future while potentially not profitable in the near term? These markets are emerging, which means that consumers in these countries have not yet reached their economic potential. Are we willing to forgo short-term profits while building a strong and positive brand/company image?

In order to examine marketing in these emerging nations, it is important to try to categorize the various individual countries into more useful groupings. One way to accomplish this would involve categorizations involving the general income levels of the populations and the sophistication of the marketing infrastructures also present. This would divide the nations into the following groupings:

1   *upper-middle income–developed infrastructure* (e.g. Singapore, South Africa, Brazil, Hungary);
2   *lower-middle income–developing infrastructure* (e.g. China, Indonesia, Poland);
3   *low income–undeveloped infrastructure* (e.g. Nigeria, India).

It is important to keep in mind that high income nations are not included as they are, by nature, developed nations. As a result of these categorizations, an illustrative example of each will be discussed to demonstrate to the reader the various marketing conditions which they represent. If the variety of different conditions in each of these illustrative examples are understood, then the marketer is better positioned to make educated decisions involving the potential viability of market entry.

Example 1 – (upper-middle income–developed infrastructure) – the case of marketing in Singapore

Singapore is a highly affluent and mature consumer-goods society. The advanced telecommunications infrastructure makes Singapore a fertile ground for sophisticated marketing tools and techniques. Advertising is available across a wealth of media vehicles. The compact size of Singapore combined with its sophisticated tele-communications capability, make it easy to reach all members of the society quickly and efficiently. Its well-developed delivery infrastructure also makes it an ideal location for distribution to the people. Here an enormous range of products and services are readily available for its affluent and demanding consumers; consumer electronic products are available in many copy-cat types of retail outlets. The Singaporeans are moving upward rapidly in their purchase interests with security and retirement now of great importance. They are concerned with the purchase of stocks and bonds, homes, expensive home furnishings and a broad range of luxury products. This would put them at a high level on Maslow's hierarchy with an interest in products which help them to reach self-actualization.

In Singapore, the challenges for the marketer are to stand out from the crowd. The maturity of the market for all ranges of products and services makes the market extremely competitive. Price becomes a main focal point for strategic differentiation of one company's offerings from those of another. What becomes important in this type of market is to look for niches that have not yet been effectively served. What comes to mind in Singapore is an opportunity like youth group segmentation. As Singapore has a standard of living which is second only to Japan in Asia, it has a youth segment which is gaining its own credibility as a purchasing market. There are growing numbers of SKIPPies (School Kids with Income and Purchasing Power), which become an important buying group for such goods as compact discs (CDs), designer clothing, video cassette recorders (VCRs) and tapes, and electronic games (like Nintendo and Sony Playstation). This type of strategic segmentation would seem to have the greatest growth potential in the marketplace. Another possibility would lie in the marketing of societal innovations and leisure time products as the society deals with the need to balance hard work with vacation time.

In terms of marketing tools and practices, Singapore is a well-developed market with all manner of marketing tools possible for use. Consumers have experience with coupons, premiums, contests/sweepstakes, trading stamps and free samples. All ranges of high-quality magazines, newspapers, televisions and even computers can be used to reach target audiences. The trick is to find the target that has not yet been developed and get into the head of the customer before anyone else and stay there with continuous innovation and value creation.

Example 2 – (lower-middle income–developing infrastructure) – marketing in the People's Republic of China

China has been an enigma to many marketers with its enormous population but daunting political instability and infrastructural limitations. The building of relationships takes time, particularly in Asian cultures where there is an inherent wariness of foreigners, but successes in China for companies like Coke and Colgate Palmolive suggest that the time in development was worth the wait.

A major change in consumer demand has been seen during this period of time as the high demand for watches, bicycles and washing machines has been replaced by the desire for cameras, VCRs, CD players and computers. The social changes that have occurred during this period have also been staggering. There is now an awareness of and desire for imported brand merchandise with material possessions being seen as one way to differentiate the person from his or her neighbours. This is surprising given the perceived homogeneous nature of the Chinese people, but, in reality, there are pockets of middle-class consumers developing with growing levels of discretionary income in the group know as the 'self-employed individuals'.

According to the *China Statistical Yearbook of 1993*, the majority of average Chinese household expenditure (53 per cent) was on food products, while the remainder was split between clothing (14.7 per cent), cultural entertainment/educational expenditure (8.9 per cent), household durables and services (8 per cent), housing (5.7 per cent), health care (2.5 per cent), transportation and communication (2.4 per cent) and other purchases (4.5 per cent). Such a large proportion of income being spent on food products is typical of other emerging nations. The remainder of the family discretionary income is taken up primarily with clothing, leaving very little else. As Maslow's hierarchy of needs demonstrates, the lowest level of needs which must be satisfied first are for food, clothing and shelter, and the implication here is that China is still a long way behind on the economic development ladder. One has to remember that the Chinese figures are averages, and there are promising pockets of more affluent consumers who exist in the urban centres of Beijing, Shanghai and Quangzhou. The streets of these cities are filled with people carrying cellular telephones and wearing branded designer clothing.

The marketer looking at entering the Chinese market must be patient. As with other Asian societies, it is necessary to build relationships over time before being fully accepted and getting the 'green light' to allow access for your products. The importance of Chinese relationships, or *quanxi*, cannot be overstated. Everything in Chinese society is based on a series of closely-interconnected relationships and networks, and the outsider must work closely within the network to have a chance of success. Marketers must build on long-term relationships and friendships to gain access to the right negotiation circles to have any hope of success. This is not the place for the 'quick-profit' marketer. This is where the patience of the organization and its principals could pay-off many times over. It must also be noted that with the weaknesses in the Chinese currency (RMB), it may be necessary to build marketing relationships through countertrade or joint venture. Chinese consumers, particularly in the urban centres, do find value in recognized imported brands, and the trick for the marketer in a joint venture operation with a Chinese partner is to make sure that the products produced are made to look like imported rather than domestic goods. The foreign marketer must also realize that the Chinese in urban centres will be more sensitized to foreign brands and products as a result of the telecommunications available there which are not yet available in the rural areas.

An important mechanism for getting Chinese consumers to try new products is to give them free samples or to have them influenced by members of their work or social groups to use the products or services. The key to Chinese customer loyalty is to build trust and credibility over time and usage. This is not a swift process, but it can be very effective in building a loyal and fast-growing customer base. Marketing opportunities in China include direct mail, telemarketing, catalogue sales and direct response marketing. While Chinese magazines have not included high-quality advertisements in the past, there has been a virtual explosion of new magazines on the Chinese market over the last five years, and advertisers can find burgeoning opportunities in cinema advertising, newspapers, television and outdoor media such as billboards and train and bus placards, not to mention the thoroughly-accepted practice in Hong Kong of painting the outsides of buses and trolleys with company advertisements which is filtering into the rest of the Mainland of China.

It is important for the advertiser to bear in mind that China is an Asian society, and consequently is more positively affected by image advertising than product-specific advertising. There are now branches of major worldwide advertising agencies establishing offices in Beijing and Shanghai, which will help the foreign marketer to use the most effective tools and techniques for the various target markets of interest. But even more relevant is that consumers do not have a wealth of experience of advertising having only recently had access to foreign media, and Chinese companies do not use advertising for domestic products. In terms of sales promotion tools, coupons and premiums are not as well recognized and used in China, but free samples are very effective in encouraging the trial of new products. There is room for marketing innovators here, but patience is the key to success.

Example 3 – (low income–undeveloped infrastructure) – the case of marketing in Nigeria

Nigeria is the largest nation in Africa with a population in excess of 100 million people (see MANAGEMENT IN NIGERIA). Its heavy resources of crude petroleum make it an economy which is particularly tied to the world market for oil. It is certainly the most economically powerful nation in Black Africa. Its economic strength and power, however, do not reflect a sophisticated infrastructure. It is faced with developmental difficulties because of its archaic infrastructure. As aid is important to African nations, one of the difficulties faced by Nigeria is that if it becomes too successful an economy, it will lose its potential for world aid, which its government is used to receiving from world organizations. Nigeria's population is made up of a series of tribes, and this tribal orientation argues strongly for marketers to use the tribe and its leaders to have the greatest chance of success with imported products or services. The infrastructure is wholly inadequate, which forced the movement of the national capital from Lagos to Abuja. Religious divisions have plagued the country with Muslims in the north and Christians in the south at constant odds with each other. Again, this presents the global marketer with a series of challenges and opportunities.

In terms of challenges, one considerable issue appears to be a basic lack of understanding of the role of marketing in business or in society. This is the result of a history of product shortages which have put the power into the hands of the sellers. As a result, many businesses have followed a production orientation – as there was never a problem finding buyers for those goods that were produced, there was little need to use marketing tools and techniques. There are not only basic infrastructural problems in Nigeria, but also a basic lack of understanding of either what marketing can do or how to use it. In the past Nigerian managers were not getting the training to allow them to effectively utilize marketing, and businesses were not sure where marketing decisions fitted into the strategic corporate decision process. Of course, this has not necessarily been true for the larger and more powerful Nigerian enterprises; however, these are few in number, and only recently have the global advances of companies such as McDonald's been felt in the larger cities. The government of Nigeria has realized the importance of telecommunications, and is moving towards a national digital telephone service, but this has suffered setbacks on its way to implementation.

Another problem for foreign marketers is to distribute goods by making use of an inefficient transportation infrastructure. Air transport uses old aircraft with frequent delays or mechanical failures, road systems are not well developed, and the vehicles used for road transport are also dilapidated and slow. Another challenge is the concept of relationship building and trust. Nigerians are not quick to embrace foreign marketers or their products and services. It is important to build consumer awareness over time. The tribal or community orientation of the population makes it imperative for foreign marketers to get to know their customers and slowly build trust. It also takes a certain amount of education, but as the populations in the larger city centres are exposed to foreign transmissions, they are sensitized to foreign products and services and their potential uses and benefits. Another daunting challenge is the lack of hard currency and the possibility of being faced with special payments to facilitate certain types of agreements being reached and contracts being signed.

These challenges would seem to be severe and daunting; however, the innovator has enormous potential. The visionary has the ability to build a large corps of brand-loyal, even brand-insistent consumers. Without much exposure to marketing messages, there is an enormous opportunity to get a marketing message into the heads of Nigerian consumers before other marketers do, potentially creating a competitive perceptual advantage for the foreign marketer. This is an enormous potential market with a population in excess of 100 million according to the World Bank's, *World Development Report 1997*. The fact that Nigerians use the large marketplaces for business as well as social purposes provides an effective mechanism for reaching many potential customers. The importance of the tribe/community can be effectively used by foreign marketers by building awareness in influential individuals about the products and services offered. If these opinion leaders adopt your products, they will undoubtedly have a strong impact upon the purchase intentions of many of the others of the same communities/tribes. The strategic importance of using local agents/distributors would be vital for successful marketing efforts. As with any developing nation, there are concentrated consumers in urban centres that can be more easily reached. There are also good opportunities for barter/countertrade to overcome currency limitations.

The point here is that there is economic development taking place in Nigeria. There is an increasing level of urbanization, which when combined with governmental initiatives to improve the infrastructure, argue for tremendous potential profits. The key is to build a position over time, to develop the necessary trust, and to offer products/services which have benefits for the group/community/tribe as well as the individual consumers themselves.

4 Conclusion

Hopefully, these past three examples will help to illustrate the various types of issues that the internationally-focused marketer will face when entering the emerging nations of the world. The three levels point to varying strategic needs and issues to make educated decisions on how to enter the markets. The highest level of emerging nation, upper-middle income–developed infrastructure, presents the marketer with a full range of marketing mix vehicles to use and a greater likelihood that the tools that they have used in their home market will be available in the target market. The problem is, however, that this type of market requires a careful differentiation strategy since this market is likely to have other competitors already entrenched. The innovative types of offerings that could work in this type of market would include leisure-time services, new technologies and new offerings for youth or elderly markets. This is a well-developed middle-class group with sophisticated tastes and needs. The key is to go for the niche that no one else has yet captured.

The middle level, lower-middle income–developing infrastructure, presents the marketer with different issues. Here the infrastructure is potentially more limited and the consumers are not as affluent. A wide range of goods and services are possible here, and there is greater opportunity for establishing a market presence since most product/service classes will not be as saturated as they would be in the upper-middle income–developed infrastructure grouping. The limitations lie in the necessary modifications inherent in a developing infrastructure with a middle class which is not as affluent. Opportunities abound given that many product classes are not yet in their maturity stages.

Finally, the low income–undeveloped infrastructure level presents a number of possible challenges, but also enormous opportunities. In this situation, the consuming markets are small and limited, and the ability to build a presence and image may take longer due to communication limitations. The types of products which appear to have greater potential here are ones which fall into the 'essential' category (e.g. food, clothing, shelter products). The optimum approach would be to build on personal selling within the group/tribe setting since the infrastructure is not supportive. The difficulty here is that the commitment must be long-term since payback will be slow during the early market development stages. A major consideration is whether there are viable target markets with the necessary education and affluence to support the products/services being marketed.

Managerial suggestions

No matter what the level of market involved, in order to understand marketing and marketing potential in any emerging nation, it is necessary to thoroughly examine the economic and political development within the country. The following questions need to be asked. What are the initiatives of the government? How stable is the present government? How stable is the currency? What infrastructural limitations are there? Where does marketing fit into the business and educational community? How developed is the infrastructure? Then it is necessary to ask about the target constituencies within the country. What are the potential target consumer populations? What are they motivated by? How can they be reached? Then individual marketing mix decisions can be made to most effectively reach each of the target populations. There is a great variety of levels of development within what are considered to be emerging nations, but there are certain commonalities which it will be helpful to keep in mind:

1   These markets have not yet reached their full potential. Market development is therefore to be encouraged.
2   Relationship building is important. Take time to develop the appropriate relationships with opinion leaders to help pave the way for future development.
3   Make use of locals wherever possible to pave the way for acceptance by locals for your products/services.
4   Gaps in infrastructure may allow for new opportunities to open doorways. Look to skills and abilities developed in other countries that might be applied in emerging markets.
5   It may be necessary to look at things from a different perspective when entering an emerging market. Barter/countertrade, joint venture, or even wholly-owned foreign production facilities may be necessary to get around infrastructural limitations.
6   Look to the existence of middle classes, which may exist and which would provide economies of scale.

The international marketer should definitely consider the emerging nations of the world for market entry. The enormous potential profits may surely offset the difficulties inherent in the market development process.

JOHN B. FORD

DEPARTMENT OF MARKETING AND INTERNATIONAL BUSINESS

OLD DOMINION UNIVERSITY, NORFOLK, VIRGINIA

Further Reading

(References cited in the text marked *)

Asian Consumer Market Atlas (1994), Hong Kong: The Economist Intelligence Unit. (This is an excellent compilation of consumer statistics for various east and southeast Asian markets by field data collection staff from *The Economist*. This provides a good overview of Asian consumers, their expenditures, and their behaviours.)

Big Emerging Markets: 1996 Outlook and Sourcebook (1995) Lanham, MD: Bernan Press. (This contains a wealth of information gathered by the US Department of Commerce on the 10 most important emerging markets in the world. The book includes essays and statistics which reveal why these countries have been designated as important emerging markets.)

Brazil Market Atlas (1998) London: The Economist Intelligence Unit. (This is an excellent compilation of market statistics for Brazil by field data collection staff from *The Economist*. This provides a good overview of Brazilian consumers and market potential.)

* *China Statistical Yearbook* (1993) Beijing. (An in-depth statistical examination of social, political and economic aspects of the People's Republic of China.)

China Market Atlas (1994) Hong Kong: The Economist Intelligence Unit. (This is an excellent compilation of market statistics for the People's Republic of China by the field data collection staff from *The Economist*. This provides a good overview of Chinese consumers and market potential.)

Eastern Europe Market Atlas (1994) Hong Kong: The Economist Intelligence Unit. (This is an excellent compilation of market statistics for various eastern European nations by the field data collection staff from *The Economist*. This provides a good overview of eastern European consumers and market potential.)

Middle East and North Africa Market Atlas (1994) Hong Kong: The Economist Intelligence Unit. (This is an excellent compilation of market statistics for various middle eastern and northern African nations by the field data collection staff from *The Economist*. This provides a good overview of middle eastern and north African consumers and market potential.)

Regional Surveys of the World: Africa South of the Sahara, 1998 (1997) 27th edn, London: Europa Publications Ltd. (This is a good overview of various southern African nations/cultures. There are reports provided for a number of different industries within each country, and a range of useful statistics are provided.)

Regional Surveys of the World: Eastern Europe and the Commonwealth of Independent States, 1994 (1993) 2nd edn, London: Europa Publications, Ltd. (This is a good overview of various eastern European nations/cultures. There are reports provided for a number of different industries within each country, and a range of useful statistics are provided.)

Regional Surveys of the World: The Far East and Australasia, 1998 (1997) 29th edn, London: Europa Publications, Ltd. (This is a good overview of various Asian nations/cultures. There are reports provided for a number of different industries within each country, and a range of useful statistics are provided.)

Regional Surveys of the World: The Middle East and North Africa, 1999 (1998) 45th edn, London: Europa Publications, Ltd. (This is a good overview of various middle eastern and northern African nations/cultures. There are reports provided for a number of different industries within each country, and a range of useful statistics are provided.)

Regional Surveys of the World: South America, Central America and the Caribbean, 1999 (1998) 7th edn, London: Europa Publications, Ltd. (This is a good overview of various Latin American nations/cultures. These are reports provided for a number of different industries within each country, and a range of useful statistics are provided.)

Subsaharan Africa Market Atlas (1994) Hong Kong: The Economist Intelligence Unit. (This is an excellent compilation of market statistics for various sub-Saharan African nations by the field data collection staff from *The Economist*. This provides a good overview of sub-Saharan African consumers and market potential.)

United Nations Demographic Yearbook 1998 (1997) New York: the United Nations. (This contains a wealth of demographic information on the populations of the member nations of the United

Nations. There are detailed explanatory sections and a variety of comparative statistics presented.)

United Nations Statistical Yearbook 1998 (1997) New York: the United Nations. (This contains a wealth of information on the populations of the member nations of the United Nations. There are detailed explanatory sections and a variety of comparative statistics presented which cover economic, political and social aspects of the countries represented.)

* *World Development Report 1997* (1996) Washington, DC: the World Bank. (This contains a wealth of information on developmental forces within most of the nations of the world. There are explanatory sections and interesting comparative statistics that cover economic, political and social aspects of each of the countries represented.)

Yearbook of International Trade Statistics 1998 (1997) New York: The United Nations. (This contains a wealth of information on international trade across most of the nations of the world. There are detailed explanatory sections and a variety of comparative statistics presented.)

Yi, X.B. (1990) *Marketing to China: One Billion New Customers*, Lincolnwood, IL: NTC Publishing Group. (This is an excellent discussion of the use of advertising and marketing practices in the People's Republic of China.)

See also: ECONOMIES OF THE EMERGING COUNTRIES; MANAGEMENT IN THE EMERGING COUNTRIES; MANAGEMENT IN NIGERIA; PERSPECTIVES ON GLOBALIZATION, BIG BUSINESS AND THE EMERGING COUNTRIES; STRATEGY IN THE EMERGING COUNTRIES

Related topics in the IEBM regional set: MANAGEMENT IN CHINA; MANAGEMENT IN SINGAPORE; MARKETING IN ASIA PACIFIC; MARKETING IN EUROPE; MARKETING IN LATIN AMERICA; MARKETING IN NORTH AMERICA; STRATEGY IN ASIA PACIFIC

Strategy in the emerging countries

1 Emerging environment of business
2 Using technology for competitive advantage
3 Competitive strategies
4 Internationalization
5 Conclusion

Overview

Many of the developing countries of Asia and Africa with large and increasing populations have been at very low levels of economic development. They are characterized by abysmally low income levels, poor infrastructure, poor health facilities, etc. But, these countries represent potentially large markets for consumer as well as industrial products. Several developing nations in these two continents are in the process of implementing large scale economic reforms as a result of which their economies are in the process of transformation from a tightly controlled one to an economy based on market forces.

In this entry we explore the broad characteristics of the emerging environment of business and competitive strategies being pursued by firms in the emerging countries of south Asia and Africa.

1 Emerging environment of business

Geographically the two regions are large and have huge populations. Most countries in the two regions have had turbulent political histories for long periods except for India which has had a relatively more stable political situation. On the whole countries in the two regions are economically poor and poverty is rampant.

The countries themselves are characterized by large agricultural sectors and relatively smaller industry and service sectors (see ECONOMIES OF THE EMERGING COUNTRIES). Productivity growth in general has been low to moderate across sectors and countries in the two regions. The role of the government in the running of the economy has been highly significant and the public sectors in these countries are large and inefficient. Several countries in these two regions are in the process of implementing major macroeconomic reform programmes under the guidance of the World Bank and International Monetary Fund (IMF) which are expected to bring about positive changes in the business environment.

Far reaching economic reforms were instituted by the Indian government in the middle of 1991. These reforms included cutting the overall government deficit, an increase in the subsidized fertilizer price, a reduction in defence spending, steps for attracting investments from non-resident Indians (NRIs), major changes in the industrial licensing policy and policy on foreign collaborations. As part of the reform programme a new industrial policy was also initiated with the objective of maintaining sustained growth in productivity and gainful employment; encouraging the growth of entrepreneurship and upgrading technology to achieve international competitiveness. With the opening up of the Indian economy to foreign competition many foreign firms have entered different sectors of the Indian economy thereby increasing the intensity of competition (see MANAGEMENT IN INDIA).

Bangladesh announced a new industrial policy in mid-1991. One of its objectives was to encourage foreign and local investment in the private sector. Specific measures included steps to remove the distinctions between local and foreign investors and to reduce the state's role in the economy, tax exemptions to exporters and permission for foreign investors to set up 100 per cent owned ventures anywhere in the country (Far Eastern Economic Review *Asia 1992*) (see MANAGEMENT IN BANGLADESH).

In 1991 Pakistan adopted a package of reforms aimed at increasing the rate of privatization and deregulation. Plans were made to disinvest over 200 public sector enterprises and steps were taken to make the local currency fully convertible. As in the case of India the pace of reforms in Bangladesh and Pakistan has varied after their inauguration due to uncertain political conditions (Far Eastern Economic Review *Asia 1992*) (see MANAGEMENT IN PAKISTAN).

Many African countries have undertaken structural adjustment programmes to accelerate economic growth. A World Bank report (World Bank 1994) points out that in the African countries that have undertaken and sustained major policy reforms, adjustment is working; however a number of countries have yet to introduce the reforms required to restore growth. No African country has yet achieved a sound macroeconomic policy profile (inflation under 10 per cent, very low budget deficit and competitive exchange rate). On the positive side the reforms have improved external competitiveness. Increased access to imports required for growth has been achieved and also the reduced taxation of agriculture has encouraged production and exports.

Reforms of agricultural pricing and marketing systems are in progress across the African continent. Almost all countries are attempting to ensure better prices for their major agricultural exports. In some cases they have abolished state marketing boards and have allowed the private sector to compete with them. Some countries have adopted pricing formulas linked to world market prices and there has been a major withdrawal of government from food crop marketing. There has also been a move to deregulate prices and markets in other sectors. In many countries commodities like rice, sugar and tea can now be imported freely by the private sector. Monopolies, however continue in important sectors as petroleum, wheat and fertilizer and infrastructure services (see MANAGEMENT IN NIGERIA).

2 Using technology for competitive advantage

The importance of the role of technology in bringing about economic transformation is being increasingly realized in the emerging countries. One of the objectives of the reform programmes initiated by emerging countries has been to attract foreign direct investments which would enable them to upgrade their industries technologically.

With the adoption of the new economic policy in India the use of technology as a competitive weapon has gained prominence. For example, with the entry of new multinational companies (MNCs) in the passenger car industry (Daewoo, Ford,

Mercedes-Benz, etc.) the existing players Maruti-Suzuki, Premier Automobiles, Hindustan Motors have signed new collaboration agreements with foreign car manufacturers to acquire new technologies for improving existing products and also to introduce new models. As a related development several auto ancillary manufacturers have also signed up foreign collaboration agreements for upgrading technology for component manufacture.

With the adoption of a new industrial policy as part of the reform programme by India the increasing trend in the number of foreign collaborations seen during the 1980s has been maintained. From 976 collaborations signed in 1991 the figure went up to 1854 during 1994. During the 1980s and 1990s there has also been an increase in the number of collaboration agreements with foreign equity. For the period 1948–96 foreign investments formed about 30 per cent of the total number of collaborations. In 1994, 57 per cent of the collaborations were with foreign equity (Chaudhuri 1997).

In the post-reform period there are three sectors that stand out: chemicals, electricals and electronics, and consultancy and other services. The chemicals sector attracted around 14 per cent; electricals and electronics about 15 per cent; consultancy and other services about 14 per cent of all collaborations. The increase in collaborative activity between Indian companies and foreign ones is a good augury, but it is posing new managerial challenges. A significant number of joint ventures (JVs) have broken up because of the foreign partners' insistence on hiking up their equity control after the establishment of the JVs. The challenge for Indian firms would be to improve their own skills through continuous learning from their partners as well as through their own R&D activities in order to continue to be wanted as JV partners by their foreign collaborators.

On an overall basis it is evident that the USA has been the most significant provider of technology to Indian firms during the period 1981–94 with an average of 20.84 per cent of the total number of approvals. Germany and the UK follow in the same order accounting for 16.15 and 13.89 per cent of the total. During the period 1991–94 companies from countries other than those traditionally known as technology suppliers became active in this field. For example Mauritius became an important source indicating the importance of tax considerations in technology transfer.

Some of the other countries in south Asia have also been attempting to upgrade their industries by acquiring new technology through foreign collaborations. As mentioned previously, Bangladesh launched its new industrial policy in 1991 and one of the features was the attraction of foreign investors who would bring in much needed foreign exchange as well as new technology. Some positive results seem to have followed from this. During the period 1995–96 Bangladesh received US$100 million in foreign investment of which US$20 million was in the form of direct investment. During the period 1997–98 Bangladesh made significant progress in attracting foreign direct investment in the energy sector (Far Eastern Economic Review *Asia 1997, Asia 1998*).

Pakistan too has been giving prominence to securing foreign investment and technology. For example, Singapore and Malaysia agreed to finance three power generation projects in Pakistan, while Malaysia offered to put up a US$100 million oil terminal near Karachi during 1996–97 (Far Eastern Economic Review *Asia 1997*: 187).

Major industries in Africa are dominated by multinational companies which are the sources of new technologies (see MANAGEMENT OF TECHNOLOGY IN THE EMERGING COUNTRIES). For example, the chemical and petrochemical industries in Africa are characterized by the presence of all the major multinationals. The mining industry also has been dominated by foreign companies but due to a break down in the rule of law in several countries new foreign investments have not been forthcoming. South Africa is struggling to keep its mining industry competitive while other countries are in the process of making changes in their mineral legislation, fiscal and foreign exchange regimes which could make their industries attractive exploration prospects. Canadian companies have been in the forefront of exploration and mining ventures in the recent past.

3 Competitive strategies

The overall cost leadership and focus strategies (Porter 1980) have been quite common in the emerging countries characterized by the predominance of natural resource based industries (see MARKETING IN THE EMERGING COUNTRIES; MANUFACTURING IN THE EMERGING COUNTRIES). However, the increasing competitiveness of the business environment in India during the last few years has seen a surge in the use of differentiation as a competitive strategy. We examine below how some companies in different industries in India are trying to achieve differentiation.

Brand building

Currently most software companies in India earn more than 90 per cent of their revenues from consultancy and projects. On average, less than 8–10 per cent of their revenues come from generic software products. However, the scenario is likely to change fast. Indian companies are now considering introducing branded software packages to boost their bottomlines. Their brand presence is expected to generate loyalty among users and strengthen long-term business prospects. Tata Consultancy Services (TCS), the leading infotech company in the country launched five branded products during 199198. Infosys, another significant IT company launched two branded products during the same period (*Financial Express* 1998: 1).

Time to market: the emerging competitive edge

Rapid product development and market launch is an important way to score over competitors. This has been seen to be true in the TRIAD countries (USA, Europe and Japan) for a long time. However, the emerging competitive scenario in India is pointing toward the need for pre-emptive launches to exploit first mover advantage. Nestlé (India) like its multinational parent has used this strategy for its products ranging from Macaroni snacks to chocolates and soups. In mid-1997 Dabur launched its Homemade Cooking Pastes ahead of Kissan's launch of a similar product. Hindustan Lever, the Indian subsidiary of Unilever, the Anglo-Dutch multinational, launched Clinic All Clear, a new anti-dandruff shampoo ahead of Procter and Gamble's launch of the world famous Head and Shoulders (*Financial Express* 1998: 2). With the progress of economic reforms in the emerging countries the intensity of competition is likely to increase thus paving the way for firms to shift from a predominant use of cost leadership to differentiation as the source of competitive advantage.

Efficiency improvement through organizational restructuring

The pressure of competition is likely to bring about a radical change in the thinking of industry leaders. In India the advent of global competition has already made a dramatic impact on the thinking of corporate leaders in India. Whereas unrelated diversification propelled by industrial licensing norms and other governmental regulations was the norm during the pre-liberalization era large multiproduct and multi-divisional firms are now rethinking their strategic approaches. During the last few years larger firms have been pursuing complex strategies, at the heart of which is the objective of building on a few core competencies. A small number of Indian examples will illustrate this process.

Foseco India

Foseco India is the market leader in speciality foundry chemicals and steel fluxes and was born as a joint venture between Greaves Cotton Limited and Foseco International in 1964. In 1992 the Thapar group as a part of their long-term strategy divested the shares of Greaves Cotton in Greaves Foseco International and brought about organizational changes that included creating strategic business units to focus on the different markets and product lines and delayering to bring down the number of managerial layers (All India Management Association (AIMA) 1995: 43).

Tata Refractories (TRL)

Tata Refractories (TRL), the market leader in the Indian refractory market was set up by Tata Steel in technical collaboration with Didier of Germany. In the late 1980s TRL discontinued its range of low quality alumina bricks due to competition from smaller players and decline in profitability. In 1992 TRL diversified into high technology products and to meet the competitive challenge it reorganized its operations into strategic business units focusing on its dolomite, mag carbon and specialty range of products. In 1994–95 TRL sold off its loss making companies, and was planning to prune its product range and make best use of tax benefits by merging with a sister company (AIMA 1995: 45).

The RP Goenka Group

The RP Goenka Group, a large, multiproduct company (sales turnover: Rs 64,000 million) is in the midst of a complex restructuring and refocusing exercise. Recently it sold off its stake in a five-year old joint venture with Goodyear Tyres of the USA. During the last few months it divested itself of or diluted its shareholding in several JVs operating in diverse business. The new parameters that are guiding the company's entry into a business line are: competitiveness, leadership and sustained profitability. The group is currently involved in a globalization effort with JVs in Saudi Arabia, Lebanon, Malaysia and Vietnam and is exploring the possibility of a JV in China for carbon black business (*Economic Times* 1998L: 1).

Public ownership as strategic constraint

Improved efficiency has been emphasized by most African governments but their efforts have at best been only moderately successful. Almost all countries have halted the increase in the number of public enterprises, and some have reduced the number. A number of governments have signed performance contracts with key enterprises but available evidence shows that they have mostly failed in improving enterprise efficiency. Most of the divestiture of government shareholdings has occurred in the small and medium-sized public enterprises. The larger ones – airlines, railroads, mining, utilities – have generally not been privatized. The experience of India, Pakistan and Bangladesh parallels that of African countries in many ways. Public sector corporations account for a major part of their respective economies.

State owned undertakings in the emerging countries are a legacy of the past. They were created at a time and stage of development of the country when private enterprise was not forthcoming due to ideological reasons. Though they played a useful role at some time there is now an increasing need to revamp them. However, their turnaround is being impeded by government ownership which has made managers of the enterprises vulnerable to the bureaucracy or their political bosses. Political interference has also often led to financial irregularities and profligacy which these corporations can ill afford.

Despite the difficulties associated with public ownership there are some well-run public enterprises. Bharat Heavy Electricals Limited and Gujarat Narmada Valley Fertilizer Corporation are some examples in India which have performed well over relatively long periods. Strategic autonomy and a high degree of professionalism of their management have contributed to their success.

4 Internationalization

Export promotion has been a major plank of the reform programmes initiated by some of the emerging countries. Major exports of the emerging countries are natural-resource based. For example, India's major exports during 1997–98 were textiles, gems and jewellery, agriculture and allied products and engineering goods. Low labour costs is one of the most important sources of competitive advantage in these industries. But there are some emerging areas, for example computer software and pharmaceuticals, which are becoming increasingly important in India's export basket. Software and pharmaceuticals are competitive not only because of low labour costs, but also due to technological competence, for example in developing software for principals based in the USA and by developing alternative technical routes to bulk-produce drugs.

An exploratory study of the internationalization process by ten of the larger Indian firms that cut across several industries revealed some interesting facts. These firms' internationalization efforts were characterized by:

1   a fairly rapid rate of internationalization;
2   a long-term orientation to their planning;
3   a global mindset;

4   a strategy of creating beach heads in critical markets other than the 'TRIAD – Europe, USA and Japan;
5   a strong emphasis on quality;
6   creation of global scale plants;
7   an emphasis on building on distinctive capabilities;
8   an international perspective on funds mobilization;
9   a willingness to change the existing product portfolio when necessary;
10   a strategy of backward integration for better quality when necessary (Chaudhuri *et al.* 1996: 35).

Pakistan's major exports are cotton yarn, cotton cloth, synthetic textiles, cotton, rice, leather, fish, carpets and rugs, petroleum products and footwear. The export industries in Pakistan are basically geared towards pursuing a cost leadership strategy targeted towards the low end of international markets.

Though the above description of Pakistan's industries does not portray a rosy picture there are some silver linings as evidenced by the relative success of the surgical instrument industry, which has emerged in the provincial town of Sialkot. Around 300 small and medium-sized enterprises (SMEs) located in Sialkot have made Pakistan a global player in the manufacture of stainless steel medical, dental and surgical instruments. Since the mid-1980s export growth in real terms for the industry has averaged approximately 10 per cent per year. Total exports sales exceeded US$100 million in 1997. Eighty-five per cent of exports were to North America and Western Europe. Pakistan's share of the world market in this industry was 20 per cent (Far Eastern Economic Review *Asia 1998*; Nadvi 1997). The success of this industry illustrates the concept of the national diamond of competitiveness as well as the working of industrial clusters (Porter 1990).

Bangladesh's major export industries are ready-made garments, jute textiles, leather products, processed fish and seafood and tea. Available evidence suggests that exporting firms are pursuing a cost leadership strategy targeting low end customers based on low wage advantage. The ready-made garment industry has expanded quite rapidly in recent years. The small industry sector seems to have shown some amount of dynamism. Within the small industry sector, industries that have experienced significant growth are the following; bakery, oil mill, ready-made garments, hosiery, wooden furniture and fixtures, printing and publishing, industrial chemicals, lime products, soap, cosmetics and perfumery, light engineering, automobile servicing and repairing, steel furniture and jewellery (Far Eastern Economic Review *Asia 1998*; Quibria, 1997). All these industries are labour intensive. Bangladesh, with a vast population has comparative advantage in these labour intensive industries which exporting firms are exploiting.

Sri Lanka's major exports include tea, rubber, coconuts, textiles and garments, petroleum, gems – all characterized by labour intensive technologies (Far Eastern Economic Review *Asia 1998*).

5 Conclusion

The emerging countries of south Asia and Africa are in a state of transition. Having been subjected to strong regulatory influence of their respective governments over long periods in the past there was negligible pressure on firms to be competitive or responsive to customer demand. However, these economies are now in flux. Many of them are in the process of implementing wide-ranging economic reforms which have resulted in a competitive industrial environment in several countries. Firms in south Asia and Africa are now under pressure to (i) improve operational efficiency and (ii) respond to customers' needs in a more flexible manner. The changing business environment has resulted in several firms experimenting with new strategic approaches. Differentiation, organizational restructuring and internationalization are strategies that are likely to become more common in the near future at least in South Asia. Africa, however, seems to be slow in responding; though there have been some improvements. The presence of a large public sector in the economies of most African nations and south Asian countries is posing a challenge to their desire for improving operational effectiveness and efficiency. Future progress on the economic front in India as well as on the sub-continent would depend on improvement in the governance processes. Political stability would be a key to further reforms and in turn industrial resurgence. Africa is going to face a very major challenge in the process of industrial development as the political situation there is far more complex with armed internecine conflicts being rampant.

SHEKHAR CHAUDHURI
INDIAN INSTITUTE OF MANAGEMENT
AHMEDABAD

Further reading

(References cited in the text marked *)

* All India Management Association (1995) *Restructuring to Change*, New Delhi. (This book contains articles describing the process of organizational restructuring and strategic refocusing in eight large companies in India.)
* Chaudhuri, S. (1997) 'International transfer of technology to India: Problems, prospects and policy issues', Indian Institute of Management, Ahmedabad: WP No.1384.
  Chaudhuri, S. and Shah, N. (1996) 'Some aspects of internationalization by larger Indian firms: Evidence from ten case studies', Indian Institute of Management, Ahmedabad, WP No.1299, March. (This paper describes briefly the internationalization strategies adopted by ten of the larger Indian firms and analyses the key aspects of the internationalization process.)
  Colletta, N.J., Kostner, M. and Wiederhofer, I. (1996) *The Transition from War to Peace in Sub-Saharan Africa*, Washington, DC: The World Bank. (This book describes the complex political, economic and cultural transitions many countries in sub-Saharan Africa are currently facing.)
  Economic Times (1998) 'Dossier', May 8–14. (The *Economic Times* is one of the top business newspapers in India. It brings out a special feature called Dossier that publishes stories about interesting developments and strategies being pursued by Indian as well as international firms operating in India.)
* Far Eastern Economic Review (1998) *Asia 1998*. (This book provides brief sketches of the political, economic, social and cultural aspects of Asian countries on an annual basis.)
  Financial Express (1998) 'Brand Wagon', September 8. (Brand Wagon is a special feature of the *Financial Express*, a business newspaper in India. It brings out stories about new developments in the field of brand management in Indian industry).

Meier, G.M. and Steel W.F. (eds) (1989) *Industrial Adjustment in Sub-Saharan Africa*, Washington DC: Oxford University Press. (This book presents a collection of papers on various aspects of industrial development in sub-Saharan Africa. Topics covered include the business environment, small scale entrepreneurs, financial intermediation, technology and public sector management.)

http://www.mbendi.co.za/indy/ming/mingaf.htm#overiew 'An MBendi Profile: The African Mining Industry'.

http://www/mbendi.co.za/indy/chem/chemaf.htm#Overview 'An MBendi Profile – African Chemical Industry'.

http://www.mbendi.co.za/afoi.htm#Overview 'An MBbendi Profile: The African Oil Industry'.

* Nadvi, K. (1997) 'The Cutting Edge: Collective Efficiency and International Competitiveness in Pakistan', Institute of Development Studies, Discussion Paper, July. (This paper explores how a cluster of predominantly small firms have made Pakistan a global player in the world market for stainless steel surgical instruments.)

Pigato, M., Farah, C., Itakura, K., Jun, K., Martin, W., Murrell, K. and Srinivasan, T.G. (1997) *South Asia's Integration into the World Economy*, Washington DC: The World Bank. (This study takes a comprehensive look at the process of integration of South Asia's economy with the world economy and explores the implications of the Uruguay Round on clothing and textiles.)

* Porter, M.E. (1980) *Competitive Strategy: Techniques for Analyzing Industries and Competitors*, New York: The Free Press. (This book was a landmark work on competitive strategy at the time of its publication. It provides techniques for industry and competitor analysis and discusses concepts to help firms design effective strategies to fight competition.)

* Porter, M.E. (1990) *The Competitive Advantage of Nations*, London: Macmillan Press. (This book builds on Porter's earlier work on competitive strategy to explore what makes a nation's firms and industries competitive in global markets.)

* Quibria, M.G. (1997) *The Bangladesh Economy in Transition*, Delhi: Oxford University Press. (This volume is a collection of papers presented on different aspects of Bangladesh's economy at a conference organized by The Asian Development Bank.)

* World Bank (1994) *Adjustment in Africa: Reforms, Results and the Road Ahead*, New York: Oxford University Press. (This book provides comprehensive data on policy changes in sub-Saharan Africa and analyses whether reforms are paying off.)

World Bank (1995) *Claiming the Future: Choosing Prosperity*, Washington DC. (This book explores the causes of the poor economic performance of countries in the Middle East and North Africa and recommends that the MENA countries must carry out reforms in the political and economic spheres to improve the lot of the people in the region.)

See also: MANAGEMENT IN BANGLADESH; MANAGEMENT IN INDIA; MANAGEMENT IN NIGERIA; MANAGEMENT IN PAKISTAN; MANAGEMENT IN SRI LANKA

Related topics in the IEBM regional set: STRATEGY IN ASIA PACIFIC; STRATEGY IN EUROPE; STRATEGY IN LATIN AMERICA; STRATEGY IN NORTH AMERICA

World Trade Organization (WTO)

1 **Origin**
2 **WTO principles**
3 **Analysis**
4 **Conclusion**

Overview

The World Trade Organization (WTO) was established on 1 January 1995. It is the umbrella organization governing the international trading system. It oversees international trade arrangements and it provides the secretariat for the General Agreement on Tariffs and Trade (GATT), which has been based in Geneva since its inception in 1948. The GATT undertook eight 'rounds' of multilateral trade negotiations, which were successful in achieving major cuts in tariffs and (after the 1970s) some reductions in related non-tariff barriers to trade. The last GATT round, the Uruguay Round, took seven years, as its agenda had broadened to include trade in services, trade in intellectual property and a revised system of dispute-settlement mechanisms.

1 Origin

Contrary to popular belief, the WTO does not replace the GATT. An amended GATT remains as one of the legal pillars of the world's trade and, to a lesser extent, investment system. The other pillars were set up in the Uruguay Round's Marrakesh Agreement of 1994 and include the General Agreement on Trade in Services (GATS) and the Agreement on trade-related aspects of intellectual property rights (TRIPS). The membership of the WTO has increased from the seventy-six founding members of 1995 to 132 members (1998). Members include virtually all the developed and most of the developing countries. A notable non-member of the WTO is the People's Republic of China, whose entry has been blocked to date by the United States on the grounds that its economy is not open enough and that intellectual property rights (IPRs) are not sufficiently protected. The members of the WTO account for well over 90 per cent of the world's trade and virtually all of its investment.

The origins of the WTO can be traced back to the Atlantic Charter of 1941 developed by the then US president Franklin Roosevelt and the then British prime minister Winston Churchill. In order to counter US isolationism, the principle of the Atlantic Charter was for an international trading system with equal access to trade for all nations. This was seen as a complement to an effective world political forum, the United Nations (UN), established in 1946, with its permanent headquarters in New York City. The United States organized an international conference on trade and employment which resulted in the Havana Charter of 1948, in which it was proposed that the International Trade Organization (ITO) be established. Concurrently, twenty-three countries agreed to a set of tariff cuts and these were ratified by the GATT, which was set up as a transition arrangement to be subsumed under the ITO. However, the ITO was never ratified and the GATT continued for forty-seven years, until the WTO finally emerged in the last stages of the Uruguay Round to take on the powers originally designed for the ITO. The WTO now stands with the World Bank and the International Monetary Fund (IMF) as the third leg of the global economic system.

2 WTO principles

The WTO carries on the key GATT principle of non-discrimination, i.e. that any barrier to trade should be applied equally to all member countries (see ECONOMIES OF THE EMERGING COUNTRIES). It also keeps the most-favoured nation (MFN) principle, i.e. that any liberalization measures, with some exceptions, should also be granted to all members. To understand what these principles mean it is fruitful to think of the WTO as a club whose membership rules require that all members receive the same treatment and that if one member rescinds a trade concession other affected members can retaliate by withdrawing their reciprocal concessions, or receive compensation to equivalent commercial effect. If trade disputes arise then they can be settled by the unified dispute-settlement mechanism of the WTO, which can ensure timely compliance, in contrast to the basically voluntary procedures of the GATT. Now decisions of a WTO dispute panel can no longer be blocked by the disputant party, as was possible under the GATT. Panel findings can be subject to review by an Appellate Body of the WTO. In addition, the publication of trade-policy reviews and the activities of the Trade Policy Review Body (which regularly monitors the trade policies of member countries) complement the WTO's dispute-settlement activities by contributing significantly to enhanced transparency.

There are four important exceptions to the key GATT principle of non-discrimination. First, developed countries can give tariff preference to developing countries. Second, countries entering into regional free-trade agreements do not need to extend the preferences negotiated in this context on an MFN basis. Third, a country can invoke temporary 'safeguard' protection of one of its industries suffering serious injury due to a surge of imports. Fourth, temporary quantitative restrictions can be invoked by a country with serious balance-of-payment problems. In the latter two cases, these measures are temporary exceptions to the member's commitment to the GATT and a public investigation has to be undertaken to allow for limited relief from GATT obligations.

Another important principle of the WTO which is a significant improvement on the GATT is the 'single undertaking'. WTO members must accept all of the obligations of the GATT, GATS, TRIPS and any other corollary agreements. This ends the 'free ride' of some developing countries under the old GATT, when they could receive the benefits of some trade concessions without having to join in and undertake their full obligations. For most developed countries in North America and western Europe the single undertaking was already being made and the WTO meant few new obligations.

3 Analysis

The major tensions in the WTO relate to the issues of agriculture, trade in services and trade-related investment measures. None of these issues were included in the original mandate of the GATT, which dealt with trade in goods. Agriculture is a sector which most governments subsidize, and it was badly neglected in the GATT. One technical advance which helps to increase the transparency of subsidies is the calculation of producers' subsidy equivalents. As a result, in the Uruguay Round some progress was made towards the future reduction of the most egregious agricultural subsidies through a process of 'tarification', i.e. the translation of existing subsidies and other barriers to trade into tariff equivalents. Much work remains to be done in future rounds to liberalize agricultural trade.

Today services account for 70 per cent of the employment and value added in advanced industrialized countries, and also for at least half the world's trade and investment. The Uruguay Round started to address issues of trade in services with the establishment of GATS. Trade-related investment measures (TRIMS) were also considered and a substantive agreement that prohibits a number of investment requirements affecting cross-border trade in goods was reached, e.g. the TRIMS agreement restricted the imposition of export requirements on foreign investors. Future negotiations at the WTO (following on the last Uruguay Round of the GATT) will need to develop a deeper and more comprehensive set of rules for multinational investment than exists in TRIMS. These may well be based on the model of the North American Free-Trade Agreement (NAFTA), using the national treatment principle as the basic logic. National treatment states that foreign investors should not be discriminated against, but receive the same treatment as domestic firms in the application of domestic laws.

The WTO round could build on a multinational agreement on investment (MAI) which was partially negotiated by the Paris-based Organization for Economic Cooperation and Development (OECD) over the 1995–98 period. Currently, investment issues are being discussed at the WTO in the context of the Working Group on the Relationship between Trade and Investment, established and given a two-year mandate at the 1996 ministerial meeting in Singapore. Another important Working Group established during the WTO Singapore meeting is that examining the interaction between trade and competition policy.

4 Conclusion

Over a fifty-year period the GATT has moved forwards to the extent that today's new constitution for international trade, embodied in the WTO, includes an even fuller agenda of policy issues than was envisaged by its pioneering founders. These issues include further reduction of tariffs; a set of rules for multinational investment and competition policy; and the development of increased linkages between trade and issues of social policy, such as the environment and labour policy. The hurdles to achieving these three sets of objectives are lowest for tariff cuts, higher for investment, and highest of all for environmental and other social issues.

ALAN M. RUGMAN

TEMPLETON COLLEGE, UNIVERSITY OF OXFORD

Further reading

Brewer, T. and Young, S. (1998) *The Multinational Investment System and Multinational Enterprises*, Oxford: Oxford University Press. (Provides the economic context for a multilateral agreement on investment, possibly at the WTO.)

Feketekuty, G. (ed.) (1998) *Trade Strategies For a New Era: Ensuring U.S. Leadership in a Global Economy*, New York: Council on Foreign Relations. (A set of 18 mainly academic essays exploring the potential agenda for a new round of the WTO.)

Jackson, J.H. (1998) *The World Trade Organization: Constitution and Jurisprudence*, London: The Royal Institute of International Affairs. (Describes the institutional fabric of the WTO and the rules and procedures of its appellate system.)

Krueger, A. O. (1998) *The WTO as an International Organization*, Chicago, IL: University of Chicago Press. (Leading US academics analyse the WTO as an institution and consider current policy issues.)

Ostry, S. (1997) *The Post-Cold War Trading System: Who's on First?*, Chicago, IL: University of Chicago Press. (Presents an analysis of the GATT and WTO by the world's leading scholar of international institutions.)

Qureshi, A.H. (1996) *The World Trade Organization: Implementing International Trade Norms*, Manchester: Manchester University Press; New York: St Martin's Press. (Explains the legal framework of the WTO, how it works in practice and presents an appendix which reprints key selected documents.)

Rugman, A.M. (1996) *Multinationals and Trade Policy: Volume 2 of the Selected Scientific Papers of Alan M. Rugman*, Cheltenham: Edward Elgar. (Contains research papers reporting tests of GATT-related dispute-settlement procedures on countervail and anti-dumping, and on trade in services.)

Schott, J.J. (1996) *WTO 2000: Setting the Course for World Trade*, Washington, DC: Institute for International Economics. (Discusses the challenges facing the WTO and the agenda for future trade negotiations.)

World Trade Organization (1995) *The Results of the Uruguay Round of Multilateral Trade Negotiations: The Legal Texts*, Geneva: WTO. (Presents the actual legal texts of the last GATT round.)

World Trade Organization (1996a) *Annual Report 1996: Special Topic: Trade and Foreign Direct Investment*, vol. I, Geneva: WTO.

World Trade Organization (1996b) *Singapore Ministerial Declaration*, Document WT/MIN/(96)/DEC/W, Geneva: WTO. (Presents the report of the first WTO ministerial meeting in December 1996, including the Working Groups on competition policy and on investment.)

World Trade Organization (1997) *Annual Report 1997: Special Topic: Trade and Competition Policy, Vol. I.* Geneva: WTO.

Further resources

http://www.wto.org

See also: ECONOMIES OF THE EMERGING COUNTRIES

Related topics in the IEBM regional set: ASIA-PACIFIC ECONOMIC COOPERATION; ASSOCIATION OF SOUTH-EAST ASIAN NATIONS; EUROPEAN UNION; NORTH AMERICAN FREE-TRADE AGREEMENT

Country profiles
Africa

Management in Africa

1 Context
2 Corporate planning
3 Authority and decision making
4 Personnel and labour relations
5 Communication
6 Management education and training

Overview

In order to analyse and understand management practices and organizational processes in a diverse continent like Africa, it is necessary to consider at the outset the socioeconomic and cultural environment within which industrial enterprises operate. Such an understanding is useful because management policies and practices are influenced by culture and a deep-rooted belief system among Africans.

Modern organizations in Africa fall into three distinct broad categories. The first comprise public enterprises, in which the state controls 50 per cent or more of the share capital. Organizations in this category are set up to discharge specific functions and attain objectives which are more readily achievable outside the civil service system. In practically all African economies, this is the dominant type of organization in the modern sector. In the era of structural economic reforms, however, several African countries have embarked on extensive privatization programmes which have substantially reduced the role of the state in business enterprises in this category.

The second category includes private indigenous enterprises, an area in which African entrepreneurs are dominant. Enterprises in this category are comparatively small in size and are prominent in certain industrial sectors such as commerce, manufacturing and service. In this same category are a large number of micro-enterprises, which operate mainly in the informal sector. The informal sector occupies a prominent place in the economies of the region, and has been particularly prominent since the introduction of economic reforms and industrial restructuring which have led to substantial contraction in the formal sector since the 1980s. In this category of African businesses, management principles are marginally or informally practised. The third category includes multinational companies, foreign subsidiaries and joint-venture organizations. There are two subgroups in this category: enterprises which originated in the advanced Western capitalist economies; and those which can be described as 'third world multinationals', that is, originating in the new industrializing Asian economies. In many cases, organizations in this category are large and are found in all sectors, particularly in the manufacturing, textiles and automobile sectors. Although there are distinct approaches to management principles among the enterprises in the two categories, the issue in debate is the extent to which national norms, traditions and beliefs influence management practices in such organizations.

This entry will focus primarily on the first two categories of enterprises. The third category is excluded mainly because management principles and practices in such organizations have been covered by national entries in this series.

I Context

In the African continent the State has traditionally been dominant in economic management (see MANAGEMENT IN THE EMERGING COUNTRIES). Beginning in colonial times, business organizations were set up as public enterprises and corporations. After political independence in the various countries, the role of government in the economy intensified, generally because private capital was scarce and also because of the widespread commitment of the ruling elites to a welfarist or socialist development path in these newly independent states. In countries where private investment capital was becoming noticeable, several governments embarked on the nationalization of enterprises, ostensibly to achieve this socialist objective. In Tanzania, for example, following the introduction of a socialist development policy in 1967, several private sector organizations were nationalized by the State. Other countries, such as Sudan and Zambia adopted similar development policies. Alternatively, governments used their legislative power to acquire majority ownership in private businesses or joint-venture enterprises. In part as a result of these, the private sector in Africa has remained small, except for the expanding indigenous entrepreneurship sector. Although the introduction of economic reform policies and a market economy system since the late 1970s has rekindled interest in private investment, the public sector continues to dominate most African economies.

Management in Africa is strongly rooted in cultural beliefs and traditions. Age features prominently in the behaviour of African traditional societies. Wisdom, which permeates all human endeavour, is measured by age; older people are regarded as wiser than younger ones, who are expected to submit to the wisdom of elders. Under this system an authoritarian managerial culture naturally evolves. In public enterprises, where government predominates and where political considerations often outweigh economic rationale, a similar belief system exists because of the assumption in government that political decision makers know what is best for the majority. As a result, the government assumes the status of the paternalistic 'father' who knows what is best for the populace. What then emerges in such organizations is what might be referred to as a 'paternalistic–authoritarian' style of management.

Side by side with this managerial philosophy is the fact that the African managers, who receive their training and education in modern management principles and concepts, naturally approach the practice of management with this background. There is thus a confluence of approaches, some deriving from African culture and belief systems and some deriving from Western management principles introduced by Western capitalist organizations or management, and also from Western-educated managers who have assumed leadership and managerial positions in the enterprises. This blend of cross-cultural management principles is however confusing, or at best incomplete, in the sense that management practice has yet to achieve efficient integration of traditional beliefs with universally acceptable management principles.

2 Corporate planning

The planning function is fundamental to all organizations. It involves the visualization and determination of a future course of actions that will lead the organization to achieving its desired objectives; that is, the setting of objectives and determination of how to achieve those objectives. No matter how rudimentary, planning is a basic function in African management. In most organizations planning departments, whose responsibility it is to transform corporate objectives into realizable operational guidelines, are normally created. In practice, however, only large organizations use their planning departments in this manner, while most use them for gathering statistics and other mundane activities.

This shortcoming derives from the poor status accorded to the planning function in many organizations and the overriding influence of top management. Planning departments are rarely staffed with experts with relevant training and experience in such areas as finance, operations, organizational development, strategic management and statistics. Consequently, and given the prevailing management philosophy and limited scope for decision making, planning is invariably confined to setting general and departmental goals and rarely includes carefully developed strategic plans for translating these goals into realizable targets.

3 Authority and decision making

Generally in Africa, management authority, or the right to command and expend resources, resides with top management. This managerial style derives from the social-cultural values under which subordinates are rarely allowed or believed to possess initiative; all that is expected of subordinates is loyalty and total submission to superior authority. In African management there exists an intolerance of several power centres in an organization, a centralized control which fits well with the traditional African societal norm of leadership and control.

In public enterprises this centralization of power is reinforced by the view that only leaders can best define and execute what is in the 'national interest'. Decisions are influenced by political realities rather than by objective and carefully planned managerial processes. Because of this overwhelming centralization of decision making, the African middle-level manager is unable or unwilling to take risks or to make any initiatives. Although authority is shared or delegated within organizations, contrary to the principles of modern management, such delegation of power is restricted by the centralization of authority within top management. Even where there is delegation, it is confined to a few trusted managers who are usually family members or close friends. The underlying reason for this seems to be the general distrust among entrepreneurs that managers who are unrelated to them by birth or family affiliation would protect their interests. Given this, the scope of delegation of authority is highly limited. This type of managerial system inhibits initiative and negatively affects corporate growth and success. For the new generation of managers, those exposed to modern techniques of management, it breeds dissatisfaction and the lowering of morale.

However, forceful environmental changes are inducing change in this approach to decision-making, particularly in organizations where competitive pressures are inducing managers to seek workers' input into decisions that can improve organizational effectiveness. It is thus not inconceivable that this new thinking will slowly but gradually spread to other categories of organizations in Africa.

4 Personnel and labour relations

Personnel and human resource management (see HUMAN RESOURCE MANAGEMENT IN THE EMERGING COUNTRIES) in Africa relies heavily on ascriptive norms, with personnel decisions being influenced by the personal relationship between managers and employees. Recruitment and selection are heavily influenced by relation rather than by objective assessment of the suitability of the job applicant.

In modern management practices the responsibility for recruitment and selection is assigned to different levels of management (see INDUSTRIAL RELATIONS IN THE EMERGING COUNTRIES). Organizations vary as to which level of management has responsibility for the recruitment of certain grades of employees. While this is the usual approach in African organizations, appointments to posts for which administrative management should exercise authority are controlled by top management. This obviously reflects the dominance of the authoritarian–paternalistic style of management which is widespread in Africa. This is not to say that merit is never taken into consideration, but that family affiliation and friendship have great influence. The question of competence is often addressed by rationalizations such as: 'the employee can learn on the job'.

In most African organizations there is little formal integration of organizational objectives and human resource management. At best, human resource activities – planning, staff training and development, etc. – are assumed to reflect organizational objectives.

With regard to trade unions, several African nations subscribe to the International Labour Conventions on freedom of association and the right to collective bargaining. However, implementation is generally half-hearted in many countries. Trade unions exist but are restricted in the scope of their activities due both to the limited spread of wage or paid employment and to unfavourable state policies which impede their ability to effectively use the bargaining machinery. Bearing in mind the authoritarian–paternalistic style of management, it becomes obvious why the idea of collective bargaining, which is based on the principle of industrial democracy, does not always receive the approval of management.

At the enterprise level, African management generally does not favour unions, the accepted view being that they limit managerial freedom. The typical African entrepreneur believes that the trade unionist is a saboteur who is out to destroy his business and, as a result, takes every step, including victimization and dismissal, to discourage trade unionism in his enterprise. There is also a general disbelief among African managers that trade unions can play a constructive and positive role in their organizations.

Nevertheless, despite this dislike for trade unions, one of the key attributes of the paternalistic managerial style is the commitment of management to the welfare of the workers. The African manager is humane and considers the well-being of subordinates to be his or her major preoccupation. While this commitment does not totally remove employee discontent or grievances, it does reduce worker alienation and serves the social and psychological needs of the employees. In such organizations, management make an effort to provide both intrinsic and extrinsic rewards for their employees. This strategy helps to strengthen the bond of loyalty between employees and employer and also to reduce the drive for unionization.

Since the 1980s an increasing number of enterprises in Africa have taken a more accommodating stance towards workers' unions. Increasingly, managers are realizing both the positive role of the union and also the inevitability of workers' organization for providing a voice for workers. Thus, what the future portends for labour relations is how to balance the organizational interests of the workers with the commitment to corporate effectiveness and competitiveness.

5 Communication

Communication relates to the exchange of information, facts and opinions by two or more people in an organization by whatever means possible. It is essential for the effective implementation of decisions, plans and a sound organizational structure. Interpersonal communication, by which managers give orders as to what is to be done and how, implies the exchange of ideas or information. Yet the authoritarian–paternalistic managerial style does not facilitate smooth communication between the various cadres of management and between the latter and employees.

At the lowest level, subordinates are not expected to show initiative, particularly if they are young and not as experienced as members of senior management. Thus, what one finds in many organizations is a downward channel of communication where the chain of command is a one-way flow from top to bottom. Orders and directives follow the hierarchy of the organization. The channel normally flows from top management, through middle management, down to employees but, quite frequently, top management communicate directly with the employees, either because they believe it is their right to deal with the employees directly, in the context of the authoritarian–paternalistic style, or because of the belief that middle management cannot effectively communicate with the employees. However, the downward communication channel can only be effective where there is a feedback mechanism by which subordinates can communicate and convey their opinions and observations to their superior officers. Where this is not feasible or does not work properly, other informal channels such as the grapevine and rumours, with their attendant pitfalls, naturally become the effective means of upward communication between top management and subordinates or workers.

6 Management education and training

African management has been shown to have taken its roots from tradition and the cultural beliefs of the African people. However, the predominance of the authoritarian–paternalistic management style can, and does in some respect inhibit the achievement of corporate goals. On the other hand, neither are the Western-oriented management theories and concepts totally suitable to serve the interests of African management.

The traditional background of the African management system implies that managers do not have sufficient motivation to use their initiative or creative ability to the fullest. Neither does it respond speedily and effectively to the rapidly changing economic, political and technological environment and the interdependence of organizations worldwide. On the other hand, Western management theories and concepts which ignore the cultural beliefs of the people tend to imply that such beliefs are the causes of underdevelopment. They fail to recognize the nature of the economies and the cultural environment within which such theories are applied. They also ignore the fact that certain aspects of such theories and principles might be too advanced or, in certain cases, unsuitable in the economic realities in Africa.

Given this unsatisfactory state of competing approaches, it needs to be borne in mind that only an acknowledgement of the virtues of the cultural beliefs which influence the behaviour of the African manager will help in achieving a satisfactory blend of such beliefs and traditions with management theories and principles. Recognition of these cultural divergencies in training and management education programmes is essential if the observed inadequacies in management practices in the region are to be removed, or if the two approaches are to be seen as complementary to each other. In other words, it is essential for management education programmes to recognize cultural peculiarities and, at the same time, accommodate universally accepted management principles and concepts which are inevitable in the inter-dependent world of business. This will require a careful and well-conceived management education and training programme designed to promote a cross-cultural approach to African management.

To achieve this objective a carefully designed management curriculum for training African entrepreneurs and managers in the art and principles of management in an African environment must be developed (see MANAGEMENT EDUCATION IN THE EMERGING COUNTRIES). Such training must prepare managers for creative and imaginative tasks, in areas such as leadership, entrepreneurship, strategic planning, financial control, organizational behaviour and human resource management. The curriculum must be developed at all levels, starting with secondary education. At higher levels training should be all-embracing and should expose trainees to all known behavioural theories and how these can help in motivating the manager for effectiveness. In other words, training must enable the African manager to transform imported theories and concepts into acceptable cultural norms which can then be applied to management practices in Africa. With regard to research, efforts must be made to forge collaboration between local and international management development institutions and business organizations in an attempt to identify which management beliefs are core to Africa and how these may be interfaced or integrated with appropriate management principles and concepts.

TAYO FASHOYIN
ILO'S SOUTHERN AFRICA MULTIDISCIPLINARY ADVISORY TEAM, HARARE

Note

This entry is confined to Africa south of the Sahara.

Further reading

Blunt, P., Jones, M.L. and Richards, D. (1993) *Managing Organizations in Africa: Readings, Cases and Exercises*, Berlin: Walter de Gruyter. (Case studies on management themes including strategy, structure, conflict and human resource management.)

Blunt, P. and Popoola, O. (1985) *Personnel Management in Africa*, London: Longman. (A useful account of human resource management policies and practices in Africa.)

Fashoyin, T. (ed.) (1992) *Industrial Relations and African Development*, New Delhi: Asia Publishers. (Analyses labour relations, and the impact of structural adjustment programmes on economic development in selected African countries.)

International Bank for Reconstruction and Development (IBRD) (1993) *Indigenous Management Practices: Lessons for Africa's Management in the '90s*, Washington, DC: IBRD. (Seeks to develop an understanding of the critical role of cultural factors in indigenous reforms in sub-Saharan Africa.)

Kayizzi-Mngerura, S. (1998) *The African Economy*, London: Routledge. (This useful book deals with the challenges to African managers and the economic problems they face.)

Kiggundu, M.N. (1991) 'Challenges of management devlopment in sub-Saharan Africa', *Journal of Management Development* 10(6): 33–47. (Discusses management processes in African institutions and provides useful information regarding the challenges facing the managerial class.)

See also: HUMAN RESOURCE MANAGEMENT IN THE EMERGING COUNTRIES; INDUSTRIAL RELATIONS IN THE EMERGING COUNTRIES; MANAGEMENT EDUCATION IN THE EMERGING COUNTRIES; MANAGEMENT IN THE EMERGING COUNTRIES; MANAGEMENT IN NIGERIA; MANAGEMENT IN SOUTH AFRICA

Related topics in the IEBM regional set: MANAGEMENT IN ASIA PACIFIC; MANAGEMENT IN EUROPE; MANAGEMENT IN LATIN AMERICA; MANAGEMENT IN NORTH AMERICA

Management in Algeria

1 **Introduction**
2 **Managerial behaviour**
3 **Conclusion**

Overview

Algeria is a country plagued at present by civil disturbance. In addition to a fundamental clash between an Islamic and a secular polity and widespread violence, the environmental and economic institutions of the country are undergoing economic change. For most of the period since the country achieved independence it has functioned as a command economy organized on lines which ensured the state's control of economic processes. Large sectors of the economy have been socialized. The prevailing model of management has had to take account also of the enduring French cultural influence, which has continued to be important in the field of education and training. The transition from an essentially state-driven economic system to one in which economic deliberalization and privatization have been attempted demarcates the context under which managers in Algeria are starting to confront new challenges. These are not necessarily unique to Algeria, but the political situation gives them great force.

Since 1988 the Algerian economy has therefore moved away from a reliance on a centralized planning of state ownership to a more localized decision making, greater emphasis on market signals and more private ownership. None the less, today there are still around 300 state-owned enterprises, which account for about 60 per cent of the output of the Algerian economy. About one-fifth of these are regularly loss making. More than 70 per cent of all investment in Algeria still flows into the state-owned sector. Three hundred and fifty state-owned *local* enterprises (SOEs) account for a further 10 per cent of output and the remainder is accounted for by other ownership forms that are mainly private enterprises and joint venture. Thus, less than a quarter of the Algerian economy, at the present time, is in the private sector as understood in most other economies.

1 Introduction

Algerian public enterprises typically operate under the complex apparatus of state control (see ECONOMIES OF THE EMERGING COUNTRIES). Management decisions, therefore, require permits, authorizations and subsidies. None the less, in the emerging system such enterprises are, in some respects, autonomous to make their own economic choices. It has become a condition of state investment that state enterprises aim towards profitability. At the present time the state has completely withdrawn from the management of public enterprises, while retaining ownership. The ownership rights have been transferred to shareholders organized in the form of holdings. These are expected to produce the best possible results from a portfolio of public enterprise shares entrusted to them by the state. These participation funds are organized in eleven holding companies acting on behalf of the state to effect strategic control over the public enterprises in which they have shares.

Since 1988, foreign-owned companies have been permitted to invest in Algeria. The government is expected as an object of policy to refrain from interfering in joint ventures and creating disincentives for foreign direct investment. Most foreign joint ventures are in the oil and gas sectors. The ultimate control of ministers, in close association with party officials, in the allocation of labour and appointment of managers has determined the career choices and aspirations of most senior managers in Algerian enterprises. Wages and salaries were unrelated to individual performance and recruitment was based on assignments from the state labour bureau influenced by political and party connections.

Although in principle at the present time managers of state-owned enterprises in the public sector have more freedom to make decisions and they have even owned shares in their enterprises since 1998, high levels of losses continue to occur. No such large enterprises have, however, been made bankrupt. This factor influences management attitudes and behaviour in these enterprises.

2 Managerial behaviour

Chennoufi (1998) in a landmark study undertaken in 1995 and 1996 has documented the extent of economic liberalization and the impact on attitudes and behaviour of managers in SOEs, joint ventures (JVs) and small and medium-sized enterprises (SMEs), based on a study of sixteen structures. The study aimed to discover whether managerial attitudes and behaviour differed among the various enterprises in terms of their forms of ownership and, in particular, whether a more commercialized or Western approach to management in firms would occur in those enterprises with some private ownership and, in particular, in those in which foreign capital was involved.

Other studies have suggested that while managers may have felt themselves to have more freedom of manoeuvre during the 1980s when their managerial discretion was placed alongside that of Western managers of equivalent official rank, it became quickly apparent that they had little more scope than the first-line supervisors in Western manufacturing plants and that 'the threads that tied them to their supervisory bureaucracy were as tight as ever'. Investment, moreover, was still mainly integrated into the governmental planning system.

A study by CNAT (1995) based on ten large enterprises in the North East of Algeria investigated the effect of labour market reforms. Western-style human resource policies were found not to exist and labour turnover remained low, suggesting continuing rigidity in the labour market (see HUMAN RESOURCE MANAGEMENT IN THE EMERGING COUNTRIES; MANAGEMENT IN THE EMERGING COUNTRIES). CENEAP (1992) undertook a questionnaire survey of 97 middle managers in the western region, including Oran, in 1989. They concluded that managers still attached high importance to party contacts within the organization and to ensuring that employees had the proper political attitudes. None the less, this study found that there was 'rapidly rising interest' among managers in Western management concepts.

However, other studies have shown that bureaucrats continue to intervene directly in the management of joint ventures, even in the choice of technology, personnel, salary setting and foreign exchange. Research by CNAT in Algiers in 1988 and 1989 concluded that Algerian managers demonstrated a 'passive responsibility and participative style'. They tended to be punished for committing errors rather than awarded for taking initiatives. Further studies reported within a government report of 1993 involve six SOEs in Algiers between 1988 and 1992. These enterprises were headed by reform-minded managers; none the less, although managerial autonomy had increased, the state remained a powerful part of enterprise and decision making, especially in the appointing and dismissal of managers and influence over the granting of bank loans. None the less, the reforms of 1988 had shifted power from the central government to local politicians.

Chennoufi's study finds that by 1995/6 senior managers in large enterprises tended to be males in their middle years of 45 to 50, with 10 to 15 years of professional experience in the service of the organization with an average of just above five years in the present post. Ninety-two out of 112 respondents were university graduates with at least a first degree, predominantly in economics and finance followed by social sciences and engineering. Graduates in business administration are few and far between, only four occurring in Chennoufi's sample. Some of these, however, are in non-production areas such as marketing, personnel and corporate planning. Caution should be expressed about these findings as it is possible that managers in loss-making enterprises declined to be interviewed. Therefore, the sample consists very probably disproportionately of managers in organizations that are relatively successful.

Although government legislation allows for the appointment of boards of directors, it appears that few of these have actually been instituted and that direct relations to ministerial departments are still the preferred reporting mechanism. But under the 'responsibility system' more enterprise autonomy should occur.

The most important objectives of management are stated as being to increase profits, increase output volume and maintain employment. In a situation, however, in which political considerations obtain, it is probable that the latter two objectives continue to take precedence over the first. The power of appointing and dismissing directors or general managers is still retained by the political authorities irrespective of whether the enterprise has been corporatized or not. Several chief executives and various senior managers have a political rather than an enterprise management background. In the joint venture and SOE enterprises, however, a higher level of knowledge by senior management of modern Western techniques such as ISO 2000 was found. There was also more emphasis on management training (see MANAGEMENT EDUCATION IN THE EMERGING COUNTRIES). Managers in the joint ventures tended to be younger and more recently promoted. While the study shows that in some enterprises there have been recent closures of training departments, it is probable that this is also evidence of liberalization and privatization because such departments were formally largely directed towards political objectives rather than improvement of managerial capability. There have been little downsizing of enterprises and redundancy of employees and this may be explained by the direct involvement of employee organizations in decision making at the upper levels of the enterprise through the political process. Chennoufi concludes that 'probably the degree of worker involvement in the management of the enterprise slowed down the pace of change in the collectives compared both with the JVs and SOE sector'.

Managers interviewed in some companies expressed doubt and anxiety about whether the privatization process would be allowed to work because they questioned whether that was really the objective of state policy. A number of managers also dismissed the idea of privatization on the grounds that their enterprises were too large to be sold to the private sector or because they were loss making and therefore unattractive to buyers. But most managers understood that privatization will inevitably bring large-scale rationalization, including redundancies. Off the record, several managers, none the less, indicated that they favoured privatization.

3 Conclusion

In conclusion, therefore, the development of management in Algeria is at a most interesting stage. In some ways, the transition from a command to a privatized economy has been slower and has taken a more politicized route than occurred even in Eastern Europe when there was a sudden relaxation of restraints. The emphasis and the requirement in the next few years will be on producing a cadre of trained professional managers with expertise in Western management techniques. The current political and to some extent commercial isolation of Algeria, recent experiences of political and communal violence, and the generally depressed state of the Algerian economy, which was at one time the most powerful in the African continent, are not encouraging signs for the gradual and peaceful evolution of a more Westernized and depoliticized style of management to emerge.

Chennoufi's research shows that the budget constraint on firms has become stronger in recent years, implying a reduction in managerial discretionary behaviour but also a reduction in the scope for political intervention and decision making. The managers in Chennoufi's survey place less emphasis on pursuing the goals of central administration, implying a probable decline in the influence of government departments in these enterprises. The government is becoming less important as a source of information for managerial decision making but still retains wide powers in areas such as the appointment of senior managers, recruiting and dismissing staff, investment and the expansion of capacity, sales of assets, business restructuring, ownership change and bankruptcy and closure of the firm. It was only the managers in joint ventures who believed that they would have real power over such decisions. Downsizing has occurred to a considerable extent.

The scale and pace of change are smaller in the state-owned SMEs. The attitude of managers in the joint ventures is clearly differentiated from attitudes in the other types of enterprise studied. SME management seems the least interested in the introduction of new technology and there are indications that these enterprises are falling behind in technological capability.

Interestingly, none of the enterprise managers believe that privatization was, in fact, imminent, believing that there was a gap between public rhetoric and action in this respect. Transition to a market economy has been slow given the political crisis, the harsh environment in terms of international competitiveness and the demands of servicing very heavy external debt. Reform has been accompanied by austerity policies. Managers have felt starved of investment and the opportunity to introduce new technology and management techniques. The economy will remain largely dependent on oil, gas and product earnings for the foreseeable future.

There is a major requirement to improve the skill base in terms of human capital. This is not less significant in the area of management and management development. The policies of universities, higher education establishments and the state-supported higher schools of business and management have been geared to creating managers of an administrative and functionary type whose skills are not necessarily well suited to the changing environment of international competitiveness and performance to globally accepted best standards. This situation has been exacerbated by the reliance on largely French-inspired models of higher education and knowledge transmission, which emphasize the theoretical and abstract aspects of management rather than the practical, applied and pragmatic skills essential to managerial decision making. Despite a situation of high potential, it is difficult to see progress on these matters in the near future without considerable political stabilization, increased foreign direct investment and joint venture activity, and a changed climate towards management knowledge and application.

BOUALEM CHENNOUFI
UNIVERSITY OF EASTERN CYPRUS
GAZIMAGUSA, CYPRUS

DAVID T.H. WEIR
NEWCASTLE BUSINESS SCHOOL
UNIVERSITY OF NORTHUMBRIA AT NEWCASTLE

Further reading

(References cited in text marked *)

Aylen, J. (1987) 'Privatisation in Developing Countries', *Lloyds Bank Review* January. (Reviews progress of privatization and economic reforms in the LDCs.)

Balassa, B. (1987) 'Public Enterprise in Developing Countries: Issues of Privatization', Development Research Department, 292, World Bank, Washington DC. (Notes issues in the processes of economic liberalization and privatization for the public sector in LDCs.)

Bennoune, M. (1988) *The Making of Contemporary Algeria 1830–1987*, Cambridge University Press. (Traces the history of Algeria from conquest, through colonialization, the struggle for independence, and the emergence of independent Algeria, organized around largely socialist political institutions.)

* CENEAP (1992) Rapport sur le Development de la petite et moyenne industrie Algerie. 1975–1990. (Survey of Algerian managers and managerial attitudes to the organization.)

* Chennoufi, B.C. (1998) Privatisation and Liberalisation in Algeria, University of Bradford PhD Thesis. (Reviews economic policy in Algeria and reports a study of Algeria managers, public officials and political leaders on progress in privatization and economic liberalization.)

* CNAT Study (1995) Petites et Moyennes Entreprises au Niveau des Collectivites Locales en Algerie. 1978–1988. (Investigation into the effect of labour market reforms in Algeria).

Ruedy, J. (1992) *Modern Algeria: The Origins and Development of a Nation*, Indians University Press. (Describes the forms leading to the major political, social and economic structures of contemporary Algeria.)

See also: ECONOMIES OF THE EMERGING COUNTRIES; HUMAN RESOURCE MANAGEMENT IN THE EMERGING COUNTRIES; MANAGEMENT EDUCATION IN THE EMERGING COUNTRIES; MANAGEMENT IN THE EMERGING COUNTRIES

Management in Botswana

1 Introduction
2 The nature of the economy
3 Mining: diamonds and copper-nickel
4 Agriculture and cattle production
5 Employment
6 The Southern African Customs Union (SACU)
7 The development of business and management in Botswana

Overview

Management in Botswana is set within the context of a small arid and landlocked country in Southern Africa, which has been independent from colonial rule for some 32 years. From its origins as a country in the 1960s, Botswana has had a remarkable development as a country in sub-Saharan Africa in two respects; it has had both high and steady rates of economic growth and it has also combined this with a fully representative democracy. These two achievements alone single this small country out as an exception from almost all of the other countries of sub-Saharan Africa, including its much larger and more economically diverse neighbour South Africa. Botswana has made considerable economic and social progress despite of the major disadvantage of its drought prone location (much of the country is semi-arid and encompasses the Kalahari desert) and for most of the period of its existence as a country it has had to cope with an apartheid neighbour who would not have hesitated to violate its sovereignty in pursuit of its racist objectives. As a small open economy it has, since independence, been outward looking in its liberal economic policy and in its politics. Botswana is a classic example of the dualistic economy , where diamonds in the modern sector of the economy and cattle raising in the traditional sector dominate the economic activity of the country (Colclough and McCarthy 1980) The management of the economy has been highly successful, although not without serious problems, but the government has hitherto always managed to balance a harsh and unforgiving natural environment and its few opportunities for obvious economic diversification, with a political climate in South Africa that until very recently was equally harsh. It has required great skill and judgement to maintain this balance and to avoid falling foul of its neighbour.

1 Introduction

Botswana was the British protectorate Bechuanaland, until it was granted independence on 30 September 1966. All the people of Botswana are known as the Batswana although this name also refers to the major ethnic group the Tswana in South Africa. These people came into the area (from South Africa) during the period of the 1880s during the Zulu wars. The indigenous population were the bushmen of the Kalahari made famous in the writings of Laurence van der Post. The Batswana were herders and farmers who lived under traditional tribal government. Bechuanaland was given British government protection in the 1880s, since hostilities had broken out with the Batswana and the Afrikaner boers. Bechuanaland was much larger than present day Botswana, since it comprised a southern territory which is now part of Cape colony in South Africa. The majority of tswana-speaking people live in South Africa.

In 1909 the inhabitants of the Bechuanaland protectorate (and also those of Basutoland and Swaziland) asked for and received assurances from the British government that they would not be included in the proposed Union of South Africa. The expansion of British central authority during the 1920s saw the evolution of tribal authority and government. This tribal rule and powers were regularized in the 1930s. During the 1950s and early 1960s a consultative legislative council was formed which culminated in the proposal for democratic self-government in Botswana in 1964. The seat of government had, prior to independence, been in Maefeking in South Africa and with the granting of independence the British government provided the funding for the new capital, Gaborone.

Botswana was established with some controversy, since the UK government of the time whilst recognizing that Seretse Khama was both leader of the independence movement and the legitimate traditional ruler, was hesitant about dealing with the independence movement. There were elements in the Conservative government of the day that sympathized with white South Africa and attempted to thwart Khama since he was married to a white woman. Seretse Khama was elected first president, re-elected twice and died in office in 1980. The presidency passed to the vice-president Sir Ketumile Masire, who was elected in his own right in 1984 and re-elected in 1989 and 1994. The next election is to be held in 1999.

2 The nature of the economy

Botswana is a small open economy with a substantial level of foreign reserves. Foreign reserves in 1997 were some 20 billion pula, official reserves are the equivalent of some 32 months of imports of goods and services. The economy of Botswana is predominantly dualistic in so far as the modern sector is dominated by diamond production and export. Botswana has had periods of high economic growth achieving an impressive 10 per cent annually over the years since independence. In 1996 the real growth rate was some 5 per cent. Per capita income is of the order of US$3,100 (1996). The rate of unemployment at 21 per cent is a major problem facing the government. The government however has managed is trade and foreign exchange policy to achieve a positive trade balance which is substantial and has provided the basis for steady and impressive economic and social development given the underlying nature of the economy (International Monetary Fund (IMF) 1998). Inflation has averaged 10 per cent over the last 10 years (see ECONOMIES OF THE EMERGING COUNTRIES).

3 Mining: diamonds and copper-nickel

The economy is completely underwritten by the dominance of the mining industry and its economic success is due, in the main, to the way this industry has been well managed by the government. Two large mining companies, Debswana and

Bamangwato Ltd (BCL), both have substantial government equity. Debswana is a joint equal partnership operation with the South African Debeers mining company and Bamangwato concessions has substantial government equity participation. Debswana is concerned with diamond production and BCL with copper-nickel mining. Since the early 1980s Botswana has become the world's largest producer of quality diamonds. Australia and the Congo being the main competitor countries. The Congo is a good example of a country with a rich mineral industry being used as a source of wealth for the leadership of that country; namely the late Mobutu. The rich mineral resources of the Congo were squandered and the economic conditions of the population have not improved since independence, whereas in Botswana the population has benefited from the relatively prudent management of both the mining industry and the overall macroeconomy since independence (Harvey and Lewis 1990).

Three large diamond mines have opened since independence (at Orapa in 1972; Lethakane in the mid-1970s; and Jwaneng in 1982); diamonds were first discovered in the early 1970s by the Debeers company. The diamond industry is part of the international diamond cartel which is managed by Debeers from the Central Selling Organisation (CSO) in London. The CSO has been one of the more successful international cartels in so far as it has had reasonable success in stabilizing the diamond market and maintaining the price of diamonds in the world economy. 'A diamond is for ever' sums up the aim of this cartel to stabilize diamond prices through the control of the supply of diamonds on the world market. Debswana has its main fortress-like building in the capital Gaborone where diamonds are held in storage while awaiting CSO decisions on sales in the marketplace. Diamond stocks vary with world market conditions and are sold with a view to maintaining prices over the long term. Diamond sales (and mining sales) amount to some 36 per cent of GDP (gross domestic product) although employment in the diamond sector of the economy is very small. In 1997 diamonds amounted to some 74 per cent of exports; other export goods were as follows: meat 2.6 per cent; copper nickel 4.3 per cent; textiles 2.3 per cent; soda ash 1.0 per cent; vehicles 10.6 per cent and other products 5.8 per cent. The mining and quarrying sector employed some 8000 people in 1997, out of a formal sector employment total of 230,000.

BCL operates a copper-nickel mine at Selebi-Phikwe but has had a troubled financial history. However, it is an important employer in the mining sector, as it has a soda ash operation at Sua Pan opened in 1991 and supported by government, although it has also lost money.

4 Agriculture and cattle production

Agriculture is the most important sector of the economy since more than half the population lives in rural areas and is largely dependent on subsistence crops and livestock farming. Agriculture meets only a small proportion of the food needs of the economy, contributing approximately 4 per cent of GDP. This contribution to GDP is primarily through beef exports. The importance of agriculture to Botswana comes from its social and cultural influence on the society, where cattle raising plays a major part in both the social and economic life of the country. Since independence, cattle have been the defining characteristic in society, where the tribal traditions of the

Batswana are governed by the requirements of cattle rearing. The representative democracy that was established in Botswana had as much to do with this traditional communal cattle rearing society, as it had to the legacy of British colonial administration. The national cattle herd has fluctuated over the years from 1.4 million in 1966 to 2.9 million in 1982. Currently the national herd stands at 2.5 million. The national herd fluctuates from year to year due mainly to the adverse effects of drought and disease. The late 1960s and the late 1970s were particularly bad years for drought and foot and mouth disease, while kung disease in cattle has also hit the herd size and exports. In the mid-1990s, 200,000 cattle were slaughtered to prevent lung disease.

Botswana has been the beneficiary of preferential access to the EU for its cattle exports under the beef quota arrangement of the Lome convention.This arrangement has provided market access to the EU, mainly to the UK. Economic aid has also been given to the cattle sector to ensure that the exacting veterinary standards required for entry into Europe are met. The EU are currently renegotiating its Lome arrangements with all its African, Caribbean and Pacific members.

The arable sector is located at the edge of the country and crops such as white maize and sorghum are grown. The government has a policy of promoting self-sufficiency in cereal production through price support but, mainly as a result of drought, has not achieved this goal during a large part of the period since the country was founded (Cathie and Dick 1987). Food security policy is, in the main, achieved by imports of the necessary cereal requirements of the population from countries in the region. Botswana has received food aid from Western donors such as the EU, but these supplies have not been reliable during drought periods and the food security policy of the country has been underpinned by the strong foreign exchange reserves held by the government.

5 Employment

Out of a population of 1.5 million people, and a total estimated workforce of 428,000, formal sector employment in the economy amounts to some 237,500 (in 1997) and 13,377 Batswana are employed in mines in South Africa. Other migrant Batswana find employment on farms in South Africa. The remittances from these workers provide a significant source of income to the poor regions of Botswana. Employment opportunities in South Africa are subject to considerable swings, since the mines hire and fire workers from a number of countries surrounding South Africa over a period of time. The unemployment rate was estimated in 1995 at 21 per cent of the working population; those who are not in formal sector employment, in Botswana or in South Africa, are engaged in cattle raising or subsistence agriculture. The economy therefore has a large proportion of the potential workforce underemployed. As a consequence of this situation the government has given high priority to expanding employment opportunities for its citizens through policies which are designed to diversify the economy (see HUMAN RESOURCE MANAGEMENT IN THE EMERGING COUNTRIES).

Formal employment in Botswana in the private and parastatal sector of the economy was approximately 150,000 during the 1990s, with central and local government employing a further 88,000 of the workforce. Formal employment in agriculture was 4,600; in mining 8,600; manufacturing 23,900; construction 22,500;

and trade and hotels 45,900; finance and business 17,500; social and personal services 13,800. Manufacturing had a considerable boost in the early 1990s when the South Korean *chaebol*, Hyundai, established a vehicle plant in Botswana to supply to the Southern African market. In 1997 vehicle exports amounted to 10 per cent of the value of exports.

6 The Southern African Customs Union (SACU)

Botswana has been a member of the Southern African Customs Union (SACU) since it was established in 1910. SACU comprises Botswana, Namibia, Lesotho, Swaziland and South Africa. Under SACU, South Africa has collected levies from customs, sales and excise duties for all members and the proceeds are shared on the basis of each country's proportion of imports. The formula for sharing revenues and the authority for deciding duties has become increasingly controversial since South Africa has rid itself of apartheid. The arrangement is being renegotiated in the current period. Botswana has benefited considerably in the past from this arrangement through its duty free access to the large South African market. Since South Africa has joined the World Trade Organisation many of the SACU duties have declined making products from third parties much more competitive.

The currency of Botswana, the pula, is not part of the monetary union which other members of SACU have with the South African rand. The pula is fully convertible and is valued against a basket of currencies (which includes the rand). Profits and direct investment can be repatriated with little or no restrictions.

Botswana has managed its pegged exchange rate regime well over the years despite its close economic proximity to a far less stable South African rand. The exchange rate policy of Botswana has been a key to its successful macroeconomic management and to its liberal and relatively open economy which has encouraged foreign investment and foreign management activity in the economy. The policy of maintaining a stable pula–rand rate in real terms has protected the non-traditional export sector and its import substituting industries. This has in turn helped safeguard employment and also encouraged greater economic diversification in the economy.

7 The development of business and management in Botswana

Botswana has as a major aim of its economic and social policy the diversification of its economy with a view to being less dependent on the diamond and cattle sectors for the employment of its population. The importance of alternative employment for its population has been recognized by the government from its earliest years. In the mid-1990s the non-traditional sectors of the economy grew at over 5 per cent, to some degree compensating for a slight decline in the mineral sector. Foreign investment and management are welcomed in Botswana and are seen as a key element in the government's objective of diversifying growth and employment in the economy. Light manufacturing, tourism and financial services have all grown in the 1980s and 1990s. Foreign investment in Botswana has grown, with companies from the USA in production facilities and brickmaking, and from South Korea in vehicle assembly. All workers are free to join or organize unions, although the industrial or wage economy is small, unions are concentrated in the mineral, railway and banking sectors. The Botswana Federation of Trade Unions (BFTU) is independent of government and is not associated with any political party. Legal strikes are only possible after an exhaustive arbitration process. A minimum wage of a monthly 286 pula is 50 per cent less than the figure the government has calculated as necessary to meet the basic needs of a family of five.

The Department of Trade and Investment Promotion Agency (TIPA) of the Ministry of Commerce and Industry provides assistance and information to investors and traders. There are two principal chambers of commerce, the Botswana National Chamber of Commerce and Industry and the Botswana Confederation of Commerce, Industry and Manpower. In 1995 The Botswana Stock exchange was established with a market capitalization of 1.4 billion pula (approximately US$403 million).

Botswana, because of its history and its geography, has had long and deep ties to the economy of South Africa. Its major role in the Southern African Development Community (SADC), the successor to SADCC, which was concerned to free the region's economic development from dependence on the apartheid state of South Africa. The 12 nations of SADC have the broad goal of encouraging economic growth, development and integration in the region. The regional centre for SADC is in Gaborone.

Government policy towards improving transportation and communications has managed to incorporate much of its sparsely populated interior through roads connecting all major towns and a fibre optic telecommunications network has also been established.

The background for business and management in Botswana has progressively improved and strengthened over the last 30 years (see MANAGEMENT IN THE EMERGING COUNTRIES). A free and open economy provides the backdrop for a progressive growing economy, which is amongst the strongest free-market friendly environments in sub-Saharan Africa. Botswana has demonstrated that sound economic development is based upon a well-managed economy, where the riches from diamond production are deployed to provide other opportunities for employment for a fast growing population. Education is given high priority by the government and the education system produces able and literate people who are positioned to grasp the opportunities that employment growth is gradually providing through the policy of employment diversification. The government of Botswana is well aware of the importance of attracting foreign investment and management to the economy and is likely to maintain that openness of approach since it has served the society in the past and is likely to do so in the future. Although a small economy in the much larger South African region, Botswana is likely to provide a role model for other counties in the region should they examine the remarkable success story that Botswana can illustrate from its economic and political record.

Botswana has the strength that comes from a well-managed economy in a difficult and somewhat hostile natural environment, and from having made a sustained development of the society and the economy. Botswana has also managed to develop that society during some difficult years politically, when South Africa was pursuing apartheid and her vulnerability was evident both economically and in terms of her sovereign security. Botswana has, however, a number of weaknesses, including a rapid population growth that, if it remains unchecked, will outrun and possibly undo the sound progress and achievements of the last 30 years. The changes in South Africa will provide both opportunities if that economy is to grow and prosper, and challenges with the likely reduction of transfers from the customs union in the wake of the need in South Africa itself for inward investment. Botswana, although a small economy, has the potential to contribute, not least from its own experience, to the economy of southern Africa. However, Botswana is also dependent upon stability in the region; as a land-locked economy, her prosperity is very much a part of the wider prosperity in the region. Her fortunes may very well depend on the fortunes of her neighbours and their ability to manage economies that in many ways are better placed than Botswana itself. It is more than likely that Botswana will continue in a steady fashion to encourage business and foreign investment in her economy in the full realization that the future of her economic and social progress is dependent upon such an open outlook.

JOHN CATHIE
UNIVERSITY OF CAMBRIDGE

Further reading

(References cited in the text marked *)

* Cathie, J. and Dick, H. (1987) *Food Security and Macroeconomic Stabilisation: a case study of Botswana 1965–1984*, Kieler Studien no 208 Tübingen: JCB Mohr (Paul Siebeck). (A detailed account of the food security policies of Botswana and the macroeconomic policy options open to the government.The structure of the economy is given in a general equilibruim model of the economy.)
* Colclough, C. and McCarthy, S.(1980) *The Political Economy of Botswana. A Study of Growth and Distribution*, Oxford: Oxford University Press. (A good history of the early development of the economy and society of Botswana. This is a standard reference work on the economy and development of Botswana.)
  Harvey, C. (ed.) (1981) *Papers on the Economy of Botswana. Studies in the Economics of Africa*, London. (A good collection of papers on the major aspects and policy problems and options of the government in the management of the economy, *inter alia*: diamonds, aid, agriculture and government policy.)
* Harvey, C. and Lewis, S.R. (1990) *Policy Choice and Development Performance in Botswana*, London: Macmillan. (This book has analysis on all the key sectors of the economy and gives an overview of the economy from independence. The growth and structure of the economy are discussed as is development strategy, agriculture, mineral policy and mining development, manufacturing, financial development and the management of the financial surplus. It also considers infrastructure and urban bias, poverty and income distribution as well as future prospects. This work provides a good detailed introduction on the economy and society.)
* International Monetary Fund (1998) *Selected Issues and Statistical Appendix*, Washington, DC: IMF, p. 55. (Recent analysis and data on the Botswana economy .This country report from the IMF highlights the development of the exchange rate in Botswana and examines the development of this policy. This report gives a snapshot of the economy and provides the most recent macroeconomic and historical data on the economy.)

See also: ECONOMIES OF THE EMERGING COUNTRIES; HUMAN RESOURCE MANAGEMENT IN THE EMERGING COUNTRIES; MANAGEMENT IN AFRICA; MANAGEMENT IN THE EMERGING COUNTRIES; MANAGEMENT IN SOUTH AFRICA

Management in Ghana

1 **Introduction**
2 **Political changes since 1987**
3 **Structural reforms**
4 **Analysis**
5 **Evaluation**
6 **Conclusion**

Overview

Although most large organizations in Ghana follow the Western style of management, managers are confronted every day with traditional practices and customs which conflict with the Western philosophy of management. These traditions and other socio-cultural issues impose some constraints on managerial efficiency and effectiveness.

Until the early 1980s, Ghana lacked political stability, with each successive government managing the economy according to its preferred political ideology. From independence, in 1957, the economy has swung from socialist orientated, to free enterprise, to mixed economy, to the current free-enterprise system. Consequently, there have been numerous modifications to the management style in Ghana.

Management style in Ghana is characterized by centralization of decision making, authoritarian leadership style, large distance between management and rank-and-file employees and minimal teamwork, among other things.

The implementation of an economic reforms programme (1983), subsequent market liberalization and serious efforts by the government to woo foreign investors have exposed organizations to competitive pressures. Managers have, therefore, had to improve their management skills in order to attain and sustain the competitive advantage of Ghanaian organizations.

1 Introduction

Arguably, the modern Western style of management in Ghana owes its origins to colonialism. Indeed, management in Ghana has been heavily influenced by historio-political factors, not least the British colonial administration. Ghana, the former British colony of the Gold Coast, made history when it became the first Black African colony to attain political independence in 1957.

The British colonial administration, European missionary institutions and European commercial enterprises introduced Western management theory and practice into Ghana. Management was not, however, unknown in pre-colonial Africa. There is evidence that pre-colonial Africa had administrative systems, typically small in size and homogenous in terms of membership. They were often led by chiefs or hereditary kings whose relationships with their subjects were highly personalized and authoritarian. But some democratic processes/structures existed for decision making and implementation of policies, with checks and balances to deal with excessive abuses of power (Kiggundu 1991).

In many parts of Africa, particularly in East and Southern Africa, the various colonial powers first destroyed or denigrated traditional administrative institutions and replaced them with their own. In anglophone West Africa, this destruction was less severe as the British colonial administration foresaw the benefits of working through the chiefs to secure its power base. Thus, unlike the French, who pursued an *assimilation* policy in their African colonies, the British followed a policy of *indirect rule*. Essentially, British rule was exercised through, rather than in spite of, traditional rulers and customary practices. Thus, in Ghana, as in the rest of British West Africa, the aim of the colonial administration was to rule, as far as possible, through the agency of indigenous institutions (Bourret 1963). The colonial administration used all its powers to encourage the chiefs to work with the government in matters of local administration (Kimble 1965). This was, in fact, a tacit admission that the traditional systems of governance could be used to implement, enforce and administer British colonial policies.

Thus, a dual system of administration emerged in the colony. Gardiner (1976) comments on this dualism by pointing out that, in Ghana, the influences of colonialism and traditional practices have an impact on management. In her view, traditional Ghanaian behaviour, beliefs, practices and attitudes exist alongside the modern Western-orientated society.

Quite apart from the colonial influence, the various post-independence governments also shaped management in Ghana. Kwame Nkrumah, the first elected Prime Minister of Ghana, and his Convention People's Party (CPP) formed the first government. Nkrumah's government pursued a populist brand of nationalism and Pan-Africanism in its early years but later, in the early 1960s, attempted to move Ghana towards a communist/socialist path. His economic policies resulted in shortages of essential commodities and bribery and corruption were rife. Despite the expressed aims of subsequent governments (the pursuit of democracy and economic security), the populace experienced a degradation of the hopes raised by independence in 1957. Ghana has endured a succession of administrations (mainly through coup and counter-coup) that also proved to be incapable of eradicating the systemic corruption that plagued public life (Economist Intelligence Unit 1990).

2 Political changes since 1987

June 1987 saw a new government, led by Flight Lt J.J. Rawlings, which was even more populist than previous regimes. To gain the support of the masses and the working class, it initiated a *house cleaning* exercise, immediately rounding up the former members of the previous regime and executing them by firing squad. This done, it set itself the task of eradicating corruption in Ghana. After this *cleaning up operation*, the Armed Forces Revolutionary Council (AFRC) allowed the scheduled 18 June 1979 election to take place. This election was won by Dr Hilla Linmann's People's National Party (PNP), which had invoked the still popular image of Nkrumah. In September 1979, the AFRC handed over power to the PNP, but Rawlings overthrew the PNP government in December 1981. The coup was precipitated by the PNP's inability to manage the economy, corruption and internal disagreements.

Rawlings' first coup marked a watershed in Ghanaian politics. For the first time in Ghana's history, power was wrested from the hands of the middle class élite and the senior ranks of the military and police (Economist Intelligence Unit 1990). In a sense, the second Rawlings coup sought to improve the welfare of the working class. The government began with an essentially leftist and socialist ideology but has now transformed itself into an ardent promoter of privatization and a free enterprise (market) economy. Besides the effects of politics on management in Ghana, the economic policies of the various governments have had their influence on management practices.

After the 1966 coup, the government of the National Liberation Council (NLC) and that of the Second Republic (led by Dr Kofi Busia, a former Oxford University academic) sought to shift Ghana towards a Western style of management. The NLC abandoned the state-directed industrialization policy and sold off some public enterprises; Busia continued this policy, encouraging the private sector to take a more active role in the economy. The following administration of the military-cum-police junta – the National Redemption Council (NRC), led by Colonel Achampong – reversed the economic and pro-Western policies implemented by Busia's government, moved away from privatization and refocused government policy on state enterprises.

The Rawlings government initially pursued similar populist and nationalist policies but it is this government that has made the greatest strides towards a free enterprise economy. After initially pursuing an economic policy which has been described as *bootstrap* stabilization, the government, in 1983, transformed itself from being orientated towards a socialist philosophy to a pro-Western style of economic management (Economist Intelligence Unit 1990). In May 1983, the government (assisted by the International Monetary Fund (IMF) and the World Bank) launched its four-year Economic Recovery Programme (ERP), aimed at addressing economic imbalance and promoting growth through liberalization.

3 Structural reforms

A major policy objective of the ERP was structural reforms in the financial, agricultural, energy, industrial, educational and health sectors, aimed at promoting growth (see ECONOMIES OF THE EMERGING COUNTRIES). During the initial stages of the Structural Adjustment Programme (SAP), two ongoing activities were predominant: (1) workforce restructuring/retrenchment, and (2) the transfer of ownership or the liquidation of loss-making public enterprises. The objective was to expose state enterprises to competitive market forces and stimulate a more cost-effective and financially responsible management (Davis 1991). Unprofitable public enterprises have, therefore, been either liquidated or privatized to avoid the wastage of public funds. The SAP has resulted in massive job losses in the public sector – in particular the civil service.

According to Agyekum and Synge (1993) the economy has been experiencing *positive* results since the introduction of the ERP and SAP. Building on the momentum towards a free enterprise economy, the government repealed the Manufacturing

Industries Act 1971 which prohibited manufacturers from setting free market prices for their products. Furthermore, the 1985 Investment Code has been revised to encourage private investment. Along the same lines, the Ghana Investment Centre has been transformed from a regulatory body to a promotion institution. The government has also made it possible for public enterprises to privatize through the use of: (a) public share offerings on the local stock exchange or foreign stock exchanges; (b) joint ventures; and (c) worker and/or management buy-outs. To facilitate this process, a stock exchange was established in Ghana in October 1990.

Having helped to liberalize the economy, the donor countries and other foreign governments put pressure on the Rawlings Provisional National Defense Council (PNDC) government to return the country to a democratically elected government; elections were held in 1992, won by Rawlings' political party – the National Defence Congress (NDC). Rawlings became President, and his party won the majority of seats in the parliament. Hence, the military regime changed overnight to a civil administration. Although the opposition party boycotted the parliamentary elections (for alleged irregularities), the NDC managed to finish its four-year term. The last elections were held in 1996 and, again, the NDC won both the parliamentary and presidential elections. Arguably, the policies of the Rawlings government instilled a free enterprise philosophy in Ghana and there is now a serious attempt to modify and adapt Western management philosophies and practices to Ghana.

4 Analysis

Ghanaian organizations can be classified according to type, ownership and size. Civil service and public enterprises are often large bureaucratic organizations with, usually, hierarchical and mechanistic structures, exhibiting high levels of centralization and formal systems of administration. Subsidiaries of multinational companies are also large but of lower hierarchical structure and formal systems of administration. Local Ghanaian firms are usually informal, non-hierarchical (flat) and lacking in formalization but usually exhibit centralized or individual decision-making practices (Kiggundu 1988). Africa still lays a great deal of emphasis on traditions and institutions, customs and socio-cultural issues. In Ghana, as elsewhere in sub-Saharan Africa, society and environment permeate management in modern organizations. These traditional practices make operating levels inefficient and costly, exerting considerable financial pressure on the organization. They also compromise the integrity and efficiency of the formal bureaucratic system, introducing an element of subjectivity in management practices, such as recruitment, performance appraisal and compensation (see MANAGEMENT IN AFRICA).

In a society where there is a great deal of respect for the elderly (respect for age), status and people in authority, there is a high degree of subservience to the elderly and authority figures in organizations (Nzelibe 1986). Social distance between superiors and subordinates is marked, with a sharp distinction and status difference between management and rank-and-file employees. Workers are expected to do their work and follow management's instructions and directives. Subordinates rarely question or challenge those in authority, not expressing their opinions openly – but there is no shortage of opinions privately.

The extended family prevails in Ghana. People give help and support to kinsmen and expect to receive help from others when they are in need. This high sense of collectivism also has a negative impact on management. It is not uncommon for people to pester relatives in managerial positions for favours. In particular, many people exert pressure on such relatives to employ them or their children, regardless of their qualifications or whether there is a vacancy (Gardiner 1996).

Another cultural/traditional issue that imposes a heavy burden on organizations is funerals. Ghanaians have long bereavement and mourning periods. As such, organizations are also expected to be sympathetic to bereaved employees and to allow employees time off to attend the funerals of friends and members of their extended family. In addition, companies are obliged, under the terms of collective agreements, to buy the coffin for an employee who dies in service or for members of an employee's immediate family. Furthermore, organizations are obliged to provide transport for employees to attend the funerals of colleagues and those of colleagues' relatives (see BUSINESS CULTURES, THE EMERGING COUNTRIES).

Also, Ghanaians have a *culture of forgiveness* which influences management on the issue of *transgression and punishment*. Ghanaians have a tendency to beg for forgiveness for infraction of organizational rules. Gardiner (1996: 496) comments that, in the workplace, it is considered that 'regardless of the seriousness of the trans-gression, whether theft or drunkenness at work, once the transgressor goes to "beg" all should be forgiven.... He may even ask a politician or member of government to mediate on his behalf.'

Such a situation creates problems in the discipline of employees in organizations as, culturally, it is expected that the manager will forgive the transgressor, or be deemed to be a wicked and uncaring person. Consequently, managers may fail to discipline employees for even gross misconduct because they do not want to be unpopular in the organization. Respect for the elderly also makes it difficult for a young manager to discipline older subordinates. Moreover, many organizations, particularly in the public sector, base promotion and pay increases on seniority rather than merit or performance.

Another socio-cultural issue that has a negative impact on management is time keeping. African culture does not emphasize the importance of time and time keeping in organizational life. Thus, lateness is endemic in Ghanaian organizations, with many people always arriving late for work or meetings.

While there are elements of both femininity and masculinity in Ghanaian culture, in terms of organizational life, masculinity is emphasized. While the culture encourages people to be concerned about others and places importance on relationships, male chauvinistic behaviour pervades organizations. For instance, male employees often make jokes about the fragility of women and many men cannot reconcile themselves to the idea of working under a female boss. The competence or expertise of women is not, however, doubted and there are no wage differentials between males and females holding the same level of appointment.

At least in theory, if not in practice, the management philosophy of large organizations in Ghana approaches that of classical management, but the bureaucratic and impersonal system of administration of such organizations is challenged by the Ghanaian traditional culture. It is, therefore, extremely difficult for organizations to have undiluted bureaucratic systems – which are faceless, impersonal and impartial. Indeed, in a country with unreliable telephone and postal systems, many organizations respond only to those who take the trouble to make personal contact with the organization.

High inflation has brought about rising costs of living and the diminishing purchasing power of earnings. Thus, motivation essentially takes the form of financial and extrinsic compensation (salary, bonuses and fringe benefits). It is common practice for organizations to provide employees with accommodation or a rent allowance and to have schemes covering health/medical expenses. Some organizations also provide a car allowance for senior employees, partly because of a lack of good top and middle managers with managerial talents and skills. As Hug (1989: 3) put it: 'with the decline in real wages, professional people and others with talent and skills began to leave the country to take up employment abroad'.

The trend has not reversed. The few competent managers work very hard and, fearing that subordinates may not pay attention to detail, often fail to delegate responsibility. Workers rarely show a high degree of loyalty and commitment to the organization. In the view of Kiggundu (1988), individual rather than organizational goals drive employee behaviour as organizational goals remain unknown or ignored by most employees. Similarly, only a few organizations have explicit mission statements and even then they are rarely adhered to. Organizations tend to be reactive rather than proactive and long-range planning is not considered seriously. There is a perpetual state of *crisis management* and instead of confronting conflicts and dealing with root causes, these are usually avoided or smoothed over. Just as in other sub-Saharan African countries, organizations in Ghana lack dynamism. On this Kiggundu (1988: 224) comments that:

> … innovation, entrepreneurship, risk taking, and individualism are not valued or rewarded. Instead they are discouraged and, as a result, African organisations are short of 'change masters'. There is little support for change even when the status quo in these organisations is unsatisfactory.

It can be implied from the above that organizations do not pay attention to evaluation of their performance. If performance is not evaluated then there is no pressure for change.

5 Evaluation

Although formal organizational performance evaluation is unusual, it does not mean that poor performance is not detected. Most Ghanaians are well aware of the inefficiencies of organizations: the services they were set up to provide are either non-existent or of low quality. Any Ghanaian who has visited a government hospital or public sector organization will attest to this. Inefficiency is not limited to the public sector as the private sector is only marginally better. This is perhaps due to the lack of a quality culture in Ghana in general and the effects (discussed earlier) of traditional and socio-cultural issues.

In Ghana, the government is the dominant player in the regulation, control and management of organizations, particularly in the legislative arena. Management in

Ghana is heavily affected by market distortions, over-regulation and political influence. The management of organizations is influenced by the political ideology and management style of the government of the day. With the frequent changes in government, organizations have little control over their environment (political and economic) and must operate according to the wishes of the government. A socialist-orientated government (for instance, the Nkrumah government) might use the trade unions to bully employers who refuse to toe the government line. Nationalist and populist governments tend to encourage organizations to hire more people than they need. Hence, many organizations tend to be overstaffed but individual employees are under-utilized. Under such conditions, morale is poor and manifests itself in unexcused absences and work indolence rather than frequent turnover (Kiggundu 1989: 9).

6 Conclusion

Management in Ghana faces a lot of challenges, the main one being how to reconcile Western management principles and practices with Ghanaian traditions, customs and beliefs to ensure the effective management of organizations. Many of the problems in management in Ghana arise from the conflicting principles that form the basis of Western management and traditional systems of governance. Values, behaviour, attitudes and customs that are acceptable in traditional settings are not necessarily acceptable in modern, formally structured organizations that have adopted a Western style of management with laid-down procedures for decision making.

Perhaps Ghana can learn from the experiences of East Asian countries, in particular Singapore, where there is an excellent fusion of Western and Eastern philosophies of management. Singapore has always used national campaigns to educate its people about economic and national issues that have an impact on the competitiveness of the economy. Maybe it is time for Ghanaians to be sensitized to the adverse effects of traditions on management practices and organizational performance.

With the new emphasis on privatization, a relatively stable and democratic political system and the shift of the political ideology towards free enterprise, the government should endeavour to provide some management education to all levels of employees. Improvement in management should be a concerted effort from both the government and organizations.

YAW A. DEBRAH
UNIVERSITY OF WALES, CARDIFF

Further reading

(References cited in the text marked *)

Abbey, J.L.S. (1990) 'Ghana's experience with structural adjustment' in J. Pickett and H. Singer (eds), *Towards Economic Recovery in sub-Saharan Africa*, London: Routledge, pp. 32–41. (It examines the lessons that emerge from Ghana's experience with economic restructuring.)

* Agyekum, F. and Synge, R. (1993) 'Ghana' in *Africa Review 1993/4: The Economic and Business Report*, London: Kogan Page, pp. 72–6. (Provides an extensive review of political developments

in Ghana since 1992 and the attempts by the government to woo foreign investors to Ghana. It also deals with the exercise in free enterprise currently in place in Ghana.)

* Bourrett, F.M. (1963) *Ghana: The Road to Independence 1919–1957*, London: Oxford University Press. (It traces the transition of the Gold Coast from colonial status to independence and self-government. Examines the British administrative system in the colony and the political and administrative system in Ghana in the early years of independence.)

* Davis, J.T. (1991) 'Institutional impediments to workforce retrenchment and restructuring in Ghana's state enterprises', *World Development*, 19(8): 987–1005. (It reviews the problems that can be encountered in an attempt to reduce overall employment in the state enterprises sector and in restructuring workforces at the enterprise level.)

Dia, M. (1996) *Africa's Management in the 1990s and Beyond: Reconciling Indigenous and Transplanted Institutions*, Washington, DC: The World Bank. (Examines the problems in institutional capacity building in Africa and the crisis of technical capacity. It argues that management in formal institutions is at odds with societal behaviour and expectations. It therefore explores the possibility of building on indigenous best practices to enhance organizational performance in Africa.)

* Economist Intelligence Unit (1990) *West Africa: Economic Structure and Analysis*, London. (It reviews the post-independence political and economic management in Ghana. It is essentially an analysis of how the various governments have managed the economy and the effects on management, wages, employment and manufacturing.)

* Gardiner, K. (1996) 'Managing in different cultures: the case of Ghana' in B. Towers (ed.), *The Handbook of Human Resource Management*, Oxford: Blackwell, pp. 488–510. (Examines management in Ghana from a cross-cultural perspective. It highlights the impact of Ghanaian traditional culture and customs on management practices.)

* Hug, M.M. (1989) *The Economy of Ghana*, London: Macmillan. (It analyses the performance of the Ghanaian economy – from independence to 1984. As part of the analysis of economic management it provides a chronology of major events, 1957–84.)

* Kiggundu, M.N. (1988) 'Africa' in R. Nath (ed.), *Comparative Management: A Regional View*, Ballinger, pp. 169–243. (Extensive analysis of management in Africa and the context in which it takes place. The impact of socio-cultural factors on management is also explored.)

* Kiggundu, M.N. (1989) *Managing Organizations in Developing Countries: An Operational and Strategic Approach*, West Hartford: Kumarian Press. (Comprehensive analysis of management and development administration in developing countries. It deals with organization and management for economic development and social change.)

* Kiggundu, M.N. (1991) 'The challenges of management development in sub-Saharan Africa', *Journal of Management Development* 10(6): 32–47. (It provides some practical guidelines for management development professionals working in Africa.)

* Kimble, D. (1965) *A Political History of Ghana*, Oxford: Clarendon. (It examines the rise of Gold Coast Nationalism from 1850–1928 and the British colonial administration's response to nationalist agitation in the Gold Coast.)

Kusi, T.A. and Gyimah-Boakye, A.K. (1994) 'Collective bargaining in Ghana: problems and perspectives, in political transformations, structural adjustment and industrial relations in Africa: English speaking countries', *ILO Labour-Management Relations Series*, No. 78, Geneva: ILO. (A comprehensive review of labour legislation, trade unions, employment policies and labour-management relations in Ghana.)

* Nzelibe, C.O. (1986) 'The evolution of African management thought', *International Studies of Management and Organisations* XVI (2): 6–16. (It traces the historical evolution of management in Africa and explores the trends that have influenced it. It also advances a rationale for an alternative management paradigm in Africa.)

Obeng-Fosu, P. (1991) *Industrial Relations in Ghana*, Accra: Ghana University Press. (Provides useful information on the law and practice of industrial relations in Ghana. It offers suggestions for improvement of industrial relations in Ghana.)

Smith, P. (1998) 'Africa scrambles for Africa', *The World in 1999*, London: Economist Publications. (A survey of African prospects in 1999.)

See also: ECONOMIES OF THE EMERGING COUNTRIES; MANAGEMENT IN AFRICA; MANAGE-
MENT IN THE EMERGING COUNTRIES; MANAGEMENT IN NIGERIA; MANAGEMENT IN
SOUTH AFRICA

Related topics in the IEBM regional set: MANAGEMENT IN ASIA PACIFIC; MANAGEMENT
IN SINGAPORE

Management in Kenya

1 Introduction
2 Emerging characteristics of management and labour in Kenya
3 Labour relations policy
4 Kenyan management in the 1990s
5 Management in a multi-ethnic society
6 The future

Overview

Kenyan managers operate in a business environment heavily influenced by institutional structures inherited from the colonial era mediated by the ethnic politics of the independence era. Sharp distinctions also have to be made between the organizational cultures of state-owned enterprises (SOEs), the subsidiaries of multinational enterprises (MNEs), domestic enterprises owned by Kenyans of African origin and domestic enterprises owned by Kenyans who originate in the Indian subcontinent (Henley 1978). It is difficult to attribute causality simply to ownership-type because MNEs, as always, tend to be concentrated in either export-oriented commodity production (tea, coffee, cut flowers and out-of-season vegetables in particular) where tight control of labour costs is critical, or in domestic-oriented branded consumer goods manufacture where wage costs are a small portion of the production price. Domestic enterprises tend to be smaller than MNEs or SOEs and serve only the domestic market, using mature production technologies. SOEs have been subject to ethnic capture, operate with low levels of capacity utilization, have an inflated payroll and are generally in a poor commercial condition.

The Kenyan economy was heavily protectionist until the political and economic crises of the 1990s eventually forced the government to liberalize the economy in exchange for continuing International Monetary Fund (IMF) and World Bank assistance with balance of payment support. The turning point was November 1991 when donors suspended quick disbursing aid. This forced the government to liberalize interest rates, float the Kenyan shilling, abolish import licensing and introduce a retrenchment programme for the civil service (EIU 1998a). The arguments with the IMF have continued over lack of progress with privatization and corruption in the civil service but official capital inflows have partially resumed. Ultimate resolution of the struggle between the new generation of technocrats and modernizers and the old guard with its power located in ethnically defined fiefdoms will not occur until President Moi's successor assumes power at the beginning of the twenty-first century, no later than January 2003 (EIU 1998b).

1 Introduction

Kenya is a democratic republic with a population of 28.7 million people. It was under British colonial rule from the end of the nineteenth century until 1963. The UK remains Kenya's largest trading partner, taking 10.4 per cent of total exports in 1996, and the source of 13.2 per cent of total imports. Other major trading partners are neighbours Uganda and Tanzania, and Germany and South Africa. The first ten years of independence were characterized by a period of rapid economic growth; gross domestic product (GDP) grew at an annual rate of 6.2 per cent and manufacturing value added at 9.1 per cent. After the initial spurt, performance of manufacturing has decelerated significantly during the 1980s and 1990s such that the growth of manufacturing value added has rarely been higher than 5 per cent per annum. By the mid-1990s industrial output growth averaged less than 4 per cent per annum. During the same period, the real GDP growth rate averaged rather less than population growth rate at around 3 per cent per annum (EIU 1998a; Dun and Bradstreet 1997).

The manufacturing sector developed within the framework of the former East African Community and enjoyed strong protection against foreign competition and virtually tax-free access to investment in machinery and capital equipment. Consequently during the 1960s the sector grew significantly. The slowdown in the rate of growth in the following decades, particularly from the end of the 1970s, was due to foreign exchange shortages which limited industrial inputs, drought which raised the price of domestic inputs, and the collapse of the East African Community which eliminated the larger protected market. Rapid fluctuations in growth rates that have occurred since the late 1970s have ensured that structural change in the manufacturing sector has remained very limited. Leading industrial branches remain food products, beverages, textiles and fabricated metal products and electrical machinery. Over half of manufacturing value added is accounted for by consumer goods, and the share of intermediate goods, the development of which is important for industrial diversification, has remained stagnant at 25 per cent or so of Kenyan manufacturing during the 1980s and into the 1990s. Perhaps unsurprisingly, the structure of manufacturing employment has virtually remained static over the years. Large-scale manufacturing employment actually began to decline in the 1990s as a result of opening of the economy to wider competition from imports (see ECONOMIES OF THE EMERGING COUNTRIES).

2 Emerging characteristics of management and labour in Kenya

Until the late 1950s, it was conventional wisdom in East Africa that the major problem of manpower development was one of attracting and retaining sufficient numbers of workers into the European-controlled labour force (see MANAGEMENT IN AFRICA). Strategies differed radically between plantation agriculture and industry. In colonial agriculture the emphasis was on coercion and tightening up an already restrictive labour registration system to seek to punish deserters from plantation agriculture. The 'target-worker' hypothesis – that the African labourer has only limited economic needs – was used to justify reductions of hourly wages, and labour controls (Henley 1973).

By comparison, Kenyan manufacturers were more enlightened and set about seeking to remould 'natural' man as 'industrial' man by using a system of positive incentives. Since it was widely believed that African workers were suffering from the stultifying effects of hereditary, environment and upbringing, it was concluded that the best way to turn them into hard-working and productive industrial workers was by providing a complex array of employment benefits in addition to wages so that the African worker would feel disinclined to return to the rural areas. It was clear to the increasing number of professional managers who were being brought in by international companies investing in pre-independence Kenya that positive material incentives to stabilize the labour force were more efficient than the coercive low-wage strategies favoured by colonial agriculture. These latter, more cost-conscious interests preferred to rely on authoritarian control, which, of course, is relatively ineffective for securing the efficient performance of complex tasks.

By Independence in December 1963, the sharp dualism on racial lines in Kenyan agriculture had been substantially modified by the opening up of European land to African ownership. In manufacturing industry concern over the now very stable labour force was beginning to creep into official policy. The feckless migrant labourers of the colonial era had been replaced by armies of only too eager job seekers. A vicious circle of development had emerged that produced increases in GDP and average industrial wages but a static or declining proportion of the labour force in wage employment and growing inequalities in income distribution. The inequalities built into the earlier colonial economy continued into independent Kenya, perpetuated now by an African elite. This was perhaps to be expected given that the new power elite had an even closer identity of interests than their colonial predecessors, amongst its members in the state bureaucracy, industry, large-scale agriculture and in the political system (Leys 1975).

The only radical discontinuity in Kenyan management at independence and since has been ethnic. While large-scale farms, industry and the public service have come under the management of Africans, the division of the economy into rich and poor sectors remains comparable to the colonial situation (see BUSINESS CULTURES, THE EMERGING COUNTRIES). Indeed, in some respects inequality is worse today. Those who were promoted to replace the outgoing expatriate administrators were mostly already employed in the colonial bureaucracy. Since the most familiar role models were European it was hardly surprising that after independence and political stability the inequality of colonialism was reproduced in independent Kenya. What gradually changed from the late 1970s was a closing-off of employment opportunities and, particularly for the university-educated elite, a substantial restriction in the possibilities of upward mobility and progression. The shockwave of political independence and the removal of racial barriers to upward mobility in the 1960s and 1970s have today produced stagnation in the managerial (and political) elite in Kenya.

3 Labour relations policy

Kenya inherited the British Colonial Office 'voluntary' industrial relations system based on enterprise unionism and collective bargaining (Henley 1978). Shortly after independence, the government found it expedient to move towards tripartism by adding a government conciliation service and a labour court to provide binding arbitration on collective and individual disputes. Legal restrictions were imposed on the right to strike, effectively making strikes illegal. The role of the registrar of trade unions was extended to include responsibility for overseeing the unions' internal affairs and the power to settle recognition and jurisdictional disputes. Moreover, the government is represented on the Central Organization of Trade Unions (COTU) and for a brief period COTU was even affiliated to the ruling political party, KANU. In Kenya labour relations policy has basically oscillated between co-option and coercion (Henley 1989). Tractable unions have been encouraged with state patronage, while radical elements have been harassed through strict enforcement of laws relating to the conduct of union affairs (especially election of officers and preparation and auditing of accounts) (see HUMAN RESOURCE MANAGEMENT IN THE EMERGING COUNTRIES; INDUSTRIAL RELATIONS IN THE EMERGING COUNTRIES).

Kenyan trade unions face a well-organized Federation of Kenyan Employers which deals with industrial relations matters on behalf of its members, including representation in the Industrial Court. The Kenyan Association of Manufacturers handles more general business lobbying on behalf of large employers. There are a large number of private consultancy firms offering various kinds of management training loosely coordinated under the aegis of the Kenya Institute of Management (see MANAGEMENT EDUCATION IN THE EMERGING COUNTRIES).

4 Kenyan management in the 1990s

Few anticipated the intensity of competition that would prevail in the world economy during the modern era, when they were planning the development of management and employment relations in post-colonial Kenya. Multinational enterprises today assess the overall vitality of the Kenyan national business environment and find it lacking. It is perceived by international firms as being characterized by state arbitrariness, instability, corruption and bureaucratic inefficiency. Existing foreign investors have been increasingly inclined to disinvest from productive activities rather than to modernize and upgrade existing facilities. Sadly, the promising growth in investment and manufactured output achieved by Kenya in the 1960s and 1970s has failed to be sustained in the 1980s and 1990s.

The economic decline in Kenya from the late 1970s was a consequence of pursuit of an import substitution policy, that is, when tariff rates were set by the government at a higher level for finished goods compared with intermediates, with little or no attempt to discriminate on the basis of the amount of local value added or to remove tariff protection from infant industry once it had matured. Manufacturing industry responded to this tariff structure by increasing its requirements for imported intermediates, and because of this the demand for foreign exchange also rose. With rising domestic demand and the relatively slow growth rate in the agricultural exporting base, foreign exchange constraints increased over time, resulting in rationing. This in turn resulted in periodic restrictions on manufactured imports, further enhancing the effective rate of protection for low production.

In this economic environment of increased scarcities, particularly of foreign exchange, managers of the 'enabling business environment', the political elite, have great powers of redistribution and interference in business activity. This in turn increases the political risks attached to business activities and the incentives for businessmen to engage in non-market-driven behaviour (Swainson 1980). Moreover, while bureaucratic agencies can attempt to stimulate or order a stop to economic activity, and the World Bank and IMF have frequently attempted to do so, they cannot create entrepreneurship and economic efficiency. These depend on such intangibles as individual motivation and perception of incentives in the business environment. All too often in this environment negotiating skills turn out to be as important as the commitment to managerial efficiency.

5 Management in a multi-ethnic society

A previously mentioned feature of the Kenyan economy that is hostile to the development of economically rational institutions is the penetration of all spheres of life by ethnic-based clientelist politics. This is especially so in the civil service in Kenya and the public sector but it also crosses over into the private sector, especially where the latter is significantly dependent on government contracts or protection. Since government regulations have an impact on many aspects of business activity, very few are exempt from the attentions of influence peddlers even if, in most cases, they can be politely ignored (see MANAGEMENT IN AFRICA).

Managers of multinational subsidiaries in many situations feel a keen sense of remoteness: technically from industrial markets, advanced production systems and supply lines, and psychologically from great uncertainty about the basic parameters of social and economic activity (Stopford *et al.* 1991). The contradictory pulls on them from headquarters, from local officials and from their employees can seldom be resolved purely by rationality alone. To deal with the uncertainties managers rely on what Triandis (1984) calls the culture of 'personalissimo', defined as the 'social process of knowing somebody, who knows somebody, who knows the person from whom you need a service'. Under these conditions, new managers, especially expatriates, experience a sense of powerlessness even though their formal status leaves others to expect authority and expertise. Without good understanding of the local organizational climate, managers can make expensive mistakes.

The organizational culture in a developing country such as Kenya is significantly different from countries with a longer history of industrialization. The main differences revolve around the inseparability of authority and obligation. While senior managers have considerably more direct power at their disposal in relationships with subordinates than would be the case in a mature industrial economy, they are also embedded in a parallel network of social obligations which requires them to assist relatives and friends. Often, these obligations originate from the support people need during the process of adjustment from rural migrant to a fully 'captured' member of urban society. Social networks and obligations inevitably penetrate organizations because the employees cannot insulate themselves from their wider social commitments. This is not to say that relationships based purely on friendship, work and business are unimportant. They are undoubtedly increasing in importance as the class structure in modern Kenya becomes less open and fluid, but linguistic differences and Kenyan social and political geography tend to work towards ethnic closure rather than multiculturalism.

A further social consequence of ethnicity and clientelism is that it also reinforces a strongly instrumental and individualistic attitude to employment. In a country where the proportion of people in formal wage employment is very small, everyone in regular employment faces endless demands from relatives and friends for various kinds of assistance. Even the very wealthy are unable to find jobs for all their own relatives and friends' relatives. This very high level of dependency forces the typical Kenyan employee to consider first what material benefits he or she can obtain from his or her position in an organization. From the best-paid person in the corporation to the worst, each is the patron of a network of dependence. This means that it is very difficult for anyone facing constant demands for favours from friends and relatives to maintain an attitude of professional detachment at work. Because organizational commitment tends to be weak, companies establish elaborate security systems yet theft of company property remains a major concern to employers. Where many employees are heavily committed to personal networks that exist outside the enterprise it is easy to rationalize theft from 'foreigners' or the 'rich' as obtaining your just reward.

All organizations in Kenya must therefore decide whether to accept social cultural traditions or attempt to create new ones (see BUSINESS CULTURES, THE EMERGING COUNTRIES). Family and other social networks can be harnessed to form an important basis for maintaining the cohesion of formal organizations and thereby reducing the probability of transactional failure. It is clearly more effective if the formal system of rewards and sanctions used to manage organizational relationships is underpinned by a degree of moral obligation. Unfortunately the very feature that is characteristic of traditional multi-ethnic social structures and gives them their coherence and strength, that is, their exclusiveness, when translated into a modern organizational setting in a multi-ethnic society, can lead to severe inefficiency. Thus, for example, while the traditional imperative of mutual self-help may allow flexibility for the ingroup, bureaucratic standards tend to be enforced with an exacting thoroughness on the outgroup. Such behaviour is liable to set in train a process which convinces most people (the outgroup) that the organization considers them to be untrustworthy. Before long, behaviour conforms to expectations and it becomes necessary for a simple act, such as signing a cheque, to require three people where one would otherwise suffice.

Great subtlety is needed on the part of managers if they are to avoid the dangers of severe efficiency losses inherent in tight administrative controls. A further serious challenge to traditional headquarters-driven thinking about management is the need to take greater account of the availability of local management. In the past, many firms assumed they could make up for the shortages of local management talent with expatriates. Today host government restriction on work permits and the rising costs of expatriation are forcing many multinationals in Kenya to review their international personnel policies. The proportion of expatriate managers employed has dropped dramatically since the early 1980s as the profitability of Kenyan subsidiaries has declined.

6 The future

In the 1990s multinational enterprise policies have tended to focus on a limited set of businesses to which the centre could add value. Many firms now limit the geographical spread of their global businesses to large and dynamic markets. Relatively small economies with modest growth rates such as Kenya suffer from increased marginality in the strategic thinking of the world's largest corporations.

One of the illusions fostered by the political rhetoric of the independence struggle in Kenya was that existing institutional structures and processes could rapidly be transformed into modern aggressive agents of development once the colonial power had departed and national political autonomy was achieved. Western social engineers were only too happy to promote the idea that institutional structures could be designed (with the help of consultants, of course) to drive progressive political, social and economic processes. With hindsight, many expectations of Kenya at independence, as elsewhere in Africa, now seem to have lacked the most elementary historiographical understanding of the functioning of social and political institutions. The rapid drift towards protectionism, cronyism and corruption should have been obvious. The introduction of modern management methods and techniques could not alone develop a competitive investment environment and market for manufactured goods. The relationship between the beneficiaries of the manufacturing sector and the structure and political economy of the state, forged under colonialism and continued into independence, must take much of the blame.

While the forces of protectionism and rent seeking are today substantially in retreat this change has been forced on the government. It has reluctantly embraced liberalization and the active promotion of entrepreneurship and competitive behaviour because of the intervention of the IMF and the World Bank. The challenge for the twenty-first century is to create a more subtle blend of economic and social relationships that better reflects the potential of the underlying social structure and the requirements of an economy seeking to achieve competitiveness in the global economy. Without real progress in achieving this blend, the prospect for Kenyan management is bleak.

JOHN S. HENLEY
THE UNIVERSITY OF EDINBURGH MANAGEMENT SCHOOL

Further reading

(References cited in the text marked *)

* Dun and Bradstreet (1997) *Country Report – Kenya*, London: Dun and Bradstreet Limited. (Accessible reviews of political and economic development in Kenya.)
* Economist Intelligence Unit (1998a) *Country Report – Kenya*, London: EIU. (Accessible reviews of political and economic development in Kenya.)
* Economist Intelligence Unit (1998b) *Country Risk Service – Kenya*, London: EIU. (Accessible reviews of political and economic development in Kenya.)
* Henley, J.S. (1989) 'African employment relationships and the future of trade unions', *British Journal of Industrial Relations* 27(3): 295–309. (An assessment of the implications of globalization for African economies and trade unionism in particular.)
* Henley, J.S. (1978) 'Pluralism, underdevelopment and trade union power: evidence from Kenya', *British Journal of Industrial Relations* 16(2): 224–42. (Reviews the consequences of the political economy and social structure of Kenya for the development of trade unions.)
* Henley, J.S. (1973) 'Employment relationships and economic development – the Kenyan experience', *Journal of Modern African Studies* 11(4): 554–89. (An account of the colonial origins of employment practices and their development since Independence.)

* Leys, C. (1975) *Underdevelopment in Kenya*, Berkeley: University of California Press. (An incisive account of political and economic development in Kenya 1964–71.)
* Stopford, J., Strange, S. and Henley J.S. (1991) *Rival States, Rival Firms*, Cambridge: Cambridge University Press. (A comparative study of foreign investor behaviour in Brazil, Kenya and Malaysia focusing on host government relationships with investors.)
* Swainson, N. (1980) *The Development of Corporate Capitalism in Kenya 1918–77*, London: Heinemann. (A review of the development of foreign investment in Kenya and its symbiotic relationship with the state and political interests from the colonial period through to Independence.)
* Triandis, H.C. (1984) 'Towards a psychological theory of economic growth', *International Journal of Psychology* 19(1–2): 85 – 98. (An interesting speculative account of the influence of economic conditions on behaviour.)

See also: BUSINESS CULTURES, THE EMERGING COUNTRIES; ECONOMIES OF THE EMERGING COUNTRIES; HUMAN RESOURCE MANAGEMENT IN THE EMERGING COUNTRIES; INDUSTRIAL RELATIONS IN THE EMERGING COUNTRIES; MANAGEMENT IN AFRICA; MANAGEMENT IN SOUTH AFRICA; MANAGEMENT IN TANZANIA; MANAGEMENT IN UGANDA

Related topics in the IEBM regional set: MANAGEMENT IN ASIA PACIFIC

Management in Nigeria

1 Introduction – origins/context
2 Analysis – management practice in Nigeria
3 Evaluation
4 Conclusion

Overview

The style of management practised by Nigerian managers is deep rooted in the nation's political history, economy and culture. Although liberalization of the economy and the development of oil wealth have continued to constitute pressure for change towards Western models, Nigerian management philosophy has changed very little. It is characterized by centralization, masculinity, excessive control and machoism.

The period before the oil boom of the 1970s was one of business stability, when excessive competition and the struggle for corporate survival was minimal. With the oil boom, businesses expanded, new ones were set up and foreign participation in Nigerian businesses grew astronomically in a very short time. Traditional styles of management became challenged and the need for more professional and younger managers increased. Even so, the strength of the cultural trait was such that emerging management styles became a hybrid of traditional Nigerian and Western styles, rather than an outright rejection of the old.

The development of more modern management styles, however, progressed but was checked by serious economic downturns from the early 1990s. All the same, management styles today are much different and much improved from those of yesteryears. As globalization and liberalization take hold, so will the need to develop better managers for the future growth of Nigerian enterprises and the economy become increasingly important.

1 Introduction – origins/context

Industrialization

Nigeria, an independent member of the Commonwealth, has been ruled by civilian administrations for only nine of its 35 years of independence. With a population of over 100 million, composed of several ethnic groups with mutually non-intelligible languages, and a gross domestic product (GDP) of $90.6 billion, Nigeria is the most populous and second richest country in south Saharan Africa and the 42nd richest in the world. It shares a common heritage of British colonial rule with much of English-speaking West Africa and the Indian sub-continent, which also left behind similar administrative and legal systems.

Although Nigeria's early politicians committed themselves to rapid industrialization as a means of building a strong and prosperous economy soon after independence in 1962, industrial production growth has not been remarkable and today stands at just about one fifth of GDP, of which 7 per cent is manufacturing.

Nigeria fell victim to the spending disease when oil prices and public revenues rose in the 1970s and early 1980s. As revenues rose, so did the excitement to spend. Emerging export revenues were spent on non-tradeable consumption, thereby increasing the relative prices of non-tradeable goods and wages. The share of consumption in GDP is about 85 per cent. On the contrary, investment accounts for only 10 per cent. This excessive consumption hurt the development of tradeable (other than oil) products in the economy (see ECONOMIES OF THE EMERGING COUNTRIES).

Public sector participation in the economy

Nigerian economic development became hampered by political instability and the ravages of civil war in the first ten years of independence. A strong diversified agricultural nation in the 1950s and 1960s, Nigeria turned into an oil-dominated economy in the 1970s. Rising world oil prices led to a large foreign exchange inflow. Increasing availability of petrol dollars made it possible to hasten the process of indigenization. Such indigenization provided a greater opportunity for rapid social and economic development.

The large oil revenues, accruing primarily to the Federal Government, increased the role of the government as an investor and joint owner of several strategic modern industrial enterprises, such as steel, oil exploration and defence production. State governments also own several enterprises, sometimes based more on ethnic nationalism than economics. These parastatals, as they are called, may be profit or non-profit oriented. The private sector has, however, an open-ended scope for development, engaged in relatively smaller units, except the operations of multinational enterprises like Shell.

The large role of the public sector and the power and control that public officials wield over organizations and parastatals have implications for management practice and, in turn, organizational performance in Nigeria. Research indicates that differences in performance between parastatals and similar but private enterprises are accounted for by differences in the style of management (Ihimodu 1986). Among the features of management of parastatals are the role of federal or state governments in appointing chief executives without necessary regard to merit, incessant meddling by ministerial officials, relatively poor conditions of service in the civil service and the huge debt owed to parastatals by the governments themselves. Such control has hampered efficient and effective management practice in a large chunk of the economy.

Colonial heritage

Very few empirical investigations of leadership styles and practices in African organizations have been undertaken and published. The little evidence available (attested to by the author's personal experience) seems to suggest that the predominant management style is towards the authoritarian end of the spectrum. As observed in Blunt and Jones (1992), the management styles prevailing in Africa are authoritarian, personalized and politicized. Entrepreneurial and creative talents are suppressed in favour of what is described as 'bureaucratic risk averse administration based on absolute obedience'.

Explanations for this style of management can be traced partly to Africa's colonial past (see MANAGEMENT IN AFRICA). Colonial administrators had little faith in the ability of their African subordinates and therefore tended to keep all managerial authority to themselves. No real authority was delegated and this has played a major part in the development of the typical African management style, which tends to concentrate authority in the hands of a small number of people at the top of the organization. This, combined with the traditional style of leadership in African societies, has resulted in a culture that bears very much on the management style.

The socio-cultural environment

In all organizations, management consists of coordinating the activities of both human and non-human resources to achieve established or stated objectives. Management definition implies being able to deal effectively with both the human and technical sides of organizations. The existence of the human aspect of organizations requires the management process to see culture as vital in organizational decision making. To the extent that no machine or capital can achieve much without the efforts of people, all management activities are culture-based (see BUSINESS CULTURES, THE EMERGING CULTURES).

Hofstede (1984) has defined culture as 'the collective programming of the mind which distinguishes the members of one group or society from those of another'. In short, culture is a collection of how a population thinks and acts. Although ingrained in the minds of individuals, culture is manifested by the way institutions are run in particular societies, how people within those institutions react to how the institutions are managed and how decisions are made. Consequently, a manager's effectiveness at planning people's activities, organizing their time and motivating them to perform better is contingent upon his or her understanding of what it is that guides the thought processes of workers and their feelings about the directives, i.e. culture.

Machoism

Being a very masculine society, showing off in Nigeria is part of the people. Also, there is a strong belief in money. Having more money, apart from enabling the moneyed Nigerian to fulfil his family obligations is, in itself, a testimony of his success and power and therefore legitimizes his candidature to office. Thus machoism and ostentatious living is a permanent feature of the Nigerian way of life and may lead to someone attaining a top position in society regardless of acumen or technical competence (Odubogun 1992). Also, there seems to be a general acceptability of macho manager behaviour. The more an individual is able to brag about his or her achievement in public, the more, interestingly, he/she is admired.

Gender issues

The Nigerian constitution affirms equal employment opportunities for both men and women. Under Chapter 11 of the 1979 Constitution, the state is enjoined to direct its policy towards ensuring that all citizens have equal opportunity to secure employment without discrimination on any grounds. The reality is, however, different. While virtually all respondents to a survey agreed that there were no specific policies which limit women's access to employment in both public and private sectors and also impede their mobility to top management positions, in practice discrimination abounds (Olojede 1995). In certain parts of the country, discrimination based on religious practices deny women the opportunity of formal education.

There tends to be general lack of acceptability by society of women occupying top management positions. Culturally, women are considered inferior to men. Whatever training they acquire, it is believed, should be utilized at home. For many decades, this sharp division between what men should do and what women should do, except those that are determined by biological factors, have resulted in unwritten laws which men, consciously or unconsciously, implement against women in the recruitment and promotion process. Although in recent years there has been an obvious improvement in the way women are regarded, the change is very slow indeed.

Management development

The level, relevance and quality of education in general and of professional education in particular contribute significantly to the process of industrialization. Lack of adequate quality management education can inhibit efficiency in the economics of goods and services provision, thereby hampering economic growth. Traditionally, people have moved into senior positions 'through the ranks' without any formal management training.

This, to some extent, is colonial heritage, and although it seemed to have worked well in the past, increasing competition engendered the need for 'purpose-made' managers via theoretical and practical training. This need did not, however, really catch on in Nigeria until much later in the 1980s. The cultural dictat of seniority by age rather than by qualification and experience, seems to have thwarted a real take-off of undergraduate and postgraduate programmes in management. For most of the 1990s, only about 10 per cent of those graduating from Nigerian universities were from the 'Administration' discipline. Improvements in this imbalance, though necessary, has been very gradual indeed.

2 Analysis – management practice in Nigeria

In a general sense, the concern of all organizations is to obtain some desirable end and the task of management is to determine and direct how this is to be done. Basically, management determines the outcomes of the organization. It manages inputs and help transform inputs into outputs. Managers undertake the science and profession of control. How this control is exercised is partly circumscribed by environmental factors, the most important of which have been discussed above and it is to the way management is practised in Nigeria that we now turn.

Long range planning

The concept of long range planning is neither well-developed nor widespread in Nigeria (see MANAGEMENT IN AFRICA). Formal long-term planning is confined primarily to the large organizations, mostly the subsidiaries of foreign enterprises such as the UAC and Shell and very large indigenous holding companies like the Odu'a Group and the New Nigeria Development Company (Fadahunsi 1989). In general, planning in such organizations varies according to the size/scale of capital investment and usually has a horizon of 5–10 years. Since the mid-1970s, however, recurrent political instability has tended to force most firms to shorten their planning schedules to the medium term of 3–5 years.

Centralization

Apart from the subsidiaries of multinational enterprises and very large public sector firms such as the Nigerian National Petroleum Company and the National Electric Power Authority, managers of Nigerian firms tend to centralize decision making, use limited delegation and committee work and practise tight control. As the section on cultural influence indicates, top managers tend to view delegation as indecisiveness. They are also hesitant, by and large, in accepting the ability of subordinates to carry out delegated tasks and undertake the responsibility satisfactorily (Blunt and Jones 1992). There is also the issue of trust and loyalty, so that where delegation is practised, it is correlated with a high degree of trust in the subordinates. Although, the trend is increasingly to delegate more, the top man is still very much in charge and makes all the critical decisions.

In small owner-managed enterprises, the owner generally looks after all the managerial functions. The top man not only carries the whole organization, he also enjoys the power that it confers. Interestingly, this behavioural pattern is also seen in many large firms. Many chief executives prefer individual consultation to committee meetings, a behaviour embodied in the 'macho' context described above. Nigerian businessmen tend to be individualistic. This is reflected in the ratio of sole businesses to corporate partnerships, which continues to be high at about nine to one.

With regard to public sector organizations, Nigerian managers, especially those in parastatals, adhere rigidly to rules and regulations and operating procedures laid down in earlier years (rules of thumb). Most protect their positions fiercely and are usually political appointees. They thus tend to be unprepared and unable to meet the rapid pace of development in a changing world of business.

Loyalty and integrity

The extent to which top managers are willing to delegate depends, to a large extent, on the level of confidence and trust they have in their subordinates. Traditionally, an owner-manager would act as guardian and manager and would expect a strong sense of personal loyalty from the employees, especially senior staff, who would in most cases be members of the same family or village. Even in large private companies, such as ITT, and large publicly-owned companies, such as NET, this loyalty is still expected by the 'big man', although, it has been less forthcoming with time.

In the economic boom period of the late 1970s and early 1980s, such loyalty to the top man or owner waned. Job-hopping, in this era of prosperity, to take advantage of marginal increases in wages became very frequent. Even so, this loyalty model was only dormant, not dead, and indeed has become very strong again in the 1990s, with the downturn in Nigeria's economic fortunes.

Human resource management

In line with the cultural tenets expounded above, Nigerian industry has tended to indulge in hiring people who are affiliated to those already employed or hail from the same tribe, village or region. On the positive front, this behaviour was motivated by the desire to have people around the leader who could be trusted. On the negative, however, difficulties could arise, ranging from those of distant relations and friends seeking employment to those requesting financial assistance. Numerous examples abound where many people who, on the basis of merit, should not have been employed were given jobs for reasons of their relationships to the detriment of the organizations (Onah and Ejiofor 1979). The trend these days is to have young talented people with no ties but with the requisite skills to run businesses, although the preference will still be for people of the same ethnic kind.

In general, there is a reluctance to employ women, especially in top management positions. Traditionally, this was due to the acceptance of the culturally-based notion that a woman's place is in the kitchen. The evidence also indicates that excessive absenteeism is more prevalent with women. The reluctance to work overtime or night shifts and paid maternity leave are also given as some of the reasons for failing to employ women.

By and large, Nigerian industry tends to respond to age as the basis of upward mobility. It is not common, nor generally desirable, to see younger people in top positions (Onah and Ejiofor 1979). Young people themselves may not even feel confident in such positions, as one cannot reconcile giving instructions to more elderly but junior colleagues to whom one must bow in greeting. The system thus tends to perpetuate the adage that 'the older one is the wiser'. As young managers, who have been able to 'break in', give a good account of themselves in their managerial roles, one would hope that the doors will be opened for more better-trained young people to fill senior management positions (see HUMAN RESOURCE MANAGEMENT IN THE EMERGING COUNTRIES).

3 Evaluation

Nigerian and, indeed African management styles have been the subject of criticisms by many management theorists. It has been described as authoritarian, inflexible and insensitive. Others have criticized its virtual exclusion of women and its inclusion of strong social bonds as a recipe for favouritism and nepotism. It is not uncommon to find square pegs in round holes in Nigeria, arising out of family connections or ethnicity. More often than not, such favouritism accorded to incompetent people leads to inefficiency and costs to society. Also, the exclusion of talented women is a waste of a valuable resource, leads to resentment on the part of a large section of society and may constitute indifference in the direction and delivery of economic output in the society. In the public sector, management tends to be conservative, 'preferring the unacceptable present to the unpredictable future' (Blunt and Jones 1992). It tends to be more concerned with matters of internal administration than with policy issues, developmental goals and public welfare.

While these criticisms are well founded, one cannot fail to observe that such management styles as we observe in Nigeria are culturally-based and that the apparent inadequacy of current management styles stem from the importation of Western standards and ways of doing business. Cultures die hard and a criticism of a system without due regard to the cultural aspect is not only shallow but unfair as well. In a politically unstable society that is in search of stability, for example, a sharp departure from culture could be disastrous. Also, in a system where trust is shown along ethnic lines, the manager ignores this at his peril. What is more, the organization of an under-developed economy may necessitate a household role for women, although this must be in general terms only.

The truth of the matter, however, is that although the Nigerian style of management is not devoid of value, it is clearly inadequate for today's modern organization. As globalization takes hold and pressures to liberalize intensify, so will the need to train and imbue up-and-coming managers with the tools and skills necessary to enable them to manage Nigeria plc into the twenty-first century become vital.

4 Conclusion

The expansion of the Nigerian economy during the oil boom of the late 1970s and early 1980s led to substantial changes in the economics of goods and services provision in the country. On the back of substantial oil revenues, old industries were expanded and new ones ushered in. Large construction projects were also undertaken. This expansion and the competitive pressures that it induced constituted a challenge to the way 'management' was practised before the oil boom. To this was added the pressures of liberalization and globalization, demanded by international institutions like the International Monetary Fund.

Those pressures forced managers to change not only their way of thinking and their practice but also to realize that management practice in a globalizing economy needed to be different. All the same, the cultural set-up, to which the entrenched management system had hitherto been inextricably linked, has been an impediment to any desirable change. It must be said, however, that substantial improvements have occurred in the way Nigerian managers manage their organizations since the early 1970s.

Economic difficulties from the late 1980s onwards, however, dampened the growing management development process. Low industrial capacity utilization arising out of inadequate importation of vital raw materials, collapse of competitor firms, lack of adequate foreign exchange and low morale have all combined to make managers content to just 'plod on'. A new government, ushered in after the sudden death of General Sanni Abacha in 1998, promised further deregulation, easing of controls on business, privatization and a general improvement in the operation of the way the country is run. It also committed itself to civilian elections and rule. With Nigeria still producing oil at a daily rate of about 2 million barrels, good and open governance will usher in a period of prosperity once again and with this a much improved way of management practice.

PIKAY RICHARDSON
MANCHESTER BUSINESS SCHOOL

Further reading

(References cited in the text marked *)

* Blunt P. and Jones, M. (1992) *Managing Organisations in Africa*, London: Walter de Gruyter. (A synthesis of the author's as well as other writers' views.)
* Fadahunsi O. (1989) 'The holding company approach to public enterprise management' *IJPSM* 2(2): 43–54.
* Hofstede, G. (1984) 'Cultural dimensions in management and planning', *Asia Journal of Management* January: 23–40. (Discusses the relevance of culture to the practice of management.)
* Ihimodu, F. (1986) 'Managing public commercial enterprise in Nigeria', *Public Administration and Development* 6(3): 223–38. (An analysis of the management issues of a state-owned parastatal in Nigeria.)
  Nambudiri, C. and Saryadain, M. (1978) 'Management problems and practices – India and Nigeria', *Columbia Journal of World Business* Summer: 62–70.
  Kayizzi-Mugerwa, S. (1998) *The African Economy*, London: Routledge. (A useful book which looks at the prospects for Africa's economic development.)
* Odubogun, P. (1992) *Management Theory: Relevance for Management Practice in Nigeria*, Netherlands International Institute for Management, The Hague, 56–7.
* Olojede, I. (1995) *Women in Top Management in Nigeria*, Nairobi: AAPAM. (Discusses issues of discrimination against women in various aspect of human endeavour.)
  Onah, J.O. (ed.) (1981) *Management Practice in Developing Countries*, London: Cassell. (A description of the various forms of management practices in several developing countries.)
* Onah, J.O. and Ejiofor, P. (1979) *Nigerian Case in Business Management*, London; Cassell, 90, 99. (Presents several case studies of Nigerian firms.)

See also: HUMAN RESOURCE MANAGEMENT IN THE EMERGING COUNTRIES; INDUSTRIAL RELATIONS IN THE EMERGING COUNTRIES; MANAGEMENT EDUCATION IN THE EMERGING COUNTRIES; MANAGEMENT IN AFRICA; MANAGEMENT IN GHANA, MANAGEMENT IN SOUTH AFRICA

Related topics in the IEBM regional set: MANAGEMENT IN ASIA PACIFIC

Management in South Africa

1 Introduction
2 Context
3 Specific features
4 Conclusion

Overview

South Africa's re-entry into competitive global markets in the 1990s has created new managerial challenges. Although the legacy of apartheid is being eroded, little more than 14 per cent of South African managers are black. However, employment discrimination is being replaced by policies and practices aimed at recruiting and developing black managers. Management development, changes in corporate culture and black advancement have all become more prominent.

Following Western approaches to management there is an emphasis on general management at middle to senior levels. These skills are acquired through career path planning experiences such as job rotation, project assignments and cross-functional appointments; the completion of a general management education programme such as an MBA or of a shorter executive development programme either at one or more of South Africa's seven business schools or one run by management consulting firms; by *ad hoc*, informal work exposure; or by a combination of the above.

Decades of economic isolation have created tough but inward-looking managers in South Africa who are hands-on and results-orientated. Managers tend to be individualistic and directive in their styles, with a masculine orientation. Other than in the retail sector, fewer than 16 per cent of managerial jobs are held by women. Managers are appointed to such positions following 5–10 years work experience in a particular functional discipline occupation such as engineering.

1 Introduction

Management work in South Africa has in the last decade been influenced by a fluid and often volatile political climate. Complexity and change have become standard features of the decision-making process now that the simple 'right or wrong' responses of the past no longer work (see MANAGEMENT IN AFRICA).

There are certain watershed events which have shaped management practices in South Africa since 1970. These include the 1973 Natal strikes for improved working conditions and trade union recognition, the Soweto riots of 1976, the legalization of industrial relations rights and the impact of sanctions and disinvestment in the 1980s. The state of emergency introduced in 1986 created a siege economic strategy with inward-looking managerial practices, and further isolated South African business from international competition and new technology. This mindset has made re-entry into world markets in the post-apartheid era more difficult, especially for the manufacturing and service sectors.

2 Context

Labour and political rights

Several factors are important in the evolution of management in South Africa. Rapid growth of the trade union movement since 1980, from less than 10 per cent to over 30 per cent and around 3,272,999 members, has changed the nature of managerial work. The changes have consisted primarily of increasing support for human resource management, fair employment practices and equitable treatment. Authoritarian managerial styles and unilateral decisions have been eroded and expectations increased as apartheid structures have been gradually eaten away. Managers have faced demands in which the separability of political and workplace issues is unclear. As a result they have experienced a steep learning curve, being forced into acquiring negotiating skills and getting used to dealing with complex issues (see HUMAN RESOURCE MANAGEMENT IN THE EMERGING COUNTRIES).

Socio-economic factors

While an increase in economic growth has occurred since 1993, in the decade up to 1990 economic growth averaged at 1 per cent; this compared with a population growth rate of 2.5 per cent and unemployment of over 5.5 million estimated at nearly 30 per cent of the economically active population. Whereas retrenchment in the 1980s focused primarily on blue collar employees, the 1990s have seen job cuts at managerial and professional levels following organizational restructuring, de-layering and downsizing. Rising costs, poor labour and capital productivity and intense competition as South Africa re-enters global markets, coupled with poorer economies of scale and higher wage costs than the Pacific Rim economies, have led to job losses at all levels. Meanwhile, political uncertainty has limited the domestic and foreign investment necessary for job creation. Managerial work in South Africa is therefore influenced by a mix of sociopolitical and labour market factors and the prevailing organizational culture.

The labour market

A structural inequality in the skill profile exists: a shortage of occupationally and managerially skilled workers is contrasted with an excess of unskilled labour. Meanwhile both recessionary conditions and a lack of managerial skills have led to cuts in spending on training and development. The *World Competitiveness Report* (1997) has indicated, however, that organizational investment in training and development is a decisive competitive factor. In comparison to developed market economies, South Africa's per capita output is one-sixth of Switzerland's, one-fifth of that of the USA and one-quarter of Japan's. Ultimately, labour and capital productivity is a managerial function.

Whilst more than 35 per cent of managers have tertiary educational qualifications, some 60 per cent of formal sector employees working for them do not have a high school education. This is because South African companies under apartheid did not invest sufficiently in human capital. This neglect hampers successful re-entry into global markets: South Africa was rated by the 1997 *World Competitiveness Report* as one of the lowest among emerging industrial countries in terms of human resource priorities. These socioeconomic and labour market issues remain pressing managerial challenges in the transition to a post-apartheid South Africa.

Structural factors

Apartheid created a distorted labour market with economic power concentrated in a few white hands. Economic power was, until recent moves to disaggregate or unbundle large corporations such as Gencor and Barlow Rand, concentrated in eight conglomerates which controlled over 70 per cent of the share capital on the Johannesburg stock exchange. There is also a concentration of managerial control through a system of interlocking directorates where the same person(s) serve on the boards of several corporations. This has created a mechanism of social closure which has prevented the upward mobility of black managers and women. However, South Africa's re-entry into the international business community has forced an awareness about its relative uncompetitiveness in the manufacturing and services areas and, recently, the impetus has been towards affirmative action. There have been several black directors appointed to boards of directors and although less than 10 per cent of South Africa's company directors are blacks or women, this is likely to change significantly by the year 2000.

3 Specific features

Management styles

Managerial styles reflect both Western values based on individualism and meritocracy and the authoritarian legacy of apartheid. Indigenous models of leadership have not emerged in South Africa although the concept of *ubuntu* (humaneness) underlines traditional group decision making (see MANAGEMENT IN AFRICA). Transformational leadership styles are rare, with anecdotal exceptions such as Albert Koopman, former Chief Executive of Cashbuild, a building supply company, and Leon Cohen, former Chief Executive of P G Bison Ltd. Managerialism – a focus on administrative systems and risk aversion – has been reinforced by an inward-looking economy. None the less, the increasing globalization of markets coupled with rising costs and poor productivity has resulted in a reassessment of organizational strategies, restructuring and downsizing and an experimentation with Japanese work methods such as self-directed work teams and employee empowerment through task-level participation and multi-skilling. South African management now emphasizes cooperative teamwork and communal decision making, where the core is the group and not the individual. Companies such as Pick 'n' Pay in retailing and S A Breweries where significant black advancement has occurred are examples of this new approach (see HUMAN RESOURCE MANAGEMENT IN THE EMERGING COUNTRIES).

Organizational culture in South Africa thus reflects the co-existence of both Western and African leadership styles. A synergy of these ostensibly different leadership approaches is a part of organizational development in the post-apartheid era. This is evident in black-owned insurance companies such as African Life and Metropolitan Life and in National Sorghum Breweries.

Unfair labour practice jurisprudence has also eroded unilateralism and ensured more participative managerial styles. While managers retain traditional rights to hire and dismiss, how they may do so has changed. Procedural and substantive fairness are a cornerstone of managerial labour relations practice reinforced by the Labour Relations Act (1995), which defines managers as 'employees' and thus entitled to fair treatment such as a proper disciplinary hearing. Traditional managerial styles are increasingly questioned by employees. However, although behavioural change has occurred in this regard, a shift in mind-set is important for developing suitable styles for managing diversity.

Managerial culture

Management styles reflect organizational and national cultural patterns. In South Africa, while achievement is valued, group and organizational conformity is also important. Although little research has occurred on managerial culture in South Africa, a masculine dominance is evident, underlined by individualist values and a societal culture with a relatively large power distance between groups. This is based on historical racial disparities. However, an emergent black middle class has just begun to occupy decision-making positions in business and government sectors, and this class mobility is likely to have an impact on managerial culture and inform a debate about desirable values, rituals and organizational practices. Managerial ideologies also reflect unitarist ideas – the organization as a 'happy family' or team with organizational loyalty and conflict avoidance – which are similar to the Japanese notion of industrial familism. Organizational realities in South Africa reflect diversity and pluralism and the procedural regulation of inherent conflicts.

Management development

Although companies are not required by law to train and develop managers, management development programmes are run internally in larger organizations. Many send managers to MBA and executive development programmes at one or more of South Africa's business schools, or abroad. Average expenditure on training and development in general amounts to less than 2 per cent of salary budgets, with a small number of companies spending around 6 per cent. Of this expenditure, 21 per cent goes on management training. Black management development has been neglected historically, but affirmative action policies and programmes have now been introduced in more than 30 per cent of medium and large organizations. Employment policies seek to remove discriminatory policies and practices and to actively recruit and develop black managers. With the introduction of the Labour Relations Act (1995) discriminatory employment practices now constitute an unfair labour practice.

Creating employment equity in organizations dominated by white males is an important aspect of affirmative action. Black empowerment includes both advancement into positions of executive authority and the provision of equity and profit sharing. Most management development programmes set numerical goals based on workforce requirements and labour market supply of relevant occupations. Employers reject legislating quotas in favour of a goals and timetables approach. An important lobby group, the Black Management Forum (BMF), has formulated a blueprint for management development which stresses the process and importance of increasing the supply of suitable managers with requisite skills. This blueprint advocates that by the year 2000, 40 per cent of middle management positions must be held by black people, 30 per cent of senior management posts and 20 per cent of executive directors. The government has passed an Employment Equality Bill, which will soon become law. It requires employers of more than 50 people to submit employment equity plans with targets, timetables and measures to redress past discrimination.

Subtle discrimination acts as a barrier to occupational mobility. This is mitigated by pressure to build non-racial organizational structures emanating from trade unions, lobby groups, foreign multinational companies and possible legislation. However, perceptions of black inferiority have developed a white managerial mind-set which often doubts the ability of black people to perform in a so-called white managerial environment. Although higher economic growth coupled with a new political order may stimulate management development efforts, until significant numbers of black people have the decision-making authority to affect organizational outcomes, the corporate culture of South African organizations will be slow to change. None the less, a restructuring of the workforce at all levels to reflect a visible non-racial diversity is occurring, for example in parastatal organizations such as Transnet.

The historically small black managerial class is a function of a defunct political dispensation. The presence of a black majority government means more emphasis is being placed on the upward mobility of black managerial staff. Unfortunately the questions of affirmative action and black advancement are more complex in South Africa than in post-colonial African countries. The upper echelons of state bureaucracy were dominated by an Afrikaner cultural ethos: the civil service elite is predominantly male, but a rapidly increasing proportion are now held by black managers. There is also a concern among skilled and experienced civil servants that patronage appointments will occur. (This has in fact been the case, in reverse, historically.)

4 Conclusion

Participative practices are an example of a collective orientation towards motivation and work design. This is more a feature of European and Japanese organizations than part of the individualism of North American managerial culture. An important question is the extent to which teams with multicultural and inter-functional diversity can be fostered in South African organizations. A shift from a traditional to a flexible organization requires a move away from a command and control style towards cooperation and motivation. Thus, managers will have to learn new principles and practices if South African organizations are to compete effectively. This is also essential because employee expectations and attitudes to work are changing; sociopolitical change and a workforce which is becoming more educated mean higher levels of expectations for personal growth, fair treatment and better income.

Participative practices are more successful where management has restructured to create a de-layered organization in which authority and responsibility are delegated to lower levels and where workers are empowered through information sharing, knowledge and skills, recognition and rewards and the opportunity to influence shopfloor decisions. In South Africa such approaches are increasing and include a range of organizations such as Cape Cabinets, Escom, S A Nylon Spinners, Pick 'n' Pay retailers and the Delta Motor Corporation. Although not extensive, flexible work practices, multi-skilling and performance-based pay have become issues in the field of human resource management.

There is a need to reduce racial polarization, erode a tradition of adversarialism and nurture a sense of common purpose. The latter requires the visible advancement and economic empowerment of black people in order to create employment equity and the stability necessary for economic growth. The diversity of South African organizations creates an insistent need to find common goals, shared values and foster reconciliation after the divisiveness of apartheid.

Raising managerial competence in strategic management, resource utilization, negotiation and operations is vital for organizational effectiveness. Performance improvement, greater accountability and active measures to address the racial mix in the occupation structure are necessary. While management development emphasizes planned interventions, informal experiences often provide meaningful learning. There is no uniform approach to management development. Differing cultural contexts imply that for management initiatives to have a lasting effect, integration with corporate objectives, organizational structure and job design, reward systems and corporate culture is necessary.

FRANK M. HORWITZ
UNIVERSITY OF CAPE TOWN

Further reading

(References cited in the text marked *)

Adam, H. and Moodley, E. (1993) *The Negotiated Revolution: Society and Politics in a Post-Apartheid South Africa*, Los Angeles, CA: University of California Press. (An insightful and detailed analysis of sociopolitical developments in South Africa, with reference to the role of business.)

Barker, F. (1992) 'Recent labour market trends', *People Dynamics* 11(2): 53–5. (A useful summary of relevant statistics.)

Blunt, P. and Jones, M. (1993) *Managing Organisations in Africa*, Berlin: Walter de Gruyter. (A rigorous and comprehensive comparative study of management and organizations in African countries.)

Bowmaker, A., Horwitz, F., Jain, H. and Jagger, S. (1998) 'Employment equality programmes', *Industrial Relations Journal* 29(3): 1–12. (An analysis of affirmative action and human resource trends based on a longitudinal study.)

Bowmaker-Falconer, A., Horwitz, F.M. and Searll, P. (1994) 'Affirmative action and equal opportunity: a difference', *Breakwater Monitor Update* 1: 5–10. (A member publication for participating organizations in a large multi-sectoral national database on human resource development. The bi-annual survey covers one million employees.)

Horwitz, F.M. (1993) 'Elements in participation, teamwork and flexibility in South Africa', *International Journal of Human Resources Management* 4(4): 917–31. (A study of management culture and innovative human resource practices in three South African companies.)

Horwitz, F.M. (1998) 'The Employment Equality Bill', *South African Labour Bulletin* 22(3): 80–2. (An analysis of the Bill.)

Horwitz, F.M., Bowmaker-Falconer, A. and Searll, P. (1995) 'Employment equity, human resource development and institution building in South Africa', *International Journal of Human Resource Management* 6(3): 671–85. (Focuses on structural and labour market factors associated with employment equity and diversity management in South Africa, based on findings from 130 organizations.)

Human, L. (1993) *Affirmative Action and the Development of People*, Kenwyn: Juta. (A practical guide based on sound theory for effectively introducing human resource development into organizations.)

Human, P. and Horwitz, F.M. (1992) *On the Edge: How South African Companies Cope with Change*, Kenwyn: Juta. (A research project, written in a popular style, involving a large sample of organizations and managers.)

Visser, J. (1994) 'Why South Africa is not a winning nation', *Human Resource Management* 9(10): 26–8. (A factual and critical look at factors hindering South Africa's international competitiveness.)

* *World Competitiveness Report* (1993) University of Lausanne: World Economic Forum and the Institute for Management Development. (Ranks countries according to various indices such as human resource development.)

See also: HUMAN RESOURCE MANAGEMENT IN THE EMERGING COUNTRIES; INDUSTRIAL RELATIONS IN THE EMERGING COUNTRIES; MANAGEMENT EDUCATION IN THE EMERGING COUNTRIES; MANAGEMENT IN AFRICA; MANAGEMENT IN THE EMERGING COUNTRIES; MANAGEMENT IN GHANA; MANAGEMENT IN NIGERIA

Related topics in the IEBM regional set: MANAGEMENT IN EUROPE; MANAGEMENT IN JAPAN; MANAGEMENT IN NORTH AMERICA

Management in Tanzania

1 Introduction
2 Analysis
3 Evaluation
4 Conclusion

Overview

This entry introduces the key issues affecting the process and practice of management in Tanzania. Despite an abundance of natural resources, Tanzania is one of the least developed countries in the world. The endemic poverty has had a strong impact on the prevalent type of management: a tendency towards *laissez-faire*. For nearly three decades, post-independence Tanzania pursued a socialist orientation, and put the bulk of the economy into state corporations. The pattern of management in such corporations – characteristically inefficient and corrupt – came to overshadow the entire framework of management in the country. Political and economic restructuring began towards the end of the 1980s, and the country is entering the new millennium with a new outlook as well as new management perspectives.

1 Introduction

A combination of many inter-related factors has influenced the pattern of management in Tanzania. Among these factors, three stand out clearly. The first is the very low level of social and economic development in the country. The second relates to the dominant role that the state has historically played in Tanzania in practically all public affairs. Third, the social and cultural features of what is essentially a rural traditional society have also influenced the practice of management. Section 2 of this entry examines how these and other aspects have influenced the country's management pattern.

Tanzania lies on the east coast of Africa, just below the equator. Covering some 945,234 square kilometres, it is by far the largest country in the region. Tanzania is larger than neighbouring Kenya and Uganda combined. Except for a narrow belt of 900 square kilometres along the coast, most of Tanzania lies above 200 metres in altitude, and much of the country is higher than 1000 metres above sea level.

Estimates put the country's population for 1998 at just over 29 million. Close to 85 per cent of the people live in rural areas – mostly as smallholder peasants. The population growth rate is just over 3 per cent – one of the highest in the world. Indeed, the urban areas register an annual growth rate of over 8 per cent. Like other countries in Africa, Tanzania's population is relatively young – people under 15 years of age constitute more than 40 per cent of the population.

Apart from its relatively large size, the country has abundant natural resources. There are considerable deposits of minerals: gold, diamonds, gemstones, gypsum, and tanzanite – a mineral found in Tanzania only. As for agriculture, practically every tropical crop grows in one or more of the country's three main ecological zones. There is wheat, coffee, tea, potatoes, coffee and pyrethrum in the highlands lying along the frontiers. The plateau area in the centre of the country produces maize, rice, sorghum, sisal, millet, cotton and tobacco. On the other hand, coconuts, cashew nuts and many types of spices abound on the coastal strip and on the Indian Ocean islands.

Despite this apparent endowment in natural resources, however, Tanzania is one of the poorest countries in the world (see ECONOMIES OF THE EMERGING COUNTRIES). With an annual income per capita of just under US$200, the country ranks amongst the world's ten least developed countries. The mineral deposits are largely untapped, the agricultural sector is backward, and the country's infrastructure is very poor. While fairly vibrant, the industrial and commercial sectors are relatively small.

The economy, therefore, is quite shaky (Stewart *et al.* 1992). External debts – accumulated over decades – annually rob the country of the bulk of whatever surpluses the economy is able to generate. With a debt per capita value that is far above the country's per capital income, Tanzania is in the World Bank's category of *severely indebted low-income countries*. Throughout the 1980s and 1990s, the balance of payments deficit increased annually. In 1997 it constituted about 10 per cent of the country's gross domestic product.

Unlike the other countries in the region, Tanzania has had a chequered political career. The country has gone through a number of very different political regimes. The European scramble for African colonies in the nineteenth century had placed the bulk of what is now Tanzania under German rule. The defeat of Germany during the First World War shifted Tanganyika – as the mainland part was then called – into the British Empire as a United Nations trusteeship territory. Independence from Britain came at the end of 1961, and in 1964 Tanganyika united with the next door island of Zanzibar to form *The United Republic of Tanzania*. The first two and half decades of independence saw a one-party political system with a socialist orientation. Finally, the coming of multi-party politics towards the end of the 1980s coincided with the introduction of liberal policies on the economic front. The country has therefore gone through a series of very distinctive and radically different epochs that few other African countries have experienced.

Like other African countries, Tanzanian society is still in the process of formation. The landmass that Germany conquered and ruled from 1885 to 1918 consisted of more than 100 traditional societies. These were at different levels of development and had varied social structures and systems. The Germans used a variety of techniques – including very brutal 'pacification drives' – to amalgamate them into a single economic entity. The main role of the colony was to supply Germany with agricultural raw materials, particularly cotton, rubber and sisal. Using an approach that combined integration with 'divide-and-rule', the British later continued with this mission of turning the country into a true colonial appendage – not only economically, but also culturally.

The struggle for colonial independence had nationalism as its strongest expression. Its main voice was to transcend ethnic divisions, in addition to conquering foreign occupation. This appeal for nationalism was so successful that the anti-colonial movement became by far the strongest political movement in Eastern Africa. The post-independence regime pursued this same agenda of nationalism for well over two decades – vigorously championing 'nation-building' in all economic and social policies. Indeed, it is economic nationalism that drove even the socialist policies. Nationalization of the 'commanding heights of the economy' in 1967 was more of a nationalistic than a class ideology (Shivji 1985).

Having a common language, *Swahili*, the country has achieved a level of national consciousness that is unmatched in any other country in eastern and southern Africa. While ethnic cleavages do still erupt periodically, the spirit of nationhood has reached a fairly high level. The relative peace that has characterized Tanzanian society for all the years of independence is a reflection of this spirit.

2 Analysis

The social setting

The social conditions in Tanzania have a bearing on the process and pattern of managing the country's institutions. In this regard, the society's poverty is a critical factor. Tanzania is a very poor country, by any standards. Gross domestic product figures for 1997 were US$6073 million – a per capita domestic product of only about US$240 million. Close to 30 per cent of gross domestic product is not even part of the monetary sector: it represents the estimated value of household subsistence goods and services. Individual earnings for the vast majority of the people are therefore very low. Even in urban areas – where living conditions tend to be higher – people spend, on average, more than half of their incomes on food alone.

The physical and economic infrastructure is a major hindrance to organizational performance. In the countryside, practically every year sees areas experiencing a shortage of food while other areas have surpluses. It is not uncommon for villages to suffer a series of disasters emanating from floods in one season, and from drought the following season. Inadequate road and rail transport facilities are a major hindrance to productivity improvement in agriculture. Similarly, the poor calibre of financial services is an obstacle to the development of industry and commerce.

Government policy during the first 25 years of independence – from 1961 to 1986 – was socialist. The government created hundreds of state corporations to handle various sectors of the economy: banking, manufacturing, insurance, large scale farming, import and export trade, etc. Apart from wholesale and retail business, state enterprises dominated the bulk of economic activities in the country outside peasant agriculture. The 'parastatal' sector was therefore by far the largest sector in the modern economy. Its management style has had tremendous influence on the country's management pattern as a whole (Bol *et al.* 1997).

This socialist epoch contributed three important positive features to management in Tanzania. First, by putting emphasis on attaining self-reliance in technical expertise, it rapidly increased the number of skilled people in the country. For close to three decades, the government provided free or highly subsidised college education to all those who qualified – both within the country and outside. The number of training institutions for secondary school graduates increased tenfold in the first 20 years of independence. As a result, at the time of independence in 1961 Tanzania had less than a dozen graduates, but by the mid 1980s some 4000 university graduates were joining the labour market annually. In addition, 10,000 more with diplomas in various fields – engineering, nursing, agriculture, teaching, accounting, etc. – were leaving a myriad of colleges annually. For a small economy like that of Tanzania, these are not small numbers (see MANAGEMENT IN AFRICA).

By 1990 Tanzania had more high level technical and professional skills than any other country in the region. Indeed, the number of qualified staff in such areas as engineering, finance, law, medicine, etc. was far higher than the country's economy and technology could justify or support. Low earnings and growing unemployment pushed a substantial portion of these graduates into the Southern Africa labour market where wages are higher. The best ones got jobs in Europe and North America or joined international organizations.

Second, the socialist policies of the time also enhanced access to basic education in the country (United Nations Development Programme (UNDP) 1995). Enrolment in primary school increased tremendously between 1961 and 1990. As a result of various educational efforts and reforms, during the 1980s Tanzania attained one of the highest primary school enrolment rates in sub-Saharan Africa: 96 per cent. In this way, the country created a *literate* labour force. In the context of Africa, this was a major achievement. It is therefore a characteristic of the labour market in the country that technical skills are generally available, and that unskilled labour is literate.

Third, improvements in basic education also brought about gender equality in education. In the mid 1980s, primary school enrolment achieved a 50:50 representation ratio between boys and girls (UNDP 1995). This success, however, was not repeated at secondary and higher levels of the education system. Social and cultural factors were a bigger obstacle to women attaining post-primary education – and therefore acquiring management positions – than they were for men. Even at the end of the 1990s, females constituted only about 20 per cent of university students, and about 5 per cent of technical college students.

It is therefore another characteristic of management in Tanzania that it is almost entirely male. Women have fewer opportunities than men do to move into management positions. While studies show that women do not suffer wage discrimination, women nevertheless do not have the same opportunities either at the point of entry or in terms of the rate of advancement. Even during the era of 'parastatal' bodies, women constituted a tiny proportion of management staff. In 1990, there were hardly any women holding a top management positions in pubic enterprises. There was, for instance, only one female board chairperson compared to 449 males, no female managing directors, and only two female directors compared to 72 male ones. The situation in private enterprise was far worse. Things have improved somewhat since then, but not significantly.

Management education and training also benefited – albeit indirectly – from these early policies. A faculty of commerce and management opened its doors at the country's main university in the 1970s; when at least three other national institutions were beginning to give diploma level education in various aspects of management. Denied the autonomy to structure their own remuneration and incentive packages, state corporations often sent their managerial staff for training both locally and overseas as a way of rewarding them. In this way, management education and training received a notable boost (see MANAGEMENT EDUCATION IN THE EMERGING COUNTRIES).

The pattern of management

One of the glaring features of public life in Tanzania is obviously the low level of institutional capacity. It is not difficult to observe that institutions in the country generally have a very low capacity to discharge their functions. State institutions best illustrate this low level of management. Public agencies are unable to collect garbage from the streets, to carry out maintenance of the infrastructure, or even to collect revenues due to them. Similarly, public institutions that supposedly operate commercially to provide various utilities are grossly inefficient and ineffective. Within government, administrative systems and procedures are both cumbersome and outdated.

This scenario of weak management is of course not unique to Tanzania. Indeed, it is a common feature of Africa and other developing areas. There is no single factor that is the ultimate cause of this state of affairs. Rather, it is the product of a complex web of factors. Many authors (Jaeger and Kanungo 1990) have noted that institutions in developing countries operate under social, economic and political conditions that are, at once, both the *cause* and the *result* of poor performance.

As elsewhere, the private sector operates quite differently. Wholesale and retail traders dominate this sector, but medium and small-scale industries are also sprouting. The sector faces stiff competition from imports, and therefore tries to carry itself in accordance with world standards. Multinational companies began moving aggressively into the economy in the 1990s, and these are making an impact on the style and pattern of management in the country.

3 Evaluation

There are a number of features that characterize the process of management in Tanzania. The process itself is dynamic, and the features are therefore in a state of constant evolution.

First, the work ethic is relatively weak. The low levels of living standards – coupled with very small rates of economic growth – have created a sense of *powerlessness* among people. Even managers easily exhibit a *laissez-faire* attitude to duties and responsibilities. Experience with the public sector strengthened this attitude. Indeed, the policy of public enterprises banished the sense of personal accountability, extolled corruption to high levels, and created an arena where staff in organizations – including managerial staff – openly engaged in looting their employing institutions.

This feature is of course changing. In practice at least, the country abandoned this socialist orientation from the mid-1980s. With guidance and insistence from the World Bank and the International Monetary Fund, the government embarked on economic restructuring. It began selling enterprises, closing non-profitable ones, and liberalized trade and investment. Tanzania therefore entered a new epoch in the early 1990s. It is an epoch that is gradually changing the pattern of management– among many other things.

Second, the country inherited from the socialist epoch a cadre of managers that is lop-sided in its structure. The vast 'parastatal' sector that Tanzania built for over two decades consisted largely of monopolies. Its managers therefore tended to have a *production* rather than a *market* focus. They have had ample experience in overseeing the internal operational aspects of institutions, but lack the skills and experience of dealing with customer issues and problems. Tanzania is therefore left with a cadre of managers for a monopolistic environment.

For this reason, the multinational companies that – with economic liberalization – have rushed into the country have had no problems finding qualified engineers, lawyers, economists or scientists. They have, however, had difficulties finding people who can design marketing strategies. This feature is, of course, also changing fast. It will, however, take time before the lop-sided nature is fully corrected.

Third, the dominance of the state in organizational life during the socialist epoch meant that government mediated most institutional interactions in society (Shivji 1985). The state always mediated all transactions – arranging for credit, organizing distribution channels, importing and exporting, etc. The managers who therefore tended to excel in their respective organizations were those with competencies in dealing with government. Such managers had the influence to win political concessions, and the skills to manoeuvre through bureaucratic red tape. They have bequeathed a management orientation for taking short-cut measures to obtain short-term objectives. It is not a management orientation for formulating long-term strategies.

It is significant that even the private sector has tended to copy this approach to some extent. In the past, the most successful private businesses were those with connections to government officials. Thus, a tendency has grown whereby, rather than struggle to enhance its entrepreneurial capacities, the private sector also tends to look to government for solving the sector's problems.

Finally, management in Tanzania has had an inclination to be parochial in its outlook. The decades of state enterprises largely excluded foreign managers. The few who did work in the country came mainly at the behest of the state sector, and therefore had little influence over the style of management in the country. Indeed, theirs was largely a technical rather than a managerial role. As a result, Tanzanian managers have for a long time been able to shield themselves from the flow of ever-changing management ideas and practices that have been engulfing the rest of the world. For example, empowerment, total quality management, customer focus, re-engineering, etc. are generally untried management concepts in the country.

4 Conclusion

Tanzania is leaving the twentieth century on a weak footing. The country is, however, entering the new millennium with a great deal of expectations. A new political dispensation began in the early 1990s with the introduction of multi-party politics. It will take at least until the end of the first decade of the new millennium for the political system to stabilize fully. Investment in the key areas of the economy – mining, agriculture, and tourism – has now started to flow.

However, there are fundamental contradictions. For one, a de-emphasis on social services has already led to a downturn in education, health and welfare generally. The extent to which wealth generated through new investments is not siphoned out of the country is also, as yet, an open question.

Still, the prospects for a brighter future are better than at any other time. While the past bears heavily on the country's conscience, the opportunities are nevertheless irresistible. Above all, the structural reform of the civil service and the 'parastatal' sector is bringing a radically different management pattern to the country. This pattern will definitely have ramifications throughout society.

HENRY MAPOLU
REDMA – MANAGEMENT CONSULTANTS

Further reading

(References cited in the text marked *)

Austin, J.E. (1990) *Managing in Developing Countries* London: The Free Press. (A treatise on corporate management in the context of developing countries.)

* Bol, D., Luvanga, N. and Shitundu, J. (eds) (1997) *Economic Management in Tanzania*, Dar es Salaam: Tema Publishers. (Discusses the experience of different phases in the management of Tanzania's economy.)

Bryceson, D.F. (1993) *Liberalizing Tanzania's Food Trade*, Dar es Salaam: Mkuki na Nyota. (Case study on state policies on the management of the food industry in the country.)

Havnevik, K.J. (1993) *Tanzania: The Limits to Development from Above*, Dar es Salaam: Mkuki na Nyota. (Examines the interaction of policy makers, donors and experts on a major economic project in the country.)

* Jaeger, A.M. and Kanungo, R.N. (eds) (1990) *Management in Developing Countries*, London: Routledge. (Analysis of the various issues and features related to managing institutions in countries like Tanzania.)

Semboja, J. and Therkildsen, O. (eds) (1995) *Service Provision Under Stress in East Africa*, Dar es Salaam: Mkuki na Nyota. (Analysis of the role of the state and people's organizations in Kenya, Uganda and Tanzania.)

* Shivji, I.G. (ed.) (1985) *The State and the Working People in Tanzania*, Dakar: Codesria. (Contributions on the role of the state and different sectors and groups in Tanzania.)

* Stewart, F., Lall, S. and Wangwe, S. (eds) (1992) *Alternative Development Strategies in Sub-Saharan Africa*, London: The Macmillan Press. (Examines alternative policies for managing development in sub-Saharan Africa.)

* United Nations Development Programme (1995) *Human Development Report*, New York: United Nations Development Programme. (Contains very useful information on human development status in Tanzania.)

See also: BUSINESS CULTURES, THE EMERGING COUNTRIES; ECONOMIES OF THE EMERGING COUNTRIES; MANAGEMENT EDUCATION IN THE EMERGING COUNTRIES; MANAGEMENT IN AFRICA; MANAGEMENT IN THE EMERGING COUNTRIES; MANAGEMENT IN KENYA; MANAGEMENT IN NIGERIA; MANAGEMENT IN SOUTH AFRICA; MANAGEMENT IN UGANDA; MANAGEMENT IN ZAMBIA

Related topics in the IEBM regional set: MANAGEMENT IN ASIA PACIFIC

Management in Uganda

1 Introduction
2 Analysis
3 Conclusion

Overview

To the visiting foreigner, Uganda is a beautiful and scenic country with polite and friendly people. To the local business executive, entrepreneur or public service manager, however, it is a difficult country to manage. This entry discusses the factors which, over the years, have shaped the leadership, organization and management of the country's political economy. It concludes with a cautiously optimistic note about the future of the country and its management.

1 Introduction

Located at the northern shores of Lake Victoria and the source of the Nile, Uganda is an equatorial country endowed with natural beauties and resources. But it is also small, landlocked, underdeveloped, highly differentiated, and characterized by contrast, contradiction and conflict. The forces which have shaped the country's business development, leadership and management style and content include:

1   its history: pre-colonial, colonial, and post-colonial;
2   the country's variegated cultural and ethnic groupings including religious and sectarian differentiation;
3   a predominantly agricultural and resource based economy with a small but promising industrial sector;
4   socioeconomic status differentials, including sex roles. Computer information technology and globalization have not as yet had a direct significant impact on the country's development, work processes, or management thought and practice.

2 Analysis

History and management

Modern Uganda is glued together from previously independent or semi-independent traditional kingdoms and chieftancies each with its own unique governance institutions, work organizations, languages, cultural values, religious beliefs and practices. Before colonial times, administrative systems were small in size, homogenous in membership and therefore easy to manage, used local technology and indigenous knowledge systems, and co-existed in relative harmony with the natural environment. Each had a formal hierarchy with the chief or king at the apex. Authority was due to conquest, heredity or special relationships with the supernatural. Even today, leaders attempt to emulate these traditional forms of authority which were also reinforced by the colonial administrators through a system of indirect rule. Consequently, symbolism and status are important in influencing leadership behaviour and managerial style (Kiggundu 1991).

Kinship and shared cultural values helped to cement relationships across administrative hierarchies. It also helped to foster a common understanding and thereby control any excessive abuse of power with indirect but socially effective checks and balances. The weakening of the traditional social controls and sanctions has contributed to current problems of governance and economic mismanagement. In addition, organizations which cut across traditional homogenous lines are prone to conflict, and are more difficult to manage.

The current stock of leaders and managers draw their experience and inspiration from the traditional leaders and colonial administrators. Most managers in the private sector have served their time in government or the military. Accordingly, leadership and management philosophy values, styles and practices are similar across sectors (see MANAGEMENT IN AFRICA). Leadership is characterized by a formal hierarchy, and by autocratic, authoritarian and paternalistic behaviour with highly centralized decision making. Delegated participative management is rare. Symbolism, especially that drawn from traditional or even colonial images is important. Power distance is high and senior managers often take on the role of father figure towards their employees. Lower level employees are given little or no autonomy in their work; middle and junior managers exercise close supervision. Trust across hierarchical levels is low. Those in leadership roles behave like the old traditional chiefs (Blunt and Jones 1992)

Differentiation without integration

Uganda and its formation as a modern state is a complex juxtaposition of ethnicity and religion with a more recent spicing of African nationalism, Islamic fundamentalism, and post-Cold War ideology. There are about 55 tribes in Uganda with a population of just over 21 million people (1996) and a total surface area of 241,139 square kilometres (about the size of Britain) of which about 20 per cent is covered with water and swamps. Religion is important in Uganda and there is competition among the Christian churches and with the Muslim community. According to the 1995 figures, 60 per cent of the population belongs to various Christian denominations of which the Catholic church (7.8 million) and the Anglican church are the most dominant. Muslims make up only 5 per cent of the population although they are much more dominant especially in politics, trade and commerce.

The historical and socio-cultural characteristics, reinforced by colonial and post independence administrations have resulted in a highly differentiated society. Besides ethnicity, language and religion, society is differentiated by race, education, income, wealth (e.g. land, cows), opportunity, the rural–urban divide, gender, age, family connections, heredity and political affiliations. This differentiation makes management and public administration difficult, and causes a certain disconnectedness especially between traditional institutions and modern organizations (Dia 1996).

Societal differentiation manifests itself in many different ways relevant for public administration and business management. For example, it explains why a relatively small country has over 20 political parties and an equal number of small commercial banks each servicing a small segment of the population. It also explains why so many small universities are mushrooming in spite of a generalized lack of resources for post-secondary education. It also explains the existence of wide disparities in education, income, wealth and opportunity among the various segments of society. It explains some of the tensions and conflict which characterize independent Uganda (Rupesinghe 1989).

Societal differentiation and its manifestations transcend to the level of individual institutions and business organizations. At the organizational level, it complicates leadership, management and supervision. For example, national institutions such as the civil service, the military and the central bank devote a lot of resources trying to reconcile different and often conflicting regional, tribal or religious differences. This may explain why, as of 1998, the Uganda Railways, left with only a 50 mile operating line from Kampala to Jinja, still employs over 2000 workers. It may also explain why top management of the corporation, after being found wanting, was reprimanded by being sent home on six months' paid leave.

Leaders and top executives try to cope with organizational differentiation by taking on many societal extra-organizational roles. For example, a senior banking executive is president of a local youth organization, heads a religious or tribal group, chairs the board of governors of a local university, sits on the fund-raising committee for a local high school and advises political leaders. This means that these executives are spread too thinly and hardly have time to concentrate on the strategic aspects of the business or to keep up to date with industry trends. Ugandan managers tend to be more operational and tactical than strategic or long-term in their business decisions (Kiggundu 1989, 1996). This may explain at least in part the excessive dependence on outside consultants, especially in the public sector.

Differentiation contributes to organizational small size because it prevents the development of joint ventures, large scale partnerships, horizontal or vertical business integration. Indeed many organizations in Uganda suffer from being small in size, not only because of market limitations but also due to societal differentiation. This deprives management of economies of scale and results in highly cost inefficient operations. Entrepreneurs in Uganda complain of a lack of economies of scale, but are reluctant to take practical steps to merge operations because they are afraid of losing management control. Trust is low and information on corporate performance is not shared (see BUSINESS CULTURES, THE EMERGING COUNTRIES). As one CEO told me, 'we do not provide operational or performance data. If you are successful, they are jealous; if you fail, they laugh at you.'

The problem is not that differentiation in Uganda's organizations is too high. Indeed, organizations in other countries – especially in Africa – operate under similar differentiated environments. Rather, the problem is that no corresponding effective integrating mechanisms are in place. Integrating mechanisms such as shared corporate vision and how to achieve shared goals, effective horizontal linkages within and across organizations, mutual trust and a code of business ethics and employee empowerment have been difficult to institutionalize. This is the challenge for management in Uganda in the twenty-first century.

War and disease

The Ugandan population, including political, business and institutional leaders and managers has been traumatized by war and disease. By the year 2000, those who were born in the mid 1960s when the first incidents of domestic conflict started will be in their mid 30s. Those who were in their teens when Amin's 'state of blood' started in the early 1970s will be in their 40s. Those who were young adults when Obote and Muwanga's reign of terror started in the early 1980s will be in their 50s. Those who got their experiences and work values and ethics from the colonial era are retiring (Kasozi 1994).

The present generation of leaders and managers is made up of men and women who have grown up under reckless, highly stressful and traumatic conditions. There is no adult in the country who has not lost a close relative, friend, co-worker or business associate either due to conflict or disease. HIV/AIDS has been particularly devastating not only to the individuals and their families, but also to the social and economic fabric of society as a whole. It is estimated that by the mid-1990s, about 15 per cent of the adult population was infected with the human immunodeficiency virus (HIV), the causative agent for AIDS (Armstrong 1995).

Besides reducing the already limited stock of available management, entrepreneurial, professional and intellectual capital, or inexpensive unskilled rural labour, war and disease have created a generation of traumatized employees and their managers. Trauma manifests itself in many ways including fear, anger, learned helplessness, mistrust, depression, perceptual distortion, a sense of personal persecution and a variety of psychosomatic disorders. The full extent of the effects of these manifestations on the leaders and business managers in the country has never been studied. However, as a minimum, the managers' ability to analyse business decisions, take appropriate business risks, maintain healthy social and interpersonal relations, and sustain strategic thinking must be negatively affected. A lot of energy is spent camouflaging these feelings, especially when dealing with foreigners. Managers who have no faith in the future do not think strategically and tend to be corrupt. There is very limited respect for the sanctity of ordinary life. Investment decisions are made to protect capital from the consequences of war and disease rather than to maximize long-term profitability. Hoarding of capital, stock, information and other business assets is part of doing business. Yet, Ugandans are very resilient. In spite of almost 40 years of war and disease, they are busy rebuilding a society and economy which, if successful, will be the envy of all their neighbours.

Economic management

Agriculture is by far the most important sector of the economy accounting for 46 per cent of GDP (gross domestic product), 90 per cent of exports and 80 per cent of the total labour force (see ECONOMIES OF THE EMERGING COUNTRIES). It is predominantly organized by small holdings with little or no application of modern technology or management. The development of the whole economy is heavily influenced by the performance of the agricultural sector which in turn is influenced by climatic conditions, internal security, rural infrastructure, availability of local cheap labour and global pricing. The few agricultural estates for tea, sugar and coffee are owned by foreign firms with their own global management systems largely independent of local management practices (Europa Yearbook 1998).

There is a small industrial sector based on agriculture/food processing, textiles, logging, mining and quarrying, which accounts for about 5 per cent of GDP. The industrial sector was developed from the colonial period through independence on the basis of import substitution rather than global integration and contained a dominant and pervasive public enterprise sector. Like the agricultural sector, the industrial sector contains many very small firms. Over 80 per cent of the firms employ 35 people or less, and 50 per cent employ 10 people or less. These firms are too small and too undercapitalized to take advantage of modern technology or management. The larger firms are either foreign owned, or currently undergoing privatization.

Most of the manufacturing sector produces the usual 'necessities' of life in poor developing countries: processed food, beer, soft drinks, soap, cigarettes, cement, electricity, paper, etc. These products tend to be politically sensitive and the firms seek protection or concessions against foreign competition. They therefore have little incentive to adopt modern management techniques since competition is muted. Most industries are located in the Kampula-Jinja-Tororo axis while the north and western regions (outside Mbarara) have very few industries. This uneven regional distribution accentuates problems of differentiation across the country (United Nations Industrial Development Organisation (UNIDO) 1992).

The sector has been adversely affected by several factors including the leftist policies of the 1960s, the expulsion of the Asians (1972), the break up of the Easter African Community, the security problems of the 1980s and associated brain drain, and the frequent looting during successive civil conflicts. During the 1990s the government has been preoccupied with the rehabilitation, development and privatization of the public enterprise sector. By the early 1990s the entire industrial sector was performing at only 30 per cent of capacity, and manufacturing accounted for about 7.7 per cent of GDP in 1995/96. Government policy aims at creating an enabling environment for private sector development including attracting private direct foreign and domestic investment. During the period 1992–95 it identified over 1600 new investment projects in various sectors of the economy. Experience elsewhere shows that public sector administrators rarely make good private sector managers.

The new class of African entrepreneurs and managers are developing their own approach to business development and management. Rather than concentrating on the growth of a single firm in a single sector, the tendency is to develop many small firms in many different sectors. This is particularly the case with entrepreneurial family owned firms. For example, one entrepreneur who started out in the financial services sector, over a period of 10 years, has developed an 'octopus' business structure that includes real estate, hotel and recreation, food processing, export, trading and post-secondary education (Jorgensen *et al.* 1986).

The management implications and challenges of the octopus approach to business are obvious. First, individual firms are likely to remain small and therefore unable to enjoy economies of scale. Small firms do not use modern management or technology, especially if market conditions are competitive. Second, the few available management capacities are spread too thinly across different and unrelated businesses. This makes industrial specialization difficult and the octopus entrepreneur runs the risk of running out of good managers across sectors. Third, integration within the same or similar sectors is difficult as investments in individual firms are considered not in the context of their respective sectors, but as part of a sprawling octopus with social and political implications for the entrepreneur rather than purely business considerations. These implications suggest that adoption of modern management and technology by these octopus entrepreneurs is likely to be slow.

One of the issues confronting the new African entrepreneurs is corporate governance. Most of the *nouveaux riches* do not yet understand the structuring, role and responsibilities of the corporate board of directors and the separation of responsibilities with the executive senior managers. Some board members are known to get involved in the day-to-day running of the business, thus interfering with managements' prerogative to manage. At the same time, executive managers are reluctant to provide board members with corporate sensitive information for fear it will be sold to the highest bidder. This problem is particularly serious in the early stages of privatization where overlapping directorships and changing minority interests are common.

The commercial banking system is in need of significant change. In 1994, more than half of the banks made losses with a large negative core capital. Aggregate non-performing assets were in excess of 50 per cent of total loans. Banks generally lacked financial discipline and administrative efficiency thus causing high intermediation costs. Even the Central Bank's financial position and institutional capacity are in doubt. The government has responded by privatizing its own Uganda Commercial Bank forcing the closure of the worst of the non-performing banks and strengthened the supervisory capacity of the central bank. Still the majority of the small entrepreneurs have no access to open market credit.

Privatization of public enterprises is expected to attract modern management and technology as the new owners seek better returns from their investments. However, this will only happen if privatization is accompanied by increased competition in the local economy and if there is a clear distinction between the new owners and those in government and their political or military masters. Crony capitalism impedes advances in business and management development. Available evidence suggests that the difference between management before and after privatization is rather blurred. Uganda has been ranked the twelfth most corrupt country in the world.

The Asian factor in Uganda's management

No discussion of management in Uganda is complete without examining the role of the Asian community (see BUSINESS CULTURES, THE EMERGING COUNTRIES). This is a small but important group of entrepreneurs originally from the Indian subcontinent who settled in Uganda, brought capital, enterprise and expertise and dominated the country's commerce and industry both in urban centres and rural areas. Although governments before and after independence attempted to limit the role of the Asians, they remained dominant until their expulsion in 1972. In the mid-1990s, they were invited back to repossess their businesses and some have accepted the challenge and restarted their business operations or opened new ones.

In spite of their dominant role, especially in small and medium-sized enterprises, the Asian entrepreneurs have never been instrumental in introducing modern management thought and practice. Instead, their employment practices, management styles and business philosophy are traditional and paternalistic. They have tended to exploit their superior economic status but are not interested in transferring their business acumen to the indigenous entrepreneurs. They have tended to crowd out the Africans, especially in the more profitable lines of business. True business partnerships based on a level playing field between the two groups are rare. Until this happens, coexistence will be difficult, and mutual mistrust will continue.

Unions and associations

Uganda does not have a strong independent trade union movement. The small size of the agricultural and industrial firms, the problems of societal differentiation, lack of union support from overseas and restrictive government legislation have all contributed to a weak labour movement (see HUMAN RESOURCE MANAGEMENT IN THE EMERGING COUNTRIES; INDUSTRIAL RELATIONS IN THE EMERGING COUNTRIES). This gives managers a relatively free hand in shaping employee relations at their place of work.

There are several active employer associations in the country. For example, the Uganda Manufacturers Association, originally formed in 1972 and re-activated in 1989 has more than 200 medium and large-scale member companies in both the private and public sector. Together with the Federation of Uganda Employers, the Uganda Chamber of Commerce, Uganda Management Institute and the recently established Private Sector Foundation, these organizations play an active role in promoting industrial development and assisting local organizations to improve management thought and practice.

Women in management

Uganda is a basically male dominated society and this dominance pervades life in work organizations. Although the country has a long tradition of female education through christian missionary schools, few women are active in business management and entrepreneurship, except in the social sector (e.g. education, health, welfare, non-government organizations). Status differentials also prevent the advancement of women, as existing women's organizations tend to concentrate on their narrow interests rather than reaching out to the grassroots including the poor and uneducated women. Ironically, AIDS, which cuts across social status, has had the effect of bringing Ugandan women together as they cope with the challenges of widowhood, single parenting and the vulnerability of their own health. The Aids Support Organization (TASO) is a case in point.

Although there are a few high profile women who have been successful in politics and public administration, the overall role of women in society leaves much to be desired. More women are needed, especially in the higher levels of business, corporate management and entrepreneurship.

4 Conclusion

For a country that has been described as the 'pearl of Africa' and a 'state of blood', predicting the future is indeed a risky business. During the late 1990s, the country enjoyed positive international press and material support from the World Bank and Western donors. However, very little of the aid has trickled down to the poor. On the basis of monetary and economic macro-performance, these supporters predict favourable conditions for business and management development. This is particularly likely to be the case if the country's industrial strategy is linked to the agro-business sector taking advantage of a favourable climate, fertile soils, cheap unskilled labour, and a good track record of managing relatively small and simple value adding enterprises.

The real test will be the extent to which the country attracts substantial private foreign direct investment and maintains an environment within which local business can grow and eventually compete in the global economy. Critics point out that a combination of internal tensions, crony capitalism, mismanagement and poor utilization of resources and regional military adventurism may give rise to the development of 'Aminic' conditions leading to yet another reign of terror and destruction. History teaches us to be cautiously optimistic.

MOSES N. KIGGUNDU
SCHOOL OF BUSINESS
CARLETON UNIVERSITY

Further reading

(References cited in the text marked *)

* Armstrong, J. (1995) *Uganda's AIDS Crisis: Its Implications for Development*, Washington, DC: World Bank Discussion Papers, No. 298. (This field study shows that AIDS in Uganda will have a far-reaching impact on the social and economic fabric of the country's society and that it poses a serious threat to development including the rural areas where HIV is spreading rapidly.)
* Blunt, P. and Jones, M.L. (1992) *Managing Organizations in Africa*. New York: Walter de Gruyter. (Discusses the challenges and prospects for developing and managing effective organizations in Africa with illustrations from Uganda.)
* Dia, M. (1996) *Africa's Management in the 1990's and Beyond: Reconciling Indigenous and Trans- planted Institutions*, Washington, DC: The World Bank. (Presents research evidence to support the view that problems of economic management in Africa are due to a structural disconnection between formal institutions transplanted from outside and indigenous institutions born of traditional African culture.)
* Europa Yearbook (1997) 'Uganda', *Africa South of the Sahara* 27th edn, London: Europa Publications Limited. (Provides the statistics used in this section of the paper.)
* Jorgensen, J.J., Hafsi, T. and Kiggundu, M.N. (1986) 'Towards a market imperfections theory of organizational structure in developing countries', *Journal of Management Studies* 23(4): 417–42. (Develops the concept of the octopus as a structural response to market imperfections in the development of small entrepreneurial organizations. Provides illustrations particularly relevant to the newly emerging indigenous small business organizations in Uganda.)
* Kasozi, A.B.K. (1994.) *The Social Origins of Violence in Uganda 1996–1985*, Montreal: McGill-Queen's University Press. (Spirited discussion of the causes of violence from the time of independence in 1962 to 1985 by a Ugandan social historian.)
* Kiggundu, M.N. (1989) *Managing Organizations in Developing Countries: An Operational and Strategic Approach*, West Hartford, CT, Kumarian Press. (Provides a framework with illustra-

tions from Uganda for the analysis of strategic and operational aspects of organizations in developing countries.)

* Kiggundu, M.N. (1991) 'The challenge of management development in Sub-Saharan Africa', *Journal of Management Development* 10(6): 32–47. (Discusses the effects of history on management development in Africa with examples from Uganda.)

* Kiggundu, M.N. (1996) 'Integrating strategic management tasks into implementing agencies: From firefighting to prevention', *World Development* 24(9): 1417–30. (Provides a rationale and suggested approach for integrating strategic management and operational administration in organizations in Uganda.)

Mutibwa, P. (1992) *Uganda Since Independence: A Story of Unfulfilled Hopes*, London: Hurst and Co.

Ofcansky, T.P. (1996) *Uganda: Tarnished Pearl of Africa*, Boulder, Colorado, Westview Press.

* Rupesinghe, K. (ed.) (1989) *Conflict Resolution in Uganda*, Oslo: International Peace Research Institute. (Discusses the causes of conflict in Uganda. For more recent historical accounts, see Wrigley 1996; Ofcansky 1996; Mutibwa 1992; and Twaddle 1993.)

Twaddle, M. (1993) *Kakungulu and the Creation of Uganda*, London: James Currey.

* UNIDO (United Nations Industrial Development Organization) (1992) *Uganda: Industrial Revitalization and Reorientation*, Industrial Development Review Series, Geneva. (Discusses the structure and historical evolution of Uganda's industrial sector with a special emphasis on government initiatives since 1986.)

Wrigley, C. (1996) *Kingship and State: The Buganda Dynasty*, Cambridge: Cambridge University Press. (Wide-ranging and original study of one of Africa's most famous kingdoms.)

See also: ECONOMIES OF THE EMERGING COUNTRIES; HUMAN RESOURCE MANAGEMENT IN THE EMERGING COUNTRIES; INDUSTRIAL RELATIONS IN THE EMERGING COUNTRIES; MANAGEMENT IN AFRICA; MANAGEMENT IN THE EMERGING COUNTRIES; MANAGEMENT IN KENYA; MANAGEMENT IN TANZANIA

Management in Zambia

1 **Introduction**
2 **Colonial rule and its consequences**
3 **Government and administration: 1st and 2nd Republics**
4 **The civil service**
5 **Parastatal companies**
6 **Financial management**
7 **Industrial relations and trade unions**
8 **Conclusion**

Overview

Management in Zambia and the parastatal sector grew as a result of the nationalization policies which have existed since the 1970s. The overall economic policy evolved around a static command economy. This *allowed* the government to provide financial and administrative capacities to manage commerce and industry. The economy in Zambia is unbalanced and heavily dependent on supplies and markets outside the country. The political system is trying to unite disparate peoples and to establish an orderly effective mechanism for governing and for directing development.

Zambia's economy is overwhelmingly dependent on copper mining. Over 92 per cent of the values of Zambian exports and 60 per cent of government revenue are directly derived from this industry. At the time of independence, virtually all of the transportation facilities and sources of power essential to Zambia's copper industry were located in territory controlled by white minority regimes. Political tensions between Zambia and these governments necessitated the heavy costs of developing alternative transportation routes and power supplies. Imbalances in Zambia's economy are not only related to copper. Very little development has taken place in the 290,000 square miles of Zambia except along the single existing railway line that runs north–south through the centre of the country. The political and economic need of extending economic development to the rest of the country is a matter of the highest urgency.

1 Introduction

Zambia began its existence as an independent country when Northern Rhodesia, a British protectorate in central Africa, became the independent Republic of Zambia on 24 October 1964; this 1st Republic ended in December 1972. The independence constitution, which has allowed multi-party competition, was then amended to provide for a one party participatory democracy. The 2nd Republic was inaugurated and its government institutions elaborated during 1973.

Its existence as an independent country began with only 1200 citizens with secondary school certificates and 104 with college degrees. This number was hardly adequate to satisfy the demands for an improvement in the material conditions of living, to perform the non-development tasks of government and to operate the world's second most productive copper industry. Moreover, because of racial barriers to advancement during the colonial period, few Africans could claim any experience in a position of meaningful responsibility. In other words, experience did not compensate for a lack of formal training.

This entry charts the historical background of Zambia's colonial rule and analyses the emergence of the civil servants and parastatal companies in Zambia's bid to operate effectively in the world economy.

2 Colonial rule and its consequences

The BSA Company ruled Zambia from 1890 to 1924 for mainly economic reasons. It handed over its administrative role to the British Colonial office. Britain, although allowing local European settlers a progressively larger say in government, retained ultimate control of the territory until Independence. Britain did, however, permit the creation of the Central African Federation which united southern and northern Rhodesia with Nyasaland, under the control of predominantly southern Rhodesian whites.

In the 1930s, copper began to be exploited on a large scale. This lead, on the one hand, to a rapid and large increase in the number of Europeans in the country, and, on the other, to the formation of the powerful African mine workers union in 1949.

Even before this, African protest against colonial rule had begun with the emergence of the Northern Rhodesian Colonial system in the first half of the nineteenth century. It not only shaped the nationalist movement – which emerged to oppose and eventually overthrow it – but has also had consuming consequences for Zambia since Independence. Northern Rhodesia Colonialism was an extension of white South Colonial rule, which involved the introduction into northern Rhodesia of European and Asian minorities. While the former monopolized managerial, professional and skilled artisan occupations, the latter (although much smaller) conducted much of the country's mid-range retail commerce. Both groups were deeply committed to a private enterprise economy, although at the same time few of them were prepared in 1964 to take out Zambian citizenship or to invest in long-term projects essential to the development of the economy.

Paradoxically their dominant position in the economic structure forced the UNIP (a non-racialist party) to draw a non-racialist policy. It was at this time that many of its African supporters deeply resented the wealth, exploitation, social exclusiveness and arrogance of these minorities. Citizenship policy and fears of 'Paper Zambians' were recurrent issues throughout the 1st and 2nd Republics.

The European minority also successfully institutionalized racialist practices against the African majority: wage discrimination, exclusion from many occupations and social facilities, segregated public services. While racialism created a convenient target for the nationalist movement, it also created a series of post-independence problems. Many Europeans precipitately left after 1963, before indigenous citizens had been trained to replace them. And perhaps, most of all, the continuing economic clearance between Africans and other racial groups has diverted popular attention from the evolving inter-African class formation which has taken place as independence paved the way to African entry into the private sector and domination of the public bureaucracy.

3 Government and administration: 1st and 2nd Republics

Industrial participatory democracy

Under the President Dr Kenneth Kaunda, the UNIP government issued the policy of Industrial Participatory Democracy. This policy decision was to actively involve workers in the management of industries. The ideal version of the industrial participatory democracy stipulates that:

1 Workers and progressive managerial elements should seize 'power from a few who have organized to exploit the working people'.
2 Workers and progressive managers are charged with the responsibility of managing the seized industries.
3 Gaining the skills of production by workers represents the initial step towards equity in the distributing income.
4 Workers participation in industries also placed upon them the moral responsibility to promote the interests of the peasants.
5 Workers participation in industrial enterprises is essential for the realization of the moral goal and of promoting the interests of the common man. (See Industrial Relations Act 1971 Part II: 98–9.)

The more practical implementation of the industrial participatory democracy or the works council calls for the promotion of efficient participation of the workers in the affairs of industry for which the works council was established. It also envisages some considerable degree of influence by the workers in the management of industries.

The UNIP also introduced radical programmes of administrative decentralization in order to increase and widen the scope of liaison between local administration, the party, government administration and parastatal organizations. In operational terms, the policy of administrative decentralization followed in the wake of local government reforms which placed a cabinet minister at the head of each of Zambia's nine provinces with a permanent secretary who functions as Chief Civil Servant in the provinces to assist him. Industries in Zambia are either state-owned and controlled by the civil service or are parastatal companies, the interim stage of the country's privatization programme.

4 The civil service

In 1971 'grass-root' participatory structures came into effect with the introduction of the Registration and Development of Villages Act. The functions of the village productivity committees, ward councils and ward committees serve as the basic units of local administration to the rural areas, responsible for:

1 maintenance of law and order, promotion of commercial services and community interests;

2   interpreting national electives and policies in terms of their applicability to local needs and to transmit local interests and aspirations to the national decision-making structures;

3   economically, to promote rural development and the spirit of self-reliance, including the employment of the institutions and faculties provided by the government to achieve this objective;

4   formation and implementation of rural development policies, assisting in the promotion of health and education, establishment and maintenance of local welfare services or amenities.

However, the Zambian civil service suffers from a number of internal weaknesses, including the lack of sufficient coordination and communication between ministries and their field staff, over-centralization, a bureaucratic structure and procedures, a lack of financial control, and cases of official corruption and accidents. The parastatal sector has also been criticized for financial indiscipline and inefficiency, which has led to its growing dependence on central government subsidies and grants.

Over-centralization and overburdening of the top level hierarchy have had serious effects on the civil service's ability to implement the second National Development Plan. Technical departments still had to be handled by expatriate officers recruited from overseas.

The morale of the civil service has been adversely affected not only by the poor quality of personnel management but also by the erosion of the principle of political neutrality. Top civil servants worry about job security whilst those below them wonder whether proved political loyalty will be a more important criterion for promotion than administrative or technical efficiency. In these circumstances, it is not surprising that many civil servants have either resigned from the service to join private companies or have transferred to the parastatal sector (see MANAGEMENT IN AFRICA).

5 Parastatal companies

Parastatal companies refer to those institutions created by government for implementing development programmes or for supplying essential services which by the nature and magnitude of the capital involved cannot be left to free enterprise. They are set up by Acts of Parliament and are an arm of the government. The Acts of Parliament set out their objectives, duties and powers, while policy matters and the day-to-day running of these enterprises is the concern of the Board of Directors. Parastatal companies are not supposed to be bound by civil service red tape and should be in a position to take major decisions by themselves within the scope of their powers but subject to certain safeguards in the national interest. In short, parastatal companies encompass state companies, state trading corporations, utility corporations, regulatory commissions and marketing boards.

The state companies, unlike statutory corporations, are established under the ordinary company law of Zambia and some shares may be in private hands. It is the form used when governments want to enter into partnership with foreign private investors.

The economic rationale for the creation of parastatal companies is in the assumption that:

1   Efficiency can be achieved to a higher degree than is possible if the enterprise is run by a government department or ministry.
2   There will be freedom of initiative, and the possibility of quick decisions and more flexible policies and methods.
3   As a result, the corporation will be in a position to run the enterprise at a profit.
4   As a government-run organization, the people are the ultimate owners of the enterprise. Thus the profits accrued from their operations are public money and can be fully utilized in the public interest, e.g. by reducing consumer prices for the products.
5   Although public corporations are expected to operate as a business and produce a profit, they are also expected to provide better employment opportunities for citizens. It is generally believed that the big expatriate-owned commercial and industrial enterprises in the country could employ more people and offer more generous conditions than they presently do if they were less profit-orientated. Thus, public corporations should be motivated by social welfare and profit at the same time.
6   Profits made by state-owned corporations, unlike those of private enterprises, could be ploughed back into the domestic economy while most of the profit made by foreign-owned enterprises, on average, benefit the expatriates. In other words, the income from public corporations can produce and multiply economic effects of the country and bring about economic development.

Mismanagement of parastatal companies

Since the inception of parastatal companies, the experience in Zambia has shown that very few of these economic expectations have been met. Numerous factors have characterized their operation, including staffing problems, the cost of equipment and quality of service, financial management, politics and trade unions (see HUMAN RESOURCE MANAGEMENT IN THE EMERGING COUNTRIES).

Staffing

Over-staffing occurs when the staff strength of a corporation exceeds the volume of work which it is intended to cope with, and vice versa. The result is that corporations lose money through under utilization of capacity. The Zambian experience is dotted with perennial troubles arising from the threat of or actual mass retrenchments and from anxieties over delays in paying staff regular wages. Another aspect of this problem is having too much stable employment. Rather than hiring on a day-to-day basis or on a piecework basis, staff are given tenure, thus causing a perpetual burden on the funds of the corporation concerned. One of the results of this is that tenure tends to reduce alertness, dedication and diligence and therefore aggravates human obstacles.

Over-staffing not only reduces the profit margin of the enterprise concerned but also reduces the total output per person. The problems of over-staffing in Zambia have been necessitated through political patronage. Heads of parastatal companies were appointed by the President and cabinet ministers and felt an obligation to employ relatives of politicians.

Most parastatal companies follow the civil service tradition of hierarchical levels of personnel when in fact, these roles could be dispensed with and one or two persons could do the job more effectively.

The wage rate of parastatal companies in Zambia is higher than those of the government although total benefits, including job security, may compare unfavourably with those of the latter. Fringe benefits and conditions of service differ from one corporation to another. The problem here is that wage rates and fringe benefits are not determined by economic realities, such as the size of profits or output per worker, but is fixed even before the corporations begin to operate.

High cost of equipment

Many parastatal companies have to import most, if not all their capital equipment. Costs are naturally high, especially since some are not exempt from large import duties. Expectations of profit must take into account heavy maintenance costs as well as the considerable time lag needed to offset the heavy sums initially invested.

Uncompetitive or low quality products and services

Most parastatal companies produce services rather than goods. In recent years there have been constant public complaints about the quality of service provided by parastatals. As far as goods are concerned, there has been the persistent impression that locally manufactured goods are inferior in quality and much higher in price than imported goods. The result is the continued importation of foreign brands.

6 Financial management

Another serious aspect of financial mismanagement is the over-pricing of contracts and the attendant kickbacks for top level personnel. The result is that large amounts of money earmarked for investment do not take the corporations as far as they were expected to do because only part of this money is actually invested.

Socio-political factors

The intervention of politics into the affairs of parastatal companies has been a major problem both in the 1st and 2nd Republics of Zambia. Unprofitable ideologies like Humanism in Zambia and the First National Development Plan were implemented unsucessfully. Their failure is due to political interference in the running of the companies, especially through the politically influenced appointments of senior management staff. Other areas in which political intervention is manifested include the award of major contracts and determination of further investments.

7 Industrial relations and trade unions

The role of the trade unions is unclear. Labour relations are seen as merely working for the employees and working out what they can get from the corporations. Few, if any make the point of assessing the efficiency and productivity of workers as a basis for demands for higher pay and better working conditions. Cases have arisen where unions have put pressure on directors to recall workers dismissed for theft or those who have retired after reaching retrenchment age. Such frivolous or one-sided demands have resulted in a discipline problem and a workforce that is demotivated.

However, it is also important to state that labour organizations have helped in the development of public corporations generally. Unions often provide checks on board and management prone to tribalism, corruption or applying partisan political considerations in the running of the company. The extent to which they can continue to be constructive or destructive will depend on the opportunities provided at state and national levels and also on the education of trade union leadership (see HUMAN RESOURCE MANAGEMENT IN THE EMERGING COUNTRIES; INDUSTRIAL RELATIONS IN THE EMERGING COUNTRIES).

8 Conclusion

An efficient management is indispensable to the success of a public corporation, especially if it is expected to operate as a competitive business and make profits. Corporation management in Zambia is handicapped by the lack of sufficient management experience, as is seen in most developing countries.

The Movement for Multiparty Democracy (MMD), the ruling party in Zambia, have identified the parastatal sector as a primary obstacle to economic growth. They have indicated their intentions to relinquish the government's role in running business and revert back to its traditional role as a provider of services to the people – for example health, education, infrastructure and social welfare.

To ensure the Zambian economy does not collapse, a Structural Adjustment Programme is being embarked upon. Part of this programme of change is the introduction of the privatization policy and the establishment of the Zambia Privatisation Agency (ZPA). Through the privatization policy, the Zambian government intends to divest all the 150 parastatal companies except, possibly, a few public utilities.

VICTOR MUHANDU
ZAMBIA PRIVATISATION AGENCY

Further reading

(References cited in the text marked *)

Dado, R.H. (1971) *Unions, Parties and Political Development: A Study of Mineworkers Union in Zambia*, New Haven, CT and London: Yale University Press. (Useful study of trade unions and industrial relations in Zambia.)

Dresang, D.L. (1975) *The Zambia Civil Service: Entreprenuerialism and Development Adminis-tration*, Kenya: East African Publishing House. (Informative book on the emergence of the Zambian civil service and its introduction of policies and administration.)

* Industrial Relations Act No. 36 (1971) and its supplement Statutory Instrument no 206 (13/12/74) Zambia: Government Printers. (Contains Kenneth Kaunda's legal sanction of the IPD policy.)

Kaunda K.D. (1987) *Humanism in Zambia and a Guide to its Implementation Part I*, Zambia: Zambia Information Services. (Kaunda's policy of humanism and its development into national policies.)

Makoba Wagona, J. (1998) *Government Policy and Public Enterprise Performance in Sub-Saharan Africa: The case studies of Tanzania and Zambia, 1964-1984*, New York: Edwin Mellen Press. (Investigates the impact of state development policies of nationalization, Africanization and import substitution industrialization (ISI) on the activities and performance of selected industrial public enterprises or parastatal organizations.)

Mphaisha, C.J.J. (1988) *State of National Politics and Government*, Zambia: Kenneth Kaunda Foundation. (Good primary source of information on the political development of Zambia.)

Mpuku, H.C. and Zyuulu, I. (1997) *Contemporary Issues in Socio-economic Reform in Zambia*, Aldershot: Ashgate Publishing Ltd. (This text examines the attempts and potential pitfalls of the reform programme and argues that while reform is a necessary condition for economic rebirth, it needs to ensure it has the desired socioeconomic impact on Zambian society.)

Ollas, P.E. (1979) *Participatory Democracy in Zambia: The Political Economy of National Development*, Devon: Arthur H. Stockwell Ltd. (Discusses the introduction of national development in Zambia and its implications for the political economy.)

Rweyemamu, A.H. and Goran, H. (1971) *A Decade of Public Administration*, Kenya: East African Literature Bureau. (Overview of the key events of public administration policies.)

Turok, B. (1979) *A Development in Zambia: A Reader*, London: Zed Press. (Provides a detailed account of the social and political evolution of Zambia.)

United National Independence Party (UNIP) *The National Policies for the Decade 1985-1995*, Zambia: Office of the Secretary General. (Aims and objectives of the Third Phase of the Party Programme.)

Zulu, J.B. (1970) *Zambia Humanism*, Zambia: National Education Company of Zambia, Ltd. (Discussion of the spiritual and economic challenges in Zambia.)

See also: HUMAN RESOURCE MANAGEMENT IN THE EMERGING COUNTRIES; INDUSTRIAL RE-LATIONS IN THE EMERGING COUNTRIES; MANAGEMENT EDUCATION IN THE EMERGING COUNTRIES; MANAGEMENT IN AFRICA; MANAGEMENT IN THE EMERGING COUNTRIES; MANAGEMENT IN KENYA; MANAGEMENT IN SOUTH AFRICA; MANAGEMENT IN TANZANIA; MANAGEMENT IN UGANDA

Related topics in the IEBM regional set: MANAGEMENT IN CHILE

Management in Zimbabwe

1 Introduction
2 Context
3 Specific features
4 Conclusion

Overview

Contemporary business and management practices in Zimbabwe emerged during the 1960s and there has been gradual integration of the latest management styles and techniques ever since. Contemporary management approaches commonly found in the country are reflective of the long way the system has come. The new domestic economic scenario and globalization has also brought new dimensions and challenges to management in the country.

The management style in Zimbabwean organizations has been mainly inward looking and strongly defined by a top-down approach in decision making. However, over the past eight years there has been a gradual opening up accompanied by a shift toward participative management.

1 Introduction

The current practice of management in Zimbabwe is mainly defined by the economic and political milestones of the past three decades. The changes brought a number of uncertainties and sometimes anxiety to the process of management both in the private and public sector, thus, at times, rendering experiential knowledge redundant (see MANAGEMENT IN AFRICA).

The 1966 imposition of sanctions by the United Nations led to the development of business and management practices premised on protectionist tendencies reflected in policies such as import substitution, official foreign currency allocation, and domestic-oriented management. This scenario moulded a management that locked itself away from the knowledge systems that were developing outside its national boundaries. The attainment of political independence in 1980 saw the opening up of the economy, giving a jolt to the domestic oriented management which opened the economy to international competition and management practices. However, this reorientation did not to come into being until 1990 when the economy was forced to adopt an Economic Structural Adjustment programme. The adoption of the programme marked an important watershed in the practice of business and management, as the country shifted from a socialist orientation to a market oriented economy. Management had to quickly adapt to the new dispensation or risk sinking.

2 Context

Labour and political change

Changes in the labour sector have seen a sustained and consolidated growth in trade unionism over the past 18 years (see HUMAN RESOURCE MANAGEMENT IN THE EMERGING COUNTRIES; INDUSTRIAL RELATIONS IN THE EMERGING COUNTRIES). In 1980 there was no national trade union body. Labour was represented by small fragmented groups with subscriptions from a few thousand employees. To date the main trade union body has a membership of about 1.5 million members out of total national labour force of about 3.5 million. The Labour Relations Act (1985) sought to protect the worker and, in the process, made it virtually impossible for employers to dismiss or retrench some of the workers. The government, as part of its socialist philosophy, legislated minimum wages across the board. Furthermore, the government strengthened the role of trade unions and works councils in the name of the welfare of the employee. Management in both the public and the private sector had to abide by the stipulations of the legislation, to the detriment of productivity. Politically it became an anathema to challenge the position of the legislature. Thus the government usurped the management decision-making function on fundamental corporate aspects such as wages and salaries determination, market prices and investment in capital goods.

The development of labour representation has, of course, led to fair employment practices, fair promotion practices and a focusing of management's attention on the needs of general employees. Participative decision making, especially on issues directly affecting labour, is now the newly accepted culture. Since 1991 both employers and employees have had to quickly learn negotiating skills as the government adopted market policies.

Socio-economic factors

In late 1990, the government adopted an IMF–World Bank backed Economic Structural Adjustment programme that remained in operation until 1996. The thrust of the structural adjustment programme was to open up the economy and introduce free market policies. It was therefore imperative for domestic firms to adapt and adjust their management style to the new reality of external competition and the removal of protectionist policies. It was necessary to upgrade the management resource base and modernize production systems. In response, management processes in most companies have witnessed an increase in strategic planning, corporate re-engineering, marketing re-orientation and management training and development. Government, for its part, began the process of commercialization and privatization of public enterprises. In both cases there has been an apparent demand for professional and experienced managers in all sectors of the economy. Trends remain biased towards Western management principles reflecting an overlay of cultural and societal influences with respect to the conduct of managerial work. This has brought about a new management ethic with respect to leadership, competition and customer service.

Although economic growth has averaged no more than 2 per cent in the 1990s, population growth has been unsustainably high at between 2.8 per cent and 3.1 per cent over the same period. Unemployment is officially estimated at 45 per cent. Whereas employment grew by 2.4 per cent on average during the period 1985–90, it decreased to about 0.6 per cent during the period 1990–95 (Kanyenze 1998). Although during the 1980s downsizing, particularly through retrenchment, was not a common feature, since the adoption of structural adjustment in 1991 retrenchment has become one of the commonest strategies to improve or return companies to performance. During the early part of the structural adjustment programme, the retrenchments focused mainly on shopfloor workers. However managerial level employees soon got involved, as companies attempted to make management structures leaner, flatter and more focused. This is aimed at improving productivity from both ordinary employees to managers. In some instances companies have gone to the extreme of completely dispensing with the middle management layer. Bahrami (1992) noted that: 'The de-layering and down-sizing trend was initially triggered by the need to reduce costs. Increased use of information technologies … has … reduced the need for traditional middle management, whose role was to supervise others and collect, analyse, evaluate, and transmit information up, down, and across the organizational hierarchy'. Turnaround programmes have also on occasion made replacing top management a condition. The dwindling of the domestic market, the intensification of competition from imports and lack of new investment has now led to serious liquidations in sectors such as textiles and clothing. Large textile and clothing companies such as Cone Textiles and Fashion Enterprises have had to completely close their operations as the competition intensified. This is coupled with the fact that by December 1998 inflation had gone up to 45 per cent, interest rates had gone up to 48 per cent and the local currency had depreciated by 60 per cent over a one year period between November 1997 and November 1998. This has presented management with a complicated socioeconomic scenario that has seen change management becoming a topical issue (Quinn 1980).

Structural factors

The economic influence of the corporate sector has mainly been concentrated in a few companies, although this is gradually changing. Companies such as TA Holdings, Delta Corporation, Anglo American, Lonrho and Old Mutual have been wielding a lot of economic power but that scenario has recently been altering with the introduction of the concept of 'indigenization'. For example, TA Holdings, one of the largest conglomerates in the country during the 1980s, has gone through three restructuring exercises within five years. At each stage the exercise has involved trimming off some business units to concentrate on core businesses. It is now under the control of black investors. Old Mutual is undertaking a de-mutualization process that will leave local policyholders as the local shareholders of their local subsidiary.

Managerial control, especially at director level, has recently seen the introduction of some new faces. The traditional situation was a closed system with a small number of people circulating around most of the boards. The Institute of Directors, a forum representing the interests of directors in both private and public enterprises has been lobbying its members to bring in new directors with new ideas. With changes in the racial composition of top management of the most highly rated companies, blacks are now also well represented at director level. However there remains a serious lack of female representation at top management level, and especially at director level.

3 Specific features

Management styles in private companies

Management styles commonly found in Zimbabwe are a hybrid of Western approaches, the autocratic approaches of the socialist era, and the indigenous top-down approach (see MANAGEMENT IN AFRICA). The indigenous approaches mainly centre on paternalistic tendencies where seniority and good decision making are equated. This approach tends to create a senior management who favour the use of a top-down approach in decision making. Leadership is slowly shifting from a task-oriented approach to an employee-oriented approach. Change management has not been adopted easily, although some companies, such as the Commercial Bank of Zimbabwe, Merspin and Zimbabwe Spinners and Weavers, have succeeded in turning around their huge organizations, moving from a position only a few years ago of serious losses to acclaimed profit.

With high inflation, high interest rates and a depreciating currency, management in Zimbabwe has been adopting new approaches mainly centred on high productivity and the maximization of value for money (Thompson 1995) (see ECONOMIES OF THE EMERGING COUNTRIES). The unreliability of the domestic market has now made management more outwardly oriented. This is also a result of globalization, the impact of which is now being felt by industry. The management style now commonly applied is participative management where workers – through the works councils – are expected to participate in major decisions. Management wants workers at all levels to feel they have ownership of major decisions in the company. To some extent team building, with its pluralistic approach to problem solving, is becoming a widely used tool in some companies, especially high-tech companies in highly competitive sectors. Companies in the cellular phone business in Zimbabwe, i.e. Econet, Telecel and Net*One have successfully been using the teamwork approach, although with varying degrees of success.

The organizational culture now widely prevalent in companies is defined by group cooperation, where workers and employers are all of one vision. This culture has grown stronger over the past decade as companies liquidated due to economic hardships. Workers now feel just as responsible as management, for the survival of the company also means survival of their welfare and therefore they have to participate in decision making. To strengthen the idea of ownership and responsibility companies such as APEX Corporation now reward workers with stocks in the company.

Management training and development

Management training in Zimbabwe is grounded in Western concepts and the emphasis is on the gradual development of employees toward managerial positions as they attain seniority in the workplace (see MANAGEMENT EDUCATION IN THE EMERGING COUNTRIES). Although other, shorter routes to attaining managerial status are also in use, both in the private and public sector, the emphasis on seniority is still highly important in Zimbabwe. Bates (1993: 70) notes that seniority in Zimbabwe has traditionally been a major consideration in the promotion of staff especially in government and parastatal organizations. Shorter routes mainly involve employees who enter managerial positions through graduate trainee or cadet programmes. Such graduate trainees hold degrees in business or commerce. Employees with higher qualifications such as MBAs or an MSc are almost always recruited for the top posts. In the case of top posts, employers also demand a number of years of experience. Increasingly, managerial positions are now being filled by employees whose backgrounds are in disciplines such as engineering, psychology, and sometimes the hard sciences such as chemistry or biochemistry.

Managerial positions are more or less equally shared on a 50:50 basis between blacks and whites in the private sector. In the public sector, blacks occupy no less than 80 per cent of the managerial positions. Women managers occupy 15–20 per cent of positions in both the private and public sector. Women in general only account for 16.5 per cent in waged employment in the country. A complex set of factors such as socio-cultural mores and behavioural expectations, as well as organizational policies and practices do influence women's opportunities to move into decision-making management positions (Dirasse 1991).

Companies in Zimbabwe have always tended to follow one of two routes to develop their managers. First, managers have been sent to business schools for further training. Second, managers have been groomed internally through a career path that ensures their suitability, even though some may not be the products of business schools. In business schools, managers are normally enrolled onto MBAs or executive development programmes. The degrees are mainly awarded by any one of the four functional universities in the country, i.e. the University of Zimbabwe, the National University of Science and Technology, Africa University and Solusi University. The University of Zimbabwe, which was the only university in the country until 1990, has trained about 1500 MBA graduates since 1986. Professional institutes such as the Zimbabwe Institute of Management, the Institute of Personnel Management, the Chartered Institute of Secretaries and Administrators and the Institute of Chartered Accountants which all offer certificates and diplomas, have also made a significant contribution to management training in the country. To promote human resource development, the government has also offered scholarships for training nationals in countries such as the USA, the UK, Canada, Australia and others. At independence in 1980 a lot of managers who had been trained in former Eastern-bloc countries also entered both the private and the public sector. The curricular offered by business schools in Zimbabwe is naturally biased towards Western management principles. However, there is an integration of these management principles with the political and socio-cultural traditional dimensions on aspects such as loyalty and leadership (see BUSINESS CULTURES, THE EMERGING COUNTRIES).

Companies in Zimbabwe spend on average 5–10 per cent of their human resources development budgets on management development. Although in Zimbabwe there is no forum that represents the interests of particular racial groups in management, blacks in management have moved up the ladders in relatively larger proportions than other groups. This is a result of intense lobbying by the government and the Affirmative Action Group (a black empowerment group) in the country. For example, the

Affirmative Action Group has so far forced multinationals in Zimbabwe, such as Standard Chartered Bank, to identify potential understudies of the chief executive of the company. The tradition in major multinationals has been to appoint the chief executive from outside the ranks of local professionals. The argument of the Affirmative Action Group is that appointing the chief executive from outside means no Zimbabwean will ever have the opportunity of heading the company. Other multinationals, such as Anglo American Corporation, have also come under intense scrutiny by lobby groups due to their tendency to fill chief executive posts with appointees from outside the country.

Management in public enterprises

The post-independence era witnessed an increase in the number of public enterprises as the government sought to strengthen its involvement in economic affairs and broaden accessibility to services offered by such enterprises. For those public enterprises that were already in operation, the exodus of white managers due to political uncertainty created a new challenge. It created a serious management skills vacuum in public enterprises. As a result, the new government appointed mainly inexperienced black managers into key management positions in these enterprises. In an effort to bridge the skills gap, the government also introduced manpower training and development programmes, locally and abroad.

Management in public enterprises has no autonomy in determining policy and strategy, as is the culture in the private sector due to interference by politicians. Managers are more involved in programmed decisions than non-programmed decisions irrespective of rank. The only material difference between one rank and the next is in the scope and depth of programmed decisions the manager can handle. Politicians influence aspects relating to work organization, purchase and supply (through a government sanctioned tender system), corporate strategy and the selection of top management. In most cases, management ideas are considered to be at variance with government interests and thus have often led to the dismissal of managers. Companies such as Zimpapers, Zimbabwe Broadcasting Corporation, Zimbabwe Electricity Supply Authority, Zisco Steel, etc. have lost good managers due to political meddling in managerial autonomy and decision making. Managers in public enterprises are sometimes rewarded not for their managerial capability and entrepreneurial acumen but rather their capacity to adapt and enforce government policy. Overall, the management philosophy in public enterprises has been a fusion of the cultural and political factors that have sacrificed professionalism in many respects.

In view of this analysis, it is apparent that managers in public enterprises are recruited not to ensure profitability and high return to the shareholders – mainly the government – but to ensure government control. Top managers in public enterprises sometimes lack professional qualifications and have created a non-results oriented management culture. This culture is evident in the lack of accountability in most public enterprises.

4 Conclusion

The analysis above shows the fundamental shift in management styles and focus that have been necessitated by economic, political and corporate re-orientation. The new trends have been matched by the adoption of an outward-orientation and an emphasis on professional management skills. Management philosophy in Zimbabwe is thus undergoing changes that seek to competitively position organizations in the global business environment.

The attendant trade sanctions era nurtured an inward-oriented management perspective. Thus, during this era, management was preoccupied with meeting domestic demand under a plethora of restrictive economic and political regulations. The execution of management tasks was bureaucratic, rule-driven, top-down and most organizations were virtual monopolies. Ironically, the prevalent business environment to some extent forced management to be innovative in terms of survival, and the adaptation of obsolete plant and machinery and redundant technology. The key management principles revolved around a centralization of decision making, formal control systems and a paternalistic management–employee relationship that was not open to employee contribution in decision making.

In public enterprises, government has had total control over corporate policy and strategy. In contrast, the private sector has gradually filled its managerial ranks with qualified and experienced managers. In many ways, organization structures are still bureaucratic, with most decision making located at higher management levels. The prevalence of the top-down approach in the high echelons of management reflects the inequitable distribution of power in the structures.

The adoption of the structural adjustment programme in 1990 exposed local business organizations to foreign and regional competition. At the same time, the government introduced dramatic changes by way of removing trade restrictions, foreign exchange control, subsidies and privatization of state-owned enterprises. These changes required the adoption of competitive strategies in order to come into line with trends in the global business environment. As a result, competent management resources became a key success factor and organizations found themselves recruiting or developing the requisite skills. Managements in the private and public sectors now consciously realize the importance of recruiting, training and developing professional managerial and general staff in order to survive in the global competitive environment. In many ways management principles and practices in Zimbabwe have undergone a significant transformation over the past 30 years and should prepare for greater challenges in the new millennium.

Z. MURANDA AND Z. TAMANGANI
UNIVERSITY OF ZIMBABWE

Further reading

(References cited in the text marked *)

* Bahrami, H. (1992) 'The emerging flexible organization', *California Management Review* 34(4): 33–52.(A paper discussing organizational restructuring including the concept of de-layering.)

* Bates, A. (1993) *Personnel Management in Zimbabwe,* Harare: Jann Investments. (A text that extensively discusses personnel management practices in Zimbabwe.)

Carrol, G.R. (1994) 'Organizations ... the smaller they get', *California Management Review* 37(1): 28–41. (A comprehensive article that widely discusses the concept of downsizing in the American corporate world.)

* Dirasse, L. (1991) 'Reaching the top – women managers in eastern and southern Africa', *Women in Development/Women in Management Division*: 4–11. (A text discussing the current position of women in corporate governance in eastern and southern Africa.)

* Kanyenze, G. (1998) 'Youth and Self-Employment: The Role of Trade Unions', Paper presented at the ARLAC Regional Seminar on the Role of Labour Administration in Employment Promotion in Small Enterprises, Harare. (A seminar paper that discusses self-employment options for school dropouts and current unemployment statistics in Zimbabwe.)

Mparutsa, A. (1987) 'Indigenous Leadership Styles: Shaping the Future', Paper presented at the Institute of Personnel Management (Zimbabwe) National Convention, Harare. (A useful paper discussing leadership styles commonly observed among indigenous Zimbabweans.)

Nyangulu, M.N. (1992) 'An Analysis of the Issues, Concerns, Problems, and being faced by Women in Management and in Development in Zimbabwe: The implications for WIM/WID Network Objectives, Strategies, and Activities', Paper prepared for the launch of Women in Development/Women in Management, Harare. (A paper outlining problems of women in management and development.)

Montgomery, J.D. (1987) 'Probing managerial development: image and reality in southern africa', *World Development* 15(7): 911–29. (A comprehensive article discussing behavioural tendencies of African administrators in the Southern Africa region.)

* Quinn, J.B. (1980) *Strategies for Change – Logical Incrementalism*, Irwin, Illinois. (A text on change management with an emphasis on incremental change.)

Rodrik, D. (1997) 'Has globalization gone too far?' *California Management Review* 39(3): 29–53. (A comprehensive paper discussing the implications of globalization on international trade relations.)

Smit, P.J. and Cronje, G.J.de J. (ed.) (1992) *Management Principles – A Contemporary South African Edition*, Cape Town: Juta & Co. (A text on management based on South African experiences.)

* Thompson, J.L. (1995) *Strategy in Action* 1st edn, London: Chapman and Hall. (A text on strategic management.)

See also: BUSINESS CULTURES, THE EMERGING COUNTRIES; ECONOMIES OF THE EMERGING COUNTRIES; HUMAN RESOURCE MANAGEMENT IN THE EMERGING COUNTRIES; MANAGEMENT EDUCATION IN THE EMERGING COUNTRIES; MANAGEMENT IN AFRICA; MANAGEMENT IN BOTSWANA; MANAGEMENT IN KENYA; MANAGEMENT IN SOUTH AFRICA; MANAGEMENT IN TANZANIA; MANAGEMENT IN UGANDA

Related topics in the IEBM regional set: MANAGEMENT IN JAPAN

Country profiles
Asia

Management in Bangladesh

1 Introduction
2 Analysis
3 Evaluation
4 Conclusion

Overview

The management process and style of Bangladeshi managers are highly influenced by their socio-cultural background, and the economic and political situation of the country. The country has a long history and bitter experience of political ups and downs, starting at the time of independence from British colonial rule and subsequently after liberation from Pakistani dominance. These misfortunes subjected the country to a number of different political systems ranging from military rule more than once, one party dominance and one party rule, (both during the Pakistani and Bangladeshi periods) and finally through a democratic transition, which has also been threatened by the egoistic behaviour of some of the politicians. In fact, this undesirable situation stopped Bangladesh from establishing a stable basis for thinking about or deciding on any issue relating to the economic development of the country, in which management systems are but one important issue. Therefore, no standardization was developed in any field, including management systems.

However, it should be noted that the management style of Bangladeshi managers is a mixture of the legacy of a British colonial management system and of their own behaviour, which has been inherited from their own culture.

1 Introduction

It is hardly necessary to say that a country's management system is shaped by the interaction of its socio-cultural, political and economic environment. To discuss management in Bangladesh, an introduction to Bangladesh and its economy is required, so that the writings on the topic can be understood in relation to the socio-economic and other conditions of Bangladesh.

Bangladesh has been aptly described as a new state in an ancient land. It is the youngest state in south Asia. Geological evidence shows that a vast proportion of Bangladesh was formed between 1 million and 6.5 million years ago, during the time of the tertiary era. Human habitation in this region, therefore, is likely to be very old and there is evidence of palaeolithic civilization dating back about 1 million years. Having an area of 147,570 square kilometres (according to the most reliable source), Bangladesh contains a greater bio-diversity than that of many other countries. In fact, few countries of the world can match its rich and varied flora and fauna, which are not only a unique biological phenomenon but are also a great natural resource of the country. Historically the people of Bangladesh are descendants of various races and nationalities. It is said that an Austro-Asian race first inhabited this region followed by Dravidans and Aryans. There was also an influx of Mongolians from Tibet and Myanmar. Muslims started coming to this area in the early ninth century AD: Persians, Armenians, Turks, Afgans and lastly the Mughals all came in quick succession.

The population of Bangladesh has reached approximately 126 million (estimated at January 1998) at a density of 875 persons per square kilometre and it has become the ninth most populous country of the world. It is also the second largest Muslim country in the world. Traditionally it is a land of communal harmony; followers of other religions enjoy full freedom of worship. About 98 per cent of its people speak one language – Bengali. Although there are followers of different religions, their fundamental values are the same. Historically the economy of East Bengal, which is now Bangladesh, is agrarian and had no industrial base except a few small agro-based industries. At the end of the 1990s a move towards industrialization began to appear with the utilization of the country's available natural resources in addition to cheap labour and other manpower. Trade and commerce are also increasing and are widening both nationally and internationally.

Bangladesh suffered the longest colonial exploitation of any country, and which has largely denuded it of its past affluence and wealth. Independence has finally opened new vistas of prospects and opportunities. However, unfortunately due to a number of political vicissitudes (starting from Pakistani regime even after the emergence of Bangladesh) the economic prosperity of the country could not be achieved as it was originally envisaged.

Bangladesh is one of the 48 developing countries which are categorized by the United Nations as 'least developed' on the criteria of per capita income, literacy rate (44.3 percent) and the contribution of manufacturing to GDP (gross domestic product). In the World Bank's ranking of countries on the basis of per capita income, Bangladesh is thirteenth lowest (see ECONOMIES OF THE EMERGING COUNTRIES).

Bangladesh suffers from an acute resource constraint. GDP ratio is low, hovering around 8–9 per cent in the 1990s. Thus Bangladesh has become largely dependent on external assistance. Since independence in 1971, roughly 80 per cent of its development expenditure has been financed by foreign sources – the USA being the major donor. Its outstanding external debt as of June 1996 was US$17.1 billion which is over 50 per cent of the country's GDP.

The level of foreign direct investment is also frustratingly low, even though significant incentives have been declared and provided for foreign investment over the past years. It should be noted that between 1990 and 1993 most of the foreign investors and companies left the country, withdrawing investment from Bangladesh.

Factors that making the economic environment ineffective are said to be inconsistent fiscal and monetary policies, a lack of coordination between ministries and departments responsible for policy implementation, delays in making decisions because of bureaucratic sloth and hassle, corruption in government offices particularly in service providing enterprises, disturbance of business activities by terrorists, labour unrest, poor physical infrastructure, an energy crisis, etc. These factors all combine to discourage investment in business and other productive activities.

Recently, the country's fiscal management seems to have been improved significantly as evidenced by the improvement in the government's revenue collection. The country's foreign exchange reserve has, however, fallen sharply.

The country's industrial policy has been formulated in an information gap. The fate of the 1700 sick industries that were registered with the Industries Ministry in 1991 still remains unknown nine years later. Information is also needed about the fate of over 700 industries disinvested over the past two decades. Because of the defective fiscal policy and unfair competition from neighbouring competing countries, cotton textile mills have been severely hit.

The civil administration cannot escape responsibility for much of the country's economic distress. Over 1 million people are employed in public administration in Bangladesh, which is far too big for a country of this size. Every ministry or department is overstaffed, inefficient and slow performing. In addition, the administrative set up frequently appears to be top-heavy.

2 Analysis

Even before the large scale migration after 1947, different non-Bangalee expatriates migrated to this region (East Bengal) and afterwards, with the blessings and favour of Pakistani rulers, they started to be involved in trade and commerce and established their own family businesses with a family management system. These expatriates, in collaboration with non-Bangalaee Pakistanis, started many enterprises, business houses and even a few industries in what was then East Pakistan. But unfortunately these expatriates, along with West Pakistanis, did not take into their confidence the native Bangalees and, other than at the lower levels, they did not include and Bengalis in their management teams. This step-motherly attitude deterred the Bangalees from achieving managerial experience and skills for themselves. At the same time, since economic and administrative powers were vested in non-Bangalee Pakistanis, native Bangalees' entrepreneurship was hampered by a lack of state support.

The situation that had been created in the field of management after liberation in 1971, with the departure of non-Bengali and expatriate managers – especially the owner managers of family businesses – was difficult to overcome. It was hard to fill the vacuum left in middle and top management since there were few trained and experienced management personnel. When the big industries were nationalized following the election manifesto of the Bangladesh Awami League, was in power after liberation, those industries had to be managed by the bureaucrats in the ministries concerned – personnel who had no professional nor management training, nor any experience of running a business enterprise (see MANAGEMENT IN THE EMERGING COUNTRIES).

At the outset, the government put into place a set of management structures which were modified from time to time, almost without any attempt at forward planning. In order to undertake the management tasks of nationalized enterprises, the government founded a three-tier management structure. The three tiers are: ministry, corporation and individual enterprise or plant. To present this visually:

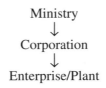

Ministry
↓
Corporation
↓
Enterprise/Plant

The management pattern of public enterprises, as developed in line with above structure, is summarized below:

Management structure in public sector industrial enterprises

1   Conglomerate sector corporation with enterprises: the Chairman is the chief executive with a full-time board. The board members are the functional heads for the corporate headquarters and they provide staff services to the enterprises.

2   Each enterprise has a board for taking major decisions; the board is headed by a Director or a General Manager (GM) from the corporate headquarters; enterprise head GM, Senior Manager (SM), and now Managing Director (MD) in the case of Bangladesh Chemical Industries Corporation (BCIC) and Bangladesh Steel and Engineering Corporation(BSEC) and one or two corporate or enterprise senior managers constitute the enterprise board. One representative from the ministry of industries of the rank of Deputy Secretary (DS), Senior Assistant Secretary (SAS) or Assistant Secretary (AS) is included on the board of the enterprise.

3   Enterprises under Bangladesh Jute Mills Corporation (BJMC) and Bangladesh Textile Mills Corporation (BTMC) operate in a fashion similar to BCIC and BSEC; however, they are controlled bytheir respective Ministries. The enterprise heads are still GM or SM in BJMC and BTMC.

4   Corporations having no separate enterprises (e.g. Bangladesh Small Industries Corporation (BSIC), Bangladesh Prajjatan Corporation, Bangladesh Biman, Trading Corporation of Bangladesh (TCB) are managed by full-time boards, a Chairman being the Chief Executive Officer; the Directors are the functional heads. The Directors work as line managers.

Management structure in nationalized banks and other financial institutions

1   These institutions are headed by boards with an honorary Chairman, the MDs, being the chief executives; the board members do not serve on a full-time basis. Board members are not selected on the basis of functional expertise. GMs under the MDs are the functional heads. The chain works as a line organization. The operation branches do not represent separate enterprises; the regional offices control the branches.

Management structure of private sector industrial enterprises (conglomerate or stand-alone)

1   Units have a traditional management structure with boards of Directors and the MD is the chief executive. The board may have a separate Chairman or the MD may act as Chairman also. In the case of public limited companies, boards

represent the shareholding interests whereas for the private limited companies with full-time boards, they also represent the equity holding.

2   The corporate headquarters of the private sector conglomerates are managed like a typical holding company.

Management structure of private sector banks and insurance companies

1   Local banks and insurance companies have a similiar management structure. They don't have full-time boards; MDs work as the chief executive officers. The functional heads are called Executive Vice Presidents and their underlinked positions are generally: Senior Vice President (SVP), Executive Vice President (EVP), Assistant VP. The functional heads, and so on down the line, represent functional expertise and they form the chain.

2   Foreign banks and insurance companies operating in Bangladesh follow different management structures consistent with their respective corporate patterns.

Unfortunately, however, in the above system – and especially in case of public enterprises – it has not been possible to create a proper and balanced distribution of power, authority and responsibility. The managers at enterprise or plant level cannot take any important decision without the approval of the corporation, which in turn may have to seek permission of the Ministry concerned on some issues. Therefore any decentralization of power and authority is largely absent.

Business as an occupation is said to be given a lower preference when choosing a career or when judging the values of occupations. Curiously enough, this present attitude does not conform to a popular Bengali proverb 'Banijje Bashati Lakkhir', i.e. 'to live in commerce is to live with luck'. In the early part of the nineteenth century, Bengalees were no less active in business than the peoples of many other parts of India, but their occupational choice shifted from business to land holding and there was a growing tendency observed for young men of the Bengalee commercial class to go into the professions and civil service (Timberg 1969). Timberg (1969) quoted Blair King who has suggested in various papers that this shifting of career choice may be partially the result of the internal and intellectual evolution of Bengal. Timberg (1969: 157) concluded. 'The Bengalis, educationally advanced and socially modern, one of the first group to enter industry, have today, relatively, no role in industry at all.' The same trend as Timberg (1969) cited above is still observable in Bangladesh, that is that the professions, civil service, etc. are more highly valued by the people in general than other occupations. This is perhaps because of the low status given to business.

3   Evaluation

If we analyse the managerial behaviour of the enterprises in Bangladesh we find that there are socio-cultural influences on some managerial actions (see BUSINESS CULTURES, THE EMERGING COUNTRIES). Very often managers are considered to be leaders and in theory there are quite a few leadership approaches which managers can follow. The leadership orientation in fact starts at home and we have mentioned the family system where the father is the head of the family and who can be said to be authoritarian in behaviour. This value system influences our view of managers as leaders.

As a result, Bangladeshi managerial behaviour is by and large authoritarian. Similarly participative management is not generally practised. Decision-making processes are generally centralized as a matter of course. Administration is top-down – bottom-up administration cannot even be considered. Because of the authoritarian character of the management, a communication gap between hierarchies can occur at times, even affecting proper coordination. Time management is very poor and cultural barriers disturb proper time schedules frequently. In the case of delegating authority, problems also arise. The principle of delegation that 'authority and responsibility should be co-extensive' is not respected; thus delegation and decentralization do not become effective. The lack of confidence in managers of subordinates' capability and trust worthiness and the fear of managers that they might lose power by delegation or decentralization of authority to subordinates creates a negative mentality. Again, it is also observed that in some cases even the subordinates become reluctant to accept delegated authority because of a lack of self-confidence. Delegation occasionally fails because of the lack of accountability and answerability from subordinates about delegated tasks.

A separate personnel department headed by a Personnel Manager is found in the majority of the industries in Bangladesh. These departments perform the functions of selection, recruitment and training, employee services, wages and salary administration, accident prevention, maintaining personnel records, etc. In performing the functions of selection, recruitment and training the Personnel Manager is unfortunately not free to make independent decisions. Interference from the top management levels and pressure from outside is an occasional phenomenon which prevents the Personnel Manager from taking proper decisions (see HUMAN RESOURCE MANAGEMENT IN THE EMERGING COUNTRIES; INDUSTRIAL RELATIONS IN THE EMERGING COUNTRIES).

Lack of skilled manpower and a lack of training for industrial management are bottlenecks in the field of industrialization. Bangladesh suffers miserably from these problems. In Bangladesh there is no shortage of training activities conducted by the enterprises themselves, or offered by professional private and public sector training institutes, colleges and universities. In company training is mainly on-the-job, or achieved through job rotation, special assignments and observation posts. In addition, the enterprises have their own training institutes where they train their employees through different methods by rotation, even countrywide. Private organizations also exist which can organize training programmes on specific issues and offer training to employees of different organizations.

The Government of Bangladesh has given a specific priority to the training of employees. It conducts training in around 350 training centres. But the contribution of the private sector in the field of training is insignificant and highly motivated commercially. Although the number of institutes mentioned above is not insignificant, the method of training is still old, out dated and traditional. The existence of a single institute with a modern training scheme would be better than hundreds like the above (see MANAGEMENT EDUCATION IN THE EMERGING COUNTRIES).

4 Conclusion

After overcoming the chaotic economic conditions of the post-independence years, the economy of Bangaldesh attained a reasonable amount of stability from time to time especially, in the early years of the 1990s. This stability, however, proved to be short-lived and much of the macroeconomic gains seems to have frittered away at the start of the second half of the 1990s. The economy experiences surging inflation, growing fiscal and external sector deficits, and a slow-down of investment. In fact, all these have happened due to the mismanagement of the economy. Keeping all these experiences in mind, it should be the endeavour of the government, politicians and concerned policy makers to proceed with utmost sincerity so that no further mistakes, negligence or vested interests can hinder the development programmes. In order to prevent another period of stagnation, strong policy action will be necessary. Inflation has to be contained without adversely affecting the growth of investment. Prudent macroeconomic policies will have to be adopted to prevent a degeneration and depression of the economy.

The country's infrastructural development should be quickened and given the utmost priority. Protectionist policies are not always good or desirable but, in some cases and perhaps at this stage, a form of protection might usefully be given to some domestic industries. Foreign direct investment should be attracted further. Bureaucratic complexities should be removed, coordination between Ministries and departments should be rationalized. Top-heavy administrative situations should be corrected and unnecessary staff could be removed through golden handshakes or other methods.

Attention should be given to the creation of a reservoir of professional managers. It has already been mentioned earlier that, even after privatization, industries are not doing as well as was hoped. One observation is relevant here. In the case of disinvested enterprises, only the ownership has changed – in most cases management has remained in the hands of the same people, who have brought with them their old management style and work culture. Again, the new enterprises which were established afresh in the private sector could also not rid themselves of this disease since they, seeking experience, etc., had to employ the executives of public enterprises with higher status and higher emoluments. But these people, by working in public enterprises, could not throw off the old habits and work culture they had developed in the public enterprises. These points justify the case of calling for professional managers with a fresh mentality.

SHAHID UDDIN AHMED
DEPARTMENT OF MANAGEMENT
UNIVERSITY OF DHAKA

Further reading

(References cited in the text marked *)

Ahmed, S.U. (1973) 'A critique of industrial management in Bangladesh', *The Business Review*, 1(1 & 2): 69–90. (Explains the post liberation management situation in industries of Bangladesh and suggest measures to improve the situation).

Ahmed, S.U. (1981) 'Entrepreneurship and management practices among immigrants from Bangladesh in the U.K.', Brunel University, UK. (The author analysed factors that make a man an entrepreneur and also explained the management practices followed by Bangladeshi migrants being influenced by their culture).

Ahmed, S.U. (1985 2nd reprint in 1998), *Management and Administration*, Dhaka: Bangla Academy. (A textbook written on general management, personnel management and office management, etc.)

Baquer, A.A.M. (1989) 'Privatisation of enterprises', *The Dhaka University Studies* Part C 10(1: 143–56. (Explains the problems and prospects of privatization in Bangladesh.)

Bhuyan, A.R. (1998) 'An overview of the Bangladesh economy: Recent performance and future challenges', *Quarterly Journal of Islamic Economics Research Bureau* 7(3, 4) January–June: 7–23. (Describes the economic picture of the country, raising vital issues relating to the Bangladesh economy including management problems).

External publicity (1999) Ministry of Information, Government of Bangladesh 'Bangladesh Diary'. (Contains an introduction to Bangladesh describing its ancient history).

Habibullah, M.(1988) 'Professional Management and industrial development', *The Dhaka University Studies Part C* IX (1): 133–46. (Points out that professional management can increase productivity sharply by the correct project identification, evaluation of economic viability and probable job creation if performed by people with managerial skills.)

Habibullah, M. *et al.*(1989) *Management*, Dhaka: Bangladesh University Grants Commission. (The authors have discuss the theory and practice of management with reference to Bangladesh.)

Haider, A.K. (1995) *Industry in Bangladesh: Problems and Prospects 'constraints of industrialisation: can they be overcome?'*. (The author comprehensively discusses the problems of industrialization in Bangladesh.)

Mannan, A. (ed.) (1987) *Entrepreneurship and Management in Bangladesh*, Bureau of Business Research, University of Chittagong. (Proceedings of the seminar held on Entrepreneurship and Management in Bangladesh in which different national and international academics and professionals contributed their valuable articles and papers.)

* Timberg, T.A. (1969) 'The origins of Marwari industrialists'. (Paper presented to Bengal studies conference, University of Illinois, May 16, 1969 in which historical analysis of industrialisation in Bengal was analysed.)

Zaidi, S.M.H. (1970) *Village Culture in Transition*, Honolulu, USA: East West Center Press. (The author describes and analyses the culture and values of the people of rural Bangladesh.)

See also: BUSINESS CULTURES, THE EMERGING COUNTRIES; ECONOMIES OF THE EMERGING COUNTRIES; HUMAN RESOURCE MANAGEMENT IN THE EMERGING COUNTRIES; INDUSTRIAL RELATIONS IN THE EMERGING COUNTRIES; MANAGEMENT IN THE EMERGING COUNTRIES; MANAGEMENT IN INDIA; MANAGEMENT IN PAKISTAN; MANAGEMENT IN SRI LANKA

Related topics in the IEBM regional set: MANAGEMENT IN ASIA PACIFIC

Management in India

1 **Cultural context**
2 **Management styles in India**
3 **The business culture**
4 **Human resource management in India**
5 **Conclusion**

Overview

Indian managers run their organizations according to a pattern derived from their cultural, political and economic background. Although both Eastern and Western traits can be found in management behaviour, the diversity of Indian culture makes for a distinct style characterized by centralization of decision making, vertical hierarchies, confrontational management–employee relationships, and dual discipline and control strategies.

The Indian economy was for a long time protectionist, shielding firms from fierce competition. As a consequence, there has been no incentive for managers to invest in product improvement; the domestic market is captive. Reinforcing this, many strategic and operative decisions, such as plant location, production technology, pricing, staffing and industrial relations, are determined by established state regulations.

The introduction of economic reforms in 1991 has brought change to India. Aimed at liberalizing the market, these reforms have opened up the country to foreign competition. In the future organizations will be forced to develop and progress if they are to survive.

1 Cultural context

India is one of the largest countries in the world, both in geographical terms (over 3,500,000 km^2) and in terms of population (over 950 million in 1998). It is also one of the oldest civilizations – India's recorded cultural heritage can be traced back to 2500 BC. An industrial power in its own right (it is listed ninth in the world), agriculture is still the mainstay of India's economy. Around two-thirds of the population are engaged in agriculture and agriculture-related activities.

India is a country made up of many and varied parts, and as such it is difficult to talk about an Indian culture. However, there are certain characteristics that many researchers and writers agree are common to the diverse peoples of India as a whole (Koestler 1966; Segal 1971; Parekh 1974; Mehta 1989; Tayeb 1988; Sinha 1990). These include arranged marriages, fatalism, respect for elders and the public expression of emotions.

In a survey conducted by Tayeb (1988) a cross-sectional sample of Indian people attributed certain characteristics to their fellow countrymen and women. Table 1 lists the results of this survey.

Table 1 Major Indian cultural characteristics

Characteristics	Rank order
Obedient to their seniors	1
Respect powerful people	2
Interested in community affairs	3
Prefer to be in a group	4
Cope well with setbacks	5
Law-abiding	6
Believe in fate	7
Friendly	7
Trustworthy	8
Strong sense of responsibility	9
Honest	10
Tolerant	11
Self-confidence	12
Self-control	13
Rational	14
Emotional	15
Copes well with new and uncertain situations	16
Respect the law to the letter	17
Caste-conscious	18
Disciplined	19
Trusting	20
Modest	21
Like to be told what to do	22
Afraid of powerful people	23
See things through	24
Prefer to merge with the crowd	25
Independence	26
Submissive	27
Willing to take account of others' opinions	28
Accept change	29
Prefer to work on their own	30
Not open to bribery	31
Outgoing	32
Play safe	33
Selfish	34

The survey highlighted some of the cultural traits attributed to Indian people in general: high power distance; collectivism; tenacity and resourcefulness; self-control; honesty; traditionalism and an aversion to change; a low opinion of other people's views; public expression of emotions; a lack of reserve; dependence; and a belief in fate.

A review of the literature on socialization processes in India demonstrates that the above characteristics, and many more, are inculcated in Indian children. They are reinforced during adulthood through institutions such as the family, religion and education. These characteristics then manifest themselves in part in political-economic institutions, including business organizations.

2 Management styles in India

For a developing country like India, on its way to full industrialization and economic development, business firms have an important role to play. The ways in which these are organized and managed are crucial (see MANAGEMENT IN THE EMERGING COUNTRIES).

India as a nation has a great deal in common with both Eastern and Western civilizations and business firms reflect this. In some respects Indian management behaviour and styles are similar to those of most other Third World countries, particularly those situated in Asia: both favour centralized decision-making processes, a low level of consultation with subordinates, an upward flow of information and a downward flow of orders and personal supervision. In some other respects Indian organizations and their management behaviour have a great deal in common with some Western developed countries, especially the UK, a former colonial power in India: both tend towards a dual-control strategy (strict control and direct supervision of manual workers and lower administrative staff), internal and subtle control of senior managers (for example, via a progress report), mistrust between management and workers and confrontational industrial relations.

Management in India, as in any other country, covers activities such as planning and strategy making, interface activities (for example, negotiation with trade partners, dealing with the government) and internal organization. These behaviours and activities take place within the Indian social context. In order to understand Indian organizations, it is therefore important to understand this context and the way in which business organizations interact with it. The section below deals with some of the major institutions and elements which constitute the context within which Indian organizations operate.

3 The business culture

The economy

Since independence in 1947, successive governments in India have pursued semi-socialist and protectionist industrial and economic policies. The private sector has been allowed to operate, in a strictly regulated market, alongside state-owned enterprises. As in many other Third World countries, the government has played an active role in the management of the economy (see ECONOMIES OF THE EMERGING COUNTRIES). Government policy has had as its focus several objectives: the eradication of poverty; industrialization of the economy; the creation of employment; redistribution of wealth; and, ultimately, economic self-reliance. In practice, however, many of these objectives have not been achieved. Massive poverty, inequality between rich and poor and high levels of illiteracy and infant mortality are still as pronounced in the country as they were in the late 1940s (Sharma 1992).

In pursuit of these policies, government embarked on a series of interventionist five-year development plans. These plans, implemented at the micro-level, essentially dictated to business firms what, how and where to produce and at what price to sell their products. The state even interfered with staffing and other internal policies of the firms. For example, firms are encouraged to employ labour-intensive technologies in order to increase the level of employment and there are set quotas for the companies to recruit workers from among lower castes and migrants from rural areas.

Such closed-door policies have created a climate in which competition from outside businesses is totally absent. As a result, business organizations have no incentive to progress, either by improving the quality of their products and services or investing in research and development, or to introduce employee training. Many companies, both private and state-owned, are characterized by inefficiency, over-manning and low productivity (Johri 1992). They are not in a position to compete in international markets against North America, western Europe and east Asia.

Since the early 1990s the scene has been slowly changing. In 1991 the government began a process of limited liberalization. The reforms have virtually dismantled investment licensing and removed government controls over private-sector firms' investment and production decisions.

Although state enterprises are not privatized, a policy of equity dilution is being implemented; that is, some of the shares in these enterprises are available for sale to the private sector. Moreover, private companies are encouraged to invest in the same industries where until mid-1991 the state held a monopoly position. The liberalization process has been extended to other economic spheres also, such as the financial sector and the exchange rate regime.

As far as foreign trade is concerned, the market has been opened up to foreign competition to some extent by the removal of some of the barriers to foreign investment, and by the reduction of import tariffs (except for consumer goods). Foreign firms may now own up to 51 per cent of a company's assets and are given considerable freedom in making strategic and operating decisions.

Despite such reforms, government bureaucracy and those with vested interests in the private sector are slowing the process down. Also, as Khalilzadeh-Shirazi and Zagha (1994) point out, in a democracy such as India the government needs the approval of both parliament and the population at large for reforms. This, too, inevitably slows down the process.

India and China

Given the similarities between China and India in their intentions to open up their large and underdeveloped markets, a comparison between the two countries is of interest.

China started its liberalization process in the 1980s and has attracted a huge amount of foreign investment, the majority of which comes from Chinese expatriates living in nearby countries. In part as a result of this move, in the 1990s China has been enjoying an average annual growth rate of 8 per cent.

In India, which lacks the large reservoir of rich expatriates and decentralized economic structure of China, the average growth rate has been more modest, at around 5 per cent. However, according to Thomas (1994), India has a greater potential for future success. The country has the necessary infrastructure for economic reform, such as a large private sector, established financial institutions and stock market, well-trained managers and English as the language of commerce and central administration. This places India in a better position in the international market than China, where this infrastructure has yet to be established.

Industrial relations

In India trade unions are either plant-based or national organizations. Both are run locally within each state. They focus their activities on the interests of their immediate members at the plant or local industry level. There are provisions for setting up works committees in factories and for worker participation in decision making at shopfloor and plant levels. However, these committees, and indeed any other form of worker participation, have not been successful (Chaudhuri 1981).

Industrial relations legislation is pro-worker and aims at protecting their employment and general well-being. There are laws concerning minimum wages, payment of wages, working conditions, equal remuneration for men and women, and security of the workers against contingencies such as industrial accidents. Labour laws and regulations tend to restrict management discretion and practices greatly. For example, it would be virtually impossible for management to fire workers or reduce their wages even if they seriously breached the terms of their contract (see INDUSTRIAL RELATIONS IN THE EMERGING COUNTRIES).

4 Human resource management in India

Indian people are, in general, resourceful and hard-working, have a keen sense of responsibility, are thrifty and entrepreneurial, and are ambitious and materialistic (see also Sinha 1990). They also have a high level of collectivism and group orientation compared to many other nations. However, these traits have not been carried over fully to the workplace or utilized by managers successfully in the form of, for instance, a high level of commitment to organizational goals. Moreover, employee productivity in India is very low compared to some of their fellow Asian counterparts, especially those in the so-called Tiger Economies (World Bank 1993).

Three basic reasons exist for this state of affairs. First, in a country which is in a state of economic transition, what matters most in human resource terms is the availability of educated and skilled manual workers. Employees need to have the skills and technological know-how to operate sophisticated machines and produce goods which are of high quality and which would sell in the international market. This calls for appropriate pre-university education and vocational training, which in India's case is not being provided. The education system in India, although impressive at the university level, is inadequate at the primary and secondary school levels. Enrolment rates for such schools are low, drop-out rates are high and vocational training is inadequate for the kind of developmental ambitions that a country like India entertains (Mehta 1989; Rao-Seshadri 1993).

Second, the collectivism of Indian culture has not been utilized in the workplace. Managers have been unable to incorporate this cultural trait into their organization culture or to build their management style around it. This is because Indian employees remain highly dedicated to their 'in-group', consisting of their extended family, friends, clan and caste, but treat their workplace as an 'out-group'. In a comparative study conducted by Tayeb (1988), Indian employees showed no more commitment to their organization than did their individualistic English counterparts (see also Sinha 1990; Singhal 1994).

Third, the country's social stratification is reflected within organizations as well. Managers and other senior staff generally come from higher castes and manual workers from lower ones, especially the unscheduled castes. Moreover, in the industrial sector, a Western-style middle-class/working-class division is superimposed on a highly divisive caste system. As a result there is a fundamental conflict of interests between the two sides of the business organization, which has contributed to a confrontational and hostile management–worker relationship (see HUMAN RESOURCE MANAGEMENT IN THE EMERGING COUNTRIES).

5 Conclusion

Management behaviour in India reflects the cultural, political and economic background of the country. Any analysis must therefore be viewed in relation to this.

The centralized structure and low level of consultation within Indian organizations reflect some of the cultural traits of their people, such as respect for seniors and large power distance. They also reflect the social stratification, which sets people in upper castes and classes against those in the lower strata. Industrial relations are beset by confrontation and mistrust.

Government policies have a major impact on Indian organizations, with all strategic and operative decisions made constrained by strict rules and regulations imposed by the state. Years of closed-door policies have protected firms from foreign competition and stunted growth. As a result, many firms are overstaffed and suffer from low productivity and inefficiency. A vast majority of their products are overpriced and cannot compete in the international market with regard to either quality or price.

The economic reforms which started in 1991 aim at liberalizing the market and reducing barriers to foreign competition. The reforms will have major implications for Indian organizations, which must adapt to a competitive and changing market where customers can no longer be taken for granted. Organizations need to invest in employee training and in technology in order to improve their productivity and efficiency, as any attempt to flourish in the new dynamic market relies heavily on employee skills. A different style of management–employee relationship is called for, one which will be based on cooperation and teamwork instead of hostility and division.

MONIR TAYEB
HERIOT-WATT UNIVERSITY

Further reading

(References cited in the text marked *)

*   Chaudhuri, K.K. (1981) 'Workers' participation in India: a review of studies, 1950–1980', working paper 41, Calcutta: Indian Institute of Management. (Discusses some aspects of industrial relations in India. Written at the beginning of the 1980s, but the situation has not changed much since then.)

    Cook, N. (1993) *India's Industrial Cities: Essays in Economy and Demography*, Oxford: Oxford University Press. (Explores the diverse demographic outcomes of industrialization in India and their social implications.)

    Crompton, P.L. and Rodriguez, G.R. (1992) 'Implications of recent trade and industrial reforms in India', *Agriculture and Resource Quarterly* 4(4): 542–53. (An analysis of the economic reforms embarked upon by the Indian government in 1990.)

    The Economist (1999) 'A Survey of India and Pakistan', 22 May: 1–18. (An up-to-date analysis of Indian and Pakistani business.)

*   Johri, C.K. (1992) *Industrialism and Employment Systems in India*, Delhi: Oxford University Press. (This book explores the possibilities of genuine industrialization in India and examines the response of labour to the development of the country's urban industrial economy.)

*   Khalilzadeh-Shirazi, J. and Zagha, R. (1994) 'Economic reforms in India: achievements and the agenda ahead', *Columbia Journal of World Business* 24 (1): 24–31. (An analysis of the background to and the process of economic reform in India.)

*   Koestler, A. (1966) *The Lotus and the Robot*, Danube edn, London: Hutchinson. (This book has several sections, one of which concerns Indian culture and Hinduism.)

*   Mehta, P. (1989) *Bureaucracy, Organisational Behaviour, and Development*, New Delhi: Sage Publications. (An analysis of Indian bureaucracy and its harmful effects on education and economic development.)

    Miller-Adams, M. (1999) *The World Bank: New Agendas in a Changing World*, London: Routledge. (New book on the World Bank and implications for the developing world.)

*   Parekh, B. (1974) 'The spectre of self-consciousness', in Parekh, B. (ed.), *Colour, Culture, and Consciousness*, London: Allen & Unwin. (This chapter highlights some Indian cultural traits and compares them with those of the English.)

*   Rao-Seshadri, S. (1993) 'An evaluation of the effectiveness of educational programs: the Indian experience', unpublished PhD thesis, Pennsylvania State University, PA. (A discussion and analysis of the educational system in India.)

    Rothermund, D. (1993) *An Economic History of India: From Pre-colonial Times to 1991*, 2nd edn, London: Routledge. (A thorough analysis of the evolution of Indian political-economic policies and institutions.)

*   Segal, R. (1971) *The Crisis of India*, Bombay: Jaico Publishing House. (Analyses India's political system and compares it with Western democracies.)

*   Sharma, S.D. (1992) 'The policies and politics of rural development and the limits to reform and redistribution: the case of post-independence India', unpublished PhD thesis, University of Toronto. (Argues why India has not succeeded in eradicating its massive poverty.)

*   Singhal, S. (1994) *Senior Management: Dynamics of Effectiveness*, New Delhi: Sage Publications. (A survey of a sample of Indian senior managers.)

*   Sinha, J.B.P. (1990) *Work Culture in the Indian Context*, New Delhi: Sage Publications. (A study of work culture in six organizations within the context of Indian culture.)

*   Tayeb, M.H. (1988) *Organizations and National Culture: A Comparative Analysis*, London: Sage Publications. (An in-depth comparison of Indian and English cultures, organizations and management styles.)

*   Thomas, E. (1994) 'Change in climate for foreign investment in India', *Columbia Journal of World Business* 24(1): 32–40. (Discusses the implications of Indian economic reforms for foreign companies.)

*   World Bank (1993) *Development Report*, Geneva: World Bank. (Discusses and compares economic and non-economic performances of member states, including India.)

See also: BUSINESS CULTURES, THE EMERGING COUNTRIES; ECONOMIES OF THE EMERGING COUNTRIES; HUMAN RESOURCE MANAGEMENT IN THE EMERGING COUNTRIES; INDUSTRIAL RELATIONS IN THE EMERGING COUNTRIES; MANAGEMENT IN BANGLADESH; MANAGEMENT IN THE EMERGING COUNTRIES; MANAGEMENT IN PAKISTAN; MANAGEMENT IN SRI LANKA

Related topics in the IEBM regional set: MANAGEMENT IN ASIA PACIFIC; MANAGEMENT IN CHINA

Management in Pakistan

1 Historical and cultural background
2 The economy
3 Employment structure
4 Management values
5 Management education
6 Labour unions
7 Human resource management
8 Conclusion

Overview

Pakistani management culture, like other cultures of the region, is characterized by allegiance to families and a predominance of relationships over rules. However, the culture differs with regard to being less centralized and believing in a dominance of humane values over material things.

The economic reforms of the 1990s have led to a healthy growth of enterprises in the private sector, creating a more competitive environment. As a response to the worldwide trend towards globalization, the significant influence of Western management education and thought, and the growing awareness of employees, public organizations are set to break away from some of age-old cultural traits, whereas many private organizations have already done so. Pakistani society has a strong familial culture, and therefore the need is to develop humane systems that specifically fulfil the psychological needs of the employees as well as financial ones.

1 Historical and cultural background

Pakistan is the seventh most populous country of the world with a total population of around 135 million people; in size it ranks 34th in the world with an area of 796,045 square kilometres; and, at 3 per cent, it has the one of the world's highest population growth rates – such that in the next two decades, its population is expected to surpass the 260 million mark.

Once a part of the United India under British rule, Pakistan gained independence in August 1947. The underlying ideology behind the split from the United India was the general belief that the Muslims of the Indian subcontinent were a separate nation, therefore they should have the freedom to establish a state in which they could freely practise Islam.

Khilji (1995) has described Pakistani culture as an amalgam of *Indian origin*, *Islamic beliefs*, *British colonialism* and *American influences*. The people of this country have been open to various cultural influences over the centuries. Being natives of one of the oldest civilizations of the world, they embraced Islam as early as the sixth century, when it was brought in by the Muslim settlers/traders from Afghanistan, Iran,

Turkey and the Arab world. This message, purporting equality of mankind, was accepted with zeal by the suppressed victims of the Hindu caste system. As all these settlers had come in from the West/North West, the Muslims population came to concentrate on the western zones of the subcontinent. Hence, it was agreed that this part of British India, comprising a majority of the Muslim population in all the provinces, should be established as Pakistan after the British left. As a result, over 97 per cent of Pakistan's population has always been of Muslim faith.

British colonialism also left some prominent marks on the educational, political and legal institutions which remain intact even after 50 years of independence. Post-independence, American culture has been filtering through the media, aid agencies and investment inflows and is significantly influencing the shaping of the emerging culture.

The above characterization describes Pakistan as a country where traditional and modern ideas are given equal importance in society and organizations.

2 The economy

Overview of the development

The economic development of Pakistan has not run smoothly on a single course in the past five decades. At the time of Independence, Pakistan inherited meagre industrial endowments. It is evidenced by the fact that out of 14,569 industrial units in British India, only 1406 (mainly unimportant units such as flour and rice mills and cotton ginning factories) were located in Pakistan. To make the situation worse, Pakistan lacked industrial credit facilities, technical institutions and research labs. Pakistan was predominantly an agriculture economy. The country produced raw jute and a high proportion of the best varieties of cotton (Khan 1997).

The first industrial policy, announced in 1949, threw almost all fields of industrial activity open to private enterprise. This policy broadly envisaged expansion of production, maximizing the scope for private enterprise and enhancing exports. Succeeding governments followed the same principle; that of seeking to make maximum use of market mechanisms. Where possible, direct control has been avoided. Public investment has been used to supplement rather than displace private investment. The only exception has been the socialist period, 1971–77, when the main thrust of the industrial policy turned sharply to nationalization. As a result, almost 900 small, medium and large industrial units were taken over by the government.

In 1990, a new government took oath when the economy was at its lowest ebb. It sought to privatize ailing state-owned enterprises and to encourage the development of a larger private sector. In fact, this privatization programme is considered to be the strongest in Asia – along with the Philippines (World Bank 1998). A liberal foreign investment policy was also put forth that was hailed from within and outside the country. As a result, foreign investment, both direct and portfolio, had increased to US$880 million by 1996.

Assessment

The growth record of Pakistan's economy compares favourably with other countries of south Asia (see ECONOMIES OF THE EMERGING COUNTRIES). The flow of goods and services from economic activities within the country, measured by GDP, has expanded thirteen fold between 1949–50 and 1996–97. Consequently, per capita income increased from Rs.370/– in 1949–50 to Rs.1,040/– in 1996–97, despite a massive increase in population from 33.4 million to around 135 million. The relative share of manufacturing has risen from 7.75 per cent of the GDP in 1949–50 to 18 per cent in 1996–97, while that of agriculture has declined from 53 per cent to around 25 per cent during the same period (see Table 1). A noteworthy feature of economic progress has been the steady achievement of respectable growth rates.

In contrast, progress in social development has been uneven and mediocre. Various quality of life indices do reflect a distinct improvement over the years but are disappointing for a country of Pakistan's economic standing. The literacy rate at 37 per cent is one of the lowest in the world. Educational facilities, although they have shown substantial expansion over the years, are inadequate and unevenly distributed.

One major shortcoming in Pakistan's case has been the rate at which the population has grown and is still growing. As a consequence, much of the gain in output has not lead to an improvement in the standard of living (especially of the rural masses). The expansion of the provision of the social services proved insufficient to satisfy the needs of such a large population. The official unemployment figure of 2.05 million people is 5.37 per cent of the labour force; and this figure triples to 15 per cent if the underemployed are included.

3 Employment structure

The total employed labour force is estimated to be around 36 million. The sectoral distribution of employed labour and its percentage share in the GDP in Table 1 shows that agriculture is the mainstay. 46.7 per cent of the labour force is employed in this sector and it contributes to 24.6 per cent of GDP. The next two important sectors of the economy are finance and services and manufacturing, employing a total of 24.77 per

Table 1 Sectoral distribution of the labour force and its percentage share of GDP (1997–98)

Sectors of the economy	Percentage distribution of the labour force	Percentage share of GDP
Agriculture	46.78	24.6
Mining and manufacturing	10.49	18.7
Construction	7.2	3.7
Wholesale/retail	14.5	15.9
Transport	5.09	9.9
Finance and services	14.28	17.2
Others	1.66	10
Total	100	100

Table 2 Employment by education (1997–98)

Major occupations	Number (millions)	Percentage
Professional	1.81	5
Administrative	0.34	1
Clerical	1.66	4.6
Sales	4.92	13.6
Services	1.59	4.4
Agriculture	16.63	46
Production	9.18	25.4
Total	36.13	100

cent of the labour force. Table 2 shows that the labour activity is concentrated in sales and production (39 per cent) after agriculture (46 per cent) (see HUMAN RESOURCE MANAGEMENT IN THE EMERGING COUNTRIES).

The main industries include textiles, pharmaceuticals, chemicals, leather products, sports goods, food processing, surgical instruments, construction materials and paper products. By and large, cotton and cotton based manufacturing account for two-thirds of the country's exports.

4 Management values

The first attempt to characterize Pakistani culture was made by Hofstede (1988). According to his research, Pakistan has one of the lowest scores on the *individualism* index depicting allegiance to families, friends and other cohesive in-groups that continue to protect individuals for unquestioning loyalty. Likewise on the *power distance* index, Pakistan scores relatively low (unlike many other developing countries included in Hofstede's sample). This predicts a management style in which subordinates and superiors consider each other as existentially equal. However, in terms of the *masculinity* index, Pakistan's score is in the middle. Such cultures are *more* likely to exhibit softer values like caring for others, warm relationships, modesty, stress for equality and sympathy for the weak. Previously, there were distinct sex roles in Pakistani society as the role of the woman was strictly defined as a sister/mother/wife. However, in the past decade or so, the trend has changed considerably in urban areas as a greater number of women have enrolled for university education and joined the work force.

The results of a survey conducted by Khilji (1995) class Pakistani culture as *family oriented, publicly displaying emotions, ascribing to status* and a *predominance of relationships over rules* (Trompenaars 1993). The basic social unit is the family, where bonds are strong and relationships tend to be diffuse. Organizations are seen as an extension of the family concept. As a result, employees expect the same rules to apply here as well. The manager–subordinate relationship is viewed as a father–son or an elder brother bond. It is common to share the problems, joys and sorrows of others at work. Firing an employee can be a highly emotive experience for other employees and the manager assigned to the task (Zakaria 1992). Praise is often an important motivational factor. As relationships come first, most business deals are based upon mutual trust and prior relationships or referrals. Ascribing to status in the workplace is a legacy of the British system and of the prevalent social systems where feudal and civil bureaucrats have remained the most powerful classes of the country for centuries. Special privileges may be granted to a person's title, age, background and the social circle he moves into. None the less, this value may have lost its foothold in the private sector, where the majority of promotions are performance based and recruitment is based on merit (see MANAGEMENT IN THE EMERGING COUNTRIES).

5 Management education

Formal management education commenced in Pakistan in 1955 with the establishment of the Institution of Business Administration in Karachi. It was founded with the support of Wharton Business School and the University of Southern California. In the 1970s, Punjab University at Lahore and Quaid-i-Azam University at Islamabad also started their own MBA programmes.

In the late 1980s, formal management education gained considerable importance as a response to the growing demands of the domestic market. This resulted in the unhindered mushrooming growth of several small private business schools in some of the major cities. These private institutions claim to have affiliation with some of the less known USA/UK based universities but generally lack educational quality in terms of faculty members and facilities.

A notable exception has been the Lahore University of Management (LUMS) that was set up in 1984 as a private university by a group of the country's leading private and public sector organizations. LUMS is actively involved in conducting research and consultancies in Pakistan and has been able to write up many case studies of Pakistani organizations. The university also offers executive development education. However LUMS, unlike other government owned universities, is a very expensive place to study and is generally termed the 'University for the Rich'.

Several management training institutes like the Pakistan Institute of Management, the Management Association of Pakistan, the National Institute of Public Administration and Staff Colleges are devoted to the education and training of professionals from the public and private sectors. These institutes specialize in holding seminars, conferences and training sessions of long duration, covering many aspects of management functions. Most of these institutes were set up in the 1950s or 1960s, while others have been established in the last ten years to capitalize on the growing awareness of the importance of training and the development of human resources. In the mid 1990s, the American Management Association (AMA) was added to this list by opening an office in Islamabad. This is the third office of the AMA in Asia after Tokyo and Shanghai. This highlights the immense potential and development of the Pakistani market in this specific field.

There is also a strong trend towards in-house training institutes. The banking industry in particular is reputed for this trend. In addition, many organizations spend large amounts of money to train their employees abroad, although this trend is far more common for the multinationals than for local organizations (see MANAGEMENT EDUCATION IN THE EMERGING COUNTRIES).

6 Labour unions

After nationalization, unions became an instrument of political patronage and a device for the accumulation of power. Consequently in large state enterprises (like Pakistan Railways, Pakistan Steel, Pakistan Postal Service and Habib/United Bank Ltd), unions were associated with recalcitrant leaders/members who posed resistance to any change. They have been blamed for overstaffing and losses borne by public organizations. However, the 1990's deregulation of the economy set out to discipline the unions. The promulgation of section 27b in 1997 has severely curtailed their activities.

Even today some pre-Independence British industrial laws like the Compensation Act 1923, the Factories Act 1934 and the Payment of Wages Act 1936 are prevalent. Post-Independence additions to these laws have been the Social Security Ordinance 1965, the Industrial and Commercial Employment Ordinance 1968, the Industrial Relation Ordinance 1969 and the Employees' Old Age Benefit Act 1976. In combination, these laws broadly deal with the provision of a safe and healthy working environment, employer's liability in case of injury caused by accident, various welfare means for the workmen, workmens' fair share in the company's profits and an employer's contribution towards social security fer every workman (Saeed 1995) (see INDUSTRIAL RELATIONS IN THE EMERGING COUNTRIES).

7 Human resource management

There is a clear distinction between the private and the public sector organizations with regard to their human resource management policies and practices. In the public sector, age-old bureaucratic systems prevail. Promotions are based on seniority. There is no systematic way of training employees even though this particular HR function is least neglected. A system of priorities that are driven by strategic considerations or career development plans of the employees has not been established. The lack of a strategic emphasis on training needs has led to the continued acceptance of a broad range of motivations in securing training places, particularly involving overseas visits (Eldridge 1992). Seniority, contacts or reward are the main deciding factors in responding to training requests. Performance appraisals are one-way, confidential, annual and personality based. Hiring is not transparent; the only exception is the annual hiring of young aspiring graduates under the competitive examinations for the civil services, where a moderately high degree of fairness is observed. Salaries are modest; but the turnover is low because people who join the public sector are committed. Their choice is guided by factors like job security, the prestige attached to the occupation, flexible working hours, a relaxed work environment and better employment facilities (like housing, hospitalization and medical cover).

On the other hand, private sector organizations are much more vibrant and progressive in their approach. Human resource departments have long replaced the traditional personnel and administration departments, though it is debated (as it is around the world) if this transformation is anything more than cosmetic (see HUMAN RESOURCE MANAGEMENT IN THE EMERGING COUNTRIES). None the less, there is a general awareness of the basic human resource management concept that the employees are *the most valuable asset* of any organization. Training is the most developed human resource function. Organizations like Citibank have led the way by developing needs-led development plans. Many more are emulating or have emulated. Performance appraisals in many multinational organizations like ICI, Lever Bros, ABN Amro are performance generated; so are the rewards. Organizations in the private sector have copied their multinational counterparts in making their performance appraisals more open and performance based. Rafiq Habib Group is quoted as a superior example of professional management; one that invests in its employees and genuinely delegates authority for enhanced efficiency.

The Management Association of Pakistan (MAP) has devised an effective technique to improve on the management systems existing in the country by giving away Corporate Excellence awards. These awards are based upon the results of an *organizational management excellence* survey. This annual survey begins by sending out questionnaires to organizations, the results of which help shortlist the top few organizations. It is followed by interviews of a small number of employees in each of the shortlisted organizations in order to cross check the management responses to the questionnaires distributed in the first stage. This finally enables the rating of the top company of the year (Management Association of Pakistan 1996).

The results of an extensive survey indicate that organizational commitment is high among Pakistani male and female employees and that the fulfilment of employees' psychological needs is a very important predictor of their commitment. Employees express greater commitment to those organizations that better take care of their psychological needs (Alvi and Ahmed 1987).

8 Conclusion

Management behaviour in Pakistan is being gradually transformed. A larger private sector presence (due to privatization of the stat-owned industrial units and the establishment of enterprises in the private sector) urbanization and influences of Western management education have triggered this change. The government itself has set out to change the culture of the state-owned enterprises by appointing professional teams of managers at the top-most levels of hierarchy.

First, management culture in Pakistan is learning to appreciate the changing needs of the employees, for example recognizing their records of achievements and basing rewards on them. Second, a high organizational commitment is a positive indicator. Organizations can capitalize on it by specifically catering to the psychological needs of employees, which is possible by taking a softer human resource management approach. It calls for an enhanced use of modern management techniques. It is indeed a challenge for the mangers in Pakistan to find novel ways of managing that would be conducive to the societal culture that the employees are a part of.

The special problem of unemployment amongst the educated youth is socially the most serious. The Prime Minister's Program presented in 1997, known as the *Better Pakistan – 2010* proposes to invest in new capital and institutions and in the improvement, management, operation and maintenance of the existing ones. It distinctly outlines the need to refashion a new work culture whose building blocks are characterized by innovation, team planning, excellence, quality and discipline

(Ministry of Planning and Development 1997). The next decade, if the above policies persist, should be promising for employees, rewarding for managers and interesting for onlookers/researchers like ourselves.

SHAISTA E. KHILJI
THE JUDGE INSTITUTE OF MANAGEMENT STUDIES
UNIVERSITY OF CAMBRIDGE

Further reading

(References cited in the text marked *)

* Alvi, S.A. and Ahmed, S.W. (1987) 'Assessing organizational commitment in a developing country', *Human Relations* 40(5): 267–80. (An extensive survey that examines the commitment of male and female employees to their organizations in Pakistan.)

Burki, S.J. (1988) 'A historical perspective on development', in Burki, S.J. and Laporte, R., Jr (eds), *Pakistan's Development Priorities: Choices for the Future*, Karachi: Oxford University Press. (Assesses the various economic policies pursued until 1988.)

* Cameron, J. and Irfan, M. (1992) 'Enabling people to help themselves. An employment and human resource development strategy for Pakistan', *World Employment Program*: 92–102. (Analyses the status of labour force and employment situation in Pakistan and logically outlays an increased need for active and long-term human resource development strategies and policies.)

Economist Intelligence Unit (1998) 'Pakistan', *EIU World Outlook*. (Provides actual and estimated figures of the economy of the country.)

The Economist (1999) 'A Survey of India and Pakistan', 22 May: 1–18. (Up-to-date survey of Indian and Pakistani business.)

* Eldridge, D. (1992) 'Strategic approach to employee development in an agriculture bank', *International Journal of Public Sector Management* 5(2): 15–20. (Investigates the link between business needs and employee development policies within a public sector bank with a view to suggesting improvements that focus on employees' performance needs.)

* Government of Pakistan (1998) *Economic Survey 1997–1998*, Islamabad: Finance Division. (The official source of the state and structure of the economy of the country.)

* Hofstede, G. (1988) *Cultures and Organizations*, London: Harper Collins Business. (In this book, Hofstede develops five dimensions on which the cultures of 50 countries are measured. Based upon cultural differences, he reveals differences amongst nations in the way businesses are managed.)

* Khan, A.A. (1997) 'Economic development' in Raza, R. (ed.), *Pakistan in Perspective 1947–1997*, Karachi: Oxford University Press. (Discusses the objectives of the economic policies pursued in the fifty years of the country's independence and their impact therein.)

* Khilji, S.E. (1995) 'Understanding the Corporate Culture of Pakistan', essay for an M.Phil degree at the University of Cambridge, England. (Explores the nature of corporate culture in Pakistan and attempts to explain the underlying issues.)

* Khilji, S.E. (1995) 'International Human Resource management in Pakistan – Case Studies of British Invested Firms in Pakistan', thesis for an M.Phil. degree at the University of Cambridge, England. (Uses an in-depth empirical analysis to study the status of human resource management in some of the multinationals in Pakistan.)

* Management Association of Pakistan (1996) *Annual Report*. (Enlists the mission, objectives and reports the activities of the association in the year under review.)

Ministry of Planning and Development, Government of Pakistan (1997) *Pakistan 2010*. (Outlines the vision of a progressive Pakistan in the year 2010 and enumerates the proposed policies to be undertaken.)

Mirza, S.A. (1995) 'Nationalisation, constitution and Islam', *Privatization in Pakistan*, Lahore: Ferozesons. (Discusses at length the position of nationalization policy of the 1970s in the light of Islamic beliefs.)

* Saeed, K.A. (1995) *Mercantile and Industrial Laws in Pakistan*, Lahore: Institute of Business Management. (A reproduction of mercantile and labour laws in Pakistan in a simple easy to understand language.)

Siddiqui, H.R. (1997) 'The missing factor in HRD', *Dawn* March 1997. (A short article that stresses the need to exhibit professionalism and innovation in the field of human resource management in Pakistan.)

* Trompenaars, F. (1993) *Riding the Waves of Culture*, London: The Economist Books. (This is about the significance of cultural differences and how they may effect the processes of doing businesses and management.)

* The World Bank Group Web Page (1998) 'Country brief – Pakistan'. http://www.worldban.org. (Provides an up-to-date analysis of the state of the economy of Pakistan.)

* Zakaria, S. (1994) 'Corporate Culture in Pakistan: Difficulties for Foreign Managers', thesis for an M.Phil. degree at the University of Cambridge, England. (Picks up on Hofstede's typology to study the difficulties faced by foreign managers in managing the people of Pakistan.)

See also: ECONOMIES OF THE EMERGING COUNTRIES; HUMAN RESOURCE MANAGEMENT IN THE EMERGING COUNTRIES; INDUSTRIAL RELATIONS IN THE EMERGING COUNTRIES; MANAGEMENT EDUCATION IN THE EMERGING COUNTRIES; MANAGEMENT IN BANGLA-DESH; MANAGEMENT IN INDIA; MANAGEMENT IN SRI LANKA

Related topics in the IEBM regional set: BUSINESS CULTURES, ASIAN PACIFIC; MANAGE-MENT IN ASIA PACIFIC

Management in Sri Lanka

1 Introduction
2 Business and management development
3 Conclusion

Overview

Management development in Sri Lanka has been influenced by many factors such as its history, political environment, and colonization by Western powers resulting in institutional structuring, economic/business conceptualizations, cultural traits, etc. The work ethics, organizational culture, systems development, entrepreneur/ employee relationships, etc. have moulded accordingly.

In a competitive situation, entrepreneurship, innovation, achievement, quality, etc. overtake *ad hocism* in management. Therein, professionalism overtakes family affiliations and the adoption of new systems/technology and scientific management embraces organizations. Thus managerial dimensions in Sri Lanka, affecting behaviour, work ethics, practices, etc. are changing fast, heading towards professionalism. Hence, future management projections will face the challenges of competition, human resources development and technology transfer with a professional outlook.

1 Introduction

Sri Lanka is a Democratic Republic with a Unitary Constitution with a population of 18.6 million living in 25,000 square miles. The demographic division of gender is equally distributed. Reduction of maternal/child deaths, 1.3 per cent population growth, per capita income of US$814 (Central Bank of Sri Lanka 1997), high literacy rates and quality of life in the South Asian context are Sri Lanka's achievements.

Its history has influenced the culture and socioeconomic environment. The *Sinhalese* (the majority race) kingdom existed up to 1815 until the British took control. Since 1505, parts of the country had been controlled by the Portuguese, Dutch or British. Economic diversification, education, physical infrastructure development, democratic governance, legal systems, administrative institutions, businesses and their practices, etc., were bases on which management systems were built. The inevitable outcome was that those systems were imprinted with the ruling management cultures, mainly the British but also with traces of the other colonial rulers.

The Constitution (1972 and 1978) conferred the status of a Republic to Sri Lanka. The 13th Amendment to the Constitution in 1987 provided for power sharing through Provincial Councils (Constitution Sri Lanka 1987). Although only partly fulfilled, it is a positive response towards decentralized management. The Local Authorities supervised by the Provincial Councils are threefold – Municipal, Urban and Divisional Councils (*Pradeshiya Sabha*), engaging mostly in environmental management.

The country's economic performance was the most important influence on management. The issues of population, unemployment, local/foreign prices, the aspirations of the younger strata of the population, etc. were all problems faced by the country. Until 1956 Sri Lanka had a capitalistic welfare economy. Nationalization of private assets and businesses was carried out from 1956 to1965. From 1965 to 1977 an attempt was made to achieve agricultural self-sufficiency, and to develop industry and tourism. An open-economic policy was implemented after 1978. Appropriate management changes accompanied these policy changes.

2 Business and management development

Since government policies are based on political philosophies, political parties are important policy determinants. Reducing public service delivery and increasing the role of the private sector highlighted public confidence in the private sector. The rule of subsidiarity (i.e. minimal government engagement in business), as accepted by the government, has helped the expansion of the private sector (see MANAGEMENT IN THE EMERGING COUNTRIES).

The historical development of management in Sri Lanka

Chronologically, Sri Lankan private businesses can be identified as: colonial (until independence), traditional (1948–56), conservative (1957–77) and new (1978 onwards). The main characteristics of these different forms are:

1 *Colonial business*: Controlled by domineering colonial masters; male dominated; with foreign managerial attitudes, mostly concerned with the repatriation of profits.

2 *Traditional businesses*: Small-scale businesses owned by nationals/non-nationals; male dominated; managers have less exposure to education/management concepts, and are inclined to consult relations, peers and elders for crucial decision making advice; are helpful to co-businessmen, generally honest, and consider business as a service.

3 *Conservative businesses*: In addition to some characteristics in number 2, above these are industrially inclined; ownership shifting towards nationals; somewhat innovative and risk taking; managers have some education in management; receiving government incentives, bank-financed; have less customer consideration.

4 *New businesses*: Larger organizations; diversified activities; national, foreign and even multi-national ownership; few females at managerial levels; more innovative; employing new management techniques, taking more risks; technically upgraded; professionals employed; large capital investments; market oriented; spendthrift; jealous of competitors; indifferent to honesty, some engaging even in anti-social businesses.

After independence, the private sector had good access to resources and enjoyed a favourable public policy. With the changing competitive business scenario, socialist thinking began to encroach upon public policy, and the business environment also changed. Nationalization of private sector assets reduced private initiatives and aggravated the fear psychosis of business managers.

The state sector was the major employer of personnel, paid from the annual budgets of the ministries/departments or statutory authorities. Privatization reduced the expenditures on personnel of statutory authorities as they came under the purview of companies, which were floated to manage them. The determination of cadres, recruitment, training, retrenchment, pension payments, etc. of public officials is the responsibility of the government. The private sector has more flexibility on hiring, but less on firing, as such action is challengeable under labour laws.

With 73 per cent of the population living in rural areas, the government was concerned about their personal and political aspirations and cultural requirements. Therefore, official language policy was changed in the mid-1950s. This has affected the performance of private sector management, as the vernacular educated joined the private sector. With more privatization, the demand for English-educated managers has increased. International schools and foreign educational opportunities have minimally improved the situation, but have not brought about miracles.

The private sector, reluctantly, had to accept the nationalization of plantations, trade, industry, services, etc. The pressure of nationalization was relieved only after 1978 with economic liberalization, again affecting business management and development. This can be seen in the increase of commercial and development banks/branches, foreign capital transfers, the establishment of consultancy firms, a relaxation of negative policies and procedures, and the introduction of new business mechanisms such as stock exchanges, capital markets and new technologies. The passage of the Companies Act gave greater encouragement to the systematic development of companies. However, the labour rights movements were not to the liking of the private sector. The Workers' Charter, benefiting labour, has been put on hold for several years, as the government seeks to retain the private sector's goodwill.

Entrepreneurship

When considering management status, we should briefly look at entrepreneurship (see BUSINESS CULTURES, THE EMERGING COUNTRIES). One study of Sri Lankan management (Perera and Buddhadasa 1992) opines that 'entrepreuneurship could be part of the solution to existing social and economic ailments'. Joseph Schumpeter has described entrepreneurs as innovators. To describe colonial or traditional Sri Lankan business managers in this way sounds unsatisfactory. However, McClelland's conclusion that power orientation is more prominent as a motivator among successful entrepreneurs has been visible in Sri Lanka.

In Sri Lanka, the need for achievement as a means of gaining social power seems to be the prime motivator of some entrepreneurs (Perera 1990). The recent intervention of the business community into the search for a solution to the ethnic crisis shows how business and social power can be extended into political power.

There have been managers and entrepreneurs, men and women, who have excelled in innovation and management acumen. The traits for success in the Sri Lankan corporate world have been identified by a leading business personality as 'boundless energy, intelligence, integrity, likeability, drive and the willingness to sacrifice' (Jayasundera 1992). This, undoubtedly, is comparable with Western thinking.

There are a number of family-centered firms controlling large businesses in Sri Lanka. In many such businesses, an ancestral entrepreneur had been positively innovative and enterprising due to extraordinary managerial capacity. Sometimes, family companies engage relations in managerial positions. Such management arrangements can be criticized as being inimical to innovation, as pointed out by Hagan (1986), who stated that 'key managerial posts given to family members may some times result in the employment of incompetents'. It is notable that there are some companies having a nominal head of the family (e.g. mother) symbolically leading the firm, although the firm is really managed by the children and other managers. However, there are also businesses in Sri Lanka which have been developed and efficiently run for long periods of time by family managers, proving the sustainability of family managed businesses in Sri Lanka. Although, it may be argued that those companies may have performed better, given the opportunity to explore an open management system.

Management styles and the cultural environment

With increasing competition and modernization, management systems have changed, showing a shift towards recruiting non-family members. A typical life-cycle for a Sri Lankan family-owned enterprise would be: the initial stage, where the owner-entrepreneur's involvement in managerial decision making is high; the growth stage, where the number of non-related managers increases; while in matured organizations, the family's participation in managerial decision making decreases, perhaps in the belief that business achievements are not a corollary to family affiliation.

Some management theoreticians argue that the affiliation motive/need is negatively correlated with the achievement motive/need. Concurrently, achievement is considered to be correlated to risk taking. Research in Sri Lanka (Perera and Buddhdasa 1992) challenges this theory by concluding that the successful Sri Lankan entrepreneur is one who takes medium risks and is highly persevering and innovative, while the less successful entrepreneur takes medium risks, is moderately persevering, but low in innovation. Hence the significant variable in Sri Lanka is innovation, although McClelland identified risk taking as a significant factor in high achievement motivated entrepreneurs. Cultural traits in the West may have created this confusion.

Hofstede (1987) identified four cultural dimensions affecting management: individualism vs. collectivism, large vs. small power distance, strong vs. weak uncertainty avoidance and masculinity vs. femininity. Although Sri Lanka was not in his study, the dimensions are relevant for Sri Lankan management. Cultural factors show that Sri Lankan management tends to be closer to collectivism, with recognizable power distance, weak in uncertainty avoidance and with 'feminine' managerial characteristics.

The collectivist approaches in Sri Lanka are not as strong as in Japan. However, group influences such as the '5-Ss' of Japanese origin are now employed by management. The influence of work values on employee involvement and the achievement of success by changing the job structures of employees have had positive effects, according to a study done in Sri Lanka (Jayawardana 1996). It is heartening to note that a few tea estates have started employing '5-Ss' to motivate workers for partnerships. A sense of belonging, group interest, tolerance of nepotism and third-party involvement of conflict resolution are some symbolic situations of collectivism.

In Sri Lanka, the issues of power distance in management are not critical as in India. The flat managerial structures are remote, but management is reasonably accessibe; age is respected; management by objectives is comparatively less in Sri Lanka. Uncertainty avoidance is reflected in weak planning in Sri Lanka. Lacking predictability, poor punctuality, minimum standardization, tolerance of deviance, etc. can all be observed in Sri Lanka, reflecting the level of uncertainty avoidance. However, planning and its importance as a management tool to maximize the use and value of limited resources, efficient management review of targets against performance, and maintenance of standards are now identified as favourable outputs of planning in Sri Lanka. The extended family relationships, people orientation, inter-dependence ideal, sympathy for the less fortunate, empathy, caring for employees, etc. exemplify the feministic behaviours of Sri Lankan managers (Fernando 1996).

A closeness to the Indian cultural dimensions reflects another facet of management (see MANAGEMENT IN INDIA). Many aspects of family and religious thought in Sri Lanka have been moulded by Indian influences. Conquering man had been the main cultural theme of Indian civilization. Research done on the influence of culture on work ethics points to the reasonableness of classifying the preferences for 'being', manipulative, negative and working for social fulfilment, as the main work relevant values in Sri Lanka (Nanayakkara 1994). It is emphasized that culture cannot adequately explain the state of work ethics in Sri Lanka. Other factors, for example colonial heritage, social welfare programmes, the structure of economic organizations, etc. also influence work ethics.

Against a background of the East Asian 'Tigers' which have shown such accelerated development (although this has slowed down considerably towards the end of the 1990s), it is interesting to compare their work ethic – such as discipline, hard work, thrift, 'this worldliness', quality achievement, etc. – with the Sri Lankan work ethic. A need to develop human resources to upgrade the work ethic, attitudes, capacities, etc. has been identified in Sri Lanka. Foreign investors have been expected to disseminate their 'imported' technical and technological expertise locally. Expertise accrued in the Middle East was expected to seep into the economy on the return of expatriate workers. These assumptions never materialized due to the establishment of less sophisticated industries in Sri Lanka and as most expatriate workers were engaged as housemaids, preventing any accumulation of technology. A void in knowledge and technology was therefore inevitable.

Management education

The universities, who increased their enrolments in commerce and management subjects (50 in 1966/67, to 800 in 1981/82 and 2000 by 1996/97) faced the void creatively. Post-graduate students increased from 40 (1981) to 300 (1997). Competition for admission is reflected by the increase in admission requirements, which have risen from the lowest in 1981/82 to the highest in 1996/97. Since independence, 7000 management graduates, 8000 commerce graduates and 1000 post-graduates have been produced by the universities. Private sector and/or foreign university collaborations have begun to offer MBA courses in the 1990s, with the Institute of Technological Studies initiating one such course. Technical institutions have supported business management as seen by the increase of institutes from 8 in 1960 to 39 by 1997. The Institute of Chartered Accountants, the Chartered Institute of Management Accountants, the Chartered Institute of Marketing of Sri Lanka, the Chartered Institute of Secretaries, the Sarvodaya Management Training Institute, the Sri Lanka Institute of Marketing, the National Institute of Business Management are major private sector training organizations (Nanayakkara 1998) (see MANAGEMENT EDUCATION IN THE EMERGING COUNTRIES).

Entrepreneurship training is undertaken by the Industrial Development Board, Small Business Development Centre, Employment Investment and Enterprise Development Division of the Ministry of Mahaweli. The private sector has also contributed to management training, with companies such as Business Consultancy Services Ltd., Business Management Bureau, etc. One important development had been the interest shown by leading companies in demonstrating to their employees the importance of work values, and using employee involvement to motivate them to become positive managers and team workers. Those interested in quality improvement have sometimes lamented that the lack of interest at the top management level is a stumbling block to making use of quality and productivity enhancement programmes, although some top managers have utilized quality improvement programmes. The critics have described many top managers as 'theory X managers' who are 'autocratic and living in the past.' (The *Sunday Leader* [paper] 22 November 1998) and explain that as the reason for negativism.

There are several problems with the training processes in Sri Lanka. The main issue is the incompatibility of graduates to the needs of employers (see HUMAN RESOURCE MANAGEMENT IN THE EMERGING COUNTRIES). Employers in Sri Lanka look for analytical, adaptation, communication and team work skills and for leadership potential. A survey conducted by Nanyakkara (1998) has shown that 47.1 per cent of graduates preferred to go into teaching rather than take risks in business. Some of the major weaknesses in the system are that little publicity is given to management education, selection processes have been found to be wanting, courses tend to have a theoretical and product orientation instead of a market orientation, and there are low levels of follow-up and weak inter-agency cooperation and coordination (Ranasinghe 1996).

Public servants have the benefit of receiving general training through Management Development Training Units and at the Sri Lanka Institute of Development Administration, for certificate courses. Even the clerical and allied grades make use of these programmes. There are many Teacher Training Colleges and a National Institute of Education to undertake major human resources development activities among educational personnel. The School of Cooperation of Sri Lanka, Institute of Cooperative Management and National Cooperative Council and its branches train cooperative employees. Sector-wise training and skill upgrading programmes are available in plantation management, textile industry, agriculture, veterinary and livestock development. With this infrastructure in place, one can satisfactorily conclude that the setting is complete for human resources development in management.

3 Conclusion

A movement towards economic success in a country has to be supported by managerial capacity. A stable private-sector-oriented economic approach has become established in Sri Lanka. Hence, the issues in management should be regarded in this light.

With increased support for liberalization and commitment to the principle of subsidiarity, the role of the government will contract in the future. Power sharing exercises will create a situation where the government will undertake a more or less regulatory function, assisting and servicing business management, in addition to centralized functions such as security, foreign exchange management, immigration/ emigration, customs, etc. Such contraction would automatically mean an expanded private sector, as non-governmental organizations cannot and will not fill the void.

In profit-motivated private sector development, entrepreneurship, innovation and productivity will be the key elements. The government and private sector organizations would like to see higher levels of entrepreneurship, which is in short supply in Sri Lanka. Human resources development towards the encouragement of entrepreneurship is one increasingly popular move. Supplementary support for the establishment of institutions, such as development banks, Sri Lanka Board of Investment, Export Development Board, research and training institutions, etc. are some of the positive recent developments to facilitate entrepreneurship.

The problems created by cultural factors are slowly changing due to political, international and socioeconomic influences. An interest in learning languages such as English, Japanese, Chinese and German; enthusiastic efforts to implement quality circles in the workplace; use of high technology in operations; contracting in non-related professionals; the use of consultants, etc. are all trends seen in management that can be called positive and proactive. The easing of cultural limitations against females, a preference for merit over seniority, and younger executives beginning to take the reins of management, etc. are changing scenarios which will have a positive effect on management.

Even the work ethic is slowly changing due to other integrated developments in the management field. The participatory approaches to management, power sharing with the periphery, etc. are serious activities, but are common issues related to the work ethic and productivity development. The culturally negative feeling of 'being' is changing as a work ethic, due to the competition among various organizations.

Therefore, the future projections on management will be centred on factors other than simply business. The social, cultural, political, economic and international factors will have an input to the successful management of both state and private sector businesses in Sri Lanka. Hence, identifying the proper mix of the various components has to be done carefully to avoid any pitfalls. This is the challenge before government, entrepreneurs, financiers and human resources developers in Sri Lanka.

AUSTIN FERNANDO
RESOURCES DEVELOPMENT CONSULTANTS LTD

Further reading

(References cited in the text marked *)

* Central Bank of Sri Lanka (1997) *Annual Report*.

Fernando, A. (1996) 'Hofstede's Cultural Dimensions – Application on Pradeshiya Sabha Manage-ment', MBA Research. (The research applies the four cultural dimensions identified by Hofstede to local government management in Sri Lanka.)

Fonseka, A.T. and Jayawardena, A.K.L. (1996) 'Self-managed teams and organisational perfor-mance: the experience of Asian Cotton Mills Ltd., Sri Lanka', *Sri Lanka Journal of Management* PIM 1(4) October–December. (Documents the experience of Asian Cotton Mills Ltd. in operating self-managed teams as a managerial innovation to meet the challenge of competition, the gains achieved in higher employee motivation, productivity and output and the lessons to be learnt from the experiences.)

Fonseka, K.B.M. (1997) 'Cost management strategies: A theoretical framework and a glimpse of Sri Lankan practice', *Sri Lanka Journal of Management*, 2(2) April–June. (Responses obtained from a sample of 44 middle and upper level managers from the services and manufacturing sectors in Sri Lanka suggest an inclination towards 'come what may type strategies' in their organizations and the unfavourable trend that requires correction.)

* Government of Sri Lanka (1987) Constitution of the Democratic Socialist Republic of Sri Lanka.

* Hagen Everett, E. (1986) *The Economics of Development*, Homewood IL: Richard D Irwin. (This study on entrepreneurship highlights innovation as doing something new and economic inno-vation as doing something new in production, products and markets.)

Hofstede, G. (1987) *Cultural Consequences* (abridged edn) Third Printing, Berkely, CA: Sage. (The extent of influence borne by societal values and culture on managerial functions has been researched in IBM and the four major dimensions described by Hofstede are dealt with in this book.)

* Jayasundara, D.S. (1992) 'Management Leadership and the Emerging Economic Order in Sri Lanka'. (Address given at the Convocation of the University of Sri Jayewardenepura, centred on the qualities of chief executives in the changing economic order and activities in Sri Lanka.)

* Jayawardena, A.K.L. (1996) 'Work values and employee involvement', *Sri Lanka Journal of Management* 1 (2). (Highlights the fact that the quantity and quality of work of autonomous groups was higher than the groups of hierarchical model and such positive results can be obtained when power, information, knowledge and skills are moved down to the lower levels through adequate changes in the organization structures.)

Nanayakkara, G. (1992) 'Work values: To be "imported" or "Made in Sri Lanka"?' in *Culture and management in Sri Lanka*, Colombo: PIM. (A book written to assist foreign experts in develop-ment to understand some important cultural aspects in the Sri Lankan work environment, especially in the public sector.)

* Nanayakkara, G. (1998) 'Development of management studies in modern Sri Lanka', PIM. (Gives an overall view of management education, the gaps between demand and supply of educational outputs, resource availability, research and related issues.)

* Nanayakkara, G. (1994) 'Sri Lankan cases in management', PIM. (A collection of Sri Lankan cases and a method of analysis that has been written with experience gathered in consultancies, teaching and training in real managerial and organizational situations.)

* Perera, T. and Buddhadasa, S. (1992) 'Characteristics of Sri Lankan Entrepreneurs: How Valid is the Schumpeterian Model?' *Sri Lanka Journal of Management*. (A study on the characteristics of Sri Lankan entrepreneurs, analysed in the light of Western literature and the authors' research.)

* Perera, T. (1990) 'Social power of low-country Sinhala entrepreneurs', MBA Research. (This research has been conducted by surveying a small number of low-country Sinhala business organizations on five hypotheses postulated within a single model relating to the concepts of: a collective work ethic, social power base, expansion of social power, level of achievement motivation and the growth of social power potential.)

* Ranasinghe, S. (1996) 'Entrepreneurship education and training in Sri Lanka', *Sri Lanka Journal of Management*. (Due to mixed success results obtained by the entrepreneur development program-

mes in Sri Lanka, the author makes a case for changing the focus, content and methodology of such programmes, taking into account the lessons learned in the past and indigenous entre-preneurial values and experiences.)

* The *Sunday Leader* (1998) 22 November, p. 19. (Discusses the difficulties faced by practitioners of quality improvement due to negative attitudes of traditional, 'old school' top managers.)

See also: BUSINESS CULTURES, THE EMERGING COUNTRIES; HUMAN RESOURCE MANAGE-MENT IN THE EMERGING COUNTRIES; MANAGEMENT EDUCATION IN THE EMERGING COUNTRIES; MANAGEMENT IN BANGLADESH; MANAGEMENT IN INDIA; MANAGEMENT IN PAKISTAN

Related topics in the IEBM regional set: MANAGEMENT IN ASIA PACIFIC; MANAGEMENT IN JAPAN

Country profiles

Middle East

Management in the Arab world

1 **Culture**
2 **Management types**
3 **Education and training**
4 **Islam**
5 **Leadership behaviour**
6 **Management styles**
7 **Conclusion**

Overview

The Arab world is extensive but management in Arab countries has been relatively little studied until recently. Hofstede's typology (1991) provides a useful framework and, more recently, Hickson and Pugh (1995) have examined the impact on Arab styles and cultures of management on the Bedouin and tribal ancestry, the religious framework of Islam, the common experience of foreign rule and the access to oil and natural resources leading to rapid economic development. Some Arab countries, however, are not oil-rich and not all have had the same experience of foreign domination. In particular there are strong differences between the largely French-influenced countries of the Maghreb and the largely British-influenced Middle East.

New typological frameworks are emerging based on empirical studies. There has been an emphasis on education and training and management development, particularly in the oil-rich areas exposed to Western influence. In many the spur to research has come through the political requirement of nationalization, the replacement of ex-patriot managers with nationals. This is increasingly true in the Gulf States.

Studies show that Arab countries, particularly in the Gulf, tend to have highly trained managerial cadres. The apparently restrictive requirements if Islamic finance and banking have not hindered economic development. Leadership control through close supervision and an absence of delegation have not inhibited effective performance. There is currently strong emphasis on the role of women and of family-owned businesses. Considerable evidence is building up that Arab management will present a 'fourth paradigm' and is *sui generis*. New studies of the impact of Islamic and Arab behaviour and belief patterns on motivation and organizational styles are, however, needed.

1 Culture

The Arab world is extensive. From north Africa to the Persian Gulf and from the Caucasus to the Sudan, Arab land and influence is dominant. Arab countries are in the main culturally homogeneous. Islam accounts for approximately twenty per cent of the world's believers. Yet the study of the cultures and behaviour of management in the Arab world is a relatively recent occurrence (Weir 1993). Even such apparently comprehensive texts as Tayeb's *The Global Business Environment* (1995) fail to deal with the Arab world at all.

One of the earliest attempts to characterize the culture of management in Arab countries is provided by Hofstede who, in a series of publications on national and corporate culture, has provided management researchers with the tools for making intercultural comparisons (Hofstede 1991). He is concerned with differences among cultures at national level and the consequences of national cultural differences for the ways in which organizations are structured and managers behave. This typology deals with the way in which individuals relate to society and handle problems of social inequality, the relationships between individuals and groups, concepts of masculinity and femininity and ways of dealing with social and interpersonal uncertainty relating to the control of aggression and the expression of emotions.

Hofstede's typology has been used to analyse the impact of cultural factors on multinational engineering companies working in the Gulf States, and provide practical advice for Arab managers in dealing with cultural problems in this work environment.

The Arab States typically score highly on the power/distance index. Societies of this kind are characterized as those in which skill, wealth, power and status go together and are reinforced by a cultural view that they should go together. Power is based on family, friends, charisma and the ability to use force. Theories of political activity which are influential in Arab countries stress the need for power and leadership. They recognize the importance of power and the requirements for decisive action in civil as well as in military society. But power needs to be exercised with restraint.

In terms of individualism and collectivism, Arab societies, according to Hofstede, rank in the middle of the individualism index. Arab societies are moderately masculine, but there are strong sex role distinctions and the role of women is clearly identified as lying within the family domain. In terms of uncertainty avoidance – the extent to which members of a culture feel threatened by uncertain or unknown situations – the Arab countries again fall in the middle. They are not frightened of other cultures, but nor do they wish to become assimilated to them. The Arab countries are classified as moderately orientated towards the avoidance of uncertainty. Arab countries also stress the importance of family and kin relations.

This fundamental characterization also points to the importance of tradition in Arab culture (see MANAGEMENT IN THE EMERGING COUNTRIES). Many writers have demonstrated that the fundamental matrix of Arab social organization is essentially hierarchical and traditional, representing in some sense a facsimile of the family and kin structures which permeate Arab society. Sulieman for example, points to the influence of family and kin relations in understanding the Arab manager's use of time and the organization of the working day. Where a close family member appears at the office of even quite a senior manager, it is regarded as improper for the merely specialist obligations of organizational hierarchy to take precedence over those of family and kin obligations (Sulieman 1984).

2 Management types

Hickson and Pugh (1995) identify four primary influences over Arabs in general and over Arab management – in the Bedouin and wider tribal inheritance, the religion of

Islam, the experience of foreign rule, and the twentieth-century impact of oil and the dependence of western Europe on the oil-rich Arab States and their oil-distorted economies (Hickson and Pugh 1995). However, not all Arab economies are in fact dominated by the oil and petrochemical industries. These four influences are also mediated by the experience of urbanization which ranges from the extremes of Cairo, one of the world's oldest continuously occupied cities, to the city states of Dubai and Abu Dhabi, for example, which have been created by the sudden experience of the enormous riches of the oil boom. The Bedouin influence, which centres on a patriarchal family, top-down authority, rests ultimately on the absolute power of the Sheikh, who none the less must take account of tribal opinion in all his decisions. This structure represents a matrix of authority which is still evident in many Arab organizations. This type of organization can be characterized as Bedouocracy or Sheikhocracy.

This typology is further developed by Dadfar (1993), who introduces a sophisticated model based on a large database of 158 in-depth interviews and several case studies. This generated 112 variables which were resolved into a number of socio cultural dimensions: macrocosmic perception, microcosmic perception, familism, practicality, determinism, time horizon, Western lifestyle, Western techniques and technology, and male/female equality. He relates the value systems to Arab personality types to create a profile intended to characterize the diverse managerial behaviours found in the Arab world. Thus he identifies eight types of management systems, based on an overview of his empirical research in Syria, Saudi and the Gulf States, which he compares to other studies he has undertaken in Hong Kong and Thailand (Dadfar 1993).

1   The tribeocrat refers to a leadership system in which tribalism values predominate. The leader has unlimited power, his words are rules and loyalty is given to the top manager. Key positions in an organization are assigned to family, tribe members and close friends. The tribeocrat leader is strongly Pan-Arabist and in personal terms is ambitious, restless and aggressive.
2   The tribeotheocrat is equally dominated by tribal values, but roots his authority in Islam.
3   The tribeo-Westernized type of manager wishes to adopt Western lifestyle, technology and techniques while disliking Western democracy and the corresponding aspects of management behaviour. This type of manager is often found in monopoly enterprises in which apparent adherence to Western management values can be legitimized by the fact that the manager does not have to become involved in competitive behaviour.
4   The theotribalized manager is prone to adopt a charismatic leadership style and a patriarchal approach, and may be prone to adopt an ethical and apparently theologically justified style of management.
5   The theo-Westernized manager may have been educated in Western countries and may have adopted Western techniques and technology. They do not adopt Western lifestyle, but wish to appropriate Western management techniques as technologies within a style of management supported by Islamic values.

6   The Western tribalized type of manager prefers a functional structure of management and may be technically very proficient, but when conflict arises gives priority to family and tribe members.

7   Western theocratic managers attempt to blend Western and Islamic values and accommodate Islam to an essentially Western capitalist mode of behaviour.

8   The Fully Westernized type of manager tends to be pragmatic, flexible and participative. This type is found most often, according to Dadfar, among managers who have had considerable experience working in the oil industry or other foreign joint ventures where they have been in the minority.

Dadfar's (1993) work is unusual in that it is based on a considerable volume of data and sophisticated data analysis. It would be very useful to test these types in other Arab countries and map the distribution of the relevant behaviours.

3 Education and training

One of the major empirical studies was that undertaken by MEIRC and published as *The Making Of Gulf Managers* (Muna 1989). A total of 140 managers were interviewed in fifty-three different organizations. The authors identify five main ingredients for success among managers in the Gulf States: a good educational head-start, early exposure to successful role-models, early responsibilities in the home or around it, the importance of an ethical system which puts a high value on hard work and commitment, and the need to take one's own initiatives in self development. The study again confirms that Gulf managers prefer a consultative decision-making process. A striking finding of this and other studies is the importance of education and training among managers in the Arab world (see MANAGEMENT EDUCATION IN THE EMERGING COUNTRIES).

Three times as many Arab managers have university degrees compared with British managers. Organizations in the Gulf countries spend three times as much money and time on their management development every year than do their counterparts in the UK. A larger proportion of managers in the Gulf hold university degrees in comparison with their counterparts in the USA, UK, France, Germany or Japan. Many organizations had formal career development systems and professional development programmes (Al Hashemi and Najjar 1989). While in the early days of development and urbanization in the Gulf countries the economies were dominated by expatriate managers, all Gulf countries now have explicit programmes of nationalization and are committed to creating a cadre of managers who are well educated, professionally trained and committed to a career in management (Attiyyah 1991).

Thus, Arab managers in the Gulf are very positive in their attitude towards management training. The MEIRC study found Gulf managers to be much better balanced than their Western counterparts in terms of work and family. Personality profiles show managers to be very similar as a population to Western managers. These are the doers rather than the thinkers and planners. Arab managers are adept at working in multinational environments. They revel in the kind of work culture which fosters good interpersonal skills and the techniques of relating well to others. Shared values are important to the managers and they value explicit corporate cultures based in ethical principles.

Above all, managers in Arab countries share a belief in the positive value of change. This is unsurprising because of course they have experienced more rapid change in their own lifetime than most managers elsewhere in the world.

4 Islam

Many writers have concentrated on the apparently all-pervading influence of Islam. Not all recognize the significance of the master division in Islam between the Suni and Sheikh traditions or the existence of the newer models of Islam represented in such societies as Pakistan and Malaysia, which are in some respects more Islamic than the core Arab countries. Abuznaid provides a concise review of the Islamic values related to managerial practice in the occupied territories (Abuznaid 1994). None the less there is a fundamental emphasis on an ethical framework for business and administration which differentiates management in Arab countries from that in the West and is in some ways more characteristic of the homogenous ethical underpinnings of Japanese management. Islam does not separate religious and state authority in the way that is normal in the more culturally diverse West.

A specialized subset of these concerns is represented by the studies of Islamic banking and financial institutions. These are characterized by differing accounting and financial concepts to those which form the basis of Western financial and accounting theory; in particular, the avoidance of interest on financial capital. This again is rooted in a basic moral concern for the avoidance of usury (see BANKING AND FINANCE IN THE EMERGING COUNTRIES).

Thus the fundamental ethic of Islamic finance is based on a profit and loss sharing concept. A joint venture is not an unusual mode of doing business in the Arab world. It is indeed the fundamental model. The rate of interest concept which entitles the original owners of financial capital to earn, regardless of the economic success or otherwise of the enterprise in which they are investing is regarded as improper in Islam.

This in turn impacts on financial and managerial concepts of risk, which leads to a greater involvement of financial institutions in the business affairs of their customers and depositors and thus approximates more closely to the German or Japanese model of long-term joint involvement in economic affairs rather than the Anglo-Saxon concept of short-termism and optimization of purely financial returns. It also involves banks and financial institutions in the realities of commercial and industrial enterprise.

This is not to say, therefore, that this system does not involve detailed controls of financial performance. Banks and financial institutions which aim to comply with Islamic law must subscribe to a system of audit that is controlled by the Sharia Supervisory Board which as well as supervising the audit function also oversees the function of Zakat (an essentially voluntary, but none the less expected donation from the wealthy and prosperous towards the less well-to-do). The concept of Zakat underlies the Islamic concept of social provision. It is not based on collectivist and universalist principles guaranteed by the state, as in Western and socialist countries, but is underpinned by the Islamic conception of responsibilities owed by individuals to other individuals. Islamic economics also prescribe that investment should support only products in services which are not forbidden by Islam.

There is variability in the extent to which these simple principles guide the actual financial behaviour of managers in Arab countries. However, there is a widespread understanding that they represent the ultimate touchstone according to which financial transactions should be judged. The enormous financial success of many Arab corporations testifies to their value.

Financial management under Islamic law and the dynamic potential of Islamic financial management is contrasted with the 'sterile mathematical models' of the West (Jabr and Amawi 1993).

The hierarchical and patrimonial nature of authority in Arab organizations does not guarantee efficiency and effectiveness either. There are many studies of the negative impacts of bureaucracy and inefficiency, often rooted in an exaggerated state of consciousness and concern for official form over the realities of commercial necessity. A reference to 'Egyptian administration' will often raise a smile among the sophisticated and more recently Westernized Arab managerial elite in other Arab states. Younis offers a useful overview of this and other problems affecting public administration in the Arab world (Younis 1993).

5 Leadership behaviour

The dual pull of tradition and modernity is evident in characteristic Arab managers' response to the problems of managing authority and relationships. Al-Rasheed is one of those who have compared managerial practices and organization systems in comparable Western and Arab situations. His study illustrates that the personalized concept of power leads to feelings of uncertainty and loss of autonomy among lower level organizational participants. Conversely, when problems occur, they tend to be ascribed to personal failure rather than to organizational or administrative shortcomings (Al-Rasheed 1994).

Leadership is a complex phenomenon in Arab organizations and is closely tied up with the concepts of shame and reputation. Arab culture may be characterized as a 'shame culture' rather than a 'guilt culture'. This governs relations in all areas of social life. For a female to lose her chastity brings shame upon her family, not least on her father and brothers for their failure to protect her honour. For a senior person to fail to provide hospitality for a guest is equally shameful. A good leader is one who arranges matters so as to protect his dependants from shame.

There are three ways by which this leadership can be exerted in the modern organization: (1) control through charisma; (2) control through close supervision; and (3) control through culture. A study of Palestinian companies indicates that the most common model is control through close supervision. Thus plant managers go to considerable length to demonstrate that they are highly active in supervising the behaviour of employees who cannot be trusted to act responsibly of their own accord (Nahas *et al.* 1995)

The most widely known study of behaviour and attitudes among Arab managers is Muna's book, *The Arab Executive* (Muna 1980). The personalization of relationships within Arab life is indicated by the fact that Muna thanks personally all the executives who participated in the study. Although it is a landmark study, this fact makes it easy to recognize that the study is in fact based on very small numbers, in fact fifty-two Arab executives. Muna's study indicates clearly that the typical form of decision making is consultative. Delegation is the least widely used technique. Loyalty is prized above all other organizational values, even efficiency. Loyalty can be guaranteed by surrounding the executive with subordinates whom he can trust.

Arab managers have a more flexible interpretation of time than Western management, and are able to run several meetings, often on quite unrelated topics, simultaneously. The basic rule of business with Arab managers is to establish the relationship first and only come to the heart of the intended business perhaps at a later meeting. Verbal contracts are absolute and an individual's word is his bond. Failure to meet verbally agreed obligations may be punished with dire penalties and will certainly lead to a termination of a business relationship. Nonetheless, the Arab world is essentially a trading world, governed by an implicit and extensive understanding of the requirements of commercial activity.

The most concise and comprehensive overview of the impact of Arab culture on Arab management practice is Al-Faleh's article on cultural influences on Arab management development in Jordan (Al-Faleh 1987). He identifies the importance of status, position and seniority as more important than ability and performance. The central control of organizations corresponds to a low level of delegation. Decision making is located in the upper reaches of the hierarchy, and authoritarian management styles predominate. Subordinates are deferential and obedient, especially in public in the presence of their hierarchical superiors. The consultation which is widely practised is done, however, on a one-to-one, rather than a team or group, basis. Decisions tend to emerge rather than to be located in a formal process of decision making. Prior affiliation and existing obligation are more influential than explicit performance objectives.

The formalities of social, family and political life are strictly preserved, even in managerial settings. Thus it is impossible to undertake any kind of meeting in an Arab organization without the ubiquitous coffee or tea rituals.

There are a growing number of studies which use standardized questionnaire methods and formal rating skills which claim to be culturally invariant, to study job satisfaction and organizational commitment. The results are difficult to interpret. Some studies report that Arab managers differ significantly in their commitment to their organization compared to Western managers, while others find that expatriates and Arabs share similar work values.

6 Management styles

Abbas Ali and his colleagues (1985) have undertaken several studies of the relationship between managerial decision styles and work satisfaction. They reinforce the general finding that Arab managers prefer consultative styles and are unhappy with delegation. They point, however, to the experience of political instability and to the growing fragmentation of traditional kinship structures as the origins of an ongoing conflict between authoritarian and consultative styles and the need for Arab managers to resolve this conflict by developing a pseudo-consultative style in order to create a supportive and cohesive environment among themselves.

They contrast Saudi-Arabian with North American managerial styles (see MANAGEMENT IN NORTH AMERICA). The Saudi managers use decision styles which are consultative rather than participative. Their value systems are 'outer-directed', tribalistic, conformist and socio-centric, compared to the 'inner-directed', egocentric, manipulative and existentialist perspectives of the North Americans. Whereas American organizations are tall, relatively decentralized and characterized by clear relationships, Saudi organizations are flat, authority relationships are vague, but decision making is centralized. In the USA, staffing and recruitment proceed on principles which are objective, based on comparability of standards, qualifications and experience. In Saudi organizations, selection is highly subjective, depending on personal contacts, nepotism, regionalism, and family name. Performance evaluation in Saudi is informal, with few systematic controls and established criteria, and the planning function is undeveloped and not highly regarded (Abbas Ali and Al-Shakhis 1985). Al-Hashemi and Najjar have documented the emergence of a managerial class in Bahrain in a series of publications (Al-Hashemi and Najjar 1989).

7 Conclusion

As educational standards rise, the emerging managerial cadres gain in confidence and are strengthened by the policies which steadily replace expatriate managers with nationals. This should reduce the pressures which Arab managers experience in the perceived absence of self-actualization at the workplace. But it may also produce a crisis of authority in the organization. These pressures are not dissimilar to those found in other cultures experiencing rapid social and economic change, an increasing globalization of business and the emerging power of multinational enterprise, not least in the petrochemical industries. But the overarching philosophy and belief system of Islam, the essential cohesiveness of the family and tribal structures, and the sheer economic strength of the Arab States should allow the emerging managerial cadres the opportunity to find their own routes to organizational effectiveness.

Among topics on which research is urgently needed is the question of women in management. Salman (1993) has documented the growing importance of women in the emerging managerial class in the occupied territories of Palestine.

Weir has argued that the Arab style is so significant and so pervasive, and internally coherent and distinctive, that it represents a fourth paradigm of managerial practice on a par with the Anglo-American, European and Japanese models. This view is criticized by Al-Rasheed who argues that there is still much diversity in practice among the varying components of the Arab world (Al-Rasheed 1994). There is a growing body of well-researched studies which will enable this issue to be resolved. The 'fourth paradigm' represents a promising research agenda.

DAVID WEIR
UNIVERSITY OF BRADFORD

Further reading

(References cited in the text marked *)

* Abbas Ali and Al-Shakhis, M. (1985) 'Managerial value systems for working in Saudi Arabia: an empirical investigation', *Group and Organization Studies* 10: 135–51. (One of a series of empirical studies on managerial attitudes and value systems in several Arab countries.)

* Abuznaid, S. (1994) 'Islam and management', Proceedings of the second Arab Management Conference, University of Bradford Management Centre. (Succinct review of common aspects of Islamic beliefs and practice applied to managerial obligations.)

* Al-Faleh, M. (1987) 'Cultural influences on Arab managerial development', *Journal of Management Development* 6(3): 19–33. (Summary of special features of Arab management, based on empirical research in Jordan.)

* Al-Hashemi, I. and Najjar, G. (1989) 'Strategic choices in management education: the Bahraini experience', in J. Davies (ed.), *The Challenge to Western Management Development*, London: Routledge. (One of a series of papers using statistical and attitudinal data on management education in Bahrain.)

* Al-Rasheed, A.M. (1994) 'Traditional Arab management: evidence from empirical comparative research', Proceedings of the second Arab Management Conference, University of Bradford Management Centre. (Paper based on empirical research characterizing traditional Arab management in terms of limited orientation to future and lack of delegation. Criticizes the excessive simplicity of the fourth paradigm argument.)

Alwani, M. and Weir, D.T.H. (1993, 1994, 1995) Proceedings of the first, second and third Arab Management Conferences, University of Bradford Management Centre. (Collected papers from the only regular international scholarly conference devoted to current theory and practice of management in Arab countries.)

* Attiyyah, Hamid S. (1991) 'Effectiveness of management training in Arab countries', *Journal of Management Development* 10(7): 22–9. (Rejects culture-specific theory of Arab management and finds that Arab management can use a variety of styles including Western-type participative styles; examines the implications for management training.)

* Dadfar, H. (1993) 'In search of Arab management, direction and identity', Proceedings of the first Arab Management Conference, University of Bradford Management Centre. (Develops a complex conceptual and analytical model identifying eight different types of management belief patterns and style, based on re-evaluation of extensive empirical research.)

The Economist (1998) 'Saudi Arabia: A Forecast', *The World in 1999*, London: Economist Publications, p.81. (Statistical update on Saudi Arabian economy.)

* Hickson, D. and Pugh, D. (1995) 'The Arabs of the Middle East', in *Management Worldwide*, Harmondsworth: Penguin. (Reviews the influence on Arab behaviour and belief patterns of Bedouin and tribal values, Islam, the experience of foreign domination and the economic impact of oil.)

* Hofstede, G. (1991) *Cultures and Organisations, Software of the Mind*, New York: McGraw-Hill. (Classic study integrating three decades of research on international comparative belief patterns of managers.)

* Jabr, H. and Amawi, S.T. (1993) 'Financial management in Islam', Proceedings of first Arab Management Conference, University of Bradford Management Centre. (Applies Islamic theories of financial management to the Palestinian situation.)

* Muna, F.M. (1980) *The Arab Executive*, New York: Macmillan. (Pathbreaking study based on a small sample of Arab executives identifying major aspects of attitude to work, use of time, and decision-making styles.)

* Muna, F.M. (1989) *The Making of Gulf Managers*, MEIRC Consultants. (Empirical study of management training and development in Gulf organizations, examining plans and prospects for nationalization of management cadres.)

* Nahas, F.V., Ritchie, J.B., Dyer, W.G. and Nakashian, S. (1995) 'The international dynamics of Palestinian family business', Proceedings of third Arab Management Conference, University of

Bradford Management Centre. (Empirical study of entrepreneurial and family-owned businesses in the Palestinian West Bank and Gaza and the implications for economic development.)

* Salman, H. (1993) 'Palestinian women and economic and social development in the West Bank and Gaza Strip', UNCTAD/DSD/SEU miscellaneous papers no. 4. (Study of women's contribution to the Palestinian economy, advocating measures to increase economic participation of women and development of women-owned businesses.)

* Sulieman, M. (1984) 'Senior managers in Iraqi society: their background and attitudes', unpublished PhD thesis, University of Glasgow. (Empirical study of managers in Iraq, illustrating the continuing importance of family and kin ties in managerial behaviour.)

* Tayeb, M. (1995) *The Global Business Environment*, London: Sage Publications. (Wide ranging and definitive account of business behaviour and impact of cultural factors on management practices.)

* Weir, D.T.H. (1993) 'Management in the Arab world', Proceedings of the first Arab Management Conference, University of Bradford Management Centre. (Proposes Arab management style as a fourth paradigm after US, Japanese and European.)

* Younis, T. (1993) 'An overview of contemporary administrative problems and practices in the Arab world', Proceedings of the first Arab Management Conference, University of Bradford Management Centre. (Reviews weaknesses in administrative systems in Arab countries.)

See also: BANKING AND FINANCE IN THE EMERGING COUNTRIES; HUMAN RESOURCE MANAGEMENT IN THE EMERGING COUNTRIES; MANAGEMENT EDUCATION IN THE EMERGING COUNTRIES; MANAGEMENT IN THE EMERGING COUNTRIES

Related topics in IEBM regional set: MANAGEMENT EDUCATION IN NORTH AMERICA; MANAGEMENT IN EUROPE; MANAGEMENT IN NORTH AMERICA; MANAGEMENT IN THE UNITED KINGDOM

Management in Egypt

1 **Introduction**
2 **The breeding environment of managerial problems in contemporary Egypt**
3 **Egyptian management versus Arab management**

Overview

Egypt is a unique country which acquired her character and that of her people through many varied historical experiences. Such a character has emerged through exposure to many cultures, religions and value systems. It is interesting to note that Egypt has been the common denominator in all the empires which have ruled or aspired to rule the world throughout history, including the USA which is the sole superpower at the present time.

Research, however, has not established a dominant mode of Egyptian managerial behaviour. For a variety of reasons – which will be explained later – generalizations cannot be drawn from other Arab countries to the Egyptian context. However, both historical developments and modern influences refer to a mixture of managerial styles practised in Egypt. They tend to differ depending on the context of the practice as well as the age and education of the practising manager.

1 Introduction

Egypt: The context of managerial practice

As to the context of managerial practice, governmental entities for the most part usually display traditional, bureaucratic, and authoritarian tendencies both in management style and organizational structure. Managers tend to manage 'by the book' and 'red tape' abounds. Hence, there are unending calls for administrative reform and equally unsuccessful attempts at that reform. An indication of that phenomena, which may be shocking, yet true, is that there are three million Egyptian government employees, receiving salaries, which the government does not need according to the present Egyptian Minister for Management Development (Fahmi 1998).

In the context of the public sector, managerial practices have differed depending on the 'personality' of the manager, his personal clout and his own ability to negotiate the corridors of powers and commerce. As much of the managerial class in the public sector was drawn from ex-army and ex-police officers, the fate of their public sector companies tended to vary according to their influence, training, personal goals and honesty. Many failures, however, were evident. Hence the recent divestiture of the public sector to 'privatization.'

As for the managers in the private sector, where profit is the ultimate measure of success, efficiency and effectiveness are critical in the employment and retention of managers. Similarly, the emphasis is on their age, training and education, at home and abroad. Their compensation is very generous by Egyptian standards. Hence, managers in the private sector tend to resemble more closely their counterparts in the more advanced parts of the world than their Egyptian peers in the government and public sector. This results in a prevalence of a more consultative and genuinely participative style, as is more common in the Western world.

To be able to understand these observations further, an examination of the political–economic as well as an administrative background of Egypt is necessary.

Egypt: a political–economic background

As in many other economically less-advanced countries, Egypt – a country of about 65 million – people has attempted to leap into the modern age since her 1952 revolution. Emerging from oppressive colonialism, Egypt has attempted to ensure mastery over her own economic destiny. Being a smaller, rather impoverished country, weary of outsiders' exploitation of her resources, the only way to create viable industrial entities of reasonably competitive size was to create a strong public sector – or at least so it seemed at the time.

Through the Nasser years (1952–70), massive public organizations were the vehicles of choice for rapid economic development. At that time, the espoused ideology was socialism. In 1970, as Sadat took over, that trend – for a variety of reasons – was brought to a grinding halt. A new economic policy that became known as the 'Open Door Policy', characterized by 'rampant capitalism' replaced the 'hesitant socialism' of the Nasser years. The public sector fell into serious disfavour. As Sadat's regime fell behind the backdoor of history and the new regime of his successor, Mubarak, came to the forefront, a more tolerant or rather ambivalent mood concerning the public sector prevailed. Yet, the controversy as to what is the proper mix between private and public enterprise was never fully resolved. Subsequently, however, under pressure from the World Bank for 'economic reform,' a vigorous programme of privatization has been taking place.

Despite the glowing picture of the economy often painted by the government and generally endorsed by the World Bank, many problems continue to confront the government and the people. Problems of poverty, inflation, constant shortages, lack of services and maintenance abound. Corruption is widespread. Various reasons and excuses for the nation's problems are constantly invented. One would be lead to believe that there are many scapegoats and few real culprits. The greatest of all scapegoats, behind which most officials and professional bureaucrats hide, is that of *lack of money*. It is often the one and only villain.

A great deal of discussion has been going on for some time about the true causes of the state of affairs just described. There seems to be reasonable agreement on the following causes, which are presented here in no particular order:

1 the population explosion;
2 limited availability of financial and other material resources;
3 a low level of productivity of the labour force;

4   the brain drain;
5   administrative inefficiency and ineffectiveness.

Obviously such problems cannot be dealt with merely through the infusion of more money. One of the fashionable solutions to such dilemmas – as we indicated – has been to resort to the privatization of many public sector entities, something which is now being carried out in earnest by Egypt.

Egypt: an administrative background

The history of 'public to private' emergence in Egypt also reflects the history of managerial emergence. From a dark bureaucratic history is now emerging a managerial class which is well-trained, modern and capable of achieving major transformations in the country. This is evidenced by their contributions to what is called the 'Great Project Era', that is the era during which the Cairo underground has been completed and the New Nile Delta project in southern Egypt is being carried out.

   Although Egypt is one of the cradles of civilization, and as such has been researched over and over in many areas, its management research has lagged far behind. And even though one of its oldest monuments, the Great Pyramids of Guiza, is a grand testimony to the practice of management, its modern managerial practices have also lagged far behind. Egyptian administrative structures as well as the actual practices of Egyptian managers represent one of the oldest bureaucratic systems and practices in the world. Egypt's river civilization since the time of the Pharaohs and the need to distribute waters fairly among its users, have forced the citizenry to surrender some of their freedoms to a higher authority – 'The Pharaoh' – in exchange for fair water distribution, an absence of conflict and a guarantee of regular and secure cultivation of their land. It is this which brought about the birth of one of the oldest authoritarian (and bureaucratic) systems of government in the world.

   The occupation of Egypt by several empires throughout history, for example the Roman, the Ottoman and the British empires, has only added to that tendency towards bureaucratization and authoritarianism, as those empires' systems of governance were both authoritarian and bureaucratic. In addition, the nature of being an-almost 'eternal colony' has fortified the tendency to adopt the systems of the rulers as well as the native-grown tendency towards submission, accepting authoritarianism and playing the bureaucratic game to the hilt. That game has its own benefits in dealing with colonialism and its natural autocratic tendencies.

2   The breeding environment of managerial problems in contemporary Egypt

El Salmi (1992: 164) a former Minister of Management Development in Egypt, a University Professor and an astute student of Egyptian Management refers to some factors, which he believes – as we do – negatively affect the contemporary Egyptian environment of management (see MANAGEMENT IN THE ARAB WORLD). Among these are societal negatives and value negatives, which will now be discussed in turn.

Societal negatives

Three main categories of societal negatives can be identified:

1 A great expansion in social ills such as bribery, nepotism, 'clique-ism' and an acceptance by large sectors of the society that these are the principal bases for getting things done and getting ahead.

2 A noticeable weakening of the authority of the law and of the executive powers of the state organs. Hence, there are widespread violations of the law in many aspects of life, making it difficult for both the average citizen as well as the professional manager to function properly (efficiently and effectively). Examples of these violations can be found in the lack of respect for traffic laws, stealing electricity, taking over public property, importing and distributing damaged goods, distributing poisoned foods to school children, selling old modified imported clothes as new, escaping tax payments, etc.)

3 A massive expansion of apathy and carelessness in dealing with problems. This has resulted from or is coupled with the deteriorating state of living conditions. The whole situation contributes to a state of national depression and hopelessness which is manifested in the tendency to accept what would normally be unacceptable living conditions.

Value negatives

In recent years, and notably since Sadat's 'Open Door Policy,' new negative values and attitudes have appeared which glorify wrong doers, encourage the emulation of negative role models, celebrate the importation of models of behaviour from abroad regardless of their appropriateness to Egyptian society, and exhalts wealth and quick profit regardless of the source, the method or the impact.

While some of these newly adopted values present hindrances to the Egyptian society and to the journey of Egyptian management towards development and prosperity, some of the old traditional values also present obstacles to managerial efforts, whether we are considering the government, the public sector, the private sector or even the non-governmental sector.

3 Egyptian management versus Arab management

If no one dominant managerial style emerges as the Egyptian style, one is tempted to extend the analysis of Arab management to Egypt – and assume that whatever is Arab must be Egyptian also (see MANAGEMENT IN THE ARAB WORLD). Indeed, many writers, Egyptian, Arab and Western, insist on identifying Egypt as an Arab country and hence claim that whatever applies to any Arab country also applies to Egypt. However, the keen observer can plainly see that Egypt is far more than being an Arab country. For example, Egypt cannot be described as an Arab Gulf country. The 'gulf' between Egypt and Gulf countries is far and wide. For example, Egyptians do not display the tribalistic mentality and the rigid and tense modes of behaviour apparent in the Gulf. Similarly, Egypt cannot be grouped with the Western part of the Arab World – Algeria, Tunisia and Morocco. For example, Egypt does not reflect the French influence found in those countries.

Indeed, once again, we state that Egypt is a unique country. She encompasses influences from many civilizations and cultures. Her present character and environment as well as the character of her people reflect those civilizations and cultures. Nasser (1953), the leader of Egypt's 1952 revolution, summarized it succinctly when he described Egypt as the centre of three circles: Arab, African and Islamic. Egypt is certainly so and more. Egypt borders three major continents, *Africa*, of which it is an integral part, *Asia*, in which her Sinai Peninsula is located geographically and from where her various rulers often came from diverse Asian empires and *Europe*, for Egypt borders the southern shore of the Mediterranean sea while Europe occupies its northern shore. Egypt has experienced both French and British colonialism, and thus their influence. Furthermore, Egypt, besides reflecting the Muslim influence, reflects the Christian Coptic orthodox influence. In addition to reflecting the pharaonic civilization, reflects the Islamic one. As well as being an ancient agricultural country, she is also a modern industrial country. In short, Egypt is a semi-Arab, semi-European, semi-African and semi-Asian country, reflecting a rich religious heritage representing the major world religions. Egypt also reflects various historical influences: ancient pharaonic, middle age Islamic and modern European.

That massive journey through history has left Egyptians, including Egyptian managers, with some unique personal characteristics, some of which are almost paradoxical. For example, Egyptians are famous for their sense of humour – a characteristic not so evident in Gulf Arab people. Yet Egypt has a massive heritage of sad and sorrowful songs. Egyptians have a tendency to be economical with the truth, condone lies and be hypocritical – behaviour which they may have developed to cope with colonialism and preserve their identity. Yet, they value honesty and goodness and trace it to their rich religious heritage. They tend to show cruelty towards subordinates while behaving submissively towards superiors, thus emulating their colonial masters. Egyptians tend to be both authoritarian and patriarchal in running their affairs, yet they are famous for their kindness and non-violence. At times, they are rigid and uncompromising while at other times they display a surprising sense of compromise and accommodation. They tend to be accepting and supportive of their superiors' opinions, yet they tend to be highly opinionated and stubborn with their peers, subordinates and children. Those characteristics are evident in Egyptian managers and as such it becomes difficult to pinpoint Egyptian managers to a particular style or a permanent mode of behaviour. Indeed, the same Egyptian manager tends to reflect a theory X orientation as well as a theory Y orientation at varying times as he faces different people and situations, making them difficult to read and predict by outsiders and often by insiders as well.

MAHMOUD SALEM
SULTAN QABOOS UNIVERSITY

Further reading

(References cited in the text marked *)

Abbas Ali (1993) 'Decision-making style, individualism, and attitudes towards risk of Arab executives', *International Studies of Management and Organization* 23(3): 53–73. (A study which focuses on testing instruments which the author sees as relevant to Arab societies.)

Al-Rasheed, A.M. (1994) 'Traditional Arab management: evidence from empirical comparative research', *Proceedings of the Second Arab Management Conference*, University of Bradford Management Centre. (Does not agree that a fourth paradigm is emerging to represent Arab management, and describes it based on empirical research – as having limited orientation to the future as well as to the process of delegation.)

Badawy, M.K. (1980) 'Styles of mid-eastern managers', *California Management Review* XXII (2): 51–8. (A study of management styles of mid-eastern executives (middle managers) from Saudi Arabia, Kuwait, Abu Dhabi, Bahrain, Oman and the United Arab Emirates.)

Elsayed-Elkhouly, S.M. and Buda, R. (1996), 'Organizational conflict: a comparative analysis of conflict styles across cultures', *The International Journal of Conflict Management* 7(1): pp. 71–81.

Elsayed-Elkhouly, S.M. and Buda, R. (1997), 'A cross-cultural comparison of value systems of Egyptian, American, African and Arab executives,' *International Journal of Commerce and Management* 7(3/4): 102–19. (An empirical study of the value systems of a large number of executives which found that Egyptian executives were least similar to American executives and to a lesser degree to African and Arabian executives.)

* El-Salmi, A. (1992) *Egyptian Management in Face of the New Realities* (In Arabic: Al-Idarah Al-Misreyah Fi Mowagahat Al-Waqee Al-Gadid): Cairo: Maktabat Gharib. (A brilliant and sincere analysis of contemporary Egyptian management, its problems and challenges as it faces the future.)

Hatem, T. (1994) 'Egypt: exploring management in the Middle East', *International Journal of Management and Organization* 24(1,2): 116–36. (An exploration of the problems of doing managerial research in Egypt.)

Hofstede, G. (1991) *Cultures and Organizations, Software of the Mind*, New York: McGraw-Hill. (A major comparative study which deals with managerial beliefs as they reflect cultural characteristics.)

Ibrahim, N.A. and Angelidis, J.A. (1994) 'Cross national differences in social responsiveness: a study of American and Egyptian business students', *International Journal of Management* 11(3): 815–26. (A study of the differences between American and Egyptian business students regarding their perceptions of corporate social responsibility.)

* Fahmi, M. (1998) 'Three million employees receive salaries, but the Government does not need them', *Rose-El-Yousif* 68 (3677): 30 (in Arabic). (An interesting interview with the Egyptian Minister of Management Development about the administrative problems of the present Egyptian Government Apparatus.)

Muna, F. (1980) *The Arab Executive*, New York: Macmillan. (Although based on a small sample of Arab executives, this ground-breaking study deals with decision-making styles, time utilization and attitudes towards work.)

* Nasser, Gamal Abd El- (1953) *Philosophy of the Revolution*. (The defining document of the Egyptian 1952 revolution that changed the face of Egypt from a monarchy to a republic.)

Pienta, D.A., Natale, S.M. and Sora, S.A. (1988) 'What is the impact of values on management?' *International Journal of Value Based Management* 1 (1). (Basically, a review of research on the impact of values on management whose understanding helps grasp the differences between some aspects of management in different cultural contexts.)

Political Handbook of the World (1998) pp. 277–85. (A handbook of up-to-date information on various countries of the world.)

Posusney, M.P. (1999) *Labor and the State in Egypt*, New York: Columbia University Press. (A monograph on the Egyptian workers and unions.)

Salem, M. (1994) 'Strategic planning for development in view of contemporary global changes', (in Arabic) *Al-EDARI* 16(57): 129–56. (Explores the impact of global contemporary changes on Arab development and its managing (especially in the Gulf country of Oman).)

Smith, B. (1999) 'Survey: Egypt', *The Economist*, 20 March, p.18. (An up-to-date overview of Egyptian economic business trends.)

Valsan, E.H. (1990) 'Egypt', in Subramaniam (ed.), *Public Administration in the Third World: An International Handbook*, pp. 131–55, New York: Greenwood Press. (A chapter containing an excellent analysis of and commentary on public administration's history and contemporary problems in Egypt.)

Weir, D.T.H. (1993) 'Management in the Arab World', *Proceedings of the First Arab Management Conference*, University of Bradford Management Centre. (An overview of management in the Arab world which suggests the potential emergence of an Arab management style comparable to the preceding American, European and Japanese styles.)

See also: BUSINESS CULTURES, THE EMERGING COUNTRIES; MANAGEMENT EDUCATION IN THE EMERGING COUNTRIES; MANAGEMENT IN THE ARAB WORLD; MANAGEMENT IN THE EMERGING COUNTRIES; MANAGEMENT IN JORDAN; MANAGEMENT IN THE GULF STATES; MANAGEMENT IN SAUDI ARABIA

Related topics in the IEBM regional set: MANAGEMENT IN ASIA PACIFIC; MANAGEMENT IN EUROPE; MANAGEMENT IN JAPAN; MANAGEMENT IN NORTH AMERICA

Management in the Gulf States

1 Introduction
2 Management in the Gulf
3 The making of Gulf managers
4 Management behaviour
5 Conclusion

Overview

The Gulf region is in some respects unique and in others demonstrates characteristics of the fast-growing economies dependent to a large extent on the immigrant, expatriate and temporary labour characteristics of such regions. In terms of income per capita the Gulf region contains some of the fastest-growing economies in the world. The Gulf regions consist almost entirely of city-state economies, including Kuwait, Bahrain, Dubai, Abu Dhabi and Sharjah. Most are linked by their common membership of the Gulf Co-operation Council, which may be seen as a nascent economic community fostering the possibilities of significant investment and employment potential. Oman is a little different in some ways but shares some common characteristics with the Gulf economies.

The emerging and evolving Gulf managerial style is neither Western nor Eastern but is greatly influenced by the distinctive culture of the Gulf and of the characteristics and values of Arab social organization. Consultation rather than centralized and autocratic decision making is a natural and preferred decision style. Management behaviour is rooted in the traditions and writings that organize Arabic society as a specific historical form. The culture of Gulf management is a culture of talking rather than writing and of interpersonal relations rather than of formal structures.

1 Introduction

The Gulf region consists of city-state economies, including Kuwait, Bahrain, Dubai, Abu Dhabi and Sharjah. Although commonly linked as one state, there are differences between the Gulf States and their economies, which should not be overlooked. The distribution of natural resources is uneven. Within the United Arab Emirates, for example, Abu Dhabi has oil and gas resources sufficient to satisfy predicted demands for over 900 years at present rates of consumption; Dubai, however, its nearest neighbour only an hour and a half drive away, has reserves for only the next 20 years. Dubai by contrast has built on the trading culture, originally developed around the port facilities of the creek and the historically significant port of Deira, which for countless generations has dominated the cross-Gulf trade. It has especially significant contacts with Iran, and has continued to look outwards and develop a free trade culture which has proven a powerful matrix for international business development and diversification. The free port facilities of Jebel Ali, the world's largest man-made hole, the airport cargo village and the dry dock facility, while impressive civil engineering projects in their own right, all stem from the same philosophy of openness to the global economy. Likewise, the routing schedules of Emirates Airlines permitting access between the markets of Western Europe, North America, Dubai and the major Far East hubs of Hong Kong and Singapore are designed to suit the arrival and destination requirements of international business travellers. This airline has for several years dominated the ratings for the best business air carrier in the world.

Kuwait's impressive economic growth in the 1970s and 1980s came to an abrupt halt with the Iraqi invasion. Its economy was supported by expatriate managers and workers from other Arab countries, notably from Iraq itself, Jordan and the Palestinian West Bank. Following the resumption of peace in Kuwait, each of these national groupings became much less significant. The problem then became one of training and developing indigenous Kuwaiti management capability. The heavy dependence on the chemical and oil-based industries was also reviewed to create the possibility of Kuwait developing capability in international financial services. The Kuwait investment office had for years, moreover, been investing steadily in good stocks in European and North American capital markets.

Bahrain has had considerable success in developing into a service-based economy. Tourism and particularly tourism from Western Europe has grown steadily as hotels and leisure facilities have developed to support it. Sport and leisure growth remains a very strong vector of development in Dubai, while in its neighbour Abu Dhabi, public sector and public service organizations have found the more bureaucratic style of government an appropriate milieu.

Despite the success of these economies in recent years, they have evaded the attention of most serious business academics (e.g. Hampden-Turner 1993). In the city-state political and economic environment, political control and centralized direction are possible. In several of the Gulf city-state economies these means have been used to develop highly competitive, open and characteristically capitalistic economies. In addition to indigenous enterprise a number of multinational companies, largely but not exclusively pointed to petro-chemical exploitation and downstream manufacturing, have continued to operate with great success. There thus exists a complicated matrix of organizational structure and management behaviour and practices. Multicultural workforces with a large proportion of expatriates are commonplace. During the past few years there have been strong political pressures towards reducing the number of expatriates and progressively nationalizing the professional, technical and managerial labour forces. Alsane (1994) describes some of the trends in governmental thinking towards emerging managerialism.

2 Management in the Gulf

Over the past thirty years in the development of the Gulf economies and societies education has been a major object of national policies (see MANAGEMENT IN THE ARAB WORLD). A classic study by Al-Hashemi and Al-Najjar (1993) in Bahrain demonstrated that between 25 and 30 per cent of managers in Bahrain organizations were educated at least to degree level in subjects related to their managerial activities. Corresponding proportions in Western societies would be rather less and in the UK at the present under 10 per cent. It is illusory to believe that the economic success of the Gulf society has been based solely on oil and is measurable in terms of camels, tents and sand. These are highly educated managerial labour forces with aspirations of career success and developing economic and professional achievement at least equivalent to those that exist in Western economy. Specifically since the oil price rise the growing relative affluence of these economies has exposed professional managers to the best of managerial models extant in other societies in the USA, Europe and Japan and the Far East.

Al-Hashemi and Najjar also find that the managerial labour force is increasingly well educated even by North American norms, and has developed a realistic self-image setting strict performance standards. Managers wish to take advantage of opportunities for professional self-renewal and, within the context of the authoritarian autocratic power structures of society, are increasingly demanding inclusion in the decision-making process at organizational, if not at national, political level.

Among the key tasks for professional managers in Bahrain are those of moderating demands for individual achievement in the interests of the largely collectivist approach to organization and society characteristic of the Arab world. Aspirations for many managers in the Gulf States have been limited towards the public sector in which status, official position, prestige and non-financial marks of achievement have been paramount. Thus the drive for qualification in some aspects of the public service can become an end in itself. Aspirations for individual managers tend to be incapable of being totally satisfied within conventional organizational hierarchies. Therefore there is a high rate of formation of many industrial and commercial groups, sometimes oriented around a mini financial institution or bank as a means of satisfying individuals' aspirational needs. Inevitably, as in most of the Arab world, these organizations tend to have familial and kin-based structures supportive of these family-type networks. Thus the very concept of 'manager' dissociated from a cultural, familial and local context is misleading applied to these managerial organizations. Nonetheless Al-Hashemi and Najjar find that there are pressures towards professionalization and increasing consciousness of management as a class within Bahraini society.

Mezal (1991) contrasted the managerial background patterns and attitudes of Arab managerial cadres in Kuwait and Egypt. His study also supports the finding of increasing educational and professional qualification among Kuwaiti managers in his sample, who are younger, better qualified and in many respects more Westernized than their counterparts in Egyptian society. But they are similarly interested in job security as a more desirable outcome even than expanded promotion opportunities.

3 The making of Gulf managers

The most authoritative source of data about management in the Gulf is the MEIRC report on 'the making of Gulf managers' (see MANAGEMENT EDUCATION IN THE EMERGING COUNTRIES). This has provided a basis for comparison for many significant studies since its publication in 1989. More Gulf managers hold university degrees than their counterparts in the USA, the UK, France, Germany and Japan and moreover receive far more management training per year even than American and UK managers. The most important characteristics for managerial success, none the less, are family upbringing, quality of education and early experience. Unsurprisingly, many subsequent studies in the Gulf have concentrated on recruitment and selection as well as training and development. Even in 1989 MEIRC found several examples of good and even 'outstanding' practice in the large Gulf employers. But he also found that amongst small and medium enterprises and developing organizations more characteristically traditional forms of management and organization are prevalent.

It is appropriate to review management in the Gulf countries as a whole because the MEIRC study finds there is a higher degree of homogeneity amongst managers from the six GCC countries, supervening nationality as a statistically significant factor. The differences, in other words, are clearly outweighed by the similarities. The study points to an emerging and evolving Gulf managerial style, which is neither Western nor Eastern but is greatly influenced 'by the distinctive and particular culture of the Gulf'. Consultation rather than centralized and autocratic decision making is a natural and preferred decision style. Subordinates in the Gulf mirror these expectations by not expecting to participate in the decision making but having high expectations that they will be consulted. These findings demonstrate that Western-style organizational democracy and Japanese bottom-up consensus decision making are equally irrelevant to the preferred style in Gulf organizations.

Gulf managers prefer structures that are stable, even fixed, but in which they have powers of discretion within predictable limits. They prefer the decision making of their superiors in office to be decisive and responsible and not to have to take out-of-range decisions at their own level. None the less, they find that decision making is illegitimate unless it is accompanied by the appropriate level of consultation. This consultation is expected to involve incorporation in thinking and explanations that lie behind the need for specific senior management decisions.

4 Management behaviour

The Arab world is a blend of traditional and modern influences (see BUSINESS CULTURES, THE EMERGING COUNTRIES). In explaining why particular forms of behaviour are appropriate, Gulf managers are likely to refer not to Western or Eastern managers and philosophies of management but to behaviours and philosophies rooted in the traditions and writings that organize Arabic society as a specific historical form. Thus explanations in terms of the responsibility of the head of tribe to consult even the most junior members of the family in a 'majlis' setting are invoked in order to justify particular contemporary management practices. 'Management by walking about', identified in the West by the writings of Tom Peters, is justified by Gulf managers by reference to the practice of Khalif Omar Ibin Al-Khattab. He visited his people regularly to see and hear at first hand their problems and grievances. Khalif Omar, known for his 'priority, justice and patriarchal simplicity and his irreproachable character', is quoted as a role model more often than Bill Gates. Respect is accorded in Gulf organizations to subordinates who approach superiors with problems to which they have already preconfigured an appropriate solution. But they do not own the solution. It is for the organizational head to make a decision on his wider knowledge of the whole situation.

Above all, the culture of Gulf management is a culture of talking rather than writing and of interpersonal relations rather than of formal structures. The more important the context and subject matter of the decision, the more necessary is personal and face-to-face interaction. A meeting even of as little as one hour on a transcontinental trip may be significant in sealing a significant business deal. The use of personal networks, connections and coalitions to support face-to-face interactions is essential. As it is difficult within the culture of the Middle East to say 'no' face to face, successful managers are seen as those who have developed the capability to give negative messages while maintaining strong interpersonal support which will become the basis for future business.

The models on which successful Gulf organizations are based are exemplified in communication practices and descriptions of roles. Thus heads of organizations will speak of themselves as the 'head of the family'. This gives the necessary empowerment for decision making and decisive intervention, and also the ability to offer social supports, assessments and development.

A key dimension, nonetheless, of management in the Gulf has been the existence, often at high organizational levels, but throughout organizations more generally, of expatriate managers. A strong dimension within Gulf societies over the past few years has been the attempt to reduce dependence on expatriate managers and to 'nationalize' the processes and practices of management. Companies such as Emirates Airlines which have produced a meld of the best practices of global management suitabll tailored to Middle Eastern conditions are nonetheless embarked on a consistent process of replacing expatriate managers with locals whenever this can be done without detriment to operating performance and economic viability. The key to the utilization of both expatriate and local managers is therefore professionalism based on training and qualifications (Wilson 1993).

Within most of the Gulf, expatriate managers comprise both Eastern and Asian and in particular Indian and Pakistani managers as well as those of Western origin. Within any particular Gulf country expatriates bring different expectations and behavioural practices which, historically, have not always been in tune with local expectations. However, increasingly a common set of behavioural patterns involving a blend of expatriate and local practices has emerged. The MEIRC study showed that expatriate managers were valued for their know-how, expertise, hard work, professional discipline, organizational attention to detail and their ability to work within and tolerate the perceived differences of local culture. In early years some expatriate managers were noted for their lack of respect for local cultural practices, arrogance, materialism and perceived opposition to the training and development of nationals. But in the ten years since the MEIRC study these differences have been modified and moderated. The present situation is one in which expatriate and national managers work in most cases well together. Nonetheless, there has been an increasing use of Western-style management practices such as assessment centres documented by Wilson, Alsane and others. Bank and Vinnicombe have studied the growth of women managers in the Gulf countries. Many of these have come from the Indian subcontinent and thus have a double set of cultural hurdles to overcome (Bank and Vinnicombe 1994).

Recent studies have built on the growing sophistication and capability and competence of the managerial labour force in Gulf countries. A recent study by Abbas Ali *et al.* (1999) has focused on perceptions by Kuwaiti managers of the requirement and innovative behaviour in the Kuwaiti market and the Gulf region in particular. Managerial practices learnt in many Western countries may have led to a lack of flexibility and variability in dealing with the increasingly sophisticated expectations of Kuwaiti managers.

Mustapha *et al.* (1997) have surveyed the implementation of quality assurance (QA) systems in the UAE. They point out that the UAE is the most buoyant market in the Gulf region, with many multinational companies operating in industry and commerce.

The determination of Gulf-based enterprise to remain at the leading edge of managerial practices is shown by the rapid implementation of QA and total quality (TQ) systems in advance in many cases of their Western counterparts. Most of the surveyed companies had implemented such systems within the last two years and had done so within the period comparable with that required by Western companies. The major reason for implementation was to gain competitive advantage and support was provided at all levels although the characteristic resistance of some middle managers found in most Western studies was also reported in the UAE survey. Training and motivation, communication, the use of external QA consultants and the organizational judgement of the cost effectiveness of the systems, once implemented, followed similar patterns to those experienced in the West.

Education continues to be of the utmost significance in the planning of the leaders of the Gulf States. Many have preferred to restrict local higher education institutions to bachelors-level programmes, preferring to benchmark their educational standing against the best international providers. This has meant that masters and doctoral work has not developed as quickly. The 1990s have seen an influx of universities from North America, Europe and Australasia offering programmes, for example, of the MBA type. Not all of these have been successful. Those that have worked best have been those that have found strong local partners and have maintained a significant permanent presence of staff in the region.

Higher education facilities for men and women have typically been segregated. The likelihood is that their tendency towards indigenization of Gulf enterprises and institutions will affect higher education and specifically management education over the next few years. We are likely therefore to see a growth in partnership and joint venture management development and training programmes rather than franchise and direct representation of Western business schools (see MANAGEMENT EDUCATION IN THE EMERGING COUNTRIES).

5 Conclusion

It is clear that the UAE and its organizations operate in a fast-developing cultural matrix in which the legal structure, tax legislation, and societal disincentives to rapid economic progress have largely been overtaken by a combination of public policy and free enterprise operating in conditions of relative affluence. In this context management is expected to operate at the leading edge and to represent state-of-the-art characteristics. Studies by Wilson and others indicate that this is true of the larger organizations. Studies by Al-Shamali and others demonstrate that sectoral and industrial characteristics are equally important (Al-Shamali and Wild 1995).

None the less, the enduring features of management in Arab countries can be endemically linked to the characteristics and values of Arab social organization. Weir has postulated that these features, far from being deviant or outlying versions of Western or Pacific Rim management models, may provide the basis for a style of management organization well suited to the growing requirements of a networked global society, based on own information transmission capabilities, city-state economies, and business and management relations based on the enduring values of professional competence rooted in the experience of strong interpersonal relationships, trust and mutuality of respect. In this way, therefore, the emerging management styles and behaviours of the Gulf region may indeed represent 'a fourth paradigm' (Weir 1990).

DAVID T.H. WEIR
NEWCASTLE BUSINESS SCHOOL
UNIVERSITY OF NORTHUMBRIA AT NEWCASTLE

Further reading

(References cited in the text marked *)

* Abbas Ali, Taqi, A.A. and Camp, R.C. (1999) 'Kuwaiti managers' perception of a lack of creativity: a three national comparison', *Middle East Business Review* 3(1). (Compares Kuwaiti managers' perceptions of creativity with Western norms.)
* Al-Hashemi, I.S.J. and Najjar, G. (1993) 'The making of Bahraini managers: Metamorphosis 2000', in *Proceedings of Arab Management Conference 1993*, University of Bradford Management Centre. (Reports on a major study of Bahraini managers, showing influence of education in developing a well-trained managerial elite. Demonstrates changing patterns of aspirations and shows pattern of 'partial' inclusion as Bahraini managers push for greater organizational mobility.)
* Alsane, N. (1994) 'Developing management in the countries of the Gulf Co-operative Council', in *Proceedings of the Arab Management Conference 1994*, University of Bradford Management Centre 4. (Reviews trends in governmental thinking from the perspective of a politician and consultant, reflecting on the emerging managerialism in Gulf countries.)
* Al-Shamali, A.D. and Wild, K.L. (1995) 'Marketing management and Middle East firms', in *Proceedings of Arab Management Conference 1995*, University of Bradford Management Centre. (Reports on a study of car dealerships in Kuwait.)
* Bank, J. and Vinnicombe, S. (1994) 'A door opens: women in management in the UAE', in *Proceedings of Arab Management Conference 1994*, University of Bradford Management Centre. (Reviews evidence for growing importance of women in management in UAE, owing to the factors of nationalization, education, national wealth, women's associations, favourable work day design, a family-friendly national culture, support for child-care arrangements and changing women's attitudes.)
* Hampden-Turner, C. (1993) *The Seven Cultures of Capitalism*, London: Piatkus. (Reviews value systems sustaining and encouraging the development of capitalism in seven cultures, comprehensively ignoring the Arab world.)
  MEIRC (1993) *The Making of Gulf Managers*, Dubai. (Reviews results of a study of 177 Gulf managers, interviews with expatriates and training managers, with commentary by Nasser Alsane.)

* Mezal, F. (1991) 'Comparison of Kuwaiti and Egyptian managers' attitudes and behaviour', Unpublished paper. (Contrasts Kuwaiti and Egyptian managers' attitudes, expectations and behaviour.)

Muna, F.M. (1980) *The Arab Executive,* New York: Macmillan. (Pathbreaking study based on a small sample of Arab executives identifying major aspects of attitude to work, use of time, and decision-making styles.)

* Mustapha, F.H., Al-Nakib, A.A.L. and Al-Hajari, N. (1997) 'Implementation of quality assurance systems in the United Arab Emirates', *Middle East Business Review* 2(1). (Shows rapid uptake and introduction of QA systems in UAE organizations, up to and ahead of Western norms.)

Ohmae, K. (1995) *The End of the Nation State*, London: Harper Collins. (Reviews the Globalization Thesis, and concludes that the most dynamic economies are those based on 'city states': cites several examples, mainly from the Far East, North America and Europe but omits the Middle East, including the Gulf region in which several very successful city-state examples may be found.)

* Weir, D.T.H. (1999) 'Management in the Arab world: a fourth paradigm', in Al-Shamali, A. and Denton, J. (eds), *Arab Business: The Globalisation Imperative*, Bristol: Bristol Academic Press. (Reviews significance of Arab world in global management, and the surprising ignorance of Arab management in Western textbook and monograph treatment: develops thesis that the behaviour and practices of management in the Arab world constitute a 'fourth paradigm' distinct from the Western, Japanese and European models.)

* Wilson, C. (1993) 'Training for quality' and 'Training the UAE managers', in *Proceedings of Arab Management Conference 1993*, University of Bradford Management Centre. (Reviews management selection, training and development practices in Emirates Airlines.)

See also: BUSINESS CULTURES, THE EMERGING COUNTRIES; MANAGEMENT EDUCATION IN THE EMERGING COUNTRIES; MANAGEMENT IN THE ARAB WORLD; MANAGEMENT IN EGYPT; MANAGEMENT IN THE EMERGING COUNTRIES; MANAGEMENT IN JORDAN

Related topics in the IEBM regional set: MANAGEMENT IN ASIA PACIFIC; MANAGEMENT IN EUROPE; MANAGEMENT IN NORTH AMERICA

Management in Iran

1 Introduction
2 Analysis
3 Conclusion

Overview

The environment within which Iranian managers operate is volatile and intensely political. The economy and indeed the society as a whole were reconstructed after the 1979 revolution on an Islamic model, which permeates both the private and public lives of peoples and organizations. In addition, the managers are constrained by certain problems such as skills shortages, inadequate infrastructure and difficulty of access to advanced technologies, which in turn deprive them of the professionalism they require and limit their scope for innovation and excellence. Also, certain cultural characteristics, such as scepticism and mistrust in others, evolved over thousands of years and influenced by various historical events, have resulted in centralized organizations with limited scope for participation and cross-fertilization of ideas.

1 Introduction

Iran, situated in the Middle East, almost at the centre of Asia in the northern hemisphere, is the seventh largest country in the world (1,648,000 sq km). Its population, estimated over 66 million in 1998, is a young one with 44 per cent under 14 and about 4 per cent over 65 years of age. The literacy rate is around 72 per cent, with the rate being higher in urban areas than rural regions and slightly higher among men than women.

Iran is OPEC's second largest oil producer and accounts for roughly 5 per cent of the global oil output. The country holds 9 per cent of the world's oil reserves and 15 per cent of its natural gas reserves. In 1992, the most recent date for which data are available, oil accounted for 23.3 per cent of GNP, but it constituted 85 per cent of export revenues as of 1996. The other 15 per cent comes mainly from carpets, fruits, nuts, iron and steel.

2 Analysis

Islamic revolution and business in Iran

Iranian managers work in a turbulent environment which has seen many changes, especially since the mid-1970s, and has not yet settled down. There are various elements in this environment which have left their imprints on the management styles of these managers. The Islamic revolution, which followed a few years of civil and industrial unrest during the last stage of the Shah's reign, set the scene. The 1980s began with a devastating and debilitating war with Iraq, which lasted for eight years and drained the country of its resources, both natural and human, and brought the

316

country's process of economic development and industrialization to a grinding halt. The war interrupted the export of oil and left much of the country's oil installation and other industries and the infrastructure in ruins. The total damage is estimated at around US$400 million in addition to some US$90 billion of the financial costs of military activities.

In addition, because of the changes in relations between Iran and major Western countries, there was an almost overnight halt to foreign direct investment which had hitherto provided some of the momentum for the economic growth. Later, for one reason or another, sanctions were piled upon sanctions which aggravated these already uneasy relations, and which in turn had serious implications for Iran's economy in general and its business in particular.

Foreign direct investment from non-Western countries, especially those in southeast Asia, was the first to flow slowly in again after the end of war with Iraq in the late 1980s and has increased gradually since then. In the late 1990s efforts were made, by all sides concerned, to improve the relations with Western nations, and a few European companies started to develop business interests in the country. However, because of internal political struggles between various factions and certain unease in the relationships between Iran and the USA and European Union, progress has been very slow on that front. Moreover, existing laws discourage foreign investment, by allowing non-Iranians only 49 per cent of the shares in any venture and no right to own property. Strict labour laws are another deterrent to investment.

The Islamic revolution in 1979 also had other profound implications for the economy and the society as a whole. Islam, it is worth noting, has been the main religion of Iran for almost 1400 years and has influenced, as well as being influenced by, the Iranian culture. Throughout history, this influence has ebbed and flowed considerably; it was perhaps at its weakest during the Shah's regime, as his father had secularized the society, to some extent, on Turkey's model.

The revolution marked another period of ascendance of Islam, which not only changed the political, economic and cultural fabric of the society but also the private lives and relationships of its people. After all, Islam, unlike many other religions, is an all-encompassing creed and governs every aspect of life, worldly and religious.

For instance, almost immediately after the new regime was established, all banks were nationalized and foreign participation in the financial sector was removed. Later, in 1984, a law came into effect that was designed to make the banking sector subject to Islamic rules, replacing the payment of interest with profit and risk sharing schemes. All organizations and institutions, such as the armed forces, universities and other educational establishments, public and private sector companies, the media, the arts and cultural events, are required to conform to Islamic laws and regulations. Women have to follow a strict Islamic dress code at work, and indeed elsewhere. A policy of segregation of the sexes is observed in prayers, wedding ceremonies, public transport, schools, sports events, television quiz shows, queues at shops and so forth.

Implications for management of Islamic values and Iranian culture

At a deeper cultural level Islam permeates people's taken-for-granted values and assumptions as well (see MANAGEMENT IN THE ARAB WORLD; MANAGEMENT IN THE

EMERGING COUNTRIES). Ultimate fear of and trust in God alone, piety and abstinence, decency, truthfulness, helping the poor and weak, respect for age and seniority, hospitality, loyalty, obedience of leaders and looking up to seniors for direction, family-orientation, uncertainty avoidance, and fatalism yet acceptance of responsibility for one's actions, are among the Islamic roots of the Iranian culture.

Islam also asserts that the nature of relationships among people should be egalitarian, and urges leaders to consult their followers in the running of their affairs (see MANAGEMENT IN THE ARAB WORLD). Translated into workplace behaviour this should mean a consultative decision-making process, and a fairly diffused power structure. Self-discipline, trustfulness, honesty, resolve, loyalty and abstinence, should encourage managers to trust their subordinates' judgement and integrity, which could in turn lead to a participative management style. Cooperation, patience, and family-like relationships among people, should encourage teamwork and mutual support within an organization and care for the community outside it. This is a speculative picture of management that one may draw on the basis of Islamic ideals (Tayeb 1997). The extent to which these ideals are translated into practice is, however, a different matter. They are by their nature open to interpretation, and the workplace is a notoriously fertile ground for such interpretations, given its varied constituencies, interests and goals.

Moreover, Islam is not the only source of Iranian national character. As Bani-Asadi (1984) points out, Iranian culture is a mixture of three different cultures which have coexisted for centuries: Ancient Persian culture, with about 6000 years of history; Islamic culture, with about 1400 years of history; and Western culture, with about 200 years of history.

Throughout its long history, the nation has experienced many unpleasant and hard times as well as happy episodes: authoritarian regimes, repression, wars, domination and invasion by foreign powers and loss of territory. Some of these events have created a deep scepticism and distrust in the national psyche and a need to take refuge in the security offered by religion and in the comfort of home and family, which alone alongside God can be trusted.

The implications of such a psyche for the management of organizations are obvious. From the employees point of view, the workplace does not belong to their in-group, as is the case for example in Japan. Their commitment to the company is at best shaky and at worst open to negotiations. As a consequence, corruption in many institutions and organizations, especially in the public sector, is endemic. Also, employees' willingness to participate in the decision-making process and the running of the organization, particularly at middle and lower levels, is almost non-existent.

From the management side, there is a deep mistrust of subordinates. As a result, organizations tend to be centralized, with power concentrated in the hands of a few and trusted senior managers.

In a study of fourteen organizations in the pre-revolutionary Iran, Tayeb (1979) found some of the managers who had been educated in American and European universities were aware of the merits of decentralization of decision making in their organizations as an appropriate response to their changing environment, but they were reluctant to employ such an approach in their own companies. They did not trust subordinates' abilities and intentions to carry out their tasks properly. Indeed these managers argued that they would stand to benefit if they tightened their control over their employees and made important decisions themselves. Some had chosen to appoint their own close friends and relatives to crucial posts, thereby to ensure the proper handling of the organization's tasks.

Mangers in general tend to adopt a paternalist approach, which has the benefit of centralization but also has a kinder and softer touch. In post-revolutionary Iran, Bani-Asadi (1984), Mortazavi and Karimi (1990) and Mortazavi and Saheli (1992) found the organizations they studied were characterized by a paternalistic culture. Mortazavi and Saheli (1992) also found a close relationship between this paternalistic behaviour of managers and the job satisfaction of their subordinates.

In order to be successful at work and create a friendly atmosphere, Iranian managers attempt to build a close and heartfelt relationship with their subordinates. This point is supported by Latifi's (1997) research. She closely observed a small sample of Iranian managers at work over a period of time and found that Iranian employees viewed their managers as sympathetic brothers and sisters or compassionate fathers and mothers. In addition, this family-like relationship appears to have been extended to include 'social' and 'teacher' roles for the managers. They were frequently involved in their subordinates' private lives and family matters. Some of those interviewed said they would make their time and organizations available for high school and university students who wished to conduct research projects or acquire work experience as part of their courses. They saw this as fulfilling a part of their responsibility to the society and to the next generation of managers.

In the euphoria which followed the 1979 revolution, people took pride in their collective action which led to the overthrow of the Shah's authoritarian regime. The country became for a while a big united family. Some of this euphoria and the shared experience might also explain the paternalistic and soft touch of some organizations.

Political economy and management

Political and economic institutions of a country also play their role in the shape of organizations and their management styles (see ECONOMIES OF THE EMERGING COUNTRIES; MANAGEMENT IN THE EMERGING COUNTRIES).

The economy, although it is a capitalist one, is run on a strict protectionist and statist model. Many industries and firms which in a large number of capitalist countries would normally be in private hands, are owned and managed by the state in Iran. It is estimated that the government's share of the ownership of the economy is 80 per cent. The government has tried in recent years to reduce subsidies and price control over certain commodities and food products but the process is inevitably a slow one. Attempts were also made to reform the economy and start a process of privatization in the early 1990s, but the programme faltered. In the late 1990s the question of privatization was aired again but the authorities admitted that the idea might remain only an idea.

Like India and some other developing countries (see MANAGEMENT IN INDIA), Iran's protectionist policy is in part a reaction to political events. Iran has never lost its independence throughout its history, as did India for instance, but foreign powers such as the USA and Great Britain influenced the country's foreign and domestic policies especially for the best part of the twentieth century. The Shah's father, the founder of the Pahlavi dynasty, came to power with the help of the British. Later, during the Second World War, because of his support for Hitler, the Allies, led by the USA and the UK, forced him to abdicate in favour of his son, who ruled the country under their patronage. A *coup d'état* in 1953, which entrenched his position of power in the country further, was staged by the Americans. This and similar historical episodes have created a need and desire in people for real political independence and economic self-reliance.

As a consequence of protectionist economic policies, however, business organizations are largely protected from both foreign competition and the rigour of a domestic market-based economy. In addition, Iran's economy is in the so-called 'demanding market' state, where demand outstrips supply. These two factors have in turn led to the almost total absence of a need for organizations to have vigorous market research, marketing, research and development and consumer relations and similar functions. There is little or no incentive for managers to emphasize product improvement and innovation. Iranian companies are, as a result, ill-prepared to face competition at home and abroad, and the country's bulk of export-related earning comes from crude oil, and not value-added manufactured goods.

There are also other aspects of management which are affected by the environment within which Iranian organizations operate. The infrastructure – from water supply, electricity, and rail, road and air travel networks to media, information technology, telecommunications, and specialist and consultant services – is not as advanced and ubiquitous as those in more developed nations.

In addition, information and statistics about the general state of the economy, such as the inflation rate, annual growth, the trade balance, unemployment, skill composition of the economically active population, and a whole host of crucial figures, are either inadequate or unreliable. The official rate of unemployment as of 1998 is for instance 11 per cent but there are other sources which estimate it at over 30 per cent. Moreover, the black economy contributes some 25 per cent to the GNP but no other reliable statistics are available. Managers often formulate their strategies and policies intuitively and informally rather than on the basis of scientific analysis, which pre-supposes availability of reliable and useful data.

This situation slows down and hinders the managers' efforts to perform their tasks effectively within their organizations and to manage their relationships with the outside world competently. The brain drain, which the country has suffered for decades, and the technological gap between what is needed and what is available also limit managers' scope for innovation and managerial professionalism.

Operating within an intensely political and at the same time volatile environment managers have instead developed the special skills necessary to cope with the situation as best they can, such as developing and maintaining informal and 'useful' networks and contacts. This is not nepotism or cronyism, it is simply a strategy for survival.

Also, whereas in Western countries managers, similar to other professionals, tend to specialize in their skills and functions, in a developing nation like Iran managers are of necessity generalists; the country simply cannot afford to have managers with focused and narrow specialisms. In addition, as was mentioned earlier, the managers' domain stretches beyond their own organization into the community. Social responsibility and participation in community affairs are not of course a monopoly of organizations in developing nations (see for instance Buchholz 1991; Smith *et al.* 1996), but the scope and emphasis are much wider and deeper compared with more advanced nations (Muna 1980; Tayeb 1988; Das 1991; Chow 1992). It is for instance a manager's social duty to help bring electricity to his small town or improve the irrigation system in the neighbouring village.

The vast majority of Iranian organizations, notwithstanding a growing army of educated managers with MBA and other business degrees from home and abroad, are run by people with little or no managerial qualifications. A study by Amirshahi (unpublished manuscript) found that of over 700 university educated executives and senior managers surveyed only 13.7 per cent had a management degree. Even these had probably not received the kind of education which would be needed to operate successfully in the current Iranian economy, as Latifi (1997) found in her study.

Latifi's research exposed the gap between Iranian managers' professional and skill needs and what is on offer in universities and business schools. MBA courses, for instance, are generally modelled after American and British ones, which are primarily designed for their own domestic needs. Marketing and financial accounting classes, for example, are intended for managers working in an open-door capitalist market with a vibrant private sector and widespread public share ownership, sophisticated consumers, easily accessible economic and demographic data, and so forth. The appropriateness of such courses for managers working in a protected economy dominated by the public sector is rather doubtful. In fact the mangers who participated in Latifi's study considered such courses as irrelevant.

As a result of the constraints and limitations inherent in their socio-cultural and political-economic environments, Iranian managers have limited strategic and organizational choices at their disposal. Using a musical metaphor, Tayeb (1979) argued that these managers have a low repertoire of modes of structure and management styles. Organizations that she studied tended to be highly centralized, formalized and standardized, irrespective of the diversity of their specific task environments and contextual factors, such as industry, product, technology, size, market share and ownership.

This low repertoire also limits the managers' ability to import and modify management practices such as participative decision making, quality circles, total quality management, teamwork and the like (Tayeb 1995). These practices presuppose, among other things, a willingness to participate in group decision making and decision implementing and a strong commitment to the workplace, on the part of employees. They also assume a certain degree of confidence and trust in employees and willingness to delegate authority to team members, on the part of their managers. Iranian culture does not appear to be as fertile a ground for such management practices as was Japan's when Japanese managers successfully imported them from the USA a few decades ago.

3 Conclusion

Iran is a developing country which started its process of modernization and industrialization nearly a century ago. It even dreamed during the 1960s of one day becoming the second Japan of Asia. Its business organizations, if assisted with supporting internal and external environments, are her obvious engines of progress to become a Western Asian tiger in the next century. There are many opportunities at the disposal of these organizations: abundant natural resources from fossil fuel to minerals, a growing domestic customer base and a young and largely educated population eager to learn new skills and participate in the economy. But there are constraints as well, such as inadequate infrastructure, shortages of skilled workforce and capital. The current banking and financial system, in which creditors share the risk as well as profit instead of charging interest, redirects loans away from long-term to short-term investment. This is because creditors will have to wait until the projects that they finance come to fruition before they can get their share of the profit, if any.

There are also cultural impediments to managerial professionalism and employment of innovative and modern management techniques, which to some extent could be overcome, with managers' good will and appropriate employee training programmes. However, protectionist and statist economic policies have removed serious incentives for managers to invest in product innovation and vigorous professionalism.

With the improvement of relations between Iran and her Western partners already appearing on the horizon, and the increase in foreign direct investment that this could entail, the economy might be injected with much needed managerial skills, advanced technologies and above all competition, both for resources and customers, in the domestic market at least.

MONIR TAYEB
HERIOT-WATT UNIVERSITY

Further reading

(References cited in the text marked *)

* Bani-Asadi, H. (1984) 'Interactive planning on the eve of the Iranian Revolution', PhD dissertation, University of Pennsylvania. (An investigation into the management culture of a sample of Iranian organizations.)
* Buchholz, R.A. (1991) 'Corporate responsibility and the good society: from economics to ecology', *Business Horizons* July–August: 19–31. (A discussion of traditional and modern views of organizations with respect to their social responsibilities.)
* Chow, I.H. (1992) 'Chinese managerial work', *Journal of General Management* 17(4): 53–67. (It discusses the implications of economic reforms for organizations especially in terms of the separation of managerial from political functions.)
  Coville, T. (1994) *The Economy of Islamic Iran: between State and Market*, Tehran: The French Institute for Research. (A collection of papers analysing various aspects of the economic reform programme initiated in the early 1990s, and its failure.)
  Daneshvar, P. (1996) *Revolution in Iran*, Basingstoke: Macmillan. (A thorough analysis of the causes and implications of the 1979 revolution.)
* Das, H. (1991) 'The nature of managerial work in India: a preliminary investigation', *ASCI Journal of Management* 12(1): 1–13. (Various facets of management functions and roles in Indian organizations are explored.)
  Goode, J.F. (1997) *The United States and Iran: In the Shadow of Musaddiq*, Basingstoke: Macmillan. (An analysis of the influence of the USA in Iran's economic and political policies, from staging a *coup d'état* to oust the nationalist prime minister in 1953 up to the 1979 revolution.)

Hashim, A. (1995) *The Crisis of the Iranian State: Domestic, Foreign and Security Policies in Post-Khomeini Iran*, Oxford: Oxford University Press. (A monograph about revolutionary Iran and the problems it faces.)

* Latifi, F.(1997) 'Management learning in national context', PhD thesis. Henley Management College. (An empirical investigation into managerial roles and educational needs in Iran.)

Mazarei, A. (1996) 'The Iranian economy under the Islamic Republic: institutional change and macroeconomic performance (1979–1990)', *Cambridge Journal of Economics* 20(3): 289–314. (An economist's view of the events which shaped the country since 1979.)

* Mortazavi, S. and Karimi, E. (1990) 'Cultural dimensions of paternalistic behaviour: a cross-cultural research in five countries', in Iwawaki, S., Kashima, Y. and Kwok, L. (eds), *Innovation in Cross-cultural Psychology*, Amsterdam, Berwyn, PA: Swets & Zeitlinger. pp. 147–51. (A discussion of Iranian paternalistic management style and its cultural roots.)

* Mortazavi, S. and Saheli, A. (1992) 'Organisational culture, paternalistic leadership and job satisfaction in Iran', paper presented at the 22nd International Congress of Applied Psychology, Erlbaum, UK. (It builds on an earlier project and examines employees' job satisfaction as a consequence of their managers' paternalistic behaviour.)

* Muna, F.A. (1980) *The Arab Executive*, London: Macmillan. (A seminal study of Arab senior managers' social as well as professional roles.)

Paidar, P. (1995) *Women and the Political Process in Twentieth-Century Iran*, Cambridge: Cambridge University Press. (An analysis of the struggles of women and their considerable success in participation in politics as well as other spheres of public life.)

* Smith, P.B., Dugan, S. and Trompenaars, F. (1996) 'National culture and the values of organisational employees: a dimensional annalaysis across 43 nations', *Journal of Cross-cultural Psychology* 27: 231–64. (A questionnaire survey of culturally-rooted work-related values of a large sample of employees from different countries.)

* Tayeb, M.H. (1979) 'Cultural determinants of organizational response to environmental demands', M,Litt, thesis. University of Oxford. (A study of national culture, work-related attitudes and values and management styles of a sample of organization in pre-revolutionary Iran).

* Tayeb, M.H. (1988) *Organizations and National Culture: A Comparative Analysis*, London: Sage Publications. (Compares Indian and English cultures, work-related attitudes and values and organizations structures.)

* Tayeb, M.H. (1995) 'The competitive advantage of nations: the role of HRM and its socio-cultural context', *International Journal of Human Resource Management* 6(3): 588–605. (A discussion of the implications of cultural characteristics for competitiveness at both macro- and micro-levels.)

* Tayeb, M.H. (1997) 'Islamic revival in Asia and human resource management', *Employee Relations* 19(4) 352–4. (A theoretical discussion on the implications of Islamic values for human resource management.)

See also: HUMAN RESOURCE MANAGEMENT IN THE EMERGING COUNTRIES; INDUSTRIAL RELATIONS IN THE EMERGING COUNTRIES; MANAGEMENT EDUCATION IN THE EMERGING COUNTRIES; MANAGEMENT IN BANGLADESH; MANAGEMENT IN INDIA; MANAGEMENT IN PAKISTAN

Related topics in the IEBM regional set: MANAGEMENT EDUCATION IN EUROPE; MANAGEMENT EDUCATION IN NORTH AMERICA; MANAGEMENT IN JAPAN

Management in Jordan

1 Introduction
2 Jordanian managerial behaviour
3 Jordanian management culture
4 Conclusion

Overview

Jordan is situated to the north west of the Arabian Peninsula, covering some 96,000 square kilometres. It is bordered by Syria to the north, Iraq to the north east and Saudi Arabia to the south east. A great deal of this area is desert or semi-desert terrain. Nonetheless, the fertile irrigated land in the Rift Valley on both sides of the River Jordan has historically been one of the most fertile and prosperous areas in the Middle East. In the highlands of the west and east bank there is other fertile cultivated land. The Dead Sea, which is 392 metres below sea level, lies to the south of the River Jordan and forms a continuation of the Rift Valley which stretches further south to Aqaba, Jordan's only port on the Red Sea. This intermediate position in the Middle East and the distribution of natural resources has led to a concentration of the population of about 4.2 million within the Rift Valley. There has been a growing urbanization and higher rate of population growth in recent years. More than half of the population lives in the conurbation comprising Amman, Zarka and Ruseifa. The second major urban growth pole is in Irbid in the north with a population of 1.13 million. Between Amman and Aqaba the terrain is mainly desert and sparsely populated. Arabic is the official language of the country but English is widely spoken in business and governmental circles.

Throughout the 1990s Jordan has continued to develop economically, though endowed with few natural resources apart from phosphates and potash. The political liberalization has been the basis of economic growth, coupled with the relative political stability over the period. A reform package based on funding from the International Monetary Fund commenced to take effect from 1989, supported by structural funding from the World Bank. The result has been a growth in inward investment and clear gains in economic performance, improved balance of payments, reduced inflation and reduced government debt. None the less, a significant proportion of the economic activity supports a high defence budget and it is clear that most indigenous Jordanian enterprise does not operate to accepted standards of international competitiveness. None the less, the picture is a brighter one than in the recent past and has permitted a growth of management confidence and capability which is quite marked.

1 Introduction

Jordan is a relatively small country, unusual among the Arab states of the Arabian sub-continent in having no oil or similar natural resource to form a solid economic base. The country is of recent origin, being formed after the Second World War out of a partition of the Arab lands based on the area previously known as 'Transjordan' and in conflict with the emerging state of Israel. Thus 'Jordanians' are Arabs, many of whom originated in what is now the Palestinian West Bank area of the state of Israel. Family and kin loyalties extend to other countries, particularly what is now Saudi Arabia and Iraq. The political and economic institutions are based on a liberal, moderate, monarchical regime in which traces of British civil service and military organizational structures, and the ubiquity of the armed forces, have combined with a developmental, modernizing and moderate philosophy of government in which a high value has been placed on education as the engine of developing national prosperity. The original two universities of Jordan and Yarmouk have in the past ten years been joined by a dozen others, and Jordan is in some ways emerging as an educational and training centre for much of the Arab Middle East. For example, the organization of Arab airlines (AACO) has recently chosen to locate its training and management development activities in Amman. Other Arab institutions and governmental and regional representational activities such as the Arab league also have prominent representation in the country.

Unsurprisingly therefore, the public sector has provided much of the impetus for management development and public policy directed through civil service and parastatal organizations which have been a powerful influence on management, ideology and practice. The pervasive evidence of the paternalistic and moderate influence of the Royal family is universally obvious in Jordan. At the time of writing, His Majesty King Hussein has just been succeeded by His Majesty King Abdullah. For fifty years the King and his brother Crown Prince Hassan have been personally identified not merely with supporting the development of an educated and highly professional cadre within Jordan but to a large extent acting as role models for the emerging managers.

The emphasis on education has worked its way through public and private sector enterprises and has produced a richer vein of research and teaching capability in the field of business and management than in many other Arab countries at the present time. Significant contributions to scholarships have been made by such scholars as Burra, Shariah, Al-Jubari, Al-Faleh, Al-Shaikh and Al-Rasheed, and a second generation of younger scholars trained in Western business schools, such as Abu-Doleh and Hala Sabri, are producing well-documented empirical research findings on the nature of management in Jordan.

2 Jordanian managerial behaviour

Al-Faleh (1987) argued that the specific cultural influences on Arab management development were likely to produce specific and different managerial behaviour and practices from those that were obtained in Western countries (see MANAGEMENT IN THE ARAB WORLD). Although many of these derive from Islam it is important to recognize that Islam as practised in Jordan represents a developing interaction between traditional and modern values. Al-Rasheed (1994) identifies the traditional culture as emphasizing fatalism against freewill, shame, conformity, past orientation, heart versus mind, form versus content, collectivity versus individuality, closed mind against open mind, obedience against rebellion, charity against justice. The dominant traditional type of Arab culture, which is in conflict with modernity, helps in explaining traditional Arab management and organization. Equally, within Jordan the behavioural tenets of this Islamic matrix have to be reinterpreted in terms of the organizational and economic imperatives of business organization. Al-Faleh (1989) depicts Jordanian business executives in a landmark study.

In many ways the evolving traditions of management in Jordan demonstrate the success of public and national policy in developing a middle way in which traditional Islamic values combine with the traditions of Bedouin life (which two generations back represents recent historical experience for many Jordanian families) and the collective aspirations of a moderate liberal monarchical regime to support a professional managerial middle class which to some extent embodies quite clear behaviours and values. Thus, Jordanian organization does not exemplify the extreme forms of centralized decision making, 'wasta', patriarchy and patronage due to the operation of power and influence working through social networks in the way often seen in other Arab societies.

Thus, while power is concentrated in Jordanian organizations, there is a tradition of relatively open information. While authority is rarely completely delegated, it is operated through a framework of rules which are quasi bureaucratic in nature, and the lack of power and authority at lower levels noted by Sharabi (1988) and others is mediated by the growing confidence of a more authentically educated managerial cadre. Many of the new managers and perhaps the majority of senior managers have by now had the benefit of exposure to Western educational models, often to Masters level. Thus Jordanian management represents an emerging meld of Arabic, Middle Eastern, urban rural, Eastern and Western influences.

Perhaps of equal significance is the emerging role of women. This can be overstated and it is undoubtedly true that most senior positions are still held by men. But there is an emerging generation of career women managers whose aspirations are justified by experience and strong educational and professional qualification. In the Palestinian West Bank indeed, this same generation of women managers has, during the experience of the Intifada, had to take major responsibility for some significant aspects of the economy and of public sector management.

Al-Rasheed (1997), in his studies of management in the banking and financial sectors, demonstrated the existence of both what we may call the traditional Arab organization in terms of management and the emerging more professionalized model. The main features of the 'traditional' Arab business organization and management include a limited future orientation, an absence of job goals and plans, systematic performance appraisal and human resource management (HRM) policies (see HUMAN RESOURCE MANAGEMENT IN THE EMERGING COUNTRIES). There is also a lack of delegation of authority, with decision making concentrated at the apex of hierarchically structured organizations. As is general throughout the Arab world, superior–subordinate relationships tend to be highly personalized and this is reflected in loyalties being expressed to individuals rather than organizations and in a generally paternalistic relationship towards subordinates.

Traditionally, Jordanian organizations did not have long-term training policies based on performance and an emphasis on appraisal and skills identification. Human resource management policies were ill developed. Organization structures were not formalized and explicit and were ill coordinated and rigid. Above all there was a narrow scope of opportunity for advancement and promotion for many managers and most specifically for women managers. However, recent research by Abu-Doleh (1997) and others have demonstrated that changes are occurring and that the needs of the Jordanian economy for a highly trained managerial cadre better qualified that its predecessors and empowered to operate in a less hierarchical and less structured manner are being addressed. Thus Abu-Doleh's research specifically contrasts organizations with effective management training and development (MTD) policies, including needs assessment and performance appraisals, use of assessment centres and the other apparatus of formalized MTD activity.

In a sample of the major companies listed in the Amman financial market he found that 87 per cent of the financial companies do undertake systematic management of performance appraisal whereas only 46 per cent of the manufacturing companies did so. Training and development needs were identified by over 60 per cent of both samples and clear procedures used at least at the supervisory level in 90 per cent of the companies sampled. These findings are consistent with equivalent levels of performance obtained by similar companies in the USA. None the less, Abu-Doleh finds there is a missing link in the process in that it is unusual for these practices to be embedded in the strategic planning and decision making of the overall organization. As Abu-Doleh rightly says, 'this finding leads us to question the value of managers training needs' assessments'.

Al-Rasheed, commenting on the research findings of a study of Jordanian bank managers, argues that the emerging generation of Jordanian managers 'reveals higher concern for achievement and power and autonomy and growth and lower concern for relationship and affiliation, security and structure and pay and comfort'. He also finds that gender 'has most statistical significant impact on bank managers' intended behaviour towards motivation and job satisfaction'. Again the finding is consistent with cross-national research in developed societies on the same theme. Al-Rasheed comments, 'the fact that women managers, especially in a country like Jordan, attempt to prove themselves in their job and work might help to explain the similarity of their intended behaviour towards motivation and job satisfaction for that of male manager.'

It is important to note that most of the research undertaken on characteristics of management in Jordan has been inevitably directed towards managers in large organizations and Western-style corporations and other research has been undertaken into the public sector. However, small-scale industries are widespread in Jordan and over 50 per cent of employment is in such small organizations. Elaian (1995) reviews the employment position in small-scale industries (SSIs) consisting of manufacturing firms employing 1 to 19 workers.

In companies of this sort, the more traditional pattern of family ownership and management is prevalent. In these companies personalized superior–subordinate relationships and undeveloped HRM policies are strengthened by the managerial practices derived from tribalism and the network of kin relations resulting in 'wasta' and patronage. In these organizations middle management, where it exists, is linked to the owner by personalized relationships. No job market for managerial skills of this kind exists and the opportunities for personal development are hindered by the complete absence of developed HRM policies.

3 Jordanian management culture

In a recent study of the impact of national culture on four Jordanian organizations, using the now widely applied Hofstede (1991) categories of national and organizational culture, Sabri (1995) distinguishes power distance, uncertainty avoidance, individualist collectiveness, and masculine and feminine aspects of Jordanian management culture. She links this with Harrison's distinction between the power, role, achievement and support orientation (Harrison and Stokes 1990). Further, she identifies the roots of Arab organization and management issues in the national culture as well as the cross-national generic cultural characteristics of Arab organizations. Her findings are significant therefore in identifying what may be more specifically Jordanian about the organizational culture of Jordanian organizations. She hypothesizes that existing organizational culture in Jordanian organizations would be higher on power and role culture than achievement and support culture, that Jordanian employees would have a stronger preference for power and role culture than achievement and support cultures, that Jordanian organizations would have high scores on existing power and role cultures and that Jordanian employers would have strong preferences for power and role cultures, in each case compared to organizations in national culture that are relatively low on power and relatively weak on uncertainty avoidance. In contrasting existing and preferred aspects of organizational cultures, she finds, indeed, that existing organizational culture and Jordanian organization are higher on power and role cultures than achievement and support. However, Jordanian employees have a stronger preference for achievement and role than power and support cultures. When she contrasts organizations of different types in the electricity, potash production and airline management and refinery sectors, she finds that the two service companies have a higher power orientation while the two production companies are higher on role orientation.

When contrasting Jordanian organizations with those found by other research in Australia, New Zealand and the United States she finds that the Jordanian organizations tend to have more power and role culture than in the USA, while US organizations tend to have more achievement and support culture than in Jordan. Organizations in Australia and New Zealand are higher on role and support culture than those in Jordan. She concludes that Jordanian organizations have high scores on existing power and role culture compared to organizations in the USA but not compared to organizations in Australia and New Zealand. There is a general preference, however, on the part of employees for a stronger emphasis on achievement and role.

Again, Sabri's detailed and careful empirical research, like that of Al-Rasheed, shows that bland and over-general depictions of management culture in Jordan tend to be misleading. Jordanian organizations and the attitudes of employees and managers who operate within them indicate a strong developmental and progressive tendency in relation to what has been recently regarded as aspects of a relatively unchanging and procrustean 'culture of Arabic management'.

In this national culture and in the organizational cultures it supports, managers are learning to operate in a way that is characteristic, it is true, of certain aspects of behaviour and culture in the Arabic and Islamic world. None the less, they are moving quite rapidly and over one or two generations to a position that is, if not characteristic of Western and developed societies, none the less quite distinct from the apparently unchanging and classically traditional practices of the recent past. The high emphasis on education, particularly to postgraduate level, and the collective drive of a whole society becoming integrated initially against immediate political and military threat but latterly in a determination to make good the lack of natural physical resource with the determination to use human capital as an investment vehicle, have combined to create a set of management practices and management styles which is distinct from others in the region and provides a model for developing economies without strong physical resources.

4 Conclusion

As Sabri concludes, 'the higher preference for achievement for Jordanian employees may reflect the changing nature of the technology and education and aspirations of the workforce. Existing organizational cultures may reflect the lower technological and educational base that characterized the economy when many of these existing organizations were founded. The rate of development in Jordan has been such that employees had developed preferences for organizational cultures which are more oriented to achieve than less oriented to power, but when compared to employees working in some other cultures they still have a relatively strong preference for power and role.'

Similar movement is demonstrated in a study by Abu-Bakr and Green (1995) on requirements for corporate social responsibility and reporting. They find that current corporate reporting practices are not consistent with the requirements of the social, economic and political environment of Jordan but that an accountability approach based on concepts of corporate social responsibility might provide an appropriate framework for determining the necessary wider disclosure. However, the main finding of their study of their survey of financial managers of Jordanian shareholding companies indicates that 'the notions of corporate social responsibility and reporting are widely accepted as desirable and feasible'.

Likewise Abu-Doleh (1997) finds enthusiasm among middle managers not merely for human resource management policies embedded in relations of mutual trust and understanding as is traditional in Arab society, but for more formalized management training and development practices. It is at the top level or in bridging the gap between what Abu-Doleh calls the covert and overt organizational strategies that management training and development needs to come together in the perceptions of the professional middle managers in these organizations. The study of management and managers is spreading into areas characteristic of Western business schools and their research, as recent research by El-Omani (1999) and others demonstrates (see

MANAGEMENT EDUCATION IN THE EMERGING COUNTRIES). In conclusion, management in Jordanian enterprises is an emergent reality. It is no longer possible, as Al-Rasheed points out, to rely on generic propositions. The results of more recent empirical research demonstrate an emerging practical reality, doubtless more attuned to the needs of Jordanian organization and enterprise.

DAVID T.H. WEIR
NEWCASTLE BUSINESS SCHOOL
UNIVERSITY OF NEWCASTLE

Further reading

(References cited in the text marked *)

* Abu-Bakr, N. and Green, C.D. (1995) 'Corporate social responsibility and reporting', *Proceedings Arab Management Conference*, University of Bradford Management Centre. (Examines the framework of corporate reporting and disclosure practices of large companies operating in Jordan.)
* Abu-Doleh, J. and Weir, D.T.H. (1997) 'Management training and development needs analysis practices in Jordanian private companies', *Middle East Business Review* 2(1). (Reviews findings from a study of major companies listed in the Amman Financial Market that have a formal MTD unit. Contrasts manufacturing and financial sectors.)
* Al-Faleh, M. (1987) 'Cultural influences on Arab managerial development', *Journal of Management Development* 6(3): 19–33. (Explains Jordanian management behaviour and beliefs in context of Arab culture values.)
* Al-Faleh, M. (1989) 'Characteristics and background of business executives in Jordan', *Dirasat* 16 (1). (Demonstrates attitudes and demographic features of business executives in Jordan.)
* Al-Rasheed, A. (1994) 'Traditional Arab management: evidence from empirical comparative research', *Proceedings Arab Management Conference*, University of Bradford Management Centre 1994. (Criticizes non-empirical typologies and relates Jordanian management behaviour to empirical research.)
* Al-Rasheed, A. (1997) 'Factors affecting managers' motivation and job satisfaction: the case of Jordanian bank managers', *Middle East Business Review* 2 (1). (Reviews findings from a major study of Jordanian bank managers finding higher concerns for achievement, power, autonomy and growth, and lower concerns for relationship, affiliation, security, structure, pay and comfort. Argues that these findings are similar to those for Western managers in similar industries.)
* Elaian, K. (1995) 'Employment generation of small-scale industry in developing countries: new evidence from Jordan', *Proceedings Arab Management Conference*, University of Bradford Management Centre. (Demonstrates continuing importance of small-scale industry in Jordanian economy.)
* El-Omani, H. (1999) 'Assessing Jordanians' willingness to buy: A consumer's point of view', *Arab Journal of Administrative Services* 6 (1), January 1999. (Demonstrates that income is not the sole determinant of purchasing decisions.)
* Harrison, R. and Stokes, H. (1990) *Working with Organization Culture: A Workbook and Manual for Diagnosing Culture*, Roffey Park Institute. (Identifies a typology of organization culture distinguishing power, role, achievement and support orientations.)
* Hofstede, G. (1991) *Cultures and Organizations*, McGraw-Hill. (Landmark study of various discussions of culture, manifested in individual behaviour, believed to offer possibilities of intercultural comparison. Identifies Arab culture as high contrast, high power distance, high collectivist, moderate masculinity, moderate uncertainty avoidance.)
* Sabri, H. (1995) 'Cultures and structures: the structure of work organization across different cultures', *Proceedings Arab Management Conference*, University of Bradford Management Centre. (Shows that Jordanian employees have a stronger preference for achievement and support than power and role cultures.)

* Sharabi, H. (1988) *Neo-Patriarchy: A Theory of Distorted Change in Arab Society*, Oxford: Oxford University Press. (Discusses neo-patriarchy, identified as a 'quasi-modern' form of social organization, embodying traditional Arab values and social structure.)

See also: HUMAN RESOURCE MANAGEMENT IN THE EMERGING COUNTRIES; MANAGEMENT EDUCATION IN THE EMERGING COUNTRIES; MANAGEMENT IN THE ARAB WORLD; MANAGEMENT IN EGYPT; MANAGEMENT IN THE EMERGING COUNTRIES; MANAGEMENT IN THE GULF STATES; MANAGEMENT IN LEBANON; MANAGEMENT IN SAUDI ARABIA

Related topics in the IEBM regional set: MANAGEMENT IN ISRAEL

Management in Lebanon

1 Introduction
2 Analysis
3 Conclusion

Overview

Lebanese Management can only be explained in terms of the myriad cultural and historical influences that affected the country over the years. Lebanon is rich in terms of its religious and historic diversity which – no doubt – transcended into various aspects of the Lebanese life including economic and management behaviours. Lebanon, being an Arab country, shares many of the characteristics found in the Arab World (see MANAGEMENT IN THE ARAB WORLD). Yet its historical strong ties with the Western world and its unique openness give the Lebanese special traits which are rarely found in the region. The distinctiveness of the Lebanese managerial behaviour is reflected in the dominance of family businesses, centralization of decision making, entrepreneurship and peculiar human resource practices.

1 Introduction

After its independence from France in 1943, Lebanon enjoyed remarkable economic growth and prosperity which was only hindered by the political and military disputes which have prevailed over the Middle East region during the past few decades. Specifically, the Lebanese civil war which erupted in 1975 and continued through to 1990 greatly disrupted economic growth and had a significant effect on people and businesses.

Lebanon prides itself for its banking secrecy laws and *laissez-faire* policies which advocate competition. The government, however, does interfere in terms of regulatory and other requirements in some industries. This has been evident since the end of the Lebanese civil war as the government still strongly regulates several key industries including banking, airlines, the media and telecommunications.

Lebanon has an economy dominated by banking and other commercial services. The services sector employs 59 per cent of working males and 68 per cent of working females (World Bank 1998). This is due in part to the small size of Lebanon (10,452 sq km) and the rarity of raw materials. Before the 1970's civil war, Beirut was the leading financial capital of the Middle East. As the civil war reached its conclusion in 1990, the Lebanese found themselves amidst rising inflation, heavy migration of Lebanese talent and expertise, and with an infrastructure which was virtually destroyed. In addition to all of this, the Lebanese local currency, the pound or 'Lira' deteriorated in value and many people found themselves either unemployed or paid very little compared to what they used to earn before the war. The government initiated moves to rebuild the infrastructure of the country, revised the tax laws to enhance collection and entice investments, and launched reform programmes in various sectors of the economy.

When analysing management in Lebanon, several authors categorize it among the other Arab countries as if all Arab countries have a homogeneous management behaviour and style. As this essay will demonstrate, the Lebanese – although being an integral part of the Arab world – display a managerial behaviour and style which are, in some instances, very different from those displayed in other Arab countries.

2 Analysis

What follows is a discussion that highlights some of the most important attributes of Lebanese management and managerial behaviour (see MANAGEMENT IN THE ARAB WORLD).

Dominance of family businesses

Lebanese firms are characterized by the dominance of family businesses. This is a result of the strong loyalty that the family commands in Lebanese society. What is meant by family is the extended family which includes brothers and sisters and cousins and other relatives. Many businesses in Lebanon are run by individuals who attach a high priority to recruiting other relatives. That is why the most common form of company is partnerships or limited liability companies whose owners do not exceed twenty individuals. This also includes corporations in many important sectors such as banking, cement, broadcasting and the soft drinks industry. Family members conservatively hold these corporations and shares are only sold to close associates or among the families themselves. This feature has important implications for management and executive behaviour – especially with respect to centralization – which is discussed in the later sections.

An example of the dominance of family businesses relates to the failure of several merger efforts especially in the banking and insurance sectors. While the government has initiated measures to encourage mergers and consolidations, they remain a rarity. Tannous Feghali, the president of the Lebanese Association of Insurance Companies (ACAL) indicates that mergers in Lebanon face the danger of one of the companies not being completely absorbed by the other: 'For a merger to succeed, one head has to disappear or it could be dangerous…. That can be difficult in a country where everybody wants to be the boss' (Tuttle 1998).

Entrepreneurship and other work values

The multitude of historic and cultural experiences that the Lebanese have passed through, have made the Lebanese famous for their innovation and entrepreneurship. Millions of Lebanese have successfully migrated and established thriving businesses in countries in North and Latin American, Africa, and Australia. The Lebanese are known in the Arab world for their aggressiveness, strong initiative and impressive customer service culture.

In addition to a relatively permissive economy, what help is this entrepreneurial spirit given by the qualifications of the Lebanese people in general and the workforce in particular? Lebanon enjoys good human resources, which are among the highest in the Middle East region in terms of education, skills and expertise. This fosters an impression of the Lebanese as being sharp-minded and bright. A phrase which is often used in Lebanon and many countries in the region, albeit sometimes in a negative sense, is *Al-Lubnani Shater* which literally translates into 'The Lebanese individual is shrewd'.

The Lebanese society is characterized by a high emphasis on what is referred to as 'masculine' traits which greatly impact social and managerial behaviour. Masculine traits mean an emphasis on concepts of success, hard work, accomplishment, assertiveness and other similar values. This remains an overwhelming attribute of Lebanese society as the Lebanese are highly ambitious and persistent. A superior work value system has not emerged, however, as Lebanon still suffers from the effects of corruption at the public governmental and private business levels. This happens in spite of continuous, though some claim futile, governmental efforts to push for administrative reform in terms of relevant laws and policies that combat corruption.

Centralization and decision making styles

Lebanese organizations are characterized by extreme centralization. This is, in part, the result of the dominance of the family businesses which are tightly controlled. However, centralization is not limited to family run businesses, as there are many examples of non-family businesses which suffer from extreme centralization. In tens of training programmes given by this author, many of them in non-family firms, the overwhelming remark by participants has always been concern about excessive centralization. This is supported by studies which indicate that Lebanese workers perceive their organizations to be low on formality and standardization, but extremely high on centralization (Sidani and Gardner 1998). This leads in many cases to problems in employee morale and motivation. Centralization remains a powerful feature even in those companies which have started to launch modern management intervention programmes such as total quality management and the team approach. One Lebanese manager noted to this author, for example, that in Lebanon modern approaches to management should be adopted but decisions should rarely, if ever, be delegated. The rationale behind this view, which is shared by many managers, is that employees either cannot be trusted or they are incompetent to handle most decisions.

The type of decision-making style used depends on the prevailing circumstances and the problem at hand. Nevertheless, Lebanese mangers seem to have a preference for the consultative style which implies that prior consultation is made with subordinates even when this process does not ultimately influence the leader's decision (Barakat 1994). This style may be used to gather consensus rather than necessarily seeking to genuinely involve subordinates in decision making.

Management education and training

Many businesses, irrespective of size, traditionally did not appreciate the long-term benefits associated with training. The importance of management education and training, however, is slowly gaining some recognition among Lebanese companies. There are wide differences, however, among different companies and economic sectors. Banks and other financial institutions and large firms, for example, usually emphasize, and can afford, continuous learning for their management and staff. Training in smaller companies is still virtually non-existent.

During the past few years several firms were formed to provide professional executive education and many of them are faring very well. This could be the result of companies becoming more aware of the impact of globalization and increased competitiveness on their well being and the need to continuously develop their employees' skills and talents.

It is interesting to note that most professional training in Lebanon copies the methodologies and norms found in the West. Many training institutes pride themselves at being affiliated with international organizations and often seize opportunities to invite European or North American trainers who are generally well received and appreciated (see MANAGEMENT EDUCATION IN THE EMERGING COUNTRIES).

Human resources practices

Lebanon is characterized by peculiar human resources practices. Recruitment in Lebanese organizations, for example, is generally based on personal contacts and nepotism. A number of factors enter into the recruitment decision which go beyond qualifications and suitability for the job. The family and religious factors are probably the primary criteria used in recruitment and other human resources decisions. Several Lebanese managers may wish to sidestep this issue or prefer not to discuss it. Others, while acknowledging this fact, might point out that this is constrained to a few firms.

Nobody would argue, however, that several job openings in the public sector, especially at the higher managerial levels are distributed proportionally among religious communities. Although not promulgated by Lebanese law, such practices are norms which are consistently applied and thus often have the power of legal statutes. The positions of General Managers in public entities and ministries, for example, are divided half for Christians and the other half for Muslims. While several Lebanese politicians and activists attack this 'sharing of the pie', several others argue that such moves, while unfair, are sometimes necessary to retain political and religious harmony in the country.

The private sector has a bigger problem in the opinion of this author. Philippe Skaff, an executive director of a regional advertising company, notes that: 'If you have five carpenters who are the right religion and you need a plumber, but the plumber isn't the right religion, you get one of the carpenters to do your plumbing ... That's what is happening here, and it is ridiculous' (Thomson 1998: 19). Unlike the public sector, no norms dictate that managerial and employment decisions should be distributed equally among religious groups. Despite the fact that any type of religious discrimination runs against the prevailing laws in Lebanon, it is still unfortunate to see that this has not lead to workplace practices which are solely based on competence and performance. Religious discrimination remains a widespread phenomenon in several private institutions. The experience of this author demonstrates, based on tens of interviews and contacts with employers and employees, the prevalence of such practices in Lebanon. What further complicates the issue is that people rarely, if ever, raise a lawsuit claiming religious discrimination.

It is fair to note that there is an increasing, albeit slow, awareness among several Lebanese executives about the problems that religious discrimination might pose for Lebanese prosperity and competitiveness. The government is trying hard, though some claim not hard enough, to improve the educational system so that newer generations would become more aware about the problems such practices lead to. While this may positively affect the workplace twenty years from now, stronger efforts should be made to free today's workplace from the peril of discrimination (see HUMAN RESOURCE MANAGEMENT IN THE EMERGING COUNTRIES).

Attitudes towards time

Virtually every book or article that tackles the concept of time in the Arab culture notes the different outlook attached to time. Arabs have a long perspective of time where 'bukra' – tomorrow in Arabic – can also mean 'some time in the future' (Deresky 1997). This also applies to Lebanon. It is not uncommon for some meetings to be delayed for various reasons including traffic conditions. Arriving late sometimes is viewed as a characteristic attributed to important personalities like some politicians who arrive late at public gatherings to foster the impression of importance. Promptness, however, is slowly creeping into the workplace. This may be the result of the increasing presence of managers at all levels who graduated from Western universities and who dealt with managers from other cultures where there is a different perspective of the value of time. Time management is slowly becoming a standard training course offered at some organizations to highlight the importance of time and its value in today's increasingly competitive world.

Gender issues

This is an area in which Lebanon differs remarkably from many other Arab countries. Females, in the traditional Arab culture, have been viewed mostly in terms of their role as mothers and caretakers of the home. The social, political and economic changes in the Arab world during the past few decades, however, changed this perception with varying degrees in many Arab countries. Lebanon is probably the leading country in the Arab world in terms of allowing women to take additional functions outside the traditional mother–home roles. This is due to several reasons, most of which are unique to Lebanon. The Lebanese have traditionally been more affected by the West than other Arab countries. In addition, the Lebanese civil war meant more men in the battlefield and more women in the workplace. Also, the heavy migration of large numbers of males, for better pay and work opportunities, to the Arab Gulf oil-producing countries in the 1970s and 1980s and to Europe and North America in the 1980s and 1990s again meant a shortage in the male workforce and an increased influx of women into non-traditional jobs. But probably the most relevant reason for the increasingly active role of women in the workforce is related to the deteriorating economic conditions in the late 1980s and 1990s where many homes can only survive if supported by dual-career couples. Females, according to the World Bank, constituted 28 per cent of the labour force in Lebanon in 1996.

Although the presence of women in the workforce is very common nowadays this does not extend to upper managerial positions. The presence of women in higher executive positions is still a rarity, although studies show that there is a positive and favourable attitude towards the work of women in general (Barakat 1994; Sidani and Gardner 1998). This means that working women are still trying to achieve equality in opportunities, pay and acceptance. In addition, studies show that although males may have favourable attitudes towards the work of women in general, there still is scepticism about their ability to emerge as leaders. Moreover, there seems to be less acceptance for women in jobs traditionally dominated by men such as engineering and medicine (Labaki 1997).

Management/labour relations

As a result of family businesses and extreme centralization in Lebanese businesses, management–labour relations have always passed through times of ups and downs. This has been reinforced in the last few years by the economic problems which resulted in a loss of purchasing power for the Lebanese worker. Despite governmental efforts which are slowly leading to improvement in the workers situation, things are still far from being resolved. Labour unions exist and are very powerful in many industries. In addition, most labour unions are united under one powerful leadership called 'The General Labour Association'. This association, however, is not totally free from political intervention, which sometimes leads to differences and disputes among workers themselves.

Employers continuously push to improve worker productivity. Most Lebanese banks, for example, have stretched their working hours hoping for better customer convenience and employee productivity. Needless to say, the move was not welcomed wholeheartedly by employees in this sector which is one of the most important sectors in the Lebanese economy. Management–labour relations can thus be summarized in terms of continuous managerial initiatives to improve productivity and efficiency, countered by continuous employees' efforts to improve pay and benefits. A lot remains to be done to improve the relationships and foster an environment of mutual trust (see HUMAN RESOURCE MANAGEMENT IN THE EMERGING COUNTRIES; INDUSTRIAL RELATIONS IN THE EMERGING COUNTRIES).

Motivation

An interesting area, which distinguishes Lebanese workers from employees in other cultures, relates to the things they look for in their jobs. Hofstede (1984) notes remarkably that in motivation research, one should be very careful with respect to limitations of some famous motivation theories when applied cross-culturally. Maslow's famous motivation theory for example, which represents a hierarchy of needs that people look to fulfil, may not be applicable in certain cultures. This is indeed the case for Lebanon, as the order proposed in Maslow's hierarchy does not seem to apply to the Lebanese worker. Despite the fact that physiological needs have a prominent place in the workers' agenda, the top two needs for the Lebanese worker in the late 1990s seem to be security and esteem. The need for security stems from the political and economic turbulence which engulfed Lebanon for the past two decades and which led to a general loss of security. The need for esteem emanates from the peculiarities of the Lebanese society where showing-off and having the acceptance, respect, and admiration of others constitute an integral part of one's esteem and some-times rank before certain physiological needs.

3 Conclusion

The above points noted the aspects which characterize management thinking and practice in Lebanon. A lot has to be done in the Lebanese workplace in order to make it more productive and friendlier. Employees have to be more empowered and they should work with management on improving their mutual relationships. Another worthwhile point to discuss relates to the fact that Lebanon does not seem to share the characteristics which some claim to be found throughout the Arab world. A problem lies with the adequacy of treating all of the Arab countries as one homogeneous entity. Almaney, for example, claims that a close analysis of that culture 'would reveal the presence of an unmistakable unity of style' (Almaney 1981: 10). This view, if carried to the extreme, neglects the effects of the political and economic changes that occurred in the Arab world in the twentieth century and the way they have affected the homogeneity of the Arab world.

For Lebanon, Phillipe Skaff describes the uniqueness of the Lebanese people by indicating that; 'The Lebanese are schizophrenic. They have one foot in the Mediterranean and one in the desert' (Thomson 1998: 19). The foot in the desert relates to the rich Arab history Lebanon shares with the other Arab countries. The foot in the Mediterranean relates to the openness to Europe and the West in general. It is this multi-culturality that Lebanon enjoys that marks its peculiarity and distinction.

YUSUF M. SIDANI
SCHOOL OF ECONOMIC SCIENCES AND BUSINESS ADMINISTRATION
THE LEBANESE UNIVERSITY

Further reading

(References cited in the text marked *)

* Almaney, A.J. (1981) 'Cultural traits of the Arabs: Growing interest for international management', *Management International Review* 21(3): 10–18. (Presents some of the attributes of Arabs and their relevance to management.)
* Barakat, S. (1994) 'Profile of the Lebanese Executive', unpublished MBA thesis, American University of Beirut, Lebanon. (An empirical study of Lebanese executives and their characteristics.)
* Deresky, H. (1997) *International Management: Managing Across Borders and Cultures*, Reading, MA: Addison Wesley. (An international management book, which addresses various issues in differences of management practices cross-culturally.)
  Haddad, Y. (1984) 'Islam, women and revolution in twentieth-century Arab thought', *The Muslim World* 74(3,4): 137–60. (Provides a good overview of women and their role in Arab societies.)
* Hofstede, G. (1984) 'The cultural relativity of the quality of life concept', *Academy of Management Review* 9(3): 389–98. (An excellent analysis on what distinguishes cultures from each other including managerial implications.)
  Hofstede, G. (1991) *Software of the Mind*, London: McGraw Hill. (A book that presents Hofstede's research, methodology, and findings on cross-cultural differences.)
* Labaki, H.N. (1997) 'Perceived acceptance of women business leaders in Lebanon', unpublished MBA thesis, American University of Beirut, Lebanon. (An empirical investigation on the acceptance of women executives in the Lebanese workplace.)

Muna, F.M. (1980) *The Arab Executive*, New York: Macmillan. (Pathbreaking study based on a small sample of Arab executives identifying major aspects of attitude to work, use of time, and decision-making styles.)

* Sidani, Y.M. and Gardner, W.L. (1998) 'Work values in the Arab culture: The case of Lebanese workers', under review. (An empirical investigation about work values in Lebanese companies.)

* Thomson, A. (1998). 'The dream account', *Executive* November: 18–19.

* Tuttle, R. (1998). 'Size does matter: Is merging the answer for the Lebanese insurance industry?' *Executive* November: 40–2.

* The World Bank (1998) *World Development Indicators 1998*, Washington, DC: World Bank Publications. (Provides an expanded view of the world economy for almost 150 countries including Lebanon.)

See also: BANKING AND FINANCE IN THE EMERGING COUNTRIES; BUSINESS CULTURES, THE EMERGING COUNTRIES; MANAGEMENT EDUCATION IN THE EMERGING COUNTRIES; MANAGEMENT IN ALGERIA; MANAGEMENT IN EGYPT; MANAGEMENT IN THE GULF STATES; MANAGEMENT IN JORDAN; MANAGEMENT IN SAUDI ARABIA

Related topics in the IEBM regional set: MANAGEMENT EDUCATION IN EUROPE; MANAGEMENT EDUCATION IN NORTH AMERICA; MANAGEMENT IN EUROPE; MANAGEMENT IN ISRAEL; MANAGEMENT IN NORTH AMERICA; MANAGEMENT IN TURKEY

Management in Saudi Arabia

1 Introduction
2 Islam and its impact on management
3 Religion versus tradition
4 Decision-making context
5 Models of organization structure and performance
6 Conclusion

Overview

Saudi Arabia is a vast desert kingdom ruled in relatively absolute terms. Until the discovery of oil in the second part of the twentieth century and the full utilization of the wealth it provided, she remained relatively primitive by modern standards. While oil allowed for major changes in economic and institutional life, the country – in general – remained tied to her pre-oil social and cultural traditions.

The vacillation between the old and the new has occasionally resulted in social and political stresses and tensions that impacted the way management was practised. Instead of the pure authoritarian style that tradition has prescribed and the consultative style that modernization may suggest, a pseudo-consultative style seems to dominate decision-making, both political and administrative.

1 Introduction

Saudi Arabia is a paradoxical country. She exhibits some of the most traditional as well as some of the most modern life styles simultaneously. Officially, Saudi Arabia follows a strict interpretation of Islam. The ordained annual pilgrimage to Maccah and Al-Madinah by all Muslims has kept Islam a central focus of life in this desert kingdom. The relatively recent discovery of oil has catapulted Saudi Arabia – until the last couple of years – into one of the richest countries in the world. This sudden wealth resulted in a major economic transformation – which given the state of skill and education in the nation – had to be aided by a massive importation of foreign labour. Hence, expatriate labour comprises about 30 per cent of the total population of about 20 million.

Social transformation, however, seems to have taken place among Saudi citizens who travel often or reside outside Saudi Arabia. These people, who exist in large numbers in various areas of Europe and the Middle East, exhibit more of the European lifestyle and appear to behave outside the restrictive boundaries of the Saudi internal environment. For example, some of the satellite television stations they control and operate in the USA, UK, Cyprus and Lebanon clearly operate outside the strict moral code practised within the national boundaries of the kingdom. Interestingly enough, these stations appear to be avidly watched by the local citizenry of Saudi Arabia.

Saudi Arabia is an absolute monarchical kingdom that was established in 1932 when one desert tribe was able to conquer the rest and subject them to their absolute rule. Naming the unified country Saudi Arabia made this country one of the few countries in the world – if not the only one – named after a particular family (Al- Saud). In terms of governance, there is a nominal consultative council that was established in 1993 with appointed – rather than elected – membership. Council sessions are not open to the public and the topics for debate must be approved in advance by the King (*Political Handbook of the World* 1998: 797).

Among the variables that impact political and managerial life beside oil wealth is Islam as the predominant cultural–social–political force (see MANAGEMENT IN THE EMERGING COUNTRIES). In addition, there is the massive number of foreign workers (including, expatriate managers) and the temporariness this casts on the work environment. Furthermore, there is the emergence of the governmental-administrative structure and regulations from the sleeves of the British and Egyptian bureaucratic experience – where most of the early advisors came.

2 Islam and its impact on management

Islam ordained a comprehensive life system in which the two pillars of the material and the spiritual must always be intertwined. Hence, every act of life has both a temporal dimension as well as a spiritual one. No act of life is to be practised solely on a material basis or be void of its spiritual significance and meaning. In Islam, God must be present in every act. When you start any activity you must start in the name of God, 'Bismillah'. When you intend to do something in the future, it must be if God wills, 'In shaa Allah'. When you finish something, you must express your gratitude to God by saying, 'Al-Hamdu Lellah' and so on.

One managerial impact of this state of mind is that the dedicated Muslim's locus of control must be within. Hence, the strong ethical connotation and the emphasis on internal, 'personal' control rather than external, 'other' control. The last act of every practising Muslim's day must be a reflecting on his daily actions and a personal accountability of every right and wrong done during the day. This must be followed with a determination to continue the right actions and discontinue the wrong ones coupled with the intention to move to correct them next day and to avoid similar ones in the future. That permeation of Islam in every aspect of life will dictate reference to it as we discuss various aspects of managerial behaviour in Saudi Arabia (see MANAGEMENT IN THE ARAB WORLD).

Decision-making style

Ordained Islam and the expected behaviour of practising Muslims must not be confused, however, with that of average Muslims – especially those of the present day. The inability to differentiate these two types of behaviour leads to all sorts of fallacies about the impact of Islam on modern day managerial practices of the Arabs and Muslims including those of Saudi Arabia. An example of this apparent confusion is reflected in the writings of Badawi (1980), Ali (1989) and others. Badawi, for example, concludes from his research that Arab executives are not inclined towards a participative management style. In contrast, Muna (1980) and Al-Jafary and

Hollingsworth (1983) claim from their findings that the decision style preferred by most Arab executives is the consultative style. Abbas Ali (1989), perhaps in an attempt to reconcile that polarity of opinions or 'findings', suggests the emergence of a pseudo-consultative style among Arab decision makers. This is an astute observation, in that it explains one way by which Arab managers reconcile the demands of modern management, the edicts of religion towards 'consultation' and their own intrinsic tendency towards authoritarianism.

That authoritarian tendency is daily reinforced by (i) the dominance of political systems that are either clearly authoritarian or pseudo-democratic; (ii) the one and only point of view of official Arab media – that is generally the only media-spread throughout the Arab World; (iii) the male-dominant one-person rule families; (iv) the authoritarian style of teachers' in schools and universities. All such influences exist in their most blatant forms in Saudi Arabia. Hence, there is no escape for the Saudi Arabian executive in practising authoritarianism and for the survival-oriented subordinate to practise submissiveness and often 'hypocritical behaviour'. This is also the reason for the prevalence of pseudo-consultative behaviour in management and pseudo-democratic behaviour in politics by those leaders (executives or rulers) who are faced by an increasingly narrowing zone of tolerance (Barnard 1983) as displayed by the more educated, affluent and media-aware population.

3 Religion versus tradition

Part of the problem appears to be in the interaction between the precepts of ordained Islam and the traditional practices in a particular culture. For example, while Islam encourages decision making by consultation, *Shura*, traditional tribal customs encourage authoritarian decision making. Although tribal opinion is taken into account, the power of the Sheikh is absolute.

Sometimes, the grip of tradition is stronger that that of religion. This is becoming especially true in modern times where the grip of religion seems to loosen relative to that of customs and traditions. It must be mentioned that attempts are occasionally made to reconcile ordained precepts with actual practice. For example, 'In October 1994 King Fahd appointed a Supreme Council on Islamic Affairs to review educational, economic, and foreign policies and ensure they are conducted in appropriate concert with Islamic precepts' (*Political Handbook of the World* 1998: 797) Such governmental actions, however, can only affect laws, regulations and governmental policies. They cannot alter the behaviour of people often affected by the media, surging materialism and the erosion of religion.

4 Decision-making context

Decision making takes place within an organizational cultural context (see BUSINESS CULTURES, THE EMERGING COUNTRIES). One of the models that can be used to interpret Arab organizational culture, which appears to apply to Saudi Arabia, is that of Hofstede (1991). Weir (1993) has discussed that model and concluded that in such a society, power is important for the acquisition of political and social influence. Sources of power in this case are family, friends, personal charisma and the ability to use force. In those societies, Weir (1993) emphasizes that skill, wealth, power and status go together and are indeed reinforced by a cultural view that they should go together.

What is interesting is that in terms of the remaining three Hofstede's dimensions, Arab societies were classified to be in the middle. This classification corresponds accurately to the Islamic precepts that the best of all courses of action is the one in the middle, 'Khairu alumoor alwasat', and the Koranic verse, 'And we made you a nation in the middle.' Hence, the organizational culture, which provides the context for decision-making, encourages the middle course and guards against excess and extremism.

At this point, one must introduce the four dimensions that differentiate a national culture from another that Hofstede (1980) isolated in his original research, where he studied organization-related values in over fifty countries for more than ten years. Out of this extensive research, Hofstede concluded that values of a particular culture or society influence all aspects of life, including organizational life, its management and the values their manager's hold and how they execute their tasks based on them. These dimensions are:

1 *Power distance*: this dimension deals with societal distribution of power among its different elements as it is reflected in how various groups deal with power and authority-related issues.
2 *Uncertainty avoidance*: this dimension deals with how a particular society relates to matters such as the unknown and the future.
3 *Individualism–collectivism*: this dimension deals with how individual behaviour in a particular society is individual-oriented or group-oriented and how an individual relates to other group members.
4 *Masculinity–femininity*: this dimension deals with society's division of roles between the sexes. In addition, it also deals with the degree of importance a particular society assigns to 'masculine' values. Masculine values refer to values such as independence, assertiveness and performance, while feminine values refer to values such as cooperation, close personal relationships and quality of life.

Kassem and Al-Modaifer (1987: 16–19) researched these dimensions plus another of their design and arrived at conclusions roughly similar to those reached by Hofstede. Their study compared Saudi Arabians and Americans along five dimensions, Hofstede's four plus their own dimension:

5 *Traditionalism–modernism*: this dimension evaluates the extent to which a society socializes its members to seek innovation, universalism, and secularism or to reject these norms. Their comments on the results probably present the best available analysis of managerial behaviour in Saudi Arabia. Because of its quality and insight, we present a good part of it in what follows:

[the] high power distance scale explains the twin phenomena of excessive centralization and autocratic leadership. Gulf Arabs simply expect their leaders to lead them autocratically and to make decisions for them. In other words, centralization and autocracy are part of the mental programming of Arab managers and Arab employees alike. They are part of the same value system. The high uncertainty avoidance score tells us that Saudis do not tolerate uncertainty and ambiguity. They prefer to work with explicit rather than implicit rules. This

reading of the Saudi cultural map explains the tendencies to delegate upward, to avert responsibility to insist on multiple signatures and stamps, and to refer every minor matter to a committee.

The low individualism and by implication the high collectivism score explains the prevalence of particularism, nepotism, and favoritism – a phenomena which cannot be entirely stamped out by legislation or administrative reforms, no matter how carefully designed they happen to be. By contrast, the relative success of recent policies, aimed at putting local nationals in the driver's seat, can be explained by their local appeal. Simply put, these policies are culturally congruent.

Finally, the combination of high uncertainty avoidance with high power distance explains the ambivalence of Gulf Arab subordinates to their superiors. Having a powerful superior whom one can both praise and blame is an easy way of satisfying a strong need for avoiding uncertainty.

5 Models of organization structure and performance

Although comprehensive and empirically tested models of structure and performance are not available in our view, one specific synthesizing effort deserves attention. It is presented by Kassem and Habib (1989) and based on the writings of various authors on a variety of aspects of the subject. Although it deals with the Arabian Peninsula in general, it clearly applies to its largest entity, Saudi Arabia. Kassem and Habib explain that the pattern of life within that area endows it with a character and personality of its own, distinctly different from other countries. They add that the way of life within this area is generally uniform. The area in mind includes the six GCC (Gulf Cooperation Council) states (Saudi Arabia, Kuwait, United Arab Emirates, Bahrain, Qatar and Oman) and Yemen. They state (1989: 9) that, 'With hardly an exception, people within the area speak Arabic, believe in Islam, and share the same physical habitat, mode of life, traditional values, and historic roots. Moreover, each of these states is experiencing the same economic, administrative and modernization dilemmas. There hardly exists another region in the world whose constituent countries have so much in common as those of the Arabian Peninsula'.

The managerial behaviour in those countries remains highly traditional and basically rooted in the tribe despite the introduction of modern methods of managerial life. Hence, one major aspect of contemporary management in the Arabian Gulf is the overlap, vacillation or outright confusion between modern and traditional methods, ideas and people. Kassem and Habib (1989: 16) summarize the indicators of the Arab organizational mode, termed as 'bedoaucracy', (from Bedouin) as follows:

1 a moderate degree of vertical and horizontal specialization;
2 a low degree of coordination stemming from the exercise of personal authority and extensive use of committees;
3 a low degree of behaviour formalization and highly 'bendable' rules;
4 personnel decisions (i.e. selection, placement, promotion, compensation, etc.) based on flexible criteria subject to wide personal preferences and judgements and leading to overstaffing and disincentives to work hard or be smart;
5 a high degree of centralization of decision making.

In addition to those indicators, the authors state that, 'Arabian bureaucracy features include over-centralization of authority, overstaffing, personalization, formalization, nepotism and corruption. These features continue to prevail because they are functional both to leaders and followers alike'.

As to managerial performance it may be helpful to present what Badawi (1980: 51–8) suggested to be the stereotype of Mideasten (Gulf Arab) managers (see Table 1) before we present Kassem and Habib's synthesis of an actual Arab Management Model. As the presentation will show the model is not far different from the stereotype.

Table 1 Badawi's stereotypes

Managerial function	Mideastern stereotype
Organizational design	Highly bureaucratic. Overcentralized with power and authority at the top. Vague relationships. Ambiguous and unpredictable organization environments.
Patterns of decision making	Ad hoc planning. Decisions made at the highest level of management. Unwillingness to take high risk inherent in decision-making.
Performance evaluation and control	Informal control mechanisms. Routine checks on performance. Lack of vigorous performance evaluation systems.
Manpower policies	Heavy reliance on personal contacts and getting individuals from the 'right social origin' to fill major positions.
Leadership	Highly authoritarian tone, rigid instructions. Too many management directives.
Communication	The tone depends on the communicants. Social position, power and family influence are ever-present factors. Chain of command must be followed rigidly. People relate to each other tightly and specifically. Friendships are intense and binding.
Management methods	Generally old and outdated.

Kassem and Habib's Arab management model

According to Kassem and Habib's (1989: 17), the Gulf Arab manager tends to behave as follows:

1   resists innovation and change;
2   seeks authority and likes to display bossiness;
3   Averts responsibility and decision making;
4   Admires and respects his superiors;
5   Plays favourites;
6   hates to plan, yet likes to control;
7   prefers secure to high-paying jobs;
8   motivates his subordinates by fear and negative strokes.

These behavioral tendencies seem to fit the cultural expectations facing a typical manager.

6 Conclusion

Beside the dearth of writing about Arab management – including Saudi Arabia – a good deal of such writing – when available – suffers from several fallacies:

1   frequently equating Islamic-ordained precepts with the actual practices of Muslims.
2   taking some non Arab – especially Western – writings about Arabs and Arab management for granted.
3   tendency to ignore insightful personal observations in favour of structured, yet, fragmented uninsightful – often inept or misleading – 'scientific' research.
4   propagating biased views if they happen to fit the writer's own biases.
5   insistence by some that there is a 'common' Arab management style or theory present or emerging. Such a view – for which there is no evidence in reality – ignores the real historical, cultural and personality differences among inhabitants of various Arab countries – including their managers.

MAHMOUD SALEM
SULTAN QABOOS UNIVERSITY

Further reading

(References cited in the text marked *)

* Abbas Ali (1989) 'Decision style and work satisfaction of Arab Gulf executives', *International Studies of Management and Organization* 19(2): 22–37. (An empirical study investigating decision styles actually practised by Arab Gulf executives.)

Abbas Ali (1993) 'Decision-making style, individualism, and attitudes toward risk of Arab executives', *International Studies of Management and Organization* 23(3): 53–73. (A study that focuses on testing instruments which the author sees as relevant to Arab societies.)

Abbas Ali and Al-Shakhis, M. (1985) 'Managerial value systems for working in Saudi Arabia: an Empirical Investigation', *Group and Organization Studies*: 10: 135–51. (An empirical exploration of managerial value systems and attitudes in Saudi Arabia.)

* Al-Jafary, A. and Hollingsworth, A.T. (1983) 'An exploration of managerial practices in the Arabian Gulf Region', *Journal of International Business Studies* Fall: 143–52. (An empirical investigation of the management style utilized in ten Arab Gulf organizations, which found that organization climate was the most potent determinant of effectiveness.)

Al-Meer, A.R.A. (1989) 'Organizational commitment: A comparison of Westerners, Asians, and Saudis', *International Studies of Management and Organization* 19(2): 74–84. (An empirical investigation designed to measure levels of organizational commitment among Westerners, Asians and Saudis. It concluded that Asians have a higher commitment to their organizations than both Westerners and Saudis who scored about the same.)

Al-Rasheed, A.M. (1994) 'Traditional Arab management: evidence from empirical comparative research', Proceedings of the second Arab Management Conference University of Bradford Management Centre. (Does not agree that a fourth paradiagram is emerging to represent Arab management, and describes it – based on empirical research – as having limited orientation to the future as well as to the process of delegation.)

Al-Tawail, M.A. (1995) *Public Administration in the Kingdom of Saudi Arabia*, Riyadh, Saudi Arabia: Institute of Public Administration. (An edited book composed of ten chapters written by different authors about the state of public administration and its history in Saudi Arabia.)

Al-Twaijri, M.I. (1989) 'A cross-cultural comparison of American-Saudi managerial values in U.S.-related firms in Saudi Arabia: An empirical investigation', *International Studies of Management and Organization* 19 (2): 58–73. (An empirical study of underlying values of managerial practices of both Saudi and American managers in American-oriented firms in Saudi Arabia.)

Al-Yassini, A. (1990) 'Saudi Arabia', in Subramaniam (ed.), *Public Administration in the Third World: An International Handbook*, New York: Greenwood Press, pp. 184–204. (One of the chapters of an edited book that offers a good summary of public administration's status and problems in Saudi Arabia.)

* Badawi, M.K. (1980) 'Styles of mideastern managers', *California Management Review* XXII (2): 51–8. (A study of management styles of mideastern executives from Saudi Arabia, Kuwait, Abu Dhabi, Bahrain, Oman and the United Arab Emirates.)

* Barnard, C.I. (1983) *The Functions of the Executive*, Cambridge, MA: Harvard University Press. (The classic study about the functions of the executives which is still widely quoted.)

The Economist (1998) 'Saudi Arabia: A Forecast', *The World in 1999*, London: Economist Publications, p.81. (A statistical forecast for 1999 regarding the Saudi economy.)

El-Ghonemy, M.R. (1998) *Affluence and Poverty in the Middle East*, London: Routledge. (A book that fills the gap in the literature.)

* Hofstede, G. (1980) *Culture's Consequences: International Differences in Work-Related Values*, Beverly Hills, CA: Sage Publications. (An important book based on a monumental study of the sales subsidiaries of a major multinational corporation which operates in 39 countries in the world.)

* Hofstede, G. (1991) *Cultures and Organizations, Software and the Mind*, New York: McGraw-Hill. (A major comparative study which deals with managerial beliefs as they reflect cultural characteristics.)

* Kassem, M.S., Habib, G.M. *et al.* (1989) *Strategic Management of Services in the Arab Gulf States*, Berlin: Walter de Gruyter. (A book of text and cases that offers an excellent synthesis of Arab gulf management practices.)

* Muna, F. (1980) *The Arab Executive*, New York: Macmillan. (Although based on a small sample of Arab executives, this groundbreaking study deals with decision-making styles, time utilization and attitudes towards work.)

Pienta, D.A., Natale, S.M. and Sora, S.A.(1988) 'What is the impact of values on management?', *International Journal of Value Based Management* 1(1). (Basically, a review of research on the impact of values on management whose understanding helps grasp the difference between some aspects of Saudi Arabian management and management in other countries.)

* *Political Handbook of the World* (1998). (A handbook of up-to-date information on various countries of the world.)

Salem, M. (1994) 'Strategic planning for development in view of contemporary global changes' (in Arabic), *Al-Edari* 16(57): 129–56. (Explores the impact of global changes on Arab development and its managing especially in Oman.)

* Weir, D.T.H. (1993) 'Management in the Arab World', Proceedings of the first Arab Management Conference, University of Bradford Management Centre. (An overview of management in the Arab world that suggests the potential emergence of an Arab management style comparable to the preceding American, European and Japanese.)

See also: BUSINESS CULTURES, THE EMERGING COUNTRIES; MANAGEMENT IN THE ARAB WORLD; MANAGEMENT IN EGYPT; MANAGEMENT IN THE EMERGING COUNTRIES; MANAGEMENT IN THE GULF STATES; MANAGEMENT IN IRAN; MANAGEMENT IN JORDAN; MANAGEMENT IN LEBANON

Related topics in the IEBM regional set: MANAGEMENT IN EUROPE; MANAGEMENT IN NORTH AMERICA

Index

4A approach 20
Abbas Ali, A. 297–8, 313, 342
Abu-Bakr, N. 329
Abu-Doleh, J. 327
accounting
    Asian crisis 42–3
    background 41–3
    Communist 47–8
    heritage
        British 44–6
        French 43–4
    no dominant tradition 46–7
    overview 41
acquisitions *see* mergers/acquistions
Adams, R.J. 101, 102
Adler, N.J. 61
Africa
    authority/decision-making 171–2
    communication 173
    context 170
    corporate planning 171
    management education/training 173–4
    overview 169–70
    personnel/labour relations 172–3
African Development Bank 53–4
agriculture 184–5
Agyekum, F. 191
Ahmed, S.W. 277
Al-Faleh, M. 297, 325, 326
Al-Hashemi, I.S.J. 294, 298, 309–10
Al-Jafary, A. 341
Al-Najjar, G. 309–10
Al-Rasheed, A.M. 296, 325, 326, 328
Al-Shamali, A.D. 314
Algeria
    background 176–7
    managerial behaviour 177–9
    overview 176
    trends/future prospects 179–80
Alsane, N. 309
Alvi, S.A. 277
Amawi, S.T. 296
American Management Association
    (AMA) 275

Amirshahi, P. 321
Amsden, A. 29, 30
Anglo-Saxon model 33–5
Aoki, M. 29
Arab world
    culture 291–2
    education/training 294–5
    Islam 295–6
    leadership behaviour 296–7
    management
        Arab vs. Egyptian 304–5
        styles 297–8
        types 292–4
    overview 291
    trends/suggestions 298
Armstrong, J. 231
Asia
    influence on Uganda 233–4
    management education 108–9
Asian Development Bank 54
Asian Tigers 71, 267, 284
Association of Chartered Certified
    Accountants (ACCA) 42
Association of South-East Asian Nations
    (ASEAN) 46
Attiyyah, H.S. 294
Austin, J.E. 10, 19, 60, 61, 112

Badawi, M.K. 341, 345
Bahrami, H. 247
Bangladesh
    analysis 257–9
    background 255–7
    evaluation 259–60
    management structure
        nationalized banks/other financial
            institutions 258
        private sector banks/insurance
            companies 259
        private sector industrial enterprises
            258–9
        public sector industrial enterprises
            258
    overview 255

trends/suggestions 259–60
Bani-Asadi, H. 318, 319
Bank of Credit and Commerce
    International (BCCI) 58
Bank for Reconstruction and Development
    see World Bank
banking/finance 20–1, 233, 242, 322
    African Development Bank 53
    Asian Development Bank 54
    background 50–1
    IMF 52–3
    inconsistent policies 256
    Inter-American Development Bank
        54–5
    key characteristics 51–2
        capital scarcity 51
        controlled/unstable exchange rates
            51
        fluctuations in monetary systems 51
        high level of risk 52
        strong informal banking sector 51
        unfavourable balance of payments
            52
        vulnerability to shocks 52
        weak institutions 51
    management structure
        nationalized 258
        privatized 259
    national institutions 55
        Brazil 55–6
        India 56–7
    overview 50
    problems/outlook 57–8
    risk
        operating exposure 21
        transaction exposure 21
        translation exposure 21
    socio-political factors 242
    transnational institutions 52
    World Bank 53
Barakat, S. 334
Barnard, C.I. 342
Bates, A. 249
Bauer, P.T. 69
Bean, R. 96
Best, M. 30
big business
    centrality of in West 27
    developmental state 30

direct importance of in advanced
    capitalism 31
East Asian latecomer countries 28
entrepreneurial state 29–30, 282–3
entrepreneurship 333–4
global Toyotism 31–2
globalization/Anglo-Saxon model 33–5
merger frenzy in 1990s 32–3
state/rise of in West 28
Blunt, P. 108, 109, 111, 112, 207, 210,
    211, 229
Bol, D. et al. 223
Bond, M. 109
Border Environment Cooperation
    Commission 54
Botswana
    agriculture/cattle production 184–5
    background 182–3
    development of business/management
        186–8
    employment 185–6
    mining 183–4
    nature of economy 183
    overview 182
    SACU 186
Boyacigiller, N. 61
Brandt Commission Report (1980) 81
Brandt, W. 69
Brazil, banking/finance in 55–6
Bretton Wood system 75, 76, 80, 101
Bronstein, A.S. 98, 99, 101
Brown, M.B. 53
Brundtland Report (1987) 83
Bucholz, R.A. 321
Buddhadasa, S. 282
business culture 66
    background 60–2
    economy 265–6
    India/China comparison 266–7
    internal work culture 65–6
    levels
        institutional 62–3
        societal 63–5
    overview 60

Camp, R.C. 314
Caribbean Development Bank 54
Carlson, P. 46
chaebols 34–5, 186
Chandler, A.D. 27

Chang, H. 30
Chaudhuri, K.K. 267
Chaudhuri, S. 156, 160
Chennoufi, B.C. 177, 178, 179
China *see* People's Republic of China (PRC)
China, compared with India 266–7
Chinese Institute of Certified Public Accountants (CICPA) 47–8
Cohen Committee (1945) 45
Colasse, B. 44
Colclough, C. 182
Collins, P. 108, 109, 113
communications, Africa 173
Crane, D.P. 86
cultural factors 15, 208
   Arab world 291–2
   business 60–6
   human nature perspective 15
   India 265–7
   internal work culture 90–1
   Islamic 317–19
   Jordan 328–9
   Lebanon 333, 337–8
   religion, language, gender 15
   Saudi Arabia 342–4
   societal 15, 63–5, 89–90, 192–3, 229, 246–7
      beliefs, values, norms 64
      feminine 64
      paternal 64, 193
      performance management 87–8
   Sri Lanka 283–4
   time/space orientation 15
Curran, W. 52

Dadfar, H. 293
Davila, C. 109, 110
Davis, J.T. 191
demographic factors 15
   age structure 16
   growth rates 15
   health 16–17
   urbanization/migration 16
Deresky, H. 336
developing countries 9
Development Assistance Committee of the OECD 54–5
Dia, M. 229
Dirasse, L. 249

Dreze, J. 83

East African Development Bank 54
East Asia 28
Economic Development Institute (EDI) 107
economics
   background 69–71
   factors 11
      capital 13
      foreign exchange 13
      infrastructure 14
      Iran 319–21
      labour 13
      natural resources 13
      technology 14
   international institutions 71–2
      EU 76
      Food and Agricultural Organization 74–5
      GATT/WTO 73–4
      IMF 72
      World Bank 72–3
   management 228–9
   Open Door policy 302, 304
   overview 68–9
   recurrent themes 70
   trade/aid policy issues (1945–89) 76–7
      Asian Tigers 82
      economic aid 80–2
      economic planning 79–80
      food and agriculture 82–4
      import substitution/industrialization policies 79
      terms of trade 78–9
education *see* management education
Egypt
   administrative background 303
   context 301–3
   management
      problems 302
      societal negatives 304
      value negatives 304
      vs. Arab 304–5
   overview 301
   political-economic background 302–3
Ejiofor, P. 211
El Salmi, A. 303
El-Omani, H. 330
Eldridge, D. 276

emerging countries
  big business/catch-up
    historical 27–30
    since 1980s 31–5
  lessons for 36
  overview 26
employment 185–6, 193
  Pakistan 273–4
  see also human resource management
environment 10–11
environmental analysis framework (EAF)
  10
Esman, M.J. 112
European Bank for Reconstruction and
  Development (EBRD) 76
European Development Bank (EDB) 76
European Investment Bank 55
European Union (EU) 45, 76, 83

Fahmi, M. 301
Faini, R. *et al.* 62
Fashoyin, T. 101
finance *see* banking/finance
Food and Agricultural Organization (FAO)
  68, 74–5, 83
Foseco India 158
Foster, P. 82
Fund for International Development 55

Gabre-Michael, M. 98, 101
Gardiner, K. 190, 193
Gardner, W.L. 334
gender issues 64, 208–9, 234, 336–7
General Agreement on Tariffs and Trade
  (GATT) 68, 73–4, 163–5
  see also World Trade Organization
  (WTO)
Ghana
  analysis 192–4
  background 189–90
  Economic Recovery Programme (ERP)
    191
  evaluation 194–5
  overview 189
  political changes since 1987 190–1
  structural reforms 191–2
  trends/future prospects 195
globalization 33–5
government
  business relations 19–20, 250, 267, 272

industrial relations 97–8, 242–3
macroeconomic policies 135–6
training initiatives 261
Graham, L.S. 113
Green, C.D. 329
Green Revolution 83
Gulf States
  background 308–10
  making managers 310–12
  management 309–11
  management behaviour 311–13
  management features 313–14
  overview 308

Habib, G.M. 345–6
Hampden-Turner, C. 309
Harrison, R. 328
Hartwick, J. 88
Harvey, C. 184
Heckscher–Ohlin theory 78
Hellheiner, G. *et al.* 52
Henley, J.S. 198, 199, 200, 201
Herzberg, F. 88
Hickson, D.J. 61, 292–3
Hofstede, G. 64, 109, 208, 274, 283, 337,
  342, 343
Hollingsworth, A.T. 342
human resource management (HRM) 211
  Africa 172–3
  background 86–7
  India 267–8, 276–7
  Jordan 326–8
  Lebanon 335–6
  nurturant-task leadership 93
  overview 86
  performance management 87–8
    internal work culture 90–1
    societal culture 89
    strategies for cultural-fit 92
  private/public distinction 276–7
  reward system 88
    internal work culture 91
    societal culture 89–90
  strategies for cultural-fit 91–3
  views 86

Ihimodu, F. 207
India
  banking/finance in 56–7
  business culture

compared with China 266–7
  economy 265–6
  industrial relations 267
cultural context 263–4
human resource management 267–8
management style 265
overview 263
trends/suggestions 268
industrial relations
  Africa 172–3
  background 95–6
  Bangladesh 260
  collective 99–100
  colonial impact 96–7
  demands of social partnership 102
  democratic challenge 101–2
  India 267, 276
  Kenya 200–1
  Lebanon 337
  nationalism, post-colonial states, crisis
    of development 97
  overview 95
  political problems/instability 97–8
  role of government 97–8, 239
  South Africa 215
  structural adjustment programmes
    100–1
  trade unions 234, 242–3
  trends/prospects 102–3
  Zimbabwe 246
information/communications technologies
  (ICTs) 117, 120–2, 126
Inter-American Development Bank
  (IADB) 54–5
International Accounting Standards
  Committee (IASC) 43
International Auditing Practices
  Committee (IAPC) 43
International Development Association
  (IDA) 73
International Federation of Accountants
  (IFAC) 46
International Fund for Agricultural
  Development 55
International Labour Office (ILO) 96, 97,
  99, 101, 102
International Monetary Fund (IMF) 52–3,
  68, 72, 154, 164, 183, 198
International Standards of Accounting and
  Reporting (ISAR) 42

Iran
  analysis
    Islamic revolution/business 316–17
      political economy/management
        319–21
      values/culture 317–19
  background 316
  education 318
  overview 316
  trends/future prospects 321–2
Islam 295–6
  cultural factors 317–19
  impact on management 341
    decision making style 341–2

Jabr, H. 296
Jaeger, A.M. 62, 65, 225
Japan, as entrepreneurial state 29–30
Jayasundera, D.S. 283
Jayawardana, A.K.L. 284
Johnson, C.A. 29
Johri, C.K. 266
joint ventures (JVs) 158, 177
Jones, M.L. 111, 207, 211, 229
Jordan
  background 325
  management behaviour 325–8
  management culture 328–9
  overview 324
  trends/future prospects 329–30
Jorgensen, J.J. 61, 63, 231

Kanungo, R.N. 62, 65, 87, 88, 89, 90, 225
Kanyenze, G. 247
Karimi, E. 319
Kasozi, A.B.K. 231
Kassem, M.S. 345–6
Katz, H.C. 99
keiretsu 35
Kenya
  background 199
  emerging characteristics of
    management/labour 199–200
  future prospects 203–4
  labour relations policy 200–1
  management in 1990s 201–2
  management in multi-ethnic society
    202–3
  overview 198
Khalilzadeh-Shirazi, J. 266

Khan, A.A. 272
Khandwalla, P.N. 62, 63
Khilji, S.E. 271, 274
Kiggundu, M.N. 60, 112, 190, 192, 194,
    195, 219, 229, 230
Kluckhohn, C. 61
Kochan, T.A. 100
Koestler, A. 263
Kohn, T.O. 112
Kraus, J. 97
Kroeber, A.L. 61

Labaki, H.N. 337
Lahore University of Management
    (LUMS) 275
Lake, D.A. 28
Lal, D. 66
Latham, G.P. 87
Latifi, F. 319, 321
Latin America, management education
    109–10
Lebanon
    attitudes towards time 336
    background 332–3
    centralization/decision making styles
        334
    characteristics 338
    dominance of family business 333
    entrepreneurship/other work values
        333–4
    gender issues 336–7
    human resource practices 335–6
    management education/training 334–5
    management/labour relations 337
    motivation 337–8
    overview 332
lesser developed countries (LDCs) 9, 256
Lewis, S.R. 184
Lewis, W.A. 72
Leys, C. 200
Locke, E.A. 87

McCarthy, S. 182
management 23–4
    Arab world 297–9
    authority/decision making 171–3,
        258–9, 334, 341–2
    business–government relations 19–20
    development 186–7, 209, 217–18
        colonial 281

conservative 281
    new 281
    traditional 281
factors 11
    cultural 15, 217
    demographic 15–16
    economic 11–14, 246–7
    environmental 12
    political 14–15
family businesses 333
finance 20–1
Gulf States 309–12
Iran 317–19, 319–21
Islamic influence 341–2
leadership behaviour 296–7
levels
    company 19
    industry 18–19
    international 17
    national 17–18
making 310–11
marketing 22–3
multi-ethnic society 202–3
organization 23
overview 9
practice 301–3
    centralization 210, 334
    long range planning 209-10
    loyalty/integrity 210–11
private companies 248, 281–2
problems 303
    societal negatives 304
    value negatives 304
production 21–2
public enterprises 250, 282
structure
    nationalized banks/other financial
        institutions 258
    private sector banks/insurance
        companies 259
    private sector industrial enterprises
        258–9
    public sector industrial enterprises
        258
styles 216–17, 248, 265, 297–8,
    311–13, 325–8
understanding environment 10–11
values 274–5
see also named countries
management education/training

Africa 173–4
Arab world 294–5
Gulf States 313
India 275
internal 260
Jordan 325
Lebanon 334–5
means for improvement 110–11
   cultural/institutional environments
     111
   teachers/curriculum design 111–13
overview 105–6
regional perspectives 106–7
   Africa 107–8
   Asia 108–9
   Latin America 109–10
Sri Lanka 284–6
Zimbabwe 248-50
Mangement Association of Pakistan
   (MAP) 277
Mankidy, J. 101
manufacturing
   capabilities 129–34
   economic environment
     colonial heritage 136
     government policies 135–6
     public enterprises 136–7
     role of FDI 137
     substantial lack of data 134–5
   factors against development of firms
     139
   management 138–9
   overview 129
marketing 22–3, 321
   analysis 148–50
     Nigeria 148–50
     People's Republic of China 147–8
     Singapore 146–7
   background 142–3
   context
     challenges of emerging markets
       144–5
     importance in emerging markets
       143–4
     nature of emerging market 143
   issues 150–1
   managerial suggestions 151
   overview 142
Marshall Plan 80
Meerhaeghe, M.A.G. 74

Mehta, P. 263, 267
Meier, G.M. 78
Mendonca, M. 91
mergers/acquisitions 27, 32–3
Mezal, F. 310
Mill, J.S. 78–9
Miner, J.B. 86
mining 183–4
Morgan Stanley Dean Witter 33, 34
Mortazavi, S. 319
Multilateral Investment Guarantee Agency
   (MIGA) 73
multinational corporations (MNCs) 78,
   155
multinational enterprises (MNEs) 198
Muna, F. 294–5, 321, 341
Mustapha, F.H. *et al.* 313

Nadvi, K. 160
Nahas, F.V. *et al.* 296
Najjar, G. 294, 298
Nanayakkara, G. 284, 285
Nembhard, J.G. 51
newly industrialized countries (NICs) 9
Nigeria
   analysis 209
     centralization 210
     human resource management 211
     long range planning 209-10
     loyalty/integrity 210–11
   evaluation 211–12
   marketing example 148–50
   origins/context
     colonial heritage 207–8
     gender issues 208–9
     industrialization 206–7
     machoism 208
     management development 209
     public sector participation 207
     socio-cultural environment 208
   overview 206
   trends/future prospects 212–13
North American Development Bank 54
North American Free-Trade Agreement
   (NAFTA) 60
North, D. 84
Nzelibe, C.O. 192

Odubogun, P. 208
Okimoto, D.A. 29

Ollier, C. 43
Olojede, I. 209
Onah, J.O. 211
organization
  issues
    design/process 23
    entry form 23
    ownership strategy 23
  Kassem–Habib model 345–6
Organization for Economic Cooperation
  and Development (OECD) 75
Organization of Petroleum Exporting
  Countries (OPEC) 55, 75, 81

Pakistan
  background 271–2
  economy
    assessment 273
    overview of development 272
  employment structure 273–4
  human resource management 276–7
  labour unions 276
  management education 275
  management values 274–5
  overview 271
  trends, future prospects 277–8
parastatal companies 240–1
    high cost of equipment 242
    staffing 241–2
    uncompetitive/low quality products/
      services 242
Parekh, B. 263
People's Republic of China (PRC),
  marketing example 147–8
Perera, T. 282, 283
Plan Comptable Générale (PCG) 43–4
planning
    corporate 171
    long range 209–10
political factors 14
  ideology 14
  institutions 14–15
Poole, M. 96
Porter, M.E. 157, 160
production 21–2
Pugh, D. 292–3
Pugh, D.S. 64

quality assurance (QA) 313
Quibria, M.G. 160

Quinn, J.B. 247

Rao-Seshadri, S. 267
Roberts, L. 107
Rocco, F. 53, 58
RP Goenka Group 158
Ruigrok, W. 28, 30, 31
Rupesinghe, K. 230

Sabri, H. 328
Safavi, F. 107
Saheli, A. 319
Salvatore, D. 20
Saudi Arabia
    background 340–1
    decision making style 342–4
    impact of Islam 341
      decision-making style 341–2
    organization structure/performance
      344–5
      Kassem–Habib model 345–6
    overview 340
    religion vs. tradition 342
Schein, E.H. 62
Schmitz, C.J. 27, 28
Seers, D. 78
Segal, R. 263
Sen, A.K. 83
Sharabi, H. 326
Sharma, S.D. 266
Shivji, I.G. 223
Sidani, Y.M. 334
Simpson, W.R. 100, 101
Singapore, marketing example 146–7
Singer–Prebisch hypothesis 78
Singh, A. 29, 30
Singhal, S. 268
Sinha, J.B.P. 93, 263, 267, 268
Smith, A. 28, 69
Smith, P.B. *et al.* 321
South Africa
    background 214–15
    context
      labour market 215–16
      labour/political rights 215
      socio-economic factors 215
      structural factors 216
    management
      culture 216
      development 217–18

styles 216–17
overview 214
trends/future development 218–19
South Korea, as developmental state 30
Southern African Customs Union (SACU) 186
Sri Lanka
  background 280–1
  business/management development
    education 284–6
    entrepreneurship 282–3
    historical 281–2
    styles/cultural environment 283–4
  overview 280
  trends/future prospects 286
Sri Lanka Institute of Public
  Administrations (SLIDA) 108
5-Ss 283–4
state-owned enterprises (SOEs) 176, 177, 178, 198
Stewart, F. *et al.* 222
Stokes, H. 328
Stopford, J. 202
strategy
  competitive 157
    brand building 157
    efficiency improvement through
      organizational restructuring 158
    public ownership as strategic
      constraint 159
    time to market 157
  emerging environment of business 154–5
  internationalization 159–60
  overview 154
  trends/future 161
  using technology for competitive
    advantage 155–7
structural adjustment programmes (SAPs) 100–1, 245, 246
Sulieman, M. 292
Suzuki, Y. 29
Swainson, N. 202
Synge, R. 191
Système Comptable Ouest-Africain
  (SYSCOA) 44

Taiwan, as developmental state 30
Talbot, R.B. 74
Tanzania

analysis
  pattern of management 225
  social setting 223–4
background 221–3
evaluation 225–6
overview 221
trends/future prospects 226–7
Taqi, A.A. 313
Tata Refractories (TRL) 158
Tayeb, M.H. 263, 318, 321
technology
  analysis of management practices 122–4
  background 117–18
  context 118–22
  evaluation of prevailing realities 124–6
  overview 117
  transfer problems 119–20
  trends/future prospects 126–7
  using for competitive advantage 155–7
Third World nations 9
Thomas, E. 267
Thomson, A. 335, 338
Tiger economies *see* Asian Tigers
Timberg, T.A. 259
time 336
total quality (TQ) systems 313
Toyotism, global 31–2
trade unions *see* industrial relations
training *see* management education/
  training
Triandis, H.C. 64, 202
Trompenaars, F. 64
Trotman, M. 44
Tung, R.L. 109
Tuttle, R. 333

Uganda
  analysis
    Asian factor 233–4
    differentiation without integration 229–30
    economic management 231–3
    history/management 228–9
    unions/associations 234
    war and disease 231
    women in management 234
  background 228
  future prospects 235
  overview 228

United Nations Conference on Trade and Development (UNCTAD) 68, 74–5, 81
United Nations Development Programme (UNDP) 55, 107, 112
United Nations (UN) 45
United States Agency for International Development (USAID) 75, 110

Van Tulder, R. 28, 30, 31
Venkata Ratnam, C.S. 63
Verma, A. *et al.* 101

Wade, R. 30
Walton, P. 45
Warner, M. 109
Warren, D.M. 112
Weir, D.T.H. 291, 314, 343
Wild, K.L. 314
Wilson, C. 312
World Bank 41, 53, 68, 72–3, 96, 99, 102, 106, 150, 198, 267, 272, 324, 332
World Food Council (WFC) 74
World Trade Organization (WTO) 68, 73–4
    analysis 165
    origin 163–4
    overview 163
    principles 164
    see also General Agreement on Tariffs and Trade (GATT)
World Wide Web 121

Yesufu, T.M. 96, 97, 98
Younis, T. 296

Zagha, R. 266
Zakaria, S. 274
Zakat, concept 295
Zambia
    background 237–8
    civil service 239–40
    colonial rule/consequences 238–9
    financial management 242
        socio-political factors 242
    future prospects 243
    government administration 239
    industrial relations/trade unions 242–3
    overview 237
    parastatal companies 240–1
        high cost of equipment 242
        staffing 241–2
        uncompetitive/low quality products/services 242
Zimbabwe
    background 245–6
    context
        labour/political change 246
        socio-economic factors 246–7
        structural factors 247–8
    overview 245
    specific features
        management in public enterprises 250
        management styles in private companies 248
        management training/development 248–50
    trends 251